LIBRARY OF NEW TESTAMENT STUDIES

360

formerly the Journal for the Study of the New Testament Supplement series

Editor
Mark Goodacre

By the same author
Read Greek by Friday: A Beginning Grammar and Exercises
Read Greek by Friday: Creative Exercises
Read Greek by Friday: The Gospel of John and 1 John
Greek at a Glance

RESURRECTION IN MARK'S LITERARY-HISTORICAL PERSPECTIVE

PAUL M. FULLMER

t&t clark

Published by T&T Clark
A Continuum imprint
The Tower Building, 11 York Road, London SE1 7NX
80 Maiden Lane, Ste 704, New York, NY 10038

www.tandtclark.com

British Library Cataloguing-in-Publication Data
A catalogue record for this book is available from the British Library

ISBN-10: HB: 0-567-04553-6
ISBN-13: HB: 978-0-567-04553-9

Typeset by Data Standards Ltd, Frome, Somerset, UK.
Printed on acid-free paper in Great Britain by MPG Books Ltd, Bodmin, Cornwall.

This study is dedicated to my loving and supportive wife Becky, to my daughter, Juliana, and to all who work to understand the Bible and its place in the life of the church and the world.

CONTENTS

Acknowledgments

I am particularly appreciative of the faithful and thoughtful review of my colleague Mary Ann Tolbert, who has repeatedly clarified the relationship of several of my own questions and observations to central issues currently facing Markan scholarship. Lawrence Wills of the Episcopal Divinity School has read the project in manuscript form. His remarks on a series of drafts resulted in many insightful questions and keen observations, often accompanied by relevant bibliographic resources. My sincere thanks also go to Anne Wire, who spent many hours reviewing, critiquing and contributing to the developing manuscript.

I have been delighted to participate in a reading group at the Graduate Theological Union, the brainchild of Joe Marchal. Together with Joe, Yong-Sung Ahn, Avaren Ipsen, and Sean Burke have offered not only acuity but also support as fellow authors. A dear friend, Sabrina Maling Volkert, has also read and re-read significant portions of this work throughout its development, offering keen insights regarding stylistics both ancient and modern.

Last and above all, my thanks go to my wife, Becky, who has read these pages with an amazing attention to detail and loving care. Her dedication to this project as well as our wonderful marriage is surely an expression of God's faithfulness and love.

LIST OF ABBREVIATIONS

A&A	*Antike und Abendland*
AASF	Annales Academiae Scientiarum Fennicae
AB	Anchor Bible
ABD	David N. Freedman (ed.), *The Anchor Bible Dictionary* (New York: Doubleday, 1992)
AGJU	Arbeiten zur Geschichte des antiken Judentums und des Urchristentums
AICAN	Acta on the International Conference on the Ancient Novel
AJN	Lawrence M. Wills, *Ancient Jewish Novels: An Anthology* (New York and Oxford: Oxford University Press, 2002).
AJPh	*American Journal of Philology*
AJT	*American Journal of Theology*
ALGHJ	Arbeiten zur Literatur und Geschichte des Hellenistischen Judentums
ALUN	Annales Litteraires de l'Université de Nantes
ARRIM	*Annual Review of the Royal Inscriptions of Mesopotamia Project*
AS	Approaches to Semiotics
ATLAMS	American Theological Library Association Monograph Series
AUUHR	Acta Universitatis Upsaliensis Historia Religionum
BDAG	Walter Bauer, William F. Arndt, F. William Gingrich and Frederick W. Danker, *A Greek–English Lexicon of the New Testament and Other Early Christian Literature* (Chicago: University of Chicago Press, 3rd edn, 2000)
BETL	Bibliotheca ephemeridum theologicarum lovaniensium
BGL	Bibliothek der Griechischen Literatur
BIS	Brill Interpretation Series
BKP	Beiträge zur Klassische Philologie
BMI	The Bible and Its Modern Interpreters
BRBS	Brill's Readers in Biblical Studies
BRS	The Biblical Resource Series
BTB	*Biblical Theology Bulletin*
ByzZ	*Byzantinische Zeitschrift*
BZ	*Biblische Zeitschrift*
BzA	Beiträge zur Altertumskunde
CAES	Cambridge Archaeological and Ethnological Series

CAGN	Bryan P. Reardon (ed.), *Collected Ancient Greek Novels* (Berkeley: University of California Press, 1989)
CBET	Contributions to Biblical Exegesis and Theology
CBQ	*Catholic Biblical Quarterly*
CBQMS	Catholic Biblical Quarterly Monograph Series
CC	Continental Commentaries
CCBS	Christian Classics Bible Studies
CCS	Cambridge Classical Studies
CCT	Classics and Contemporary Thought
CEJL	Commentaries on Early Jewish Literature
CENL	Charles Eliot Norton Lectures
CGTS	Cambridge Greek Testament Series
CHCL	Cambridge History of Classical Literature
CI	*Critical Inquiry*
CJA	Christianity and Judaism in Antiquity
CM	Classica Monacensia
COQG	Christian Origins and the Question of God
CQ	*Classical Quarterly*
CSCP	Cornell Studies in Classical Philology
CTIR	*Center of Theological Inquiry Reflections*
CTM	Calwer Theologische Monographien
CUF	Collection des Universités de France
DRLAR	Divinations: Rereading Late Ancient Religion
EEFGRB	Egypt Exploration Fund, Greco-Roman Branch
ESEC	Emory Studies in Early Christianity
ExpTimes	*Expository Times*
Fragments	Susan A. Stephens and John J. Winkler (eds), *Ancient Greek Novels: The Fragments* (Princeton: Princeton University Press, 1995)
FRLANT	Forschungen zur Religion und Literatur des Alten und Neuen Testaments
FzB	Forschung zur Bibel
GAP	Guides to Apocrypha and Pseudepigrapha
GCN	*Gröningen Colloquia on the Novel*
GRBS	*Greek, Roman and Byzantine Studies*
HALAT	Ludwig Koehler *et al.* (eds), *Hebräisches und aramäisches Lexikon zum Alten Testament* (5 vols; Leiden: E.J. Brill, 1967–95)
HBS	Herder's Biblical Studies
HCS	Hellenistic Culture and Society
HDR	Harvard Dissertations in Religion
HE	Hermes Einzelschriften
Herm.	Walter Scott (ed., trans.), *Hermetica: The Ancient Greek and Latin Writings which Contain Religious or Philosophic Teachings Ascribed to Hermes Trismegistus* (London: Dawsons of Pall Mall, 1968)
Hermes	*Hermes: Zeitschrift für Klassische Philologie*

HNT	Handbuch zum Neuen Testament
HR	*History of Religions*
HTKNT	Herders Theologischer Kommentar zum Neuen Testament
HTS	Harvard Theological Studies
HWS	History Workshop Series
ISFCJ	International Studies in Formative Christianity and Judaism
JBL	*Journal of Biblical Literature*
JBQ	*Jewish Bible Quarterly*
JECS	*Journal of Early Christian Studies*
JL	Jerome Lectures
JSJSup	*Journal for the Study of Judaism*, Supplement Series
JSNTSup	*Journal for the Study of the New Testament*, Supplement Series
JSOT	*Journal for the Study of the Old Testament*
JSOTSup	*Journal for the Study of the Old Testament*, Supplement Series
JSP	*Journal for the Study of the Pseudepigrapha*
JSPSup	*Journal for the Study of the Pseudepigrapha*, Supplement Series
KEK	Kritisch-Exegetischer Kommentar über das Neuen Testament
KGEZ	Die Kultur der Gegenwart: Ihre Entwickelung und Ihre Ziele
LCL	Loeb Classical Library
LSJ	Henry G. Liddell and Robert Scott, *A Greek-English Lexicon* (rev. Sir Henry S. Jones, Roderick McKenzie; Oxford: Clarendon, with supplement, 1996)
LUA	Lunds Universitets Arsskrift
M&P	Myth and Poetics
MB	Le Monde de la Bible
MBPS	Mellen Biblical Press Series
ML	The Modern Library
MLBS	Mercer Library of Biblical Studies
MS	Mnemosyne Supplements
NA[27]	Eberhard and Erwin Nestle, and Barbara and Kurt Aland, *et al.* (eds), *Novum Testamentum Graece* (27th rev. edn; Stuttgart: Deutsche Bibelgesellschaft, 1993)
NAW	Gareth Schmeling (ed.), *The Novel in the Ancient World* (Boston and Leiden: Brill Academic, rev., 2003)
NCB	New Century Bible
NIA	Tomas Hägg, *The Novel in Antiquity* (Berkeley and Los Angeles: University of California Press, English edn, 1983)
NICNT	New International Commentary on the New Testament
NICOT	New International Commentary on the Old Testament
NIGTC	New International Greek Testament Commentary
NovT	*Novum Testamentum*
NovTSup	Supplements to *Novum Testamentum*
NRSV	New Revised Standard Version
NTS	*New Testament Studies*
OBO	Orbis Biblicus et Orientalis
OBT	Overtures to Biblical Theology
OCD	Simon Hornblower and Antony Spawforth (eds), *The Oxford*

	Classical Dictionary (New York and Oxford: Oxford University Press, 3rd rev. edn, 2002)
OCM	Oxford Classical Monographs
OPR	Oxford Paperback Reference
OTL	Old Testament Library
OTM	Oxford Theological Monographs
OTP	James H. Charlesworth (ed.), *The Old Testament Pseudepigrapha* (2 vols; New York: Doubleday, 1985)
P.	Michael. Papyri Michaelidae
PPFBR	Publications of the Perry Foundation for Biblical Research
PRS	*Perspectives in Religious Studies*
PT	Playing the Texts
RAC	Theodor Klausner, et al. (eds), *Reallexikon für Antike und Christentum* (Stuttgart: Anton Hiersemann, 1950–)
RAI	Rencontre Assyriologique Internationale
RBS	Resources for Biblical Studies
RE	August Pauly, Georg Wissowa, and Wilhelm Kroll (ed.), *Paulys Real-Encyclopädie der classischen Altertumswissenschaft: Neue Bearbeitung und der Mitwirkung zahlreicher Fachgenossen* (24 vols; Stuttgart: J. B. Metzler, 1893–1963)
RHT	*Revue d'Histoire des Textes*
RSR	*Religious Studies Review*
SAAA	Studies on the Apocryphal Acts of the Apostles
SAC	Studies in Antiquity and Christianity
SB	Stuttgarter Bibelstudien
S-B	Hermann L. Strack and Paul Billerbeck (eds), *Kommentar zum Neuen Testament aus Talmud und Midrasch* (6 vols; Munich: Beck, 1961–3)
SBFA	Studium Biblicum Franciscanum Analecta
SBL	Studies in Biblical Literature
SBLAB	Society of Biblical Literature Academia Biblica
SBLDS	Society of Biblical Literature Dissertation Series
SBS	Sources for Biblical Study
SBT	Studies in Biblical Theology
SBTS	Sources for Biblical and Theological Studies
SCL	Sather Classical Lectures
SFLL	Symbolae Facultatis Litterarum Lovaniensis
SG	Serta Graeca
SHCT	Studies in the History of Christian Thought
SLJS	Stroum Lectures in Jewish Studies
SNTSMS	Society for New Testament Studies Monograph Series
SNTU	Studien zum Neuen Testament und seiner Umwelt
SPB	Studia postbiblica
SSEJC	Studies in Scripture in Early Judaism and Christianity
SSN	Studia Semitica Neerlandica
ST	Sammlung Tusculum
SUNT	Studien zur Umwelt des Neuen Testaments

SVF	Hans Friedrich A. von Arnim (ed.), *Stoicorum Veterum Fragmenta* (Stuttgart and Leipzig: B. G. Teubner, 1921–4)
SVTP	Studia in Veteris Testamenti Pseudepigrapha
TDNT	Gerhard Kittel and Gerhard Friedrich (eds), *The Theological Dictionary of the New Testament* (trans. Geoffrey W. Bromiley; 10 vols; Grand Rapids, Mich.: Eerdmans, 1964–76)
THKNT	Theologischer Handkommentar zum Neuen Testament
TSAJ	Texts and Studies in Ancient Judaism
TU	Texte und Untersuchungen
TWAS	Twayne's World Authors Series
VPT	Voices in Performance and Text
VTSup	*Vetus Testamentum*, Supplements
WBC	Word Biblical Commentary
WdF	Wege der Forschung
WestBC	Westminster Bible Companion
WUNT	Wissenschaftliche Untersuchungen zum Neuen Testament
ZNW	*Zeitschrift für die Neutestamentliche Wissenschaft und die Kunde der Älteren Kirche*
ZPE	*Zeitschrift für Papyrologie und Epigraphik*

INTRODUCTION

Narratives of death and revival occur throughout the Gospel of Mark. In the opening chapters of the Gospel, the author concludes a series of miraculous healings with a story in which Jesus raises a little girl from the dead (Mk 5.36-43). A second such narrative occurs about midway between this story and the end of the Gospel: Jesus raises a boy even though his body looks 'like a corpse' and many say 'he is dead' (9.14-29, esp. 9.26). At the close of the Gospel, the main character, Jesus himself, is said to have risen from the dead. This final event is anticipated by three predictions, each framed in a similar manner: 'the Son of Man must undergo great suffering, and be rejected ..., and be killed, and after three days rise again' (8.31; see also 9.31, 10.34). In addition, themes of death and revival mark the beginning of the story of the death of John the Baptist whom Herod believes 'has been raised from the dead' (6.14-16). Moreover, 'the resurrection' is a central issue in certain controversies between Jesus and the Pharisees (12.18-27).

The recurrence of the theme of death and revival throughout the Gospel of Mark is particularly striking when the Gospel is compared to the source it cites more than any other, the Hebrew Bible.[1] Despite its immense size and scope, references to death followed by a return to life in Hebrew Bible texts are rare, occurring only on occasion in prophetic imagery (Hosea and Ezekiel), prophetic miracle stories (Elijah and Elisha), the psalms, and apocalyptic literature.[2] Novelistic literature of the Hellenistic period, on the other hand, has a predilection for themes of death and revival. These themes occur throughout Chariton's ancient novel, *Callirhoë*, for example.[3] At the outset of the story, a swift kick in the diaphragm sends the heroine, Callirhoë, to the tomb in which she will eventually

---

1. See Thomas R. Hatina, *In Search of a Context: The Function of Scripture in Mark's Narrative* (JSNTSup, 232; SSEJC, 8; Sheffield, Engl.: Sheffield Academic, 2002); Joel Marcus, *The Way of the Lord: Christological Exegesis of the Old Testament in the Gospel of Mark* (ed. John Riches; SNTW; Edinburgh: T & T Clark, 1993).

2. Robert Martin-Achard, 'Resurrection (Old Testament)', in *ABD* 5: 680–4 (683).

3. Due to the witness of ancient documents, I refer to Chariton's novel as *Callirhoë* (abbreviated *Callir.*) throughout this study rather than *Chaereas and Callirhoë*. See Section 2.3.5.

return to life (*Callir.* 1.4–8). This death and revival is referred to 26 times throughout the remainder of the story.[4] Then, at the central turning point of the story, Callirhoë's lover, Chaereas, is summoned back to life after a widely assumed death and an elaborate funeral (5.8.5–7). Finally, at the end of the novel, the two lovers experience a type of death and revival as a couple during their much-anticipated reunion (8.1.5–12).

The Goal of the Study

In this study, I read themes of death and revival in ancient texts that bear a close literary-historical relationship to the Gospel of Mark: Hellenistic novelistic literature; its progenitor, Homeric epic; and biblical literature. With the ancients, I apply the term 'resurrection' to these themes taken collectively even in those instances where death is asserted but qualified.[5] Indeed, as I will demonstrate, a majority of resurrection narratives – both broadly Greco-Roman and specifically Christian – qualify the presentation of death preceding revival. I have organized my readings and the implications for interpretation into three parts: prolegomena, texts, and theory.

Two chapters in Part I (Prolegomena) prepare for the readings. Chapter 1 establishes the relationship of the Gospel to novelistic literature, appreciating the novelistic quality of the Gospel's narrative style, motifs, themes, structure, and rhetoric. This chapter introduces several literary terms and concepts that will inform the remainder of the study. In Chapter 2, a review of significant pre-Christian texts establishes the presence of the resurrection theme within popular mythology of the Hellenistic period. Of particular importance in this chapter is introductory material related to Chariton's novel, *Callirhoë*, a pre-Christian novelistic text that will serve as a primary point of comparison for a subsequent examination of the theme of death and revival in the Gospel of Mark.

Three additional chapters in Part II (Texts) are dedicated to the close reading of resurrection narratives in specific ancient texts. Chapter 3 begins with an analysis of the theme of death and revival in Hellenistic novelistic literature and Homeric epic. A constellation of similar motifs within these narratives as well as a recurring placement of the theme itself suggests the circulation of an Epic resurrection topos operative among storytellers of the ancient eastern Mediterranean basin. These resurrection narratives begin with a sense of confusion and proceed through death and resurrection to arrive at a place of enlightenment. Reactive crowds witness these events and exert dramatic emotions. Perhaps most distinctively, the

---

4. See Section 3.1.2.1. At Ch. 3, n. 17 the occurrences are listed in their entirety.
5. As παλιγγενεσία at Chariton 1.8.1. See Section 3.1.2.1.

nature of the death experience before the revival is explicitly qualified. All of these elements, taken collectively, occur at a strategic point in a story as a whole.

In Chapter 4 I analyze expressions of the resurrection theme in several texts of the Hebrew Bible. The texts are in many ways distinct from Homeric epic and yet also bear a close literary relationship to the Gospel of Mark. A consideration of the motifs, placement, and function of these narratives results in the identification of a Prophetic resurrection topos that may be compared to the Epic topos. This Prophetic resurrection topos repeatedly begins with a breach of divine trust that results in a death. Following resurrection, communion with the divine is reestablished. Unlike the qualified death of the Epic topos, in the Prophetic topos the element of death is presented in stark terms. In this chapter I also read themes of death and a return to life in several Hellenistic Jewish writings such as Tobit, Greek Esther, and *Joseph & Aseneth*, noting an amalgamation of the elements of the two earlier topoi that is characteristic of the extensive cultural assimilation of the Hellenistic period.[6]

In Chapter 5 I compare the placement, function, and motifs of stories about death and resurrection in the Epic and Prophetic topoi to the Gospel of Mark. The analysis suggests that Mark's resurrection narratives manifest many of the characteristics of Hellenistic novelistic literature, particularly those novelistic writings which draw upon an epic tradition: the narratives occur at strategic points throughout the story, crowds play an emotive-reactive role, the motifs of resurrection progress from confusion to enlightenment and, perhaps most distinctively, the element of death in these narratives is qualified more often than not.

It is not until the completion of the textual observations in Part II that I attempt in Part III (Theory) to assess the primary implications of the study for interpreting the Gospel of Mark. The two sections of the sixth and final chapter draw conclusions from the reading for modern appreciation of (1) the literary context in which the Gospel of Mark was written and (2) the historical context of Hellenism that produced such an abundance of resurrection narratives. Literarily, the dominant characteristics of resurrection narratives in Mark correspond to similar narratives in Hellenistic novelistic literature, affirming an identification of

---

6. The use of 'Jewish' here, as throughout this study, is not to be understood as designating a religious identity established via loyalty to a certain canon of traditions or principles. See Daniel Boyarin, *Border Lines: The Partition of Judaeo-Christianity* [DRLAR; Philadelphia: University of Pennsylvania Press, 2004], pp. 12, 17). Neither is the use of 'Jewish' in this study to be understood as contrasting with 'Hellenistic'. Rather, the study contributes to an appreciation of the Hellenistic character of the first-century Judaism that produced the Gospel of Mark.

the genre of the Gospel of Mark as novelistic.[7] I also demonstrate the influence of epic, non-biblical traditions upon the Gospel without necessitating direct dependence upon Homeric epic.[8] Scholars of the Gospel of Mark have new incentive to read Mark in relationship to ancient works of novelistic literature, regardless of whether or not that literature manifests the influence of biblical traditions.

Historically, the study supports a growing appreciation of the ethnic hybridity dominant during the period that produced the text, bringing into question an often overdrawn dichotomy between Jewish and Hellenistic cultures in the first century.[9] Deductions in this section also suggest that resurrection narratives flourished throughout Hellenistic novelistic literature because the intensity of the combined concepts of death and a return to life resonates with the intensity of experiences effected by the markedly increased physical, ethnic, and social mobility of the period. Finally, some concluding reflections have implications for the postmodern Christian church of the twenty-first century.

The particular focus of this study upon themes of resurrection in two texts, Mark's Gospel and Chariton's novel, allows for the identification of specific literary characteristics that will be noted with less attention to detail in several other ancient texts. This focus upon these two texts moderates any presumptive and absolute conclusions. While I do not claim to have the last word in the Markan debates that arise in the course of my reading, it is my hope that this study will provide a model by which other scholars will examine specific themes of the Gospel in light of literature that bears a close relationship to the Gospel, and so continue to enhance a collective understanding and appreciation of this ancient story.

---

7. See Mary A. Tolbert, *Sowing the Gospel: Mark's World in Literary-Historical Perspective* (Minneapolis: Fortress, 1989) and Lawrence M. Wills, *The Quest of the Historical Gospel: Mark, John and the Origins of the Gospel Genre* (New York and London: Routledge, 1997).

8. Compare the work of Dennis R. MacDonald (*The Homeric Epics and the Gospel of Mark* [New Haven, Conn.: Yale University Press, 2000]) and the recent response by Robert B. Coote and Mary P. Coote ('Homer and Scripture in the Gospel of Mark', in Hearon (ed.), *Distant Voices Drawing Near: Essays in Honor of Antoinette Clark Wire*, pp. 189–201). I consider both in Section 6.1.2.

9. See, for example, the collection of essays in Engberg-Pedersen (ed.), *Paul Beyond the Judaism/Hellenism Divide* as well as Denise Kimber Buell and Caroline Johnson Hodge, 'The Politics of Interpretation: The Rhetoric of Race and Ethnicity in Paul', *JBL* 123 (2004), pp. 235–51.

Part I: Prolegomena

Chapter 1

THE GOSPEL OF MARK AS NOVELISTIC LITERATURE

A comparison of the narrative style of the Gospel of Mark with that of the vast majority of Classical literature surviving from the ancient Greco-Roman world reveals some remarkable differences. For example, a salient characteristic of the Gospel of Mark is *parataxis*, a term that is a transliteration of the Greek word παράταξις, meaning an arranging (τάξις) side by side (παρά). Over and over again, the author of the Gospel of Mark places two independent phrases, each possessing their own finite verb, side by side through the use of the simple coordinating particle καί ('and').[1] In contrast, a salient characteristic of the vast majority of extant ancient Greek literature is the high frequency with which authors employ *hypotaxis*, the arranging (τάξις) of one clause 'under' (ὑπό) another through the use of subordinating conjunctions such as 'because' (γάρ), 'as' (ὡς), 'that' (ὅτι), and 'whether' (εἴτε) as well as through the use of participles and infinitives. As a result of such hypotactic stylistics, sentences in ancient Greek literature are often quite complex.

This fundamental difference between the Gospel of Mark and other Classical literature written in Greek is so striking as to become manifest even in the briefest of passages, even if these passages are translated into English. Consider, for example, the following selection from a biography of the orator Demosthenes written by Plutarch, a wealthy biographer and philosopher of the late first century, as part of his larger project entitled *Lives*. The selection follows a few items of prolegomena in which Plutarch introduces his project of setting the lives of Demosthenes and Cicero in parallel. Note how Plutarch introduces Demosthenes in a hypotactic style (that is characteristic of the majority of the writing). In order to present hypotaxis visually, I have indented participial modifiers five spaces and subordinating clauses with a finite verb ten spaces (see p. 8).

Plutarch's lengthy sentences consist of independent, finite verbs (bold above) embedded within a complex series of participles and subordinated clauses which function circumstantially ('as Theopompus tells . . .'; line 2),

---

1. Antoinette C. Wire and others would see this style as essentially oral (see, for example, *Holy Lives, Holy Deaths: A Close Hearing of Early Jewish Storytellers* [SBL, 1; Atlanta: Society of Biblical Literature, 2002], p. 80).

Demosthenes, the father of Demosthenes, **belonged** to the better class of citizens,
>> as (ὡς) Theopompus tells us,
and (δέ) **was surnamed** Cutler,
>> because he had (participle) a large factory and slaves
>> who were skilled workmen (participle) in this business.
>>> But as for what (ἃ δ') Aeschines the orator says of the mother of Demosthenes,
>>> that (ὡς) she was a daughter of one Gylon,
>>> who (τινος) was banished from the city on a charge of treason,
>>> and of a barbarian woman,

5 I **cannot say**
>> whether (εἴτ') he speaks truly or (εἴτε) is uttering slander and lies.
>> However (δ'), at the age of seven (participle),
Demosthenes **was wronged** by his guardians
>> after being left (participle) by his father in affluence,
>> since (γάρ) the total value of his estate fell little short of fifteen talents;
>> [his guardians] who appropriated (participle) some of his property to their own uses
>> and neglected (participle) the rest,
>> so that (ὥστε) even his teachers were deprived of their pay.

15 Indeed (δή) it **seems**
>> that it was for (διά τε) this reason
>> that he did not pursue (participle) the studies
>> which were suitable and proper (participle) for a well-born boy....
>>> (Plutarch, *Dem.* 1.4.1-3 [Perrin, LCL 99 with minor adaptations])

Figure 1   Plutarch, *Demosthenes* 1.4.1-3

causally ('because ...'; line 4), relatively ('who were ...'; line 5),
concessively ('but as for what ...'; line 6), conditionally ('whether he
speaks truly ...'; line 11), and to express result (' ... so that ...'; line 18),
among other functions. He employs a great deal of hypotaxis, as is typical
among writers of elite literature.

Like Plutarch, the author of the Gospel of Mark positions the
introduction of his central character (Jesus) after a few items of
prolegomena (related to John the Baptist). Unlike Plutarch, however,
Mark's introduction is remarkably paratactic (see p. 9).

Even in the few instances where subordination does occur, its
expression is limited to the use of the participle (as noted). There are no
subordinating clauses with a finite verb. Such limited stylistics results in a
narrative which is 'fairly crude, repetitious, and conventionalized,'[2]
though – as I will demonstrate below – parataxis does contribute a
certain dynamism to the story.

Within the scope of extant Classical Greek texts, the simple, paratactic
structuring of sentences in the Gospel of Mark is unusual. However, there
are certain texts which do exhibit this simple style. Chariton's novel
Callirhoë is one such text. I turn once more to the introduction of the
central figures near the outset of the story, which follow a few prolegomena
about the author and the main characters (see Figure 3, p. 10).

Some variety of connectors in Chariton's text (καί, δέ;, οὖν) outdoes the
Evangelist's heavy dependence upon the connector καί, yet there remains

2.   Tolbert, *Sowing*, p. 65.

And (καί) **it happened** in those days:
Jesus **came** from Nazareth of Galilee
and (καί) he **was baptized** in the Jordan by John.
And (καί) immediately he **saw**
  the heavens which had been torn apart (participle)
  and (καί) the Spirit which was descending (participle) on him like a dove.
  as he was coming up (participle) out of the water,
And (καί) a voice **came** from heaven:
"You **are** my Son, the Beloved; with you I **am** well pleased."
And (καί) the Spirit immediately **drove** him out into the wilderness.
And (καί) he **was** in the wilderness forty days,
  being tempted by Satan (participle);
and (καί) he **was** with the wild beasts;
and (καί) the angels **waited** on him.
(Mk 1.9-13)

Figure 2 Mark 1.9-13

considerable repetition in Chariton's passages as well as an occurrence of principal verbs that Plutarch does not require. Like Mark's Gospel, subordination in *Callirhoë* occurs primarily through the participle. Only twice does subordination occur as a result of a clause (lines 8–9 and 13), a far cry from the variety of subordinations in the selection from Plutarch. Overall, *Callirhoë* offers more stylization than the Gospel, yet the narrative does not reach the example set by Plutarch's elite writing. Like the Gospel of Mark, Chariton's style is largely paratactic.

In several other ancient Greek texts, parataxis serves as a basis of style. A thorough-going analysis of the parataxis in the Gospel of Mark in relationship to its literary environment has been undertaken by Marius Reiser in his impressively documented study, *Syntax und Stil des Markusevangeliums*.[3] Reiser examines the language of several ancient popular writings to conclude that 'der Gebrauch der Parataxe mit καί im Markusevangelium zeigt nichts Ungewöhnliches verglichen mit dem anderer volkstümlicher Erzähltexte hellenistischer Zeit': the Gospel of Mark participates in the genre of Hellenistic novelistic literature whose audience was popular rather than elite.[4]

This chapter introduces literature that is popular and novelistic, beginning with a consideration of these two terms (Section 1.1). Observations regarding the narrative style (Section 1.2), motifs (Section 1.3), themes (Section 1.4), narrative structure (Section 1.5), and rhetoric (Section 1.6) that are characteristic of novelistic literature set in contrast to the dissimilar characteristics of elite literature further develop a sense of this genre. In the process, I highlight novelistic characteristics of the

3. Marius Reiser, *Syntax und Stil des Markusevangeliums im Licht der hellenistischen Volksliteratur* (WUNT, 2.11; Tübingen: J.C.B. Mohr [Paul Siebeck], 1984).

4. Reiser, *Syntax*, p. 136. See also Hägg, *NIA*, p. 112; J.P. Sullivan, 'Introduction' to Pseudo-Lucian, *The Ass*, in *CAGN*, p. 591.

There **was** a public feast of Aphrodite,
and (καί) almost every woman **had gone** to her temple.
And (δέ) her mother **took** Callirhoë to do homage to the goddess
    who had not appeared in public (participle) before,
    at the prompting (participle) of Love.
And (δέ) at that time Chaereas **was walking** home from the gymnasium,
    gleaming like a star (participle)
            for (γάρ) the ruddiness of exercise bloomed on his shining face like gold
            on silver.
Then (οὖν) by chance at a certain narrow intersection they **fell over** one another
    as they met (participle)
    – a meeting contrived (participle) by the god
        in order to (ἵνα) make sure that they saw each other.
Then (οὖν) erotic love quickly **handed them over** to each other.
                     (*Callir.* 1.1.4-6 [Goold, LCL 481])

Figure 3   Chariton, *Callirhoe* 1.1.4-6

Gospel of Mark.[5] The chapter concludes with a survey of ancient texts
that are generally considered to be 'novelistic' (Section 1.7). My purposes
in the chapter are two-fold. First and foremost, I seek to demonstrate that
Mark participates in the genre of popular novelistic literature. I will also
argue that, although Mark is novelistic, a radical eclecticism that
characterizes both this genre and the Gospel disallows any further specific
designation of genre for the Gospel. The demonstration of these
conclusions substantiates the in-depth comparison of the resurrection
theme in the Gospel of Mark and other novelistic literature that will
follow in Part II.

1.1 *Introduction to Popular Novelistic Literature*

An appreciation of the popular, novelistic qualities of the Gospel of Mark
necessarily begins with a definition of the terms 'popular' and 'novelistic'.
Though introductory, the work of this section plunges the study into the
literary and historical context of the Gospel of Mark.

    Clyde W. Votaw, a scholar of the early twentieth century, was the first
New Testament scholar to position the Gospels among the 'popular'
works of the Greco-Roman world. In his seminal essay on 'The Gospels
and Contemporary Biographies', Votaw defined popular literature as
writings in which 'the didactic aim has operated to the neglect or the
obscuration of the historical facts'.[6] In contrast to these popular works,
Votaw suggested that another genre, 'historical biography', 'presents a
man's life ... out of an adequate knowledge of the facts'.[7] As an

    5. Tolbert undertakes similar tasks with different operating procedures. See *Sowing*, pp.
70–83.
    6. Clyde W. Votaw, 'The Gospels and Contemporary Biographies', *AJT* 19 (1915), pp.
45–73 (51).
    7. Votaw, 'Gospels', 51.

alternative to Votaw's categorization, Karl L. Schmidt posited a corpus of '*Kleinliteratur*', which he considered to be an aggregation of religious traditions written collectively by an ancient religious community that is distinct from what Schmidt termed '*Hochliteratur*', literature written by sophisticated individual authors.[8] For Schmidt, the Gospel of Mark is a primary example of *Kleinliteratur*.

Schmidt's proposal, which continues to have a substantial audience today, has been criticized on two lines of reasoning.[9] Tolbert rejects the idea of a collective author behind the Gospel of Mark: 'most biblical critics now recognize the distinctive hand of individual authors behind each of the Gospels ... [so that] the categorization that Schmidt proposed ... no longer serves any useful purpose.'[10] She argues for an appreciation of popular literature in contrast to elite literature, defining 'popular literature' broadly as 'literature composed so as to be accessible to a wide spectrum of society'.[11] Harry Gamble takes issue with the binary approach of Schmidt's work, claiming that an attempt 'to posit two categories ... oversimplifies ... a far more variegated literary situation'.[12] His work exemplifies a general movement within biblical scholarship that seeks to nuance the overdrawn dichotomies which often characterize approaches to the Hellenistic world.[13] Certainly, scholars undertaking generic analyses of ancient literature need not limit their work to two mutually exclusive categories. However, a significant bifurcation that marks the economy of the Imperial period indicates that such an approach to the literature may be instructive. In general agreement with Votaw and Tolbert, this study appreciates a genre of popular, novelistic literature in contrast to elite literature. I suggest that the popular, novelistic literary form is a product of a historical context in which the economic environment was significantly bifurcated.

A recent study by Justin Meggitt describes Roman economy in binary terms – wide-scale destitution and a small super-wealthy elite.[14] In an attempt to nuance this work, Steven J. Friesen identifies seven economic

---

8. See Karl L. Schmidt, 'Die Stellung der Evangelien in der allgemeinen Literaturgeschichte', in Hans Schmidt (ed.), *Eucharisterion: Studien zur Religion und Literatur des Alten und Neuen Testament: Hermann Gunkel zum 60 Geburtstage, 2 Band*, pp. 50–134.

9. Several reprintings, as well as an English translation in 2002, witness to the significant influence of Schmidt's proposal.

10. Tolbert, *Sowing*, p. 60, n. 39.

11. Tolbert, *Sowing*, p. 70.

12. Harry Y. Gamble, *Books and Readers in the Early Church: A History of Early Christian Texts* (New Haven: Yale University Press, 1995), p. 18.

13. See Section 6.2.1.

14. Justin J. Meggitt, *Paul, Poverty and Survival* (SNTW; Edinburgh: T&T Clark, 1998).

levels within the Roman empire.[15] Yet even Friesen's study acknowledges that 'there was an enormous difference in financial resources between the few people in the top three categories', Friesen's 'elite', 'and the majority who lived near the subsistence level', producing a significant 'gap between the majority of the population and the super-wealthy elites'[16]:

> Relatively few people had incomes between the lower three groups and the super-wealthy three groups, and these people did not comprise a 'middle class' ... Since most wealth in the Roman empire's advanced agrarian economy was based on the ownership of land rather than on entrepreneurial activity, there were very few mechanisms by which individuals or families could accumulate financial resources.[17]

So Friesen, like Meggitt, affirms a substantial economic gap that effectively bifurcates the Roman empire of the first century. Although the economic nature of this gap does not necessitate dualistic approaches to gender or ethnicity in this context, an appreciation of two basic categories of literature does follow insofar as the elite had resources that allowed for the luxury of producing and preserving literary works, whereas the majority of the population did not.

Further consideration of the class system of the Roman Empire in the first century C.E. contributes to an appreciation of the nature of the 'wide spectrum of society' for whom novelistic literature was composed.[18] According to Friesen, only a very narrow segment of the population – specifically 1.23% of the 50–60 million inhabitants of the Roman Empire equaling approximately 675,000 people – were 'elite': imperial elites, provincial elites and municipal elites.[19] Plutarch, for example, was born into an elite family of Chaeronea and associated with extremely wealthy and influential friends.[20] His own wealth afforded him the luxury to study, practice and employ literary niceties such as hypotaxis.[21]

The remaining 98.77% of the population – approximately 55,000,000 people – constitutes the 'wide spectrum' of society which was not elite.

15.   Steven J. Friesen, 'Poverty in Pauline Studies: Beyond the So-called New Consensus', *JSNT* 26 (2004), pp. 323–61.

16.   Friesen, 'Poverty', p. 345.

17.   Friesen, 'Poverty', p. 346.

18.   Tolbert, *Sowing*, p. 70.

19.   Friesen, 'Poverty', pp. 340–1.

20.   See Philip A. Stadter, 'Setting Plutarch in his Context', in Stadter (ed.), *Sage and Emperor: Plutarch, Greek Intellectuals, and Roman Power in the Time of Trajan*, pp. 1–26 (2–4).

21.   See the sources and commentary in Jo-Ann Shelton, *As the Romans Did: A Sourcebook in Roman Social History* (New York, Oxford: Oxford University Press, 2nd edn, 1998), pp. 114–22, 320–3.

(1) people having "moderate surplus resources," being
some merchants, traders, freedpersons, artisans, and veterans,
constituting roughly 7% of the population

(2) people who are "stable near subsistence level," being
many merchants, traders, artisans, and others
constituting roughly 22% of the population

(3) people living "at subsistence level," being
small farm families, laborers, and others
constituting roughly 40% of the population, and

(4) people living "below subsistence level," being
widows, orphans, beggars, disabled, and prisoners
constituting roughly 28% of the population.

Figure 4   Friesen, 'Poverty', 341 (reformatted)

Acknowledging a high level of generalization, Friesen divides this spectrum into four groups, described in Figure 4 above.[22]

Notice that members of each category are described largely according to occupation. The vast majority of the population spent most of their time in trade or on the farm; they would probably not have had the luxury of studying literature for extended periods of time as the elite did.

Explicit indications in his text as well as the paratactic stylistics of his text suggest that Chariton is perhaps best situated among the artisans of the first or second category, constituting roughly 30% of the population. In the opening of his novel, Chariton describes himself as a 'clerk of the lawyer Athenagoras' (*Callir.* 1.1.1). Such a skilled occupation under the employment of another skilled citizen – perhaps the lawyer Athenagoras was a member of the elite classes – would allow Chariton a certain degree of stability as opposed to subsistence. Assigning Chariton to a mid-range social position receives further support from the extent of parataxis in his novel, which does not reach the example set by Plutarch's elite writing, yet is not as basic as the parataxis of the Gospel of Mark. So Chariton may participate in and write primarily for an audience with surplus or stable resources, representing approximately 30% of the population (categories 1 and 2 in Friesen's schema, above).

If – as I have hypothesized for *Callirhoë* – the literary stylistics of the Gospel of Mark correlate to the social status of both the author and his audience, then Mark's parataxis suggests that his audience falls somewhere below Chariton's audience on the scale proposed by Friesen. Lawrence Wills draws a similar connection between literary stylistics and social status in relation to the Gospel of Mark when he describes the

22.   See Friesen, 'Poverty', pp. 340–7 (341). The presentation is mine.

popular *Ninus Romance* and *The Alexander Romance* as 'novels from a lower, more indigenous social level, which are shorter and written in a style much closer to Mark'.[23] If the style of Mark's Gospel suggests that the social level of the text looks up at novels such as *Callirhoë* from below, perhaps its author holds a social status that is 'stable near subsistence level' or 'at subsistence level' or lower (categories 2, 3 and 4 above), representing approximately 90% of the population.

Admittedly, determining a specific scale of poverty is 'messy and multidimensional'.[24] For example, as will become apparent in the investigation that follows, certain aspects of Mark's literary work suggest that its author had an advanced knowledge of ancient rhetorical techniques, suggesting that the text might also appeal to people having 'moderate surplus resources' (category 1 above).[25] We must allow for opportunities in public venues that would afford even authors with subsistence-level resources exposure to highly refined literature and its devices.[26] Equating literary stylistics with social status is hypothetical, as is the further extension of this status from author to audience. However, the rather conventional and crude style of their texts suggests that neither Mark nor Chariton write for the likes of Plutarch's audience. Their novelistic literature seeks the wide popular audience constituting 98% of the population who – being necessarily preoccupied with life-sustaining endeavors – were not sufficiently trained to appreciate extensive hypotaxis.[27]

And yet – although the luxury of advanced literary training was not accessible – an increasing number of people in the late Hellenistic period were learning to read and write.[28] This spread of writing enabled the popular class to develop a new (novel) art form: *novelistic literature*.[29] People from middle and lower status levels in many different geographical regions began to write down *engaging stories and tales in prose narrative*

---

23.   Wills, *Quest*, 11. See also Reardon, 'Chariton', *NAW*, pp. 309–35 (324).

24.   Peter Oakes, 'Constructing Poverty Scales for Graeco-Roman Society: A Response to Steven Friesen's "Poverty in Pauline Studies" ', *JSNT* 26 (2004), pp. 367–71 (371).

25.   See Section 1.5.3.

26.   The caveat is Gamble's (*Books and Readers*, p. 18). On public readings, see Shelton, *As the Romans Did*, pp. 318–20.

27.   Tomas Hägg presents several compelling arguments that novelistic literature seeks a wide audience in his 'Orality, Literacy, and the "Readership" of the Early Greek Novel', on pp. 47–81 of Eriksen (ed.), *Contexts of Pre-Novel Narrative: The European Tradition*.

28.   On the increase of literacy in the Hellenistic period, see Teresa Morgan, *Literate Education in the Hellenistic and Roman Worlds* (CCS; New York and Cambridge, Engl.: Cambridge University Press, 1998).

29.   This heritage from a largely illiterate oral-based social class results in a genre that shares many characteristics with the literary expressions of oral traditions.

for a popular audience.[30] The resulting literature is as diverse and complex as the Hellenistic milieu in which it arose. Nevertheless, the essence of the genre is discernible, as the following survey of novelistic characteristics and texts demonstrates.

1.2 *Novelistic Narrative Style*

One of the primary characteristics of the novelistic genre is the manner in which novelistic writings tell a story. In essence, novelistic literature promotes a heightened sense of emotion and drama. In this section I will consider three other devices of novelistic literature that further enhance this general style. I first note the recurrence of asyndeton, a literary device that takes the austere approach of parataxis one step further by juxtaposing two or more sentences without any connective (Section 1.2.1). Secondly, I observe an episodic plot development in novelistic literature that mimics the style of parataxis on the broader level of plot element (Section 1.2.2). Thirdly, I note a frequent occurrence of explicit temporal markers in novelistic literature that significantly enlivens the pace of the narrative (Section 1.2.3). The Gospel of Mark shares each of these narrative stylistics.

1.2.1. *Parataxis and Asyndeton*

The paratactic arrangement of phrases I have considered at the introduction of this chapter may be the single most salient characteristic of the narrative style of the novelistic genre. Capitalizing upon this concept, novelistic authors who would further heighten the pace and intensity of a particular episode within a story often do so by eliminating all connectives whatsoever. Grammarians refer to the absence of connectives as *asyndeton*.[31] One particularly illustrative example occurs as Chaereas stands before Callirhoë's father and the assembled council of Syracuse in order to accuse himself of killing Callirhoë:

δημοσίᾳ με καταλεύσατε· ἀπεστεφάνωσα τὸν δῆμον. φιλάνθρωπόν ἐστιν ἄν παραδῶτε με δημίῳ. τοῦτο ὤφελον παθεῖν, εἰ καὶ θεραπαινίδα Ἑρμοκράτους ἀπέκτεινα. τρόπον ζητήσατε κολάσεως ἀπόρρητον. χείρονα δέδρακα ἱεροσύλων καὶ πατροκτόνων. μὴ θάπητέ με, μὴ μιάνητε τὴν γῆν, ἀλλὰ τὸ ἀσεβὲς καταποντώσατε σῶμα.

---

30. See Lawrence M. Wills, *The Jewish Novel in the Ancient World* (M&P; Ithaca and London, 1995), pp. 4–10 as well as his *Ancient Jewish Novels: An Anthology* (Oxford; New York: Oxford University Press, 2002), pp. 5–15; and William Hansen (ed.), *Anthology of Ancient Greek Popular Literature*, pp. xx-xxiii.

31. The word derives from a compound of the Greek words, α- (alpha privative) meaning 'without' and the word σύνδετον, meaning 'binding'. The plural is 'asyndeta'.

> Stone me to death in public. I have robbed the people of its chief
> distinction. It would be merciful to hand me over to the executioner. I
> should have deserved this, had I only killed Hermocrates' maidservant.
> Look for some condign form of punishment. I have committed a crime
> worse than temple-robbing or parricide. Do not bury me. Do not
> pollute the earth but plunge my wicked body to the bottom of the sea!
>
> (Chariton, *Callir.* 1.5.4–5 [Goold, LCL 481])

In this passionate episode, Chaereas discharges nine statements rapid-fire, without allowing for any conjunctions until his final proclamation: 'but (ἀλλά) plunge my wicked body to the bottom of the sea!' Because connectives occur with such regularity and richness in Greek, their absence throughout this lengthy speech is particularly striking. Yet the function of that absence is correspondingly clear. As grammarian Herbert Smyth has noted, 'Asyndeton generally expresses emotion of some sort, and is the mark of liveliness, rapidity, passion, or impressiveness, of thought, each idea being set forth separately and distinctly.'[32] Due to this unique quality, authors most often employ asyndeton in association with the direct speech of a character, be that in the speech itself, in the introduction of direct speech, or in the continuation of a narrative following the speech of a character,[33] though it may occur apart from any connection with direct speech for rhetorical effect.[34] Asyndeton is a characteristic of lively, conversational speech.[35]

Writers of elite as well as novelistic literature make use of this literary device. Demosthenes (384–322 B.C.E.), a 'consummate orator' whose speeches were studied as exemplary literature in the Hellenistic period, occasionally employs asyndeton in his own orations for emotional effect (e.g. *Timocr.* 11–13, 106; *1 Aristog.* 63).[36] However, there is an accumulation of asyndeta in novelistic literature which is distinctive. In his analysis of asyndeton throughout Hellenistic literature, Reiser declares that Chariton, as one example among several novelistic writings, makes extensive application of asyndeta.[37] In fact, he cites 31 passages in *Callirhoë* which employ the device.[38]

---

32. Herbert W. Smyth, *Greek Grammar* (Cambridge, Mass. and London: Harvard University Press, rev. edn, 1984), §2165a.

33. Reiser's study presents textual examples of each. See *Syntax*, p. 154.

34. See Reiser, *Syntax*, pp. 157–8 for some specific examples.

35. So Reiser: 'Das Asyndeton gehört vor allem der Umgangssprache an' (*Syntax*, p. 141).

36. Ian Worthington (ed.), 'Introduction' to *Demosthenes: Statesman and Orator*, p. 5.

37. Reiser, *Syntax*, p. 140: 'wirkt die Häufung des Asyndetons in den Romanen oft rhetorisch stilisiert und gekünstelt, so namentlich bei Chariton, der den ausgiebigsten Gebrauch davon macht.'

38. See Reiser, *Syntax*, pp. 138–62.

Asyndeton also occurs frequently in the Gospel of Mark. Consider, for example, Jesus' statements following his time of prayer at Gethsemane:

καὶ ἔρχεται τὸ τρίτον καὶ λέγει αὐτοῖς, Καθεύδετε τὸ λοιπὸν καὶ ἀναπαύεσθε; ἀπέχει· ἦλθεν ἡ ὥρα, ἰδοὺ παραδίδοται ὁ υἱὸς τοῦ ἀνθρώπου εἰς τὰς χεῖρας τῶν ἁμαρτωλῶν. ἐγείρεσθε ἄγωμεν· ἰδοὺ ὁ παραδιδούς με ἤγγικεν.

And he comes a third time and says to them, 'Are you still sleeping and taking your rest? That is enough! The hour has come! Look, the Son of Man is betrayed into the hands of sinners. Get up! Let us be going! Look, my betrayer is at hand!' (Mk 14.41-42)

The situation has a dramatic tenor comparable to that of Chaereas in the example from *Callirhoë*, above: like Chaereas, Jesus ardently acknowledges his own impending death. There is also a strong component of frustration: this is the third time Jesus has come to his disciples and found them sleeping, despite repeated exhortations to prayer.[39] So the author transitions from language employing his customary connective, καί (καὶ ἔρχεται τὸ τρίτον καὶ λέγει αὐτοῖς ...), to a direct speech in which conjunctives are either absent or replaced by the exclamation 'behold!' (ἰδού). Like Chariton's exasperated Chaereas, Jesus delivers short, staccato statements: seven in a row. This is a scene crafted with the artistry of novelistic literature.

Asyndeton occurs throughout the Gospel in the introduction of direct speech (Mk 8.19, 29; 14.19), within direct speech itself (1.41; 4.27; 5.36; 6.50; 7.29; 9.7, 24, 43-47; 10.49; 11.2; 15.31; 16.6-8), in the transition from direct speech to third person narration (5.35; 8.1; 10.27), and elsewhere for rhetorical effect (12.6).[40] Its pervasive presence, Reiser concludes, communicates 'the style of popular literature'.[41]

1.2.2. *Episodic Plot Development*
The rate at which episodes develop within a literary work has a significant impact on the overall narrative tempo of that work. Writers of novelistic literature typically write narratives that consist of many brief, sequential

---

39. Episodes presented in a series of three progressive repetitions are 'perhaps the most recognizable pattern of repetition in Mark' (David Rhoads, Joanna Dewey, and Donald Michie, *Mark as Story: An Introduction to the Narrative of a Gospel* [Minneapolis: Fortress, 2nd edn, 1999], p. 54). Frans Neirynck identifies 23 'series of three' in the Gospel in his study, *Duality in Mark: Contributions to the Study of the Markan Redaction* (BETL, 31; Leuven, Belgium: Leuven University Press, 1972), pp. 110–12. See also Werner H. Kelber, *The Oral and the Written Gospel: The Hermeneutics of Speaking and Writing in the Synoptic Tradition, Mark, Paul and Q*, (VPT; Bloomington and Indianapolis: Indiana University Press, 2nd edn, 1997), p. 59.

40. Reiser, *Syntax* (Chapter 5: 'Das Asyndeton').

41. Reiser, *Syntax*, p. 162: 'den Stil der einfachen Volksliteratur'.

episodes and minimal description. Elite authors, on the other hand, tend to write fewer, highly detailed episodes that have a complex relation one to another. A comparison of passages from Chariton's *Callirhoë* (Section 1.2.2.1), Appian's *History of Rome* (Section 1.2.2.2) and the Gospel of Mark (Section 1.2.2.3) illustrate the characteristics of plot development within novelistic literature as well as in the Gospel of Mark. In particular, I will consider (1) the description of the episode, (2) geographical description within the episode, (3) character description, (4) the use of metaphor in each of these writings, and (5) the extent to which direct speech is present.

1.2.2.1. *Episodic Plot Development in Novelistic Literature*

From the outset of his story, Chariton's *Callirhoë* contains an abundance of brief episodes.[42] Immediately following their initial collision, Callirhoë and Chaereas separate (*Callir.* 1.1.5), pine for one another (1.1.5–14), eventually marry (1.1.15–16), are separated again (1.4.11), and continue to experience a series of episodes which are briefly and dramatically described until the text arrives at a final reunion of the two lovers in Book Eight. The scene in which Callirhoë is given as a bride to Chaereas illustrates some key characteristics of episodic plot development:

> [11] A regular assembly occurred. When the people had taken their seats, their first and only cry was this, 'Excellent Hermocrates, mighty leader, save Chaereas! This will be your greatest triumph. The city petitions for the marriage today of a couple worthy of each other.' [12] Who could describe that assembly, at which Love was the spokesperson? The patriotic Hermocrates was unable to refuse the appeals of the city. When he gave his consent, the people all rushed from the theater: the young men went to find Chaereas while the council and magistrates escorted Hermocrates. [13] Even the women of Syracuse were there to attend the bride. The marriage hymn sounded throughout the city; the streets were filled with garlands and torches, and the doorways sprinkled with wine and perfume. The Syracusans celebrated this day with more joy than the day of their victory over the Athenians.
>
> (Chariton, *Callir.* 1.1.11–13 [Goold, LCL 481])

This brief scene consists of two basic episodes: the assembly (1.1.11–12) and preparations for a wedding (1.1.12–13). Note how these episodes directly relate to one another in terms of cause and effect: because the assembly calls for a wedding, the wedding occurs. Note also that Chariton describes the initial event in the barest of terms – 'a regular assembly occurred' (1.1.11) – giving no indication as to how many attend. The brief

---

42. See Anderson, 'Introduction' to Xenophon of Ephesus, *An Ephesian Tale*, in *CAGN*, p. 12; Hägg, *NIA*, pp. 32–3, and Sullivan, 'Introduction' to Pseudo-Lucian, *The Ass*, in *CAGN*, pp. 591–2.

description indicates only that the crowd includes the council, magistrates, and 'even the women' (1.1.13). Sounds of the rushing crowd; hymns; smells of garlands, wine, and perfume; and visions of celebrating crowds fill the scene, though the detail is not elaborate.

Furthermore, Chariton's text informs us only partially about the *geography* and characters related to the scene. He makes brief mention of the theater and the city filled with people. What remains unexplained is where the men went to find Chaereas, or specifically to where the council and magistrates are escorting Hermocrates (1.1.12).[43]

The *character descriptions* which occur throughout the text are most often limited to a single word. Hermocrates is described only sporadically throughout this text as 'excellent', 'mighty', and 'patriotic' (1.1.11–12). In fact, there is no extensive narrative describing the virtues of this national hero to be found throughout the entirety of Chariton's text.[44]

Chariton employs several metaphors in his story as if to compensate for a lack of description. Chariton's use of metaphor evokes the participation of the reader.[45] For example, a rhetorical question in Section 11 effectually calls upon the reader to fill in the blanks: 'Who could describe that assembly, at which Love was the spokesperson?' the narrator asks, without providing further guidance. The description of the celebratory wedding preparations depends ultimately upon the readers' imagination. The text also alludes to the Syracusan victory over the Athenians, calling upon the audience members to apply their own mental images of this past celebration to this matrimonial episode that Chariton narrates so briefly.

Direct speech, on the other hand, plays a significant role in *Callirhoë*. A direct proclamation from the crowd calls for a response that furthers the action (*Callir.* 1.1.11). The inclusion of this public outcry introduces a vividness to the text. 'A rich admixture of direct speech ...', Tomas Hägg concurs, '[is] very typical of Chariton.'[46]

---

43. See Shelton, *As the Romans*, pp. 39–43.

44. See Anderson, 'Introduction' to Xenophon of Ephesus, *An Ephesian Tale*, in *CAGN*, p. 126). Like Xenophon's Hippothous, the Gospel's Peter goes in extremes in two opposing directions: proclamation of faith (Mk 14.29) and lack of faith (14.37, 66-72).

45. 'Similes ... are common in the novels. Instead of a lengthy verbal description, the author evokes a mental image in his reader ... (Hägg, *NIA*, p. 7).

46. *NIA*, pp. 8–9. 'Nearly half of [Chariton's] text consists of direct speech .... Besides speeches and monologues there are also passages of lively and rapid dialogue' (*NIA*, p. 16). Bryan P. Reardon concurs: 'The greater part of [Chariton's] text is occupied by dramatic presentation of the story, and much of that is actually in direct speech' ('General Introduction', in *CAGN*, p. 20). In Xenophon's *An Ephesian Tale* also, 'certain episodes, especially at the beginning of the novel, are embroidered with ... direct speech' (*NIA*, p. 21). For an in-depth study of direct speech in three ancient novels, see Tomas Hägg, *Narrative Technique in Ancient Greek Romances: Studies of Chariton, Xenophon Ephesius and Achilles Tatius* (Stockholm: Svenska Institutet i Athen, 1971).

1.2.2.2. *Episodic Plot Development in Elite Literature*

The distinctiveness of the episodic plot development in novelistic literature grows in definition when set in contrast to elite texts. *The History of Rome* by Appian, a wealthy and highly educated historian who lived in the late first and early second century C.E., has a narrative pace that is markedly slower than that of Chariton's *Callirhoë*. Appian's retelling of Hannibal's attack on Rome in 217 B.C.E. (Appian, *Hann.* 2.8–10) compares to the technique of Chariton in that Appian relates this episode to the material which proceeds through a cause and effect relationship: Hannibal's movement is the motivation behind the description of the Roman preparations. Unlike Chariton, however, the *description of the event* in this text might be described as profuse. Whereas Chariton provides sparse details regarding the assembly at the wedding, for example, Appian gives extensive details regarding the cause for the levy, the size and constituency of the new army, the leadership, and the locations to which they travel. Particular attention is given to *geography*. As often is the case in his writings, so in the second half of Section 8 Appian describes not only the location of the geography, but also its history and inhabitants.[47]

The portrayal of *characters* in Appian's narrative not only pays careful attention to their motivations and movements, but also uses detailed information about the characters to further the artistry of the scene described. The 'rash' and 'inexperienced' Roman leader, Flaminius, 'had been wafted into power on a popular breeze' (*Hann.* 2. 9). Maharbal, Hannibal's lieutenant, on the other hand, is next described as having 'acquired very great renown in war' (2.10). These character descriptions prepare Appian's audience for the eventual outcome of the battle: the Carthaginians defeat the Romans.

There is neither simile nor explicit metaphor in this passage. Appian assumes the entirety of the work of description, relying on his many details to paint a picture of the episode for his audience. Yet Appian's *History*, as many other elite texts, only rarely employs *direct speech*. At no point in this excerpt do the characters themselves speak: narrative summary takes the place of direct speech or dialogue. Appian gives no indication as to what specifically is said among the parties involved as the armies are levied or dispatched. He does not detail the report by which Hannibal learns of this Roman activity and positions himself to attack. Third person narration dominates the passage.

---

47. In Sections 9 and 10, marshes, a mountain, a lake, and narrow passages receive specific mention. However, these details enhance an appreciation of the battle scene that Appian describes in those sections. They are not simply narrative coloring, as in the description of the Apennines (Section 8) and elsewhere in his texts.

1.2.2.3. *Episodic Plot Development in the Gospel of Mark*

Even a dynamic writer of history such as Appian seems quite slow-going in comparison with the lightning-fast pace of the Gospel of Mark. Although the pace of the plot development in the Gospel does not compare with the detailed style of this elite text, Mark's rapid pace has an analog in novelistic writings such as *Callirhoë*.

After a few sentences of introduction, Mark launches his fast-paced portrayal of Jesus as he begins his ministry in Galilee. Jesus makes public proclamations (Mk 1.14-15), calls disciples (1.16-20), teaches in synagogues (1.21-22), performs exorcisms (1.23-28), and heals many people (1.29-34) in a series of brief, dramatic narrative units that continue through the Passion Narrative at the end of the story. A brief examination of the first four of these episodes (Mk 1.14-15, 16-18, 19-20, 21-22) illustrates the rapid tempo of Mark's plot development.

Rather than cause and effect, Mark presents one independent episode after another in a linear series related only as the result of the movements of an individual. An emphasis upon action in these events takes the place of any lengthy verbal *description of the events* such as I noted in relation to Appian's text. The author treats each episode in approximately one to three sentences, sparing the details in a manner comparable to Chariton's description of his wedding assembly. In fact, Mark spares details even when full appreciation of the story seems to depend upon such. In the first episode, for example, the mention of John's arrest ends as abruptly as it begins (1.14), leaving the audience without any explanation of this event until several episodes later (Mk 6.14-29).

Unlike Appian's text, the *geographical location* of each Markan episode receives mention only in the starkest of terms, particularly in the third episode which is described simply as 'a little farther' along in Jesus' travels. Other locations such as Galilee (1.14), the Sea of Galilee (1.16), and Capernaum (1.21) are mentioned in name only without any accompanying description. So the treatment of geography is similar to that noted in Chariton's text. Apparently, Mark's rapid narrative pace will not allow for elaborations such as where Galilee is in relation to the River Jordan, what kind of place Capernaum is in comparison to the place of Galilee, or the physical descriptions of any of the places mentioned.

Furthermore, neither Jesus' physical characteristics, nor his personal *character* – not even his astounding teaching – receives a substantial description. Like Chariton's *Callirhoë*, 'one stereotypical adjective, if that, is all most characters receive' in Mark's Gospel.[48] The author employs a simple *simile* in his description of Jesus, applicable only to his teaching: Jesus teaches 'as one having authority, and not as the scribes' (1.22).

---

48. Tolbert, *Sowing*, p. 67.

Rather than supplying his own description of Jesus' teaching in the form of an extensive narrative passage, Mark, as does Chariton, prompts his audience members to supply the details through the use of a simile.[49]

The occurrence of any dialogue must be inferred from simple *direct speech* in the form of proclamations made on the part of Jesus (1.15, 17). Thus direct speech plays a role similar to the role it plays in Chariton's *Callirhoë*. In Chariton, a direct proclamation from the crowd also calls for a response that furthers the action (*Callir.* 1.1.11). In Mark, Jesus calls the disciples to a response that establishes a relationship and prepares for future action (Mk 1.17). By the third and fourth episode these proclamations are themselves deemed unnecessary as narrative summary serves to accelerate the pace even more: Jesus merely calls (1.20) and teaches (1.21). Response is immediate and unburdened by either dialogue or discussions of motivation, highlighting the remarkable power of Jesus' teaching. Furthermore, the author has juxtaposed the second, third, and fourth episodes so that this response is repeated three times in a row, further emphasizing the powerful impact of Jesus' teaching.

Minimizing the description of events, characters, places, or dialogue allows for the passage of four episodes in just nine short verses. Although the pace does slow at times – as when Jesus encounters a demoniac in ch. 5 – the development of the plot via short episodes continues throughout the story.

1.2.2.4. *Conclusion*
An attenuation of description in novelistic literature allows for an episodic plot development that progresses at a much quicker rate than elite literature. This novelistic characteristic also dominates the Gospel of Mark. In fact, when compared to the popular novel by Chariton, the Gospel of Mark is particularly fast-paced and action-packed, perhaps indicating a source from a lower social position.[50]

1.2.3 *Explicit Temporal Markers*
Authors of novelistic literature also enliven the pace of their narratives through the frequent employment of temporal markers such as adverbs which indicate the rapidity of an action ('immediately', 'suddenly') or brief phrases marking time ('on the next day', 'at three o'clock'). That this technique is a distinctive characteristic of novelistic literature employed

---

49. Elsewhere, the author of Mark employs simile in place of lengthy description (1) as the Spirit descends upon Jesus 'like a dove' (Mk 1.10), (2) when Jesus' garments become 'as no one on earth could bleach them' (9.3), and (3) when he is arrested 'as though a bandit' (14.48).

50. Again, perhaps Mark's extremely novelistic character indicates a target audience that is 'lower' and thereby 'wider' than Chariton's audience. See Section 1.1.

throughout novelistic texts as well as the Gospel of Mark becomes apparent through philological analysis.

The text of the Gospel of Mark employs the adverb 'immediately' (εὐθύς) to an extreme that correlates to the excesses of its καί-parataxis and episodic plot development. Most often, the adverb occurs in transitional phrases, creating a sense of perpetual action. Within the approximately 11,110 words between Mk 1.10 and 15.1, the word εὐθύς occurs 51 times – even twice in one verse on one occasion.[51] In all, this single word accounts for an impressive 0.46% of the words in the NA[27] text of the Gospel. Indeed, the repetitiveness of this adverb becomes apparent in even the most lackadaisical reading. There is only one instance in which Mark makes use of a different adverb to increase the sense of speed within his narrative: the adverb ταχύς occurs in Mk 9.39. Taking this single adverb into account, adverbs evoking a sense of urgency constitute 0.47% of the text of the Gospel of Mark.

Chariton also employs the Greek word εὐθύς to enhance the liveliness of his narrative, though as might be expected, he does so with greater moderation. In the first of his eight books, for example, the word occurs six times, representing merely 0.12% of the approximately 5,100 words of that book.[52] However, a broader investigation of a wider variety of words reveals an occurrence of adverbs which accelerate the pace of the narrative that is closer to the occurrence of such adverbs in the Gospel of Mark. The adverb ταχύς occurs seven times in Book 1 of *Callirhoë*,[53] the adverb αἰφνίδιον ('suddenly') – which is not found in the Gospel of Mark – occurs twice,[54] and the adverb σπουδῆς ('with haste') – also not found in Mark's Gospel – occurs once,[55] so that the total percentage of adverbs that increase the narrative pace within Book 1 is 0.29%.

This number is still significantly lower than the 0.47% that I identified within the Gospel of Mark. However, Chariton increases the use of such temporal adverbs toward the climactic end of his novel. In the approximately 4,800 words of Book 8, Chariton makes use of the word εὐθύς an impressive twelve times – three times in the closing paragraphs of the novel – representing 0.25% of that text.[56] Other adverbs of urgency in Book 8 include ταχύς which occurs a total of nine times,[57] αἰφνίδιον

---

51. See Mark 1.10, 12, 18, 20, 21, 23, 28, 29, 30, 42, 43; 2.8, 12; 3.6; 4.5, 15, 16, 17, 29; 5.2, 29, 30, 42 (2x); 6.25, 27, 45, 50, 54; 7.25; 8.10; 9.15, 20, 24; 10.52; 11.2, 3; 14.43, 45, 72; 15.1. One of the two occurrences in Mark 5.42 is deemed a textual variant by NA[27].

52. *Callir.* 1.1.14; 1.4.11; 1.7.5; 1.11.7, 8; 1.13.8.

53. *Callir.* 1.1.3, 6, 15; 1.3.7; 1.8.4; 1.9.2; 1.14.6.

54. *Callir.* 1.9.2; 1.14.1.

55. *Callir.* 1.3.4

56. *Callir.* 8.1.7, 16; 8.2.11; 8.3.3, 5; 8.5.4; 8.6.12; 8.7.3, 10; 8.8.5, 6, 14.

57. *Callir.* 8.2.5; 8.3.6, 9; 8.4.3; 8.5.10, 15; 8.6.3, 10; 8.8.4.

which occurs once,[58] and σπουδῆς which occurs once,[59] bringing the total percentage of such adverbs to 0.48%, a figure remarkably similar to the Gospel of Mark. Although Chariton increases his use of adverbs at the end of his story, both *Callirhoë* and the Gospel employ a significant number of adverbs of urgency; Chariton simply does so with greater variation.[60]

These percentage rates do not occur in the more formal writings of elite literature. Two familiar elite texts, Plutarch's *Demosthenes* and Appian's *History*, provide helpful comparisons from both elite biography and elite history (respectively). There are very few adverbs that convey a sense of urgency in Plutarch's biography of Demosthenes: εὐθύς is found only six times in 10,700 words, or in 0.06 percent of the text.[61] The adverb ταχύς occurs five times,[62] and ἐξαίφνης occurs once.[63] The words αἰφνίδιον and σπουδῆς do not occur at all. Overall, adverbs of urgency occur in only 0.11% of the text. The Gospel of Mark and the final book of *Callirhoë* employ adverbs of urgency four times more frequently that Plutarch's elite biography.

Like the Gospel of Mark, Appian seems to have had a preference for the word εὐθύς, though he does not use it nearly as often: there are 16 occurrences of this word in the approximately 9,700 words in Appian's narrative on the Hannibalic War, totaling 0.16% of the text.[64] This percentage represents a greater frequency than I noted in Book 1 of the popular novel by Chariton. However, unlike Chariton, Appian does not employ many other adverbs of urgency: the word ταχύς occurs nowhere in the text, αἰφνίδιον occurs twice,[65] ἐξαίφνης occurs once,[66] and σπουδῆς occurs once.[67] The total percentage of adverbs which seek to increase the narrative pace of this elite text is only 0.20%, a figure that is significantly lower than Mark at 0.47% and Chariton at 0.48%.

My findings can be summarized into tabular format:

---

58.   *Callir.* 8.6.7.

59.   *Callir.* 8.2.1.

60.   I would again grant that the prominence of such adverbs in novelistic literature may be a function of the close relationship of the genre to oral tradition.

61.   Plutarch, *Dem.* 18.3; 22.1; 23.3; 24.2; 25.1; 26.5. The word is used only towards the end of the text and is concentrated in chapters 22–26.

62.   Plutarch, *Dem.* 7.2; 8.1; 12.3; 25.3; 28.1. I have not included the occurrence at 9.3 that Plutarch applies adjectivally when he writes of Demosthenes' forbearance from speaking 'that happens on the sudden', i.e. extemporaneous speech.

63.   Plutarch, *Dem.* 18.1.

64.   Appian, *Hann.* 2.6, 10, 11 (2x); 4.22, 26; 5.31; 6.32, 34, 35; 7.43, 45, 46, 47; 8.51; 9.55. Notice the concentration of occurrences that are limited to 6.32–35 and 7.43–47.

65.   Appian, *Hann.* 3.15; 8.54.

66.   Appian, *Hann.* 7.46.

67.   Appian, *Hann.* 2.9.

TABLE 1: Adverbs of Urgency in Four Ancient Texts							
Text	εὐθύς	Percentage of Text	ταχύς	αἰφνίδιον	ἐξαίφνης	σπουδῆς	Total Percentage of Text
Gospel of Mark	51	0.46	1	---	---	---	0.47
Book 1 of Chariton's *Callirhoë*	6	0.12	7	2	---	1	0.29
Book 8 of Chariton's *Callirhoë*	12	0.25	9	1	---	1	0.48
Plutarch's *Demosthenes*	6	0.06	5	---	1	---	0.11
Appian's *Hannibalic Wars*	16	0.16	---	2	1	1	0.20

A use of adverbs comparable to the climactic end of Chariton's novel occurs throughout the Gospel of Mark. The use of adverbs in both popular texts far exceeds the elite texts of Plutarch and Appian.

Just as Chariton shifts to an increased use of the adverb εὐθύς at the end of his story, so the Gospel of Mark also shifts. However, Mark further enhances the tempo of his narrative through another novelistic technique. As Mark's story progresses, the author replaces the active adverb 'immediately' with specific, controlled time designations.[68] In the closing chapters, these temporal designations carry the audience through the entire day on which Jesus is crucified, from dawn (Mk 15.1) to 'nine o'clock in the morning' (15.25) to noon (15.33) and then on to 'three o'clock' (15.34). 'When evening had come' Joseph of Arimathea removes the body (15.42), which the women seek 'early on the first day of the week' (16.2).[69] Tolbert identifies such specific, controlled time-designations at the end of *An Ephesian Tale*: 'Finally ... Habrocomes and Anthia are reunited .... The whole sequence is carefully plotted over a three-day period and tied together by reference to time: "the following day", "when

68. In the Book of Tobit, for example, three major events happen all on the same day (Tob. 2.12; 3.7, 10; 4.1; cf. 3.16).

69. John R. Donahue and Daniel J. Harrington describe a progression from general indications of time such as 'in those days' (Mk 1.9; 8.1) and 'after some days' (2.1) to more specific indications of the morning or evening of particular days (1.32, 35; 4.35; 6.47) so that 'after Jesus enters Jerusalem (11.1), the time is designated in carefully designated days (11.11-12, 19; 14.1, 12, 17; 15.1, 42; 16.2), and the final day of Jesus' life is carefully demarcated by hours (15.1, 25, 33, 34)' (John R. Donahue and Daniel J. Harrington, *The Gospel of Mark* [SPS, 2; Collegeville, Minn.: Liturgical, 2002], p. 18).

night came", and so forth.'[70] This ending propels the narrative pace into a dramatic flurry that accelerates exponentially so that by the end of the story a lifetime is but a phrase: 'and they themselves lived happily ever after; the rest of their life together was one long festival' (*Eph. Tale* 5.15; [G. Anderson, *CAGN*]).[71]

1.2.4 *Conclusion*

Novelistic authors attain a fast-paced and lively narrative tempo through their characteristic manner of telling a story. Like these authors, Mark writes in a dramatic parataxis that occasionally intensifies to asyndeton, developing his plot through brief episodes and frequently employing adverbs of urgency in an effort to maintain the pace.[72]

1.3 *Novelistic Motifs*

The stylistics and narrative devices of the Gospel of Mark are not the only literary characteristics that suggest the kinship of the Gospel to Hellenistic novelistic literature. Many of the same motifs that enliven ancient novelistic writings play a significant role in Mark's story. In this section I will demonstrate the fact that both novelistic literature and Mark's Gospel repeatedly incorporate displays of intense emotion (Section 1.3.1), crowds (Section 1.3.2), and trials (Section 1.3.3). Other shared motifs draw upon a human fascination with the macabre: morbid descriptions that diverge from the norm (Section 1.3.4) and incidences of violence and torture (Section 1.3.5). Although the exploration that follows incorporates examples from a broad spectrum of novelistic literature, my primary focus remains specifically on *Callirhoë* and the Gospel of Mark.

1.3.1 *Displays of Intense Emotion*

The brisk pace of novelistic literature does occasionally slow for topics that are especially engaging, such as displays of intense emotion.[73] This novelistic motif is particularly apparent in romantic novels such as those by Chariton, Xenophon of Ephesus, Achilles Tatius, Longus, and Heliodorus – fully extant texts built around the theme of romantic love. In describing the narrative of *Callirhoë*, for example, Tomas Hägg writes:

---

70. Tolbert, *Sowing*, p. 75.

71. See also Gareth Schmeling, *Xenophon of Ephesus* (TWAS, 613; Boston: Twayne, 1980), pp. 118–24 (as noted by Tolbert, *Sowing*, p. 76, n. 97).

72. See Hägg, *NIA*, pp. 8–9, 21, 81; Reardon, 'Introduction' to Lucian, *A True Story*, in *CAGN*, p. 620.

73. See also Section 1.3.4, 'Teachings and Descriptions that Diverge from the Norm'.

> The 'inner process,' the sorrow and happiness of the characters, their
> hopes and fears, not least their irresolution in difficult situations
> involving choice – the author devotes much more attention to all this
> than he does to the external course of events, which is often dismissed in
> a few short sentences.[74]

'One way or another,' Bryan Reardon remarks about novelistic literature,
'the reader's attention is constantly directed towards the emotion
generated by his hero's situation.'[75]

Chariton's attention to internal emotions is particularly apparent at the
conclusion of Book 1. Callirhoë has been pulled from her tomb by the
pirate Theron only to be confined within a pirate ship, where the motley
crew decides to sell her as a slave in Miletus (*Callir.* 1.9–11). As a result of a
couple of hurried excursions into the town, Theron is able to sell Callirhoë
to Leonas, the household manager of wealthy Dionysius (1.12.1 – 1.14.5).
Once these dealings are complete, Chariton slows his pace to focus upon
Callirhoë's personal reaction to the situation (*Callir.* 1.14.6–10).

The scene is rife with emotion. Isolated on the waves of the sea (*Callir.*
1.1.6), Callirhoë struggles to calm the waves of intense despair which rise
within her. She 'bewails' her fate (1.1.6) in a lengthy monologue that
includes harsh sarcasm (1.1.8) and a fitful condemnation of the god
Fortune (1.1.9). Yet no comfort follows for in the beating of her breast the
tide turns from intense anger to passionate love. Callirhoë notices her
ring, which reminds her in turn of her husband, Chaereas. So powerful are
her emotions that she kisses this surrogate symbol, speaking to it as if
Chaereas were present, confessing her sorry situation with a lamentation
so intense as to keep her from sleep for a time (1.1.10).

Not only is the romantic heroine affected by this emotional high tide,
but the hero and even the gods are also swept up in its current. Callirhoë
perceives our hero, Chaereas, bringing her a 'tribute of tears' (1.1.7). The
'murderer' is portrayed here as a 'lover' who is 'loved' in turn by Callirhoë
(1.1.7) and the recipient of her passionate kiss (1.1.9). She consistently
envisions him as though he too were overcome by emotion, 'repenting in
grief' (1.1.10). Perhaps most striking of all, however, is the emotion
attributed to divine Fortune. Callirhoë accuses the god of being motivated
by fear: 'You were afraid, Fortune!' she defiantly proclaims (1.1.9). No
level of the text, be it human or divine, is left unaffected as Chariton seeks
to inundate his narrative with emotion.

Such extremely intense monologues occur often throughout *Callirhoë*
and other romantic novels of the Greco-Roman world.[76] However, on the
whole, emotions involving romantic love are not the only emotions

---

74. Hägg, *NIA*, p. 16.
75. Reardon, 'General Introduction', in *CAGN*, p. 20.
76. Also Reardon, 'General Introduction', in *CAGN*, p. 10.

emphasized throughout novelistic literature. Writing about the novel *Greek Esther*, Lawrence Wills notes how 'the prayer scenes of Mordecai and Esther provide two different perspectives on the inner life of the protagonists. While Mordecai's prayer is full of bravery and steadfast piety, Esther's is penitent and rending and reflects her vulnerability.'[77] The love incorporated into this presentation of emotions is not romantic, but pious. Feelings of security (Mordecai0 or the lack thereof (Esther) are also operative.

So romantic texts are not the only novelistic texts to emphasize emotions. Indeed, 'emotion is central to all novelistic literature ... it is in the very fabric of the narrative.'[78] Emotions and internal processes are the centerpiece of Pseudo-Lucian's *The Ass* (second century C.E.), for example, a novelistic writing that does not center on romance. This story tells of a man who is transformed into a donkey. Because he cannot speak as a donkey, he cannot communicate with the human beings he encounters along his journeys. Nevertheless, the story is narrated by the donkey himself, who speaks exclusively through his internal voice. So when some humans speak of castrating the donkey, the humans do not know that there is an emotional reaction. The audience, however, is privy to the internal processing of the ass:

> I was already in tears at the thought of the instant loss of my manhood in my ass's skin and told myself that I had no wish to go on living if I were to become a eunuch. So I became determined to refuse all food from then on or throw myself from the mountain, where, although falling to a most pathetic death, I would die with my body whole and intact.
>
> Ps. Luc. *Ass* 33 (J.P. Sullivan)

Ancient audiences delighted in this first-person presentation dominated by the emotional, internal voice of the hero: the story was rewritten in several languages, among which Apuleius' *Golden Ass* (a Latin retelling and expansion) is best known today.

Recent biblical scholarship often attributes the recurrent descriptions of emotion in the Gospel of Mark to an attempt at realism:

> Mark writes about Jesus with a great human realism that Matthew and Luke often omit or tone down; see for example, 1.41 (his compassion); 1.43 (strong displeasure); 6.5 (surprise at disbelief); 8.12 (deep sigh); 10.14 (indignation); and 10.21 (love).[79]

Here Donahue and Harrington present some striking instances of emotion in Mark's Gospel, claiming as motivation an authorial concern for 'great

---

77. Wills, *AJN*, p. 28.
78. Wills, *Jewish Novel*, p. 213; see also pp. 19–20.
79. Donahue and Harrington, *Gospel of Mark*, p. 17.

human realism'. The inclusion of these emotions, however, is more likely a product of the emphases of the ancient popular context in which they arise rather than from concern for realism characteristic of the Renaissance and post-Enlightenment periods. Consider the emotion which accompanies the voice from heaven at the outset of Jesus' ministry (Mk 1.9-13). It conveys feelings of love ('the Beloved'; 1.11) and acceptance ('with you I am well pleased'; 1.11), but the concern is not 'great human realism'. The mythical context in which these emotions are expressed – the heavens torn apart, a Spirit descending like a dove, and a voice coming from heaven – gives no indication of a concern for realism.

Perhaps the most sustained expression of intense emotion in the Gospel is Jesus' prayer in Gethsemane (14.32-42). The author of the Gospel of Mark employs this prayer for the same purpose that the prayers of Mordecai and Esther serve in *Greek Esther*: both provide a perspective of the inner life of the protagonist. For a significant moment, Mark's narrative forfeits the dynamism of perpetual activity in order to address questions of internal conflict and resolution. Mary Ann Tolbert has commented on the function of this passage in light of ancient novelistic literature: 'like the monologues in Xenophon's *Ephesian Tale*, which can also be quite brief, Jesus' prayer comes at a crucial moment, expresses an internal state of dispute between desire and will, and resolves the situation in appropriate action.'[80] For Tolbert, the emotion conveys conflict and resolution rather than human realism. This assessment takes into consideration both (1) the functions of the narrative within the text and (2) the ancient literary-historical context of the Gospel as a whole in a way that appeals to realism do not.

1.3.2 *Crowds*

In his article, 'Narrative Technique and Generic Designation: Crowd Scenes in Luke-Acts and in Chariton', Richard S. Ascough notes five functions of the crowd within *Callirhoë* that are strikingly similar to the function of crowds in the Gospel of Luke and the book of Acts,[81] suggesting that 'when Luke presents crowds in his narrative he uses the technique of presenting crowds found in the novels'.[82] However, the conclusion rightly belongs to Mark rather than Luke, because the vast

---

80. Tolbert, *Sowing*, p. 76; see also p. 214.

81. Richard S. Ascough, 'Narrative Technique and Generic Designation: Crowd Scenes in Luke-Acts and in Chariton', *CBQ* 58 (1996), pp. 69–81.

82. Bultmann identifies 'the impression the miracle creates upon the crowd' as an element of the ancient miracle stories in the Gospels (*The History of the Synoptic Tradition* [trans. John Marsh; New York: Harper and Row, 1972], pp. 225–6). Ascough is correct to identify a novelistic impulse behind this element of the ancient miracle story as it occurs in the Gospels.

majority of Lukan examples that Ascough cites have parallels in Mark. [83]
So Mark, not Luke, first uses the technique of presenting crowds found in
the novels.[84] As Ascough notes, crowds in novelistic literature (1) serve as
an audience, (2) indicate popularity, (3) prevent hostile action, (4) incite
disturbances, and (5) generally facilitate the narrative flow of the text.[85]

1.3.3 *Trials*

Another motif common to Mark and novelistic literature is the
dramatization of court trials, which 'were excellent settings for astonish-
ing revelations, recognitions, and denouements, as well as impressive
oratory'.[86] Chariton places a majestic trial in Babylon at the center of his
story (Book 5). At this trial Callirhoë and Chaereas see each other again,
though briefly ... only to be separated once more. Two trials toward the
end of the Gospel of Mark may be considered part of Mark's tragic
denouement (Mk 14.55-65; 15.1-15). Both are patently unjust – the first
marred by false testimony (14.56-59) and the second by a leader who
succumbs to a riotous mob (15.11-14). They function, in part, to prepare
the audience for the unjust and tragic death of a teacher abandoned by all
of his disciples (cf. 15.40; 16.8).

1.3.4 *Teachings and Descriptions that Diverge from the Norm*

As with displays of intense emotion, Chariton's narrative also slows its
pace and indulges in description for story elements that 'diverge from the
norm', such as 'Callirhoë's beauty, the lovesickness of her admirers,
Theron's villainy' ....[87] and Chariton's elaborate rendering of Callirhoë's
funeral procession, which honors a very young maiden who really is not
dead at all (*Callir.* 1.6.1-5). Certainly, novelistic literature revels in
moribund divergences from the norm. The *Iolaus* fragment refers to a
father's lamentations over an unburied body.[88] One of the characters in
Petronius' popular Roman novel, *The Satyricon* (early first century C.E.),

---

83.   The one Lukan text without Markan parallel occurs at Lk. 23.48, in which the crowd
repents for desiring Jesus' death. This single act, however, may derive from a particular
Lukan emphasis upon an exculpation of the crowd and placement of blame for Jesus' death
elsewhere, rather than from Luke's unique emulation of novelistic qualities.

84.   It is quite likely that the author of Luke was, in fact, familiar with novelistic
techniques. Richard I. Pervo has demonstrated such to be the case from his work specifically
on the book of Acts. See Pervo, *Profit*.

85.   Ascough, 'Narrative', p. 76.

86.   Pervo, *Profit*, p. 47. Column 1 of *Metiochus and Parthenope* witnesses to the
prominence of this theme in novelistic literature. See also Sus 1.28–64; Apuleius, *Met.* 10.7–8;
Philostratus, *Ap. Ty.* 7.9–16; Achilles Tatius, *Leuc. Clit.* 7.7–8.14.

87.   Goold, introduction to *Callirhoë*, p. 15.

88.   See *CAGN*, p. 817.

tells a story of 'The Widow of Ephesus' who refuses to leave the tomb of her husband only to be seduced by a robber there. After three passionate nights in the tomb, the widow saves the robber from crucifixion by placing her husband's corpse on the cross in his stead.[89] In Xenophon's *An Ephesian Tale* (second century C.E.), the hero temporarily lodges with a man who keeps the corpse of his dead wife in an inner room of the house, 'embalmed in the Egyptian style'.[90] The man confides to Habrocomes: 'I still talk to her as if she is alive, and lie down beside her and have my meals with her ....'[91]

The Gospel of Mark also appeals to this 'shock value', slowing its fast pace to describe the unusual and macabre:

> The attempts to bind the Gerasene demoniac are vividly described, as are his cries and self-inflicted wounds; the dire medical condition of the bleeding woman is detailed, and in the narratives of the epileptic boy both Matthew and Luke omit the vivid descriptions of his convulsions, foaming at the mouth, and the cry of the father ....[92]

These excerpts read like a trailer for a B-grade horror film produced with the goal of providing shocking material to a popular audience. This list could in fact be expanded to include the scouring and abusive mockery detailed in Mk 15.15-20.[93]

'The motif of apparent death (*Scheintod*) recurs with persistent regularity', yet also with an amazing diversity of expression.[94] In Antonius Diogenes' novel, both a man and a woman are cursed to experience a return to life daily, 'living at night, but being corpses each day'.[95] Achilles Tatius crafts several apparent death scenes of the most sensational type in which his heroine returns to life (1) after her intestines are (seemingly) extracted from her abdomen,[96] (2) after her head is (seemingly) cut off,[97] and yet again (less dramatically) (3) when she is reported to be dead, but in fact lives.[98] Apuleius writes his resurrection narratives with yet a different type of character in mind: a young boy. In *The Golden Ass*, a grieving father learns that his son actually had swallowed a somnolent, rather than poisonous potion. He arrives at the

89. Petronius, *Sat.* 111.

90. Xenophon of Ephesus, *Eph. Tale*, 5.1.11.

91. Xenophon of Ephesus, *Eph. Tale*, 5.1.11.

92. Donahue and Harrington, *Gospel of Mark*, 16–17.

93. The Mel Gibson film, *The Passion of Christ*, enacts this passage literally with a gruesome rendering more than 30 minutes long.

94. Hägg, *NIA*, p. 9.

95. Photius, *Bibliotheca* 110a-b.

96. Achilles Tatius, *Leuc. Clit.* 3.15–17 (late second century C.E.).

97. Decapitation occurs at Achilles Tatius, *Leuc. Clit.* 5.7.4, after which Leucippe is found to be alive at 5.19.2.

98. The report comes at Achilles Tatius, *Leuc. Clit.* 7.1.4–6 and is proven false at 7.16.3.

tomb just as his shrouded son is in the very act of returning to life.[99] In *Callirhoë*, the heroine experiences a return to life in her very own tomb.[100] Like Chariton, Xenophon of Ephesus also tells of an apparent death of his heroine that is followed by an incident of tomb robbery in which the 'deceased' returns to life.[101] The similarities suggest that Xenophon was influenced by Chariton in one way or another, though they may both simply share in a common resurrection topos (the subject of investigation in Chapter 3).[102] Chariton's account of Callirhoë's empty tomb (*Callir.* 3.3.1–7) also shares many of the elements of the empty tomb story in the Gospel of Mark (Mk 16.4-6).[103] In both narratives, characters visit the tomb of a beloved one to find the entrance unexpectedly opened.[104] Upon further investigation, it is determined that the tomb is in fact empty, resulting in the conclusion that divine intervention has brought a corpse back to a state of health.[105] Such similarities – in addition to the common provenance, date, and novelistic style of the texts by Xenophon, Chariton, and Mark – are sufficiently comparable (1) to raise the question of whether one of these two authors intentionally imitates another, or if they perhaps both share some common source and (2) to merit an in-depth analysis of the treatment of resurrection narratives throughout these two texts. These tasks constitute the substance of this study.[106]

1.3.5 *Violence and Torture*

Tomas Hägg's survey of the ancient novel identifies violence as one of its 'main constituents'.[107] Such a claim garners support from the Hellenistic Jewish novel about Judith that venerates a young woman after she cuts off the head of the commander of the Assyrian army (Jdt. 13.8) and shows it to her fellow townspeople (13.15).[108] Violence is also a central element in the story of *The Ass*, pseudepigraphically attributed to the popular author

99. Apuleius, *The Golden Ass*, 10.12 (second century C.E.). Resurrection is also alluded to throughout this story. See 2.28, 3.24, 11.23.

100. Chariton, *Callir.* 1.8.1 (mid-first century C.E.).

101. See Chariton, *Callir.* 1.7–10; Xenophon of Ephesus, *Eph. Tale* 3.8.

102. In a brief reference, Conte reads the motif a bit broader: 'The intervention of the savior god ... must have been already trivialized as a narrative scheme, since it is later found as a cliché in Chariton ...' (Gian Biagio Conte, *The Hidden Author: An Interpretation of Petronius' Satyricon* [SCL, 60; Berkeley: University of California Press, 1996], p. 101).

103. See the introduction to Chapter Two, below.

104. Chariton has 'stones shaken [down]' and Mark describes a single 'stone rolled away'.

105. In Chariton this determination results from individual witnesses at the scene, including Chaereas himself; in Mark the witness is made by a mysterious man in white and three women at the tomb.

106. See Chapter 3, in particular.

107. Hägg, *NIA*, p. 3.

108. Iamblichus' *Babylonian Story* narrates a similar event (15).

Lucian.[109] Indeed, violence is the grist of Pseudo-Lucian's mill. Even after the narrator is restored to his humanity, his former girlfriend casts him from her chambers out onto the streets before he has a chance to get dressed (56). Another novelistic text, *Life of Aesop*, tells of a miserable mute slave who forces regurgitation upon himself to avoid being whipped for eating his master's prized figs (*Life* 2–3). Even though he is able to reverse many of his misfortunes throughout the remainder of the story – Aesop becomes an influential orator! – the inhabitants of Delphi ultimately call for his execution, forcing him to jump from a cliff to his death (126–142). In the fragmentary *A Phoenician Story*, a gang of robbers murders a young man, cuts out his heart, and roasts it.[110]

Violence plays a central role in Chariton's romantic novel. No character suffers more than the heroine, who is gravely injured by her husband (*Callir*. 1.4.12), trapped within a dark tomb (1.8.1–4), captured by pirates to be sold in a foreign land (1.9.1–7), and compelled to marry a man she does not love (see 3.2.12–13), among other tribulations. Although the bulk of violence that Callirhoë endures occurs in the first half of the novel, Chariton maintains its centrality via six *peristaseis* (περιστάσεις)[111] placed throughout the story in which the heroine dramatically recalls her sufferings.[112]

The Gospel of Mark also repeatedly asserts themes of violence and suffering, particularly through predictions of violence that occur at the beginning of the story (Mk 3.6) and three times at the center of the Gospel: 'the Son of Man will be handed over to the chief priests and the scribes, and they will condemn him to death; then they will hand him over to the Gentiles; they will mock him, and spit upon him, and flog him, and kill him …' (10.34; see also 8.31; 9.31). In ch. 12, a lengthy parable revolves around several slaves and a beloved son who are beaten, insulted and killed (12.2-8) before the abusers themselves are destroyed (12.9). All of this violence works together to prepare the reader for the violent end of the Gospel in which the main character is insulted, beaten, and killed (15.1-39).

Perhaps the ultimate act of violence in the Gospel of Mark is crucifixion. Although crucifixion is 'rarely present in the elite literature

109. Once the main character becomes an ass against his will (*Ass* 13), he must endure repeated beatings (e.g. 16, 30, 42), exploitation (43), exhaustion (30–31), the threat of castration (33), and several threats of death (25, 33), among other acts of violence.

110. The text of *A Phoenician Story* (*Phoinikika*) breaks off before the author reveals whether or not the men eat the heart.

111. The term *peristaseis* is a Greek literary term for lists of trials endured (*Art of Rhet.* 2.8.2). See Epictetus, *Diss*. 1.11, 18, 22, 33 and 2.19, 24; Seneca, *Epistles* 41.4, 82.14; Rom. 8.35-39; 1 Cor. 4.10-13; 2 Cor. 4.8-10; 6.4-10; 11.21b-33.

112. *Callir*. 2.5.10; 3.8.9; 5.1.4; 5.5.2–3; 6.6.4; 6.7.9.

of the period', it occurs frequently in popular literature.[113] Chariton narrates the crucifixion of his secondary character, Theron (*Callir.* 3.4.18), and Iamblichus tells of the crucifixion of his secondary character, Soraechus (*Bab. Tale*, 21). Primary characters also face crucifixion, but they typically find redemption before the process is complete. For example, Chaereas faces crucifixion in Chariton's novel, but receives reprieve from the king just as he mounts his cross (*Callir.* 4.3.5–6). Rhodanes, the hero of Iamblichus' *Babylonian Tale* (second century C.E.), is also removed from the cross on which he hangs (*Bab. Tale* 22). And Habrocomes, the hero of *An Ephesian Tale*, survives crucifixion: a gust of wind causes his cross to tip over into the Nile (*Eph. Tale* 4.2). The occurrence of crucifixion in the Gospel of Mark is not unique among the writings of novelistic literature. What is unique, however, is the death of the protagonist (Mk 15.37). Bystanders, including the religious officials, call for Jesus to 'come down' from his cross just before he dies, a timely request given the crucifixions of Chaereas, Rhodanes, and Habrocomes. However, redemption comes late in Mark, verified only through the testimony of a stranger: 'He has been raised' (16.6). This redemption comes, in fact, after Jesus is actually dead (cf. 15.37).

1.4 *Novelistic Themes*

Each of the novelistic *motifs* of the preceding section are ideas or images that recur at select points in a literary work. Literary *themes* are distinct from motifs in that these ideas or images are associated throughout a work as a whole. In this section I will examine three prominent novelistic themes that also find expression in the Gospel of Mark: travel (Section 1.4.1), history (Section 1.4.2), and the divine realm (Section 1.4.3). Novelistic themes that are *not* prominent in the Gospel of Mark, such as romantic love, are also considered throughout this examination.

1.4.1 *Travel*
The greatest works of Greek literature, *The Iliad* and *The Odyssey*, merit their distinction neither as a result of their great length,[114] nor even primarily as a result of their great age,[115] but rather due to the tremendous influence these writings had in the development of Western civilization. Throughout the Classical and Hellenistic periods, the Homeric texts

113. See Tolbert, *Sowing*, p. 68.

114. *The Iliad* consists of over 15,600 lines, and *The Odyssey* is about 12,000 lines long (Malcolm M. Willcock, 'Homer', *OCD*, pp. 718–20 [718]).

115. General scholarly consensus dates *The Iliad* around 750 B.C.E. and *The Odyssey* around 725 B.C.E. (Willcock, 'Homer', *OCD*, p. 718).

served as a basis of education,[116] with the result that 'in all periods of Greek literature, from the archaic to the Byzantine period, Homer is the natural point of departure for literary work'.[117] An attractive feature of the epics that has intrigued audiences over the centuries is the theme of travel. This theme is particularly dynamic, allowing for the introduction of a variety of adventures such as an encounter with the Cyclops (Book 9 of *The Odyssey*) or a trip to the Underworld (Book 11 of *The Odyssey*), inserted as the author deems effective.

Many early Greek novels capitalize upon this epic theme. Two 'travel novels' can be dated to the third century B.C.E., though they survive only in digest form as found within the notes of a few ancient bibliophiles, principally the summaries in the *Bibliotheca* of Diodorus Siculus. In the novel *Sacred Scripture* by Euhemerus of Messene, Diodorus has read about a fantastic journey through the peloponnesus of the Indian Ocean.[118] On the main island, Panchaea, Euhemerus claims to gain access to 'sacred scriptures' in which he discovers that the gods Uranus, Cronos, and Zeus were once human and served as kings over these very islands. In *Island of the Sun* by Iambulus, Diodorus has read of Iambulus' journey to an incredible utopia in which the eldest male is king, a collective community of men support all women and children, and everyone lives for 150 years.[119] Antonius Diogenes' travel novel, *The Wonders beyond Thule*, which also survives only in fragmentary and summary forms, contains full-blown tales of horses whose skin changes color, a city whose inhabitants see only by night, and a graveyard of the future whose inscriptions reveal the length of one's life, among other fabulous narratives.[120] Despite its fragmentary remains, the travel novel was probably quite popular in the ancient world. The type even engenders a satirical response, as indicated in an extant novel by Lucian, facetiously entitled *A True Story*. In this story, Lucian and a group of adventurers tell tales of their travel to the moon, to the underworld, and even to the belly of a whale.

Lucian's novel, along with the second century C.E. writings of Antonius Diogenes, testify to the prominence of travel as a novelistic theme even after first-century romantic novelists reunited the Homeric themes of

116. See Teresa Morgan, *Literate Education*; Yun Lee Too, ed. *Education in Greek and Roman Antiquity*; and Ronald F. Hock, 'Homer in Greco-Roman Education', in MacDonald (ed.), *Mimesis and Intertextuality in Antiquity and Christianity*, pp. 56–77. 'We cannot miss the ... models: Achilles' anger ..., Aeneas on the last night of Troy ..., the last act of his [Cicero's] political career. All these are schoolroom pieces ... as ... Hamlet's "To be or not to be"' (Conte, *Hidden Author*, p. 51).

117. Hägg, *NIA*, p. 110.

118. Diodorus Siculus, *Biblio.* 6.1.

119. Diodorus Siculus, *Biblio.* 2.55–60.

120. See Photius (*CAGN*, pp. 777–82).

travel and sexual fidelity. Just as the goal of Odysseus' travel is reunion with his faithful wife, Penelope – a reunion continually threatened by a series of challenges and tests of fidelity – so Chariton's dislocated lovers travel throughout the Mediterranean basin and even into Babylon enduring many challenges and temptations before reuniting.[121] The travels of *An Ephesian Tale* all occur within the Mediterranean basin 'in the same Near East, governed by the Romans, as the New Testament'.[122]

Although the Gospel does not incorporate the romantic theme, like the earlier travel novels the Gospel capitalizes upon the itinerant theme, portraying Jesus 'as a traveler, constantly journeying from town to town'.[123] Along his journey, Jesus' adventures include encounters with demoniacs (Mk 1.23-27, 32-34; 5.1-20), mobs of sick people after dark (1.32-34), a leper (1.40-45), a bleeding woman (5.25–36), blind men (8.22-26; 10.46-52), a deaf mute in the Decapolis (7.31–37), a Syro-Phoenician woman in Tyre (7.24-30), and even Moses and Elijah from the afterlife (9.2-8) before Jesus is confronted and condemned by the high priest himself in the great holy city, Jerusalem (14.60-64). Mark's Gospel is a travel adventure of epic proportions.

1.4.2 *History*

The predisposition of novelistic literature to adventurous travel, however, does not exclude history as an affiliated theme. Extant evidence of three novels suggests that history was a significant theme within the novelistic genre. Xenophon of Athens' *Cyropaedia*, written in the fourth century B.C.E., is a highly adventurous, historical novel that tells about the life of the founder of the Persian Empire, Cyrus the Great. In the same century, Ctesius of Cnidus wrote *History of Persia* in which 'historical facts fight a losing battle with the desire to shock, move, excite, and dazzle'.[124] And fragments of Artapanus' *On Moses* suggest that a substantial Jewish historical novel from the third or second century B.C.E. has been lost.[125]

In the later romantic novels, history is not a central focus, but rather serves primarily as a framework for a core of imaginative and entertaining material. Consider, for example, the historical figures behind the lead characters in the romantic novel about *Metiochus and Parthenope*:

The heroine of the novel, Parthenope, is to all appearances identical

---

121. For a visual summary of the travels undertaken in *Callirhoë*, see the map of 'Callirhoë's Journeys' between pp. 7 and 8 of George P. Goold, *Callirhoë* (LCL, 481). See also the collection of maps in *NAW*, pp. 801–14.

122. Hägg, *NIA*, p. 30. See the map opposite the frontispiece of this book.

123. Tolbert, *Sowing*, p. 39.

124. Hägg, *NIA*, pp. 113–14.

125. See, in particular, the summary of Alexander Polyhistor as it is quoted in Eusebius, *Praep. Ev.* 9.27.

with the daughter of Polycrates whom Herodotus mentions, though not by name. The hero, Metiochus, seems to be the eldest son (born c. 530–520 B.C.E.) of Miltiades, the Marathon general, by an anachronism typical of the novelists. As the toastmaster of the symposium we find the philosopher Anaximenes of Miletus ....[126]

In Chariton's *Callirhoë* also, the hero and heroine are the children of historical persons of earlier periods.[127] Furthermore, their adventures – dramatic though they may be – are told in a serious tone.[128] They encounter real people (pirates, governors, and kings) in customary situations (business exchanges, court trials, wedding and funeral processions ...) at real places such as Syracuse, Ionia, and Babylon.[129] This intentional effort to contain the narrative within the bounds of credibility, this emphasis upon verisimilitude, suggests that in some sense and in varying degrees, novelistic writings are offered as true accounts.

The Gospel of Mark also 'is not fiction, in the sense of an invented world that is recognized as such by both author and reader'.[130] Like the majority of novelistic literature, references to particular, identifiable figures (John the Baptist, Pilate) set the dramatic adventures within a specific historical setting. These adventures are related in a serious tone, involving real people (crowds, disciples, Pharisees, governors, Roman centurions) in customary situations (synagogue meetings, fishing, on boats, at meals) at real places (Galilee, Jerusalem, and Tyre). Mark offers his writings as true accounts, though historical verifiability is clearly not his primary concern. Rather, Mark prefers the techniques of popular literature over those of elite biography in order to make his accounts widely accessible.[131]

1.4.3 *The Divine Realm*

The theme of an otherworldly realm is also highly characteristic of Hellenistic novelistic literature. Throughout these writings, 'the action is conducted simultaneously on two levels: "divine and human motivation," as in Homer'.[132] Gods and goddesses are invariably present throughout

126. Hägg, *NIA*, p. 18.

127. See Section 2.3.3 for a detailed treatment of the incorporation of historical figures in novelistic literature.

128. Chariton 'is hardly writing farce: his love story is serious from beginning to end' (Goold, introduction to *Callirhoë*, p. 15).

129. See also Tolbert, *Sowing*, p. 65.

130. Wills, *Quest*, p. 12.

131. I consider further possible motivation for Mark's blending of history and fiction in Section 6.1.1.

132. Hägg, *NIA*, p. 6. The analysis here is of *Callirhoë*, though the concept applies to many of the novelistic writings. See Tolbert, *Sowing*, p. 74.

novelistic literature, though their specific identity varies largely as a result of the location of the human characters in the plot: Xenophon of Ephesus, for example, 'is not interested in controlling the variety of his divine forces: he is content to make [his heroes] worship the local deity wherever they happen to be'.[133] So, as a result of the extensive travels of Xenophon's heroes, Anthia and Habrocomes, 'we meet the living gods and goddesses of the time: The Ephesian Artemis, the Rhodian Helius, the Egyptian Isis, who threaten, are worshipped and conciliated, and come to the rescue .... In the end [of the novel] a written account of the tribulations suffered by hero and heroine is deposited in the shrine of Artemis' at Ephesus.[134]

According to one hypothesis from the 1920s, the form of romance novels is the end-product of a set of traditions that developed around the divine figure Isis.[135] Although scholarship initially dismissed the suggestion,[136] Reinhold Merkelbach successfully resumed consideration of the possibility in the 1960s, claiming that – with the exception of *Callirhoë* – all of the Greco-Roman romance novels are cultic texts of the Hellenistic mystery religions, fully comprehensible only to those who participated in their cult.[137] Such a broad theory applied in broad strokes with claims that at times appear arbitrary[138] led to negative criticism so extensive that the whole question of religion and the novels lay unexplored for some time.[139] However, the pendulum is now returning its swing in favor of religious influences. As anachronistically secular assumptions are increasingly identified within the work of Merkelbach's critics,[140] scholarship is experiencing a renewed – albeit cautious – willingness to identify

---

133. Graham Anderson, 'Introduction' to Xenophon of Ephesus, *An Ephesian Tale*, in *CAGN*, p. 127.

134. Hägg, *NIA*, p. 26.

135. Karoly Kerényi, *Die griechisch-orientalische Romanliteratur in religionsgeschichtlicher Beleuchtung* (Tübingen: Mohr, 1927; 2nd edn: Darmstadt: Wissenschaftliche Buchgesellschaft, 1962; 3rd edn: Darmstadt: Wissenschaftliche Buchgesellschaft, 1973).

136. The chief arguments against Kerényi are contained in Arthur D. Nock, 'Greek Novels and Egyptian Religion', *Gnomon* 4 (1928), pp. 485–92, frequently cited as decisive.

137. Reinhold Merkelbach, *Roman und Mysterium in der Antike* (Munich and Berlin: C.H. Beck, 1962).

138. One must assume, for example, that the emphasis placed upon Artemis in Achilles Tatius' novel (for whom there is no evidence of an ancient mystery religion) surreptitiously communicates aspects of the cult of Isis.

139. Perhaps the most influential of Merkelbach's early critics was Ben E. Perry. See *Ancient Romances: A Literary-Historical Account of Their Origins* (SCL, 37; Berkeley: University of California Press, 1967).

140. As noted by Richard I. Pervo, *Profit with Delight: The Literary Genre of the Acts of the Apostles* (Philadelphia: Fortress, 1987), p. 95.

religious influences within the novels.[141] Even though they may not have been religious tracts, the presence of religious influence within these texts continually woos the interest of scholars.[142]

Michael Vines notes the engagement with the divine realm in the Gospel of Mark in his assertion that the Gospel of Mark and Jewish novels are the same genre: 'they [Mark and the Jewish novels] are both engaged in a similar conversation about the nature of divine presence and action in the midst of crisis. Both are convinced that God can and will save those who trust in God's compassion and mercy.'[143] Indeed, several parallels between Jewish novels and the Gospel are noticeable. The book of Tobit, for example, dedicates extensive passages to cultic concerns (Tob. 1.3-13; 13.9-18; 14.5-7), as does Mark (Mk 7.1-23). The author of Tobit repeatedly portrays the protagonist in prayer (Tob. 3.1-6; 13.1-8), as does Mark (Mk 6.46; 14.32-42). Another novelistic Jewish text, the addition to Daniel commonly referred to as Bel and the Dragon, introduces the prophet Habakkuk into its narrative in a manner that is characteristic of the inclusion of John the Baptist/Elijah in the book of Mark (Bel 1.33-39; cf. Mk 1.4-8).[144]

However, as this study will demonstrate, the identification of the Gospel of Mark as a Jewish novel in particular is unduly restrictive, even in consideration of the Gospel's treatment of theological motifs and themes. References to the divine realm in the Gospel of Mark parallel many differing expressions of the divine realm within a broad spectrum of novelistic literature from the Hellenistic period. For example, characters in both *Callirhoë* (*Callir.* 3.3.1–7) and the Gospel of Mark (Mk 16.4-6) encounter respective 'empty tombs' and subsequently conclude that the emptiness is the work of the divine.[145] Compare also the declaration of the Romans after Habrocomes returns from his crucifixion – 'the gods were looking after' him (Xenophon, *An Ephesian Tale* 4.2) – with the declaration of the Roman soldier at the cross of Jesus – 'Truly this man was God's Son!' (Mk 15.39). Charles W. Hedrick's comparison of Mark's presentation of Jesus' prayer at Gethsemane (14.32-42) and prayers in *Callirhoë* reveals that 'in terms of Chariton's novel and literary fiction of the first century, [Jesus at prayer in connection with his sufferings] is what

141. See Hägg, *NIA*, p. 104; Pervo, *Profit*, p. 94; Tolbert, *Sowing the Gospels*, p. 65, n. 57; Reardon, 'General Introduction' to *CAGN*, p. 12.

142. A reconsideration of the work of Kerényi and Merkelbach was the topic of consideration at the Annual Meeting of the Society of Biblical Literature in 2004.

143. Vines, *Problem*, p. 159.

144. The prophetic character is introduced at the beginning of both novelistic stories in a limited, 'cameo' appearance.

145. See E.M. Sidebottom, 'The So-called Divine Passive in the Gospel Tradition', *ExpTimes* 87 (1978), pp. 200–4, who suggests that the passive occurs to emphasize process as much as to avoid the use of God's name.

one would expect a pious man to do under similar circumstances'.[146] The theme of the divine realm in Mark's Gospel is influenced by non-Jewish as well as Jewish themes.

Certainly, Mark's Gospel is popular literature of a distinctively religious nature. Even before the narrative begins in earnest, the narrator employs the religious terms 'Christ' and 'son of God' (Mk 1.1) and quotes from Jewish sacred scripture (1.2-3). John 'the baptizer' is the first character of the story, who speaks in religious terms of 'repentance', 'forgiveness', 'sins', 'confessions' and a 'holy spirit' and dresses in the attire of the Jewish prophets (1.4-8).[147] In the second episode of the Gospel, the divine itself plays a role in the action (1.11), vocally legitimizing the one who throughout the remainder of the story will proclaim the 'Kingdom of God' (1.15) in miracle, controversy, parable, and death.[148] Yet this characteristic does not necessitate a generic affiliation that is confined to or even predominantly associated with Hellenistic Jewish novels. Indeed, the explicit and prominent nature of religious concerns in the Gospel far outweigh even the religious concerns of the Jewish novels, which exhibit a religious concern comparable to that of other Hellenistic novels. Mark's religious concern seems to exceed novels of all sorts.[149]

Although Vines argues that 'the Gospel of Mark most closely resembles . . . the Jewish novels', he also acknowledges that his observation 'is not to deny other influences on the composition of the Gospel'.[150] At the end of his study, he notes that 'in the context of the first century, it would not be surprising to find that Mark, to one degree or another, borrowed from both Greek and Jewish literary forms'.[151] Indeed, as the textual observations in Part II of this study will substantiate, a non-biblical Epic resurrection topos seems to exert more influence upon the Gospel of Mark than a biblically based Prophetic resurrection topos.

1.4.4 *Conclusion*

Not only literary stylistics and narrative tempo, but also many of the motifs and themes within the Gospel of Mark suggest the Gospel's

---

146. Charles W. Hedrick, 'Representing Prayer in Mark and Chariton's *Chaereas and Callirhoë*', *PRS* 22 (1995), pp. 239–57 (257).

147. Compare Mk 1.6 and 2 Kgs 1.8.

148. For an in-depth analysis of references to biblical literature in the first 15 verses of Mark, see Robert B. Coote, 'Mark 1.1: ἀρχή, "Scriptural Lemma"', in Carroll (ed.), *Text as Pretext: Essays in Honour of Robert Davidson*, pp. 86–90.

149. See Wills' treatment of 'Myth in the Jewish Novel', in *Jewish Novel*, pp. 235–44; Erich S. Gruen, *Heritage and Hellenism: The Reinvention of Jewish Tradition* (HCS, 30; Berkeley: University of California Press, 1998), pp. 179–86.

150. Vines, *Problem*, p. 153.

151. Vines, *Problem*, p. 163.

participation within the genre of Hellenistic novelistic literature. The significant diversity of these motifs and themes – travel, history, religious expression, horror – suggests a conclusion that I will develop further at the end of the chapter: the presence of any one motif or theme does not necessitate a generic affiliation that is confined to travel, history, tract, horror, or otherwise.

1.5 *Novelistic Narrative Structure*

Another distinctive characteristic of novelistic literature as a literary genre is a basic, recurrent structure that is sufficiently flexible for many and various applications, yet identifiable in three basic components. Ancient novels typically begin *in medias res*, incorporate a 'turning point' at the middle of the story, and conclude with a 'final recognition'.[152] Crediting the literary theory presented in Aristotle's *Poetics* is one way of explaining the frequent presence of this structure in the ancient novel, as is assigning the influence to Classical Greek tragedy, though this study considers neither to be necessary antecedents.[153] As will become clear in the presentation below, these structural features are simply the very 'stuff' of effective drama. They manifest themselves with particular clarity both in the dramatic, prose literary presentations that are so distinctive in novelistic writings as well as in the Gospel of Mark.

1.5.1 *A Beginning* 'in medias res'

Novelistic texts spend few words before arriving at an event which advances the plot. As with many other characteristics of novelistic literature, the practice derives from Homeric tradition.[154] In his treatise on *The Art of Poetry* (*Ars Poetica*), Horace (65–8 B.C.E.) describes the artistry of Homer, 'that poet whose every endeavor is to the point'[155]:

> Semper ad eventum festinat et *in medias res*
> Non secus ac notas auditorem rapit.

> He always hastens to the event and *into the middle of things*
> He hurries his hearers, as if they knew it already.

> Horace, *Ars* 148–149

152. See Tolbert, *Sowing*, pp. 74–5.
153. Aristotle discusses turning points and final recognition scenes in the context of ancient tragedy in his *Poetics* 1452a22–1452b13.
154. Other indications of the significant influence of Homeric epic upon novelistic literature are noted in Sections 1.3.4, 1.4.5, 2.4, et al.
155. Horace, *Ars* 140.

So Horace inspires the literary term '*in medias res*', but Homer inspires the practice of beginnings 'in the middle of things'.[156] In the excerpt from *Callir.* 1.1.4–6 at the introduction to this chapter, nothing short of a physical collision brings these two most beautiful of people to fall in love shortly after the novel has begun. Similarly abrupt beginnings initiate other novelistic writings such as Tobit, *The Ass*, *An Ephesian Tale*, *An Ethiopian Story*, and *The Alexander Romance*, among others.[157] In contrast, Plutarch's elite narrative seeks to engage the audience with literary rather than physical acrobatics. His biography of Demosthenes begins – as most ancient biographies – at the beginning, with a linguistically ornate treatment of the parents of the subject under consideration.

Perhaps it is in the interest of enhancing the biographical nature of the Christian narrative that both Matthew and Luke add traditions about Jesus' father, mother, birth, and education to its beginning. Mark's story, however, like Chariton's, begins *in medias res*, when a mature Jesus, participating in the baptism of John, receives divine affirmation (Mk 1.1-13).[158]

1.5.2 *Central Turning Point*

Aristotle defines a 'turning point' as a change 'from one state of things to its opposite', after which the plot moves steadily to its denouement.[159] Due to this transformative nature, the turning point typically occurs at a significant point in a story.[160] In novelistic literature specifically, 'the dramatic action "turns" in the middle of the book.'[161] Chariton, for

---

156.   Neither *The Iliad* nor *The Odyssey* begins at the beginning of the Trojan War or with a formal introduction of their main characters. Both begin *in medias res*.

157.   A sampling of examples occurs at Tobit 1.1-2; *The Ass* 1.1; Pseudo-Callisthenes, *Alex. Rom.* 1.1.

158.   Klaus Baltzer claims that Mark's Gospel begins as it does because the Gospel is an example of a so-called 'prophetic biography' which typically commences with a divine call (*Die Biographie der Propheten* [Neukirchen-Vluyn: Neukirchener, 1975]; cf. Helmut Koester, *Ancient Christian Gospels: Their History and Development* [Philadelphia: Trinity, 1990], pp. 27–9). However, the very few texts which scholars claim were influential upon Mark either manifest a radically different literary style (Dieter Lührmann identifies one such biography in the poetry of Isaiah 42–53 ['Biographie des Gerechten als Evangelium: Vorstellungen zu einem Markus Kommentar', *Wort und Dienst* 14 (1977), pp. 25–50]) or are not *pre*-Markan (Tolbert, *Sowing*, pp. 55–6). Contra Koester, see also Robert Guelich, 'The Gospel Genre', in Stuhlmacher (ed.), *The Gospel and the Gospels*, pp. 173–208 (177); Vines, *Problem*, p. 144.

159.   'ἔστι δὲ περιπέτεια μὲν ἡ εἰς τὸ ἐναντίον τῶν πραττομένων μεταβολή ...' (Aristotle, *Poetics* 1452a22).

160.   For an appreciation of peripeteia in novelistic literature, see Frank Kermode, *The Sense of an Ending: Studies in the Theory of Fiction* (Oxford, New York: Oxford University Press, 2nd edn, 2000), p. 18.

161.   Hägg, *NIA*, p. 1.

example, narrates a court scene in the center of his novel (Book 5 of *Callirhoë*). All of the characters have traveled to Babylon for a trial that will decide who will be Callirhoë's husband. In court, Chaereas sees Callirhoë in person for the first time since he kicked her in Book 1. Although they are separated once more following this trial, Section 5.8 marks a dramatic change in their fortunes: the plot begins to move toward reunion.[162]

The Gospel of Mark also has a turning point at the center of its story, specifically at Mk 8.29 as Peter proclaims Jesus to be 'the Messiah'. Up to this point in the story, Jesus' special identity has been known only in the cosmic realm, proclaimed three times by 'unclean spirits' (Mk 1.24; 3.11; 5.7) whom Jesus consistently silences. Society, however, has not recognized this role before Peter's declaration, a situation that the text intentionally reaffirms just before the peripeteia: popular opinion has regarded Jesus as a prophet (8.27-28). Peter is the first human to acknowledge Jesus' identity (8.29). Immediately after this recognition, the plot begins its steady movement toward the denouement. Jesus predicts his suffering for the first of three times (8.31; cf. 9.31; 10.33), after which the Passion Narrative proper commences (11.1), ultimately leading to Jesus' death (15.37).[163]

1.5.3 *Final Recognition*

Aristotle also defines 'recognition' as a key component of plot: it is 'a change from ignorance to knowledge'.[164] In a key passage of a text by the popular author Apuleius that is now referred to as *Florida*, one of the characters comments upon the literary talents of a certain Philemon. Through these comments Apuleius very likely expresses what he himself appreciates in fine literature: 'We find in him [Philemon] much wit: plot ingeniously involved; *recognitions clearly made out* ....'[165] The recognition device is placed second on this ancient list of admirable literary techniques.

While acknowledging that there are many kinds of recognitions, Aristotle considers 'the finest recognition [to be] that which occurs simultaneously with reversal'.[166] Also noted as significant by Aristotle are final recognitions because of their ability to produce a happy ending, often

162. For a similar assessment of this scene as a *peripeteia*, see Hägg, *NIA*, p. 13, and Tolbert, *Sowing*, pp. 74–5.

163. There is also a change of direction at this point of the story: the direction of travel shifts from a northward movement (Mk 8.27) toward the south (8.31, 33), particularly toward the city of Jerusalem (Charles W. Hedrick, 'What is a Gospel: Geography, Time, and Narrative Structure', *PRS* 10 [1983], pp. 255–68 [266]).

164. Aristotle, *Poet.* 1452a31.

165. ' ... agnitus lucide explicatos ...', Apuleius, *Fl.* 16.7. See Vincent Hunink, 'Comedy in Apuleius' Apology', *GCN* 9 (1998), pp. 97–113.

166. Aristotle, *Poet.* 1452a31–34.

as the culmination of a series.[167] A prominent example from epic literature is the dramatic final recognition at the end of Homer's epic, *The Odyssey*, when the returning hero is recognized by his nurse (*Od.* 19.392–394), his wife (23.205–246), and his father (24.345–355). In the Hellenistic Jewish novel Tobit also, one recognition immediately follows another as Tobias is recognized by his mother and father at the end of the story proper (Tob. 11.5-15).[168]

The stories by Chariton and Mark also appreciate the value of this device.[169] Chariton presents a final recognition in his novel as Callirhoë and Chaereas are reunited in the eighth book (8.1.8–10).[170] The Gospel of Mark contains a particularly remarkable final recognition scene. Tolbert notes how this scene includes both a sequential recognition and an antitype of a recognition as the author prepares the audience for Mark's unhappy ending. Here is Tolbert's analysis of these final themes:

> Jesus announces his identity (Mk 14.60–63): he is 'the Christ, the Son of the Blessed'. Later his rightful position as 'King of the Jews' is given a backhanded acknowledgement by Pilate, and finally, after his death, the centurion recognizes him as 'Son of God' (15.39). In this light, it is interesting to note that Peter's denial (14.66–72), following immediately after the trial of Jesus, is almost an exact antitype of the recognition scene. In a series of questions, a maid of the high priest recognizes Peter as one of Jesus' followers, but Peter three times denies this correct information. To anyone familiar with the conventions of recognition scenes in the ancient world, such a denial of correct identification would rule out any final happy reunion.[171]

Four distinct recognitions can be identified in this analysis, none of which match the typical use of the device. There is a self-proclaimed 'recognition', a satirical recognition (Tolbert's 'backhanded acknowledgement'), an ironic recognition (made by a Roman centurion rather than a disciple), and (as Tolbert points out) an antitype of the recognition scene. Mark's adroit application of this novelistic technique is comparable to that of Petronius, Nero's own *arbitrator elegantiae*, whose satire on the popular novel 'presents farcical recognitions like that of Lichas who, by casting a

167. 'ἔτι δὲ καὶ τὸ ἀτυχεῖν καὶ τὸ εὐτυχεῖν ἐπὶ τῶν τοιούτων συμβήσεται' (Aristotle, *Poet.* 1452b 2–3).

168. See William R. Robins, 'Romance and Renunciation at the Turn of the Fifth Century', *JECS* 8 (2000), pp. 531–57.

169. Other novels with final recognition scenes include Xenophon of Ephesus. Tolbert comments upon this sequential recognition in her analysis of Mark as novelistic literature. See *Sowing*, p. 75.

170. Hägg also recognizes this passage as the final recognition scene (*NIA*, p. 13). I treat this scene in greater detail in Section 3.1.3.

171. Tolbert, *Sowing*, pp. 75–6. Agusti Borrell has undertaken a book-length study of the rhetorical effects of this passage: *The Good News of Peter's Denial*.

glance at the genitals of Encolpius, rediscovers an old acquaintance'.[172] In fact, the comparison reveals that the four-fold final recognition at the end of the Gospel of Mark is even more ingenious, showing signs of an exceptional ability to work intentionally with novelistic techniques.

1.5.4 *Conclusion*

A few disclaimers are in order regarding these observations about the similarity of the narrative structure of the Gospel of Mark to the general narrative structure of ancient novelistic literature. First, the extended separation of the hero and heroine of many romantic novels necessitates dual lines of action, both of which the author must manipulate.[173] The resulting complexity evokes a narrative structure that is quite different from the Gospel of Mark, in which the author treats one basic plot line. Secondly, it is important to note that the identification of markers at the beginning, middle, and end of a work by no means exhausts the structural possibilities. Many other ways of appreciating the structures of individual ancient novels as well as the Gospel of Mark exist. For example, in addition to the three structural features identified in this section, Mark shapes his Gospel using a technique of intercalation which is prominent in novelistic literature.[174] However, our observations do indicate a significant parallel which suggests that the Gospel of Mark is, in fact, literature that seeks to appeal to a wide audience. Like other novelistic literature, the Gospel emphasizes the very 'stuff' of good drama: a beginning *in medias res*, a central turning point, and a final recognition.

1.6 *Novelistic Rhetoric*

A comprehensive treatment of the rhetorical devices and strategies of novelistic literature set in relation to the Gospel of Mark would require a separate monograph. However, one rhetorical technique distinguishes itself in both novelistic literature and the Gospel, meriting our attention. Novelistic literature revels in irony. Irony can take many forms and occurs at many levels in novelistic texts. Fundamentally, irony is the intentional, rhetorical use of *incongruence*.[175]

Literary examples are helpful in appreciating irony. The Jewish novel

172. Conte, *Hidden Author*, p. 53.

173. See Hägg, *NIA*, p. 26, who analyses throughout the course of his study the different approaches to this situation undertaken by each of the five fully extant romantic novelists.

174. On intercalation in novelistic literature, see Craig A. Evans, '"Peter Warming Himself": The Problem of an Editorial "Seam"', *JBL* 101 (1982), pp. 245–9; Wills, *Quest*, p. 132; and Section 5.1.1., below.

175. For an in-depth theoretical treatment, see Wayne C. Booth, *A Rhetoric of Irony* (Chicago: University of Chicago Press, 1974).

Judith is 'quintessentially ironic'.[176] Incongruity acts upon the story as early as the very first line of the novel in which the author situates the story in 'the twelfth year of the reign of Nebuchadnezzar, who ruled over the Assyrians' (Jdt. 1.1). Despite the attempt at historical precision in the reference to 'the twelfth year', the sentence is blatantly erroneous. Its assertion that Nebuchadnezzar ruled over the Assyrians contradicts popular knowledge about Nebuchadnezzar, *the great king of Babylon*, rendering this statement comparable to a claim that George Washington ruled over England. Carey Moore suggests that an ancient reader of the text might even have given his listeners 'a sly wink' during a reading of the verse.[177]

Chariton also draws advantages from irony through a variety of means. His use of situational irony is particularly striking, as in his description of the crucifixion of Theron: 'Many of the crowd went with Theron as he was taken away; he was crucified in front of Callirhoë's tomb and from the cross gazing out upon that sea over which he had carried Hermocrates' daughter captive ...' (*Callir.* 3.4.18 [Goold, LCL 481]). Chariton ironically locates Theron's execution in front of Callirhoë's tomb as though the (once presumed) dead woman were present to appreciate her vindication. The Mediterranean Sea provides the setting for two opposing functions: the offense that separated the heroes and the act that atoned for that offense. In another move of irony, Chariton portrays the hero Chaereas as regretting the fact that he has been spared crucifixion: 'the executioner stopped his work, and Chaereas descended from the cross, regretfully, for he had been glad to be leaving his miserable life and unhappy love' (4.3.5–6). This salvation is ironic in that it is not salvation at all. In fact, like Judith, the entire plot of *Callirhoë* is inherently ironic. The initial text presents the union of the two most beautiful people in the world as nothing less than the outworking of divine plan, 'as chance (i.e. the divine Τύχη) would have it' (1.1.6). How ironic, then, that the two lovers are separated at all, let alone for the duration of the story.

Observations of the many instances of irony in the Gospel of Mark have sustained the writing of several monographs.[178] The irony of this text is sufficiently salient to attract the attention of Wayne C. Booth early in his expansive treatment of irony in literature in general, *A Rhetoric of*

---

176. Carey A. Moore, *Judith* (AB, 40; New York: Doubleday, 1985), p. 78. Many of the examples incorporated into this treatment of irony receive greater attention throughout Moore's commentary.

177. Moore, *Judith*, p. 79.

178. E.g. Jerry Camery-Hoggatt, *Irony in Mark's Gospel: Text and Subtext* (SNTSMS, 72; New York and Cambridge, Engl.: Cambridge University Press, 1992); Glyndle M. Feagin, *Irony and the Kingdom in Mark: A Literary-Critical Study* (MBPS, 56; Lewiston, N.Y.: Edwin Mellen, 1997); and Fowler, *Let the Reader Understand*.

Irony.[179] In this book, Booth points out how the presentation of Jesus' crucifixion scene in Mark is highly ironic. Observers of this crucifixion refer to Jesus as 'the Christ' and 'the King of Israel' (Mk 15.31-32), an identification which they employ mockingly, but which is, in fact, true for the audience. In this particular instance, as throughout the Gospel, irony manifests itself not primarily at the level of story – though it does occur at the story level quite frequently, as in the case of the centurion's confession as 'disciple' – but at the level of narration.[180] Incongruity exists between the understanding of the audience, who is informed about Jesus' unique status as 'the Son of God' (1.1) at the very beginning as well as throughout the story, and the understanding of the characters in the story, who continually do not perceive the 'true nature' of who Jesus is.[181] Unlike the irony of the book of Judith and the romantic novels, however, this is an incongruity that is never fully resolved. The story leaves the audience with a frustration that is, ironically, motivating: since the characters who knew Jesus best have all fled in ignorance (Mk 14.50; 16.8), they themselves, the audience, must make Jesus' role as the Messiah of God known to the world.

1.7 *The Diversity of Content in Novelistic Literature*

Throughout this survey of the characteristics of novelistic literature, I have introduced a diverse sampling of ancient novelistic texts that contain a wide variety of content: history (*History of Persia, On Moses*), biography (*On Moses, Life of Aesop, The Alexander Romance*), travel (*The Alexander Romance, Wonders beyond Thule, Sacred Scripture, Island of the Sun, Callirhoë*), and romance (*Callirhoë, An Ephesian Tale, Leucippe and Clitophon, Ninus Romance*). The categorization of these few examples is merely illustrative. As the repetition of the parenthetical examples suggests (*On Moses, The Alexander Romance, Callirhoë*), the majority of novelistic texts defy classification based upon content. An appreciation for this diversity is crucial for students of both the Gospel and the novel who would identify and thereby avoid the misconceptions of past scholarship.

Traditionally, scholars have defined the novelistic genre largely on the basis of five lengthy romance novels written between the first and fourth century C.E.: *Callirhoë* by Chariton (mid-first century C.E.), *An Ephesian Tale* by Xenophon of Ephesus (mid-second century C.E.), *Leucippe and*

---

179. Booth, *Rhetoric of Irony*, pp. 28–9.

180. Jesus' own family, including his own mother, thinks that he is crazy (Mk 3.14-21, 31). The crowd in the Gospel chooses the criminal 'son of the father' ('Barabbas') rather than the one designated by divine proclamation (15.1-18; see also 1.11; 9.7).

181. The disciples in the Gospel of Mark, for example, ultimately fail to understand who Jesus is. See Section 5.2.1.

Clitophon by Achilles Tatius (late second century C.E.), *Daphnis and Chloë* by Longus (early third century C.E.), and *An Ethiopian Story* by Heliodorus (fourth century C.E.). Ancient novelistic writings as a whole have been frequently referred to as 'romances'.[182] According to this approach, the novels are said to contain a common plot in which: (1) the two most beautiful people in the world fall in love and marry; (2) in a twist of fate, they are separated;[183] (3) while apart, each endures many hardships as they travel throughout the Mediterranean basin in search of one another, endeavoring all the while to remain faithful to each other; and (4) fate relents and the two lovers are reunited to live happily ever after, resulting in the conclusion that ancient novelistic literature consists of 'a substantial core of love-romance, and around it a fringe of non-erotic forms'.[184]

However, several indications suggest that this description of Greco-Roman novelistic literature is inadequate. Only infrequently is admission made that the textual witness for four of these five texts consists of only one medieval manuscript. All four derive, in fact, from the *same* medieval manuscript: Codex Florentinus, a thirteenth-century parchment currently under the care of the Laurentian Library in Florence, Italy.[185] The description of novelistic literature as substantially romantic 'must remain highly speculative'.[186] The survival of these five texts may, in fact, say 'more about the tastes of subsequent late antique and Byzantine readers than it does about the field of ancient novels itself'.[187]

Also problematic for the current assessment of novelistic literature is the assumption that the romance novels which are supposed to be at its 'core' constitute such a uniform group because, as Ewen L. Bowie has demonstrated, there is significant diversity in the way in which this 'common plot' is expressed, even within this small collection of romantic novels. The extent to which the heroine preserves her virginity/fidelity for

---

182. See, for example, Perry, *Ancient Romances* (1967); Jean Radford, *The Progress of Romance: The Politics of Popular Fiction* (HWS; New York and London: Routledge and Kegan Paul, 1986); B.P. Reardon, *The Form of Greek Romance* (Princeton: Princeton University Press, 1991); Ronald F. Hock, 'An Extraordinary Friend in Chariton's *Callirhoë*: The Importance of Friendship in the Greek Romances', in John T. Fitzgerald (ed.), *Greco-Roman Perspectives on Friendship* (1997), pp. 145–62. Some scholars may continue to use the term due to the popular ('romantic') nature of the language in which they are written. Note also that the German word for 'novel' is 'Roman'.

183. Marriage occurs before separation in Chariton and Xenophon, but after separation in Achilles Tatius and Heliodorus.

184. Reardon, 'General Introduction', in *CAGN*, p. 7.

185. See Goold, introduction to *Callirhoë*, p. 16.

186. Due to the limited nature of the evidence for *all* forms of novelistic literature, any conceptions of novelistic literature as romantic, historical, biographical, travel-based, or otherwise are necessarily speculative.

187. Stephens and Winkler (eds), *Fragments*, p. 5.

her husband, for example, varies among the narratives: 'Chariton's accepts a cultivated Greek as her second husband ..., Achilles' hero ... succumbs to a married Ephesian, and Longus' receives sexual instruction ... from a married city woman.'[188] Moreover, Longus' *Daphnis and Chloë*, unlike the other lengthy romance novels, is a pastoral novel: the characters do not travel outside of the bounds of the island of Lesbos. The two lovers are separated not by geography, but by sexual naïveté.[189] 'Longus has tried to merge the narrative form of the Greek romantic novel ... with elements of the genre of pastoral poetry created by Theocritus in the third century B.C.E.'[190] The tendency to create new forms through the combination of a variety of literary elements – a characteristic of novelistic literature – is apparent even in this small collection of specifically romantic novels. There are also substantial differences in the literary styles of these five romantic novels. The romances by Chariton and Xenophon are written in an unambitious manner marked by simple diction and parataxis.[191] The romance novels by Achilles Tatius, Longus, and Heliodorus, on the other hand, 'are three highly individual works of literature, ill suited to serve as typical representatives of a popular genre' due to their elaborate and complex writing style.[192]

The conception of novelistic literature as essentially romantic has also collapsed under the weight of two significant academic studies. Susan A. Stephens and John J. Winkler's collection of fragmentary novels and plot summaries not only gathers into a single volume such sources of histories, biographies, satires, and travel novella; in addition, the volume explicitly concludes that 'the so-called ideal romantic novel is no more than a subclass of the whole'.[193] Furthermore, a study of Jewish novels of the Hellenistic era by Lawrence M. Wills suggests their participation in the class of ancient novelistic literature.[194] His anthology of ancient Jewish

---

188. Ewen L. Bowie, 'Novel, Greek', *OCD*, pp. 1049–50 (1050); Hägg, *NIA*, p. 4–6); Pervo, *Profit*, pp. 90–1.

189. So Bowie, 'Novel, Greek'. See also Ronald F. Hock, 'The Greek Novel', in Aune (ed.), *Greco-Roman Literature and the New Testament: Selected Forms and Genres*, pp. 127–46 (esp. 130–1).

190. Christopher Gill, 'Introduction' to Longus, *Daphnis and Chloe*, in *CAGN*, p. 285.

191. Anderson, 'Introduction' to Xenophon of Ephesus, *An Ephesian Tale*, in *CAGN*, p. 126.

192. Hägg, *NIA*, p. 35.

193. Stephens and Winkler (eds), *Fragments*, p. 4. Reardon concurs that 'sometimes ... love is given little space, or none at all, and the excitement lies entirely in the adventure' ('General Introduction', in *CAGN*, p. 2). See also Christine M. Thomas, *The* Acts of Peter, *Gospel Literature and the Ancient Novel: Rewriting the Past* (Oxford: Oxford University Press, 2003), pp. 8–10.

194. See Wills, *Jewish Novel*, p. 32: 'The appropriate poetics to investigate this genre is to be derived from popular literature.'

novels includes 'novels proper', 'historical novels', and 'novelistic testaments', further widening the field.[195]

Novelistic literature is not primarily romantic but incorporates a variety of diverse texts, as the   chart on pp. 51–4 of extant ancient novelistic literature demonstrates. The inclusion of a text in this chart is merited by the consideration of that text within four anthologies of ancient novelistic literature and one influential introduction to the novel. In all, the chart incorporates writings considered to be novelistic in the work of six leading scholars in the field: Lawrence M. Wills (*AJN*), Bryan P. Reardon (*CAGN*), Susan A. Stephens and John J. Winkler (*Fragments*),[196] Gareth Schmeling (*NAW*), and Tomas Hägg (*NIA*).[197] This chart aims neither at completeness, nor does it claim to be definitive in its chronology: the precise dating of most of these writings is not possible. The texts, ordered according to a rough chronology from oldest to most recent, date through the Imperial Age only (though Hägg continues into Byzantine). Neither do the assessments of genre assigned to each work presume to be definitive.[198] Readers are encouraged to consult these works in the anthologies in which they occur. I offer Table 2 primarily as an illustration of the diversity of contents within the genre of novelistic literature.

The table demonstrates the wide variety of writings which can possibly be designated as 'novelistic'. The earliest writings are dominated by a plot that is biographical (*Cyropaedia*), historiographical (*History of Persia, On Moses*), or rooted in travel (*Sacred Scriptures, Island of the Sun*).[199] In fact, the romantic writings (*Ninus Romance, Callirhoë* and others) appear to be a later development.[200]

Scholars who oppose the association of the Gospel of Mark with novelistic literature, operating from a primarily romantic paradigm, often fail to appreciate the diversity of content that characterizes the genre. For example, New Testament scholar Vernon Robbins argues that a *striking difference in contents* between the Gospels and novelistic literature limits

---

195.   Wills, *AJN*.

196.   I have not included the short list of questionable 'testimonia' to [presumably] lost prose narratives that mention neither text nor summary. See *Fragments*, pp. 473–7 for a list of these texts.

197.   Reardon describes this introduction as the 'best general account in English' ('General Introduction', in *CAGN*, 16).

198.   Generic assessments of highly fragmentary texts are the hypotheses represented in Stephens and Winkler, *Fragments*.

199.   See Sara Raup Johnson, *Historical Fictions and Hellenistic Jewish Identity: Third Maccabees in Its Cultural Context* (HCS, 43; Berkeley: University of California Press, 2004).

200.   MacQueen argues that the Greek romance novel developed within an earlier tradition of novelistic history writing (*Myth, Rhetoric, and Fiction*, pp. 144–5).

TABLE 2: Novelistic Literature of the Greco-Roman World					
Author	**Assigned Title**	**Approximate Date**	**Earliest Manuscript Evidence**	**Basic Contents**	**Inclusion in Anthologies**
---	*Story of Ahiqar*	6th cen. B.C.E.	*Fragments:* 5th cen. B.C.E. *Manuscripts:* 2nd cen. C.E.	Prose National Hero Story	*AJN* 4, 20, 166
Herodotus	*Histories* (Short stories as at *Hist.* 4.14-15, 95)	5th cen. B.C.E.	*Fragments:* 2nd cen. C.E. *Manuscripts:* 10th cen. C.E.	Novelistic Historiography	*CAGN* 6 *NLA* 112-113
Plato	*Republic* (Short stories as "The Myth of Er" at *Rep.* 10)	4th cen. B.C.E.	*Fragments:* 2nd cen. C.E. *Manuscripts:* 10th cen. C.E.	Novelistic Prose Fiction	*CAGN* 6
Xenophon of Athens	*Cyropaedia*	4th cen. B.C.E.	*Fragments:* 3rd cen. C.E. *Manuscripts:* 10th cen. C.E.	Historical/ Biographical Novel	*AJN* 4, 11 *CAGN* 3, 6 *NAW* 581-600 *NLA* 113
Ctesias of Cnidus	*History of Persia*	4th cen. B.C.E.	*Summary:* Photius 72 9th cen. C.E.	Historical Novel	*CAGN* 6 *NAW* 629-632 *NLA* 113-114
Euhemerus of Messene	*Sacred Scripture*	3rd cen. B.C.E.	*Summary:* Diod. Sic. 6.1 1st cen. B.C.E.	Travel Novel	*NAW* 621-628 *NLA* 117
Iambulus	*Island of the Sun*	3rd cen. B.C.E.	*Summary:* Diod. Sic. 2.55-60 1st cen. B.C.E.	Travel Novel	*NAW* 621-628 *NLA* 117
Artapanus	*On Moses*	3rd cen. B.C.E.	*Citations:* Clement 2nd cen. C.E. *Summary:* Eusebius 4th cen. C.E.	Historical Novel	*AJN* 165-173 *NAW* 687-688
---	Tobit	2nd cen. B.C.E.	*Fragments:* 1st cen. B.C.E. *Manuscripts:* 4th cen. C.E.	Jewish Novel Proper	*AJN* 62-88 *NAW* 688
---	Judith	2nd cen. B.C.E.	*Fragments:* 3rd cen. C.E. *Manuscripts:* 4th cen. C.E.	Jewish Novel Proper	*AJN* 89-120 *NAW* 688
---	Greek Esther	2nd cen. B.C.E.	*Manuscripts:* 4th cen. C.E.	Jewish Novel Proper	*AJN* 27-50 *NAW* 688
---	Greek Daniel	1st cen. B.C.E.	*Manuscripts:* 4th cen. C.E.	Jewish Novel Proper	*AJN* 51-61 *NAW* 688
---	*Ninus Romance*	1st cen. B.C.E.	*Fragments:* 1st cen. C.E.	Romance Novel	*AJN* 4, 20 *CAGN* 803-808 *NAW* 663-665 *NLA* 17 *Fragments* 23-71
---	*The Marriage & Conversion of Asenath*	1st cen. C.E.	*Manuscripts:* 6th cen. C.E.	Jewish Novel Proper	*AJN* 121-162 *NAW* 688 *NLA* 161 *CAGN* 3
---	Third Maccabees	1st cen. C.E.	*Manuscripts:* 5th cen. C.E.	Historical Novel	*AJN* 174-197

---	Life of Aesop	1st cen. C.E.	*Fragments:* 2nd cen. C.E. *Manuscripts:* 6th cen. C.E.	Novelistic Biography	*AJN* 4, 200 *Fragments* 4 *NAW* 633-639
Chariton	Callirhoë	1st cen. C.E.	*Fragments:* 2nd cen. C.E. *Manuscript:* 13th cen. C.E.	Romance Novel	*AJN* 3 *CAGN* 17-124 *Fragments* 4 *NAW* 309-355 *NLA* 5-17
Petronius	Satyricon	1st cen. C.E.	*Manuscripts:* 9th cen. C.E.	Satirical Romance Novel	*AJN* 3 *CAGN* 4 *Fragments* 3 *NAW* 457-490 *NLA* 168-175
---	Testament of Job	1st cen. C.E.	*Fragments:* 5th cen. C.E. *Manuscripts:* 11th cen. C.E.	Novelistic Testament	*AJN* 242-268
---	Metiochus and Parthenope	1st cen. C.E.	*Fragments:* 2nd cen. C.E.	Romance Novel	*CAGN* 813-815 *Fragments* 72-100 *NAW* 657-660 *NLA* 18
---	The Love Drug	1st cen. C.E.	*Fragment* 2nd cen. C.E.	Travel Novel	*Fragments* 173-178
---	Calligone	1st cen. C.E.	*Fragment* 2nd cen. C.E.	Romance Novel	*CAGN* 826-827 *Fragments* 267-276 *NAW* 666-667
Lollianus	A Phoenician Story	1st cen. C.E.	*Fragments:* 2nd cen. C.E.	Satirical Novel	*CAGN* 809-812 *Fragments* 314-357 *NAW* 669-672 *NLA* 92
---	Iolaus	1st cen. C.E.	*Fragment* 2nd cen. C.E.	Criminal-Satiric Novel	*CAGN* 816-818 *Fragments* 358-374 *NAW* 669-672
Josephus	The Tobiad Romance in *Ant.* 12.4.1-11	1st cen. C.E.	*Fragments:* 6th cen. C.E. *Manuscripts:* 9th cen. C.E.	Historical Novel	*AJN* 198-212
Josephus	The Royal Family of Adiabene in *Ant.* 20.2.1-20.4.3	1st cen. C.E.	*Fragments:* 6th cen. C.E. *Manuscripts:* 9th cen. C.E.	Historical Novel	*AJN* 213-225
Antonius Diogenes	Herpyllis	2nd cen. C.E.	*Fragment* 2nd cen. C.E.	Travel Novel	*CAGN* 822-823 *Fragments* 158-172 *NAW* 683
Xenophon of Ephesus	An Ephesian Tale	2nd cen. C.E.	*Manuscript:* 13th cen. C.E.	Romance Novel	*AJN* 3 *CAGN* 125-169 *Fragments* 4 *NAW* 336-360 *NLA* 18-32
Antonius Diogenes	The Wonders beyond Thule	2nd cen. C.E.	*Fragments:* 3rd cen. C.E. *Summary:* Photius 166 9th cen. C.E.	Travel Novel	*CAGN* 775-782 *Fragments* 101-157 *NAW* 674-680 *NLA* 118-121
Lucian	A True Story	2nd cen. C.E.	*Fragments:* 5th cen. C.E. *Manuscripts:* 9th cen. C.E.	Satire of the Travel Novel	*CAGN* 619-649 *NAW* 555-562 *NLA* 118

Pseudo-Lucian	*The Ass*	2nd cen. C.E.	*Fragments:* 4th cen. C.E. *Manuscripts:* 9th cen. C.E.	Comic Novel	*CAGN* 589-618 *Fragments* 4, 323-325 *NAW* 13-15 *NLA* 176-181
Iamblichus	*A Babylonian Story*	2nd cen. C.E.	*Summary:* Photius 94 9th cen. C.E.	Romance Novel	*CAGN* 783-797 *Fragments* 179-245 *NAW* 667-669 *NLA* 32-34
Achilles Tatius	*Leucippe and Clitophon*	2nd cen. C.E.	*Fragments:* 2nd cen. C.E. *Manuscript:* 13th cen. C.E.	Romance Novel	*AJN* 3 *Fragments* 4 *NAW* 387-416 *NLA* 41-54 *CAGN* 170-284
Apuleius	*The Golden Ass*	2nd cen. C.E.	*Manuscript:* 11th cen. C.E.	Comic Novel	*AJN* 3 *Fragments* 3, 7 *NAW* 491-516 *NLA* 181-190 *CAGN* 4
---	*Acts of Paul & Thecla*	2nd cen. C.E.	*Fragments:* 3rd cen. C.E. *Manuscripts:* 11th cen. C.E.	Christian Novel	*NAW* 699-702 *NLA* 154-162
---	*Testament of Joseph*	2nd cen. C.E.	*Manuscripts:* 10th cen. C.E.	Novelistic Testament	*AJN* 229-241 *NAW* 688
---	*Petubastis*	2nd cen. C.E.	*Fragments:* 2nd cen. C.E. *Manuscripts:* 11th cen. C.E.	Historical Novel	*AJN* 4, 20
---	*Testament of Abraham*	2nd cen. C.E.	*Manuscripts:* 11th cen. C.E.	Satiric Novelistic Testament	*AJN* 269-293
---	*Antheia*	2nd cen. C.E.	*Fragment* 2nd cen. C.E.	Romance Novel	*Fragments* 277-288 *NAW* 661
---	*Chione*	2nd cen. C.E.	*Fragments:* 2nd cen. C.E.	Romance Novel	*CAGN* 824-825 *Fragments* 289-313 *NAW* 645-661
---	*Daulis*	2nd cen. C.E.	*Fragment* 2nd cen. C.E.	Aretalogy	*Fragments* 375-388
---	*Tinouphis*	2nd cen. C.E.	*Fragment* 2nd cen. C.E.	Criminal Novel	*Fragments* 400-408 *NAW* 673-674
---	*Acts of Peter*	2nd cen. C.E.	*Fragments:* 4th cen. C.E. *Manuscripts:* 4th cen. C.E.	Christian Novel	*NAW* 702-704
---	*Nightmare*	2nd cen. C.E.	*Fragment* 2nd cen. C.E.	Dream Novel	*Fragments* 422-428
---	*Staphulos*	2nd cen. C.E.	*Fragment* 2nd cen. C.E.	Comic Novel (Dionysian Novel)	*Fragments* 429-437
---	*Inundation*	2nd cen. C.E.	*Fragment* 2nd cen. C.E.	Ecphrasis	*Fragments* 451-460
---	*Theano*	2nd cen. C.E.	*Fragment* 3rd cen. C.E.	Tragic Novel	*Fragments* 438-443
---	*Acts of Andrew*	2nd cen. C.E.	*Manuscripts:* 6th cen. C.E.	Christian Novel	*NAW* 695-697
---	*Initiation*	2nd cen. C.E.	*Fragment* 3rd cen. C.E.	Criminal-Satiric Novel	*Fragments* 461-466
Dictys of Crete	*Diary of the Trojan War*	2nd cen. C.E.	*Fragments:* 2nd cen. C.E. *Manuscripts:* 4th cen. C.E.	Epic Novel	*Fragments* ix *NAW* 563-580 *NLA* 143-146

Author	Title	Date	Evidence	Genre	References
Dares	*The Destruction of Troy*	2nd cen. C.E.	*Fragments:* 2nd cen. C.E. *Manuscripts:* 6th cen. C.E.	Epic Novel	*NAW* 563-580 *NLA* 143-146
Pseudo-Clement	*Homilies* (Gk)/ *Recognitions* (Lt)	3rd cen. C.E.	*Manuscripts:* 3rd cen. C.E.	Christian Novel	*CAGN* 3 *NAW* 706-707 *NLA* 162-164
Longus	*Daphnis and Chloe*	3rd cen. C.E.	*Manuscript:* 13th cen. C.E.	Romance Novel	*AJN* 3 *CAGN* 285-348 *Fragments* 4 *NAW* 361-386 *NLA* 35-41
---	*Sesonchosis*	3rd cen. C.E.	*Fragments:* 3rd cen. C.E.	Historical Novel	*AJN* 4, 20 *CAGN* 819-821 *Fragments* 246-266 *NAW* 665-666 *NLA* 17-18
---	*Acts of Thomas*	3rd cen. C.E.	*Fragments:* 5th cen. C.E. *Manuscripts:* 10th cen. C.E.	Christian Novel	*NAW* 704-706
---	*Apollonius*	3rd cen. C.E.	*Fragments:* 4th cen. C.E.	Historical Novel	*Fragments* 391-399
---	*The Apparition*	3rd cen. C.E.	*Fragments:* 4th cen. C.E.	Ghost Story	*Fragments* 409-415
---	*Acts of John*	3rd cen. C.E.	*Fragments:* 4th cen. C.E. *Manuscripts:* 10th cen. C.E.	Christian Novel	*NAW* 697-699
---	*Goatherd and the Palace Guard*	3rd cen. C.E.	*Fragment:* 3rd cen. C.E.	Pastoral Romance	*Fragments* 416-421
---	*The Festival*	3rd cen. C.E.	*Fragment:* 3rd cen. C.E.	Ecphrasis	*Fragments* 444-450
Pseudo-Callisthenes	*The Alexander Romance*	3rd cen. C.E.	*Manuscripts:* 3rd cen. C.E.	Biography/ Travel Tale	*AJN* 4, 20 *CAGN* 650-735 *Fragments* 4, 16-17 *NAW* 601-612 *NLA* 115-117, 125-143
Philostratus	*Life of Apollonius of Tyana*	3rd cen. C.E.	*Citation:* Eusebius 4th cen. C.E. *Manuscripts:* 10th cen. C.E.	Biographical Novel	*CAGN* 3 *NAW* 613-618 *NLA* 115-16
---	*Acts of Xanthippe and Polyxena*	3rd cen. C.E.	*Manuscripts:* 11th cen. C.E.	Christian Novel	*NAW* 707-708
---	*Apollonius King of Tyre*	3rd cen. C.E.	*Manuscripts:* 5th cen. C.E.	Romance Novel	*AJN* 21 *CAGN* 736-772 *NAW* 517-554 *NLA* 147-153
Heliodorus	*An Ethiopian Story*	4th cen. C.E.	*Fragment:* 6th cen. C.E. *Manuscripts:* 11th cen. C.E.	Romance Novel	*AJN* 3 *CAGN* 349-588 *Fragments* 3-4 *NAW* 417-456 *NLA* 54-73
---	*Baarlam & Joasaph*	6th cen. C.E.	*Manuscripts:* 6th cen. C.E.	Christian Novel	*NAW* 708

the usefulness of this generic identification.[201] In particular, Robbins claims that the theme of romantic love prominent in the romantic novels greatly differentiates all popular literature from the Gospel of Mark. Robbins argues that the Gospel is a 'memorabilia' of Jesus as teacher, similar to the extant *Memorabilia* that Xenophon of Athens wrote about Socrates in the fourth century B.C.E., despite (1) its drastically different literary style, (2) its almost exclusive focus upon teaching, and (3) the fact that there are no known novelistic 'memorabilia' in complete, fragmentary, summary, or testimonial form.[202]

It is true that neither romantic love nor the concomitant concern for sexual fidelity plays a substantial role in Mark.[203] Pirates, moreover, do not play a significant role (though there are sinners and tax collectors). None of the characters are submitted to slavery or prostitution (though John the Baptist is captured), and dreams are not particularly instrumental.[204] However, as Table 2 illustrates, novelistic literature deals in a wide range of themes and content. Like the Gospel of Mark, much of this literature deals in biography, history, and travel. In fact, the ambiguity that results from the Gospel's diverse content is in itself a characteristic of novelistic literature: 'the fact that Gospels seem to lie "between" several genres simply reflects the innovations that can be seen in popular literature.'[205] Although this characteristic is not always appropriately recognized (as Robbins), Greco-Roman novelistic literature is a remarkably 'open form', particularly in regard to content.[206]

1.8 *Conclusion*

Not content, but the nature of its composition distinguishes novelistic literature from other ancient genres. The paratactic style of the Gospel of

201. Vernon K. Robbins, 'Text and Context in Recent Studies of the Gospel of Mark', *RSR* 17 (Jan. 1991), pp. 16–22.

202. See Vernon K. Robbins, *Jesus the Teacher: A Socio-Rhetorical Interpretation of Mark* (Philadelphia: Fortress, 1984).

203. Reardon claims sexual fidelity as central to Chariton's entire story ('General Introduction', in *CAGN*, p. 20). Tomas Hägg notes this emphasis throughout the novel by Xenophon (*NIA*, p. 32). Regarding the romantic novel in general, Reardon writes: 'Virginity or chastity, at least in the female, is of crucial importance, and fidelity to one's partner, together often with trust in the gods, will ultimately guarantee a happy ending' ('General Introduction', in *CAGN*, p. 2).

204. 'Dreams of a more or less directly symbolic kind are a common feature of the novels' (Hägg, *NIA*, p. 13).

205. Wills, *Quest*, p. 11.

206. Reardon, 'General Introduction', in *CAGN*, p. 9: 'The novel is the open form for the open society' of Hellenism. See also Perry, *Ancient Romances*, p. 47, and his chapter 2, 'The Form Romance in Historical Perspective'. Tomas Hägg expresses the concept botanically: 'The novelists gather their flowers in the most widely different localities' (*NIA*, p. 122).

Mark; its frequent use of asyndeton; its fast-paced narrative tempo that slows only for the anomalous and the emotional; the prominence of particular themes such as crucifixion, resurrection, religion, travel, and crowds set within a 'historical' framework; its narrative structure that begins *in medias res*, climaxes at a central turning point, and concludes with a recognition; and its extensive use of the rhetorical technique of irony all contribute to the conclusion that the Gospel of Mark is not elite literature but a work of popular, novelistic literature. Characteristics such as these have prompted several scholars investigating the genre of the Gospel to arrive at similar conclusions.[207]

Even among those who affirm the influence of novelistic literature upon the Gospel of Mark, however, there is no consensus regarding the importance of the conclusion. Reiser and Wills contend that the Gospel is a specific manifestation of novelistic literature, with Reiser placing Mark in the same genre as the travel biography *Alexander Romance*.[208] Wills finds a specific analogy within a 'subset of ... popular, novelistic biography' that is the 'cult narrative' novelized as *Life of Aesop*.[209] Tolbert applies her findings – derived largely from the romantic novels – with broader strokes as she attempts to approximate a native reading of Mark against the backdrop of the cultural environment and social conditions of the first century. At one point in her study, she describes Mark as an 'apocalyptic message in a popular narrative framework'.[210] Vines opts to include novelistic literature as one aspect of a cross-section of ancient literature to which he applies Bakhtin's modern theory of genre, arriving at the conclusion that Mark most closely approximates the Jewish novel.

The present study will apply this observation that the Gospel of Mark participates in the genre of novelistic literature in yet another direction. I prefer an approach similar to that espoused by Richard I. Pervo who, noting the extreme diversity within both Hellenistic culture and its novelistic literature, finds the novel to be 'too complex a phenomenon to be reduced to a single impetus'.[211] Tomas Hägg draws a similar conclusion in his assessment of the relationship of the Apocryphal Acts to the ancient novels: 'On the whole, it is inadvisable, as has sometimes been attempted, to press a paternity suit, categorically proving that the

---

207. See Reiser, *Syntax,* p. 168; Tolbert, *Sowing,* pp. 59–79; Wills, *Quest,* p. 12. Vines, *Problem,* p. 19; Pervo, *Profit,* p. 11.

208. Marius Reiser, 'Der Alexanderroman und das Markusevangelium', pp. 131–63 in Cancik (ed.), *Markus-Philologie: Historische, literargeschichtliche und stilistische Untersuchungen zum zweiten Evangelium.*

209. Wills, *Quest,* pp. 16–17.

210. Tolbert, *Sowing,* p. 302.

211. Pervo, *Profit,* p. 101.

[Apocryphal] Acts are "descended" from one genre or another ....'[212] Hägg's recommendation echoes the advice of the scholars of other (non-Gospel) novels among whom 'the effort to account for the novels by [a] kind of unitary hypothesis ... has reached a stage of dissolution'.[213] They, too, propose an approach which affirms a radical eclecticism.[214] 'Rather than seek to trace its development', Pervo summarizes, 'these scholars are beginning to produce a series of sophisticated studies of individual works.'[215] If the Gospel of Mark is a novel, as these similarities seem to indicate, the conclusion of these seasoned scholars of the novel may be equally true for the Gospel of Mark.

This study, therefore, seeks not to argue for a specific generic designation, but suggests that novelistic literature provided the author of the Gospel of Mark with a style, a set of motifs and themes, and a basic narrative structure which he could follow without necessarily envisioning his work to be a biography, history, apocalypse, midrash, or memorabilia. This study seeks, rather, to undertake a sophisticated analysis of an individual topic within novelistic literature: the motif of resurrection. I will review literary evidence which suggests that this motif served as a topos among ancient storytellers. I will also identify literary patterns indicating that these ancient storytellers associate this topos of resurrection with specific functions, suggesting a 'curriculum' of novelistic devices which may have guided these ancient storytellers in their craft. Although 'popular narrative is too broad a category to constitute a literary genre', the operations of specific ancient *topoi* provide information about ancient storytelling and its implications for reading not only the Gospel of Mark but also other works within its family of origin, Greco-Roman novelistic literature.[216]

---

212. Hägg, *NIA*, pp. 160–1.
213. Pervo, *Profit*, p. 100.
214. In an essay reviewing a 1976 conference of classical scholars of novelistic literature, Graham Anderson wrote on the question of origins: 'We are all eclectics now' (Graham Anderson, 'The Greek Novel', in Reardon (ed.), *Erotica Antiqua*, pp. 165–71 (169) as quoted in Pervo, *Profit*, p. 100.
215. Pervo, *Profit*, p. 100.
216. Vines, *Problem*, p. 19.

Chapter 2

RESURRECTION AS A POPULAR THEME

A study of ancient Greek influences upon the Gospel of Mark must first address the contention among ancient historians – both past and present – that the Greeks had no conception of resurrection that might influence the Gospels. A number of influential studies in both biblical and classical scholarship argue for a surprisingly limited scenario of conceptions of the afterlife in the diverse and extensive societies around the Mediterranean basin commonly referred to as the 'Greco-Roman world'. These studies assert that resurrection is wholly unknown to Greco-Roman thought before the advent of Christianity. Biblical scholar Johannes Munck, for example, commenting on a passage in which a group of philosophers mock Paul's mention of resurrection (Acts 17.32), writes: 'The idea of a resurrection of the dead was foreign to Greek thought, as can be seen also in I Cor xv. The individual soul might well be immortal, but Greeks were unwilling to think of a resurrection of the body.'[1] For Munck, members of the Greco-Roman world never entertained ideas of bodily resurrection because society as a whole held that the soul is immortal but the body is not. In an article published just two years before the appearance of Munck's commentary, Oscar Cullmann also asserts that resurrection is foreign to ancient Greek ideology. Like Munck, Cullmann bases this assertion on a dualistic interpretation of Greco-Roman philosophy which he applies to Greco-Roman society as a whole: an undisputed conception of life after death in which the soul is immortal, but the body is not.[2]

Among classicists, Glen W. Bowersock has recently sought to renew this assertion, citing the first volume of the *Reallexicon für Antike und Christentum* to argue 'that the whole concept of resurrection, although

---

1. Munck, *The Acts of the Apostles* (AB, 31; New York: Doubleday, 1967), p. 172. See also F.F. Bruce, *Paul: Apostle of the Heart Set Free* [Grand Rapids, Mich.: Eerdmans, 1977], p. 246). Pieter W. van der Horst describes resurrection as 'typically Jewish and very un-Greek' (*The Sentences of Pseudo-Phocylides* [SVTP, 4; New York and Leiden: Brill, 1978], p. 185).

2. See Oscar Cullmann, 'Immortality of the Soul or Resurrection of the Dead' in Stendhal (ed.), *Immortality and Resurrection*, pp. 9–53 (24–25), an influential essay critiqued by George W.E. Nickelsburg (*Resurrection, Immortality, and Eternal Life in Intertestamental Judaism* [HTS, 26; Cambridge, Mass. and London: Harvard University Press, 1972], pp. 177–80).

attested among other peoples, was altogether alien to Graeco-Roman thought'.[3] Bowersock grants that stories in which a character returns from the Underworld to the land of the living are quite frequent in Greco-Roman literature, citing narratives such as those in which 'Orpheus brought back Eurydice, and Heracles brought back Theseus'[4] or 'Euripides' play *Alcestis*'.[5] He rightly notes that 'negotiations for passage in and out of the world of the dead are obviously of a very different character from bodily resurrection after the corpse has grown cold'.[6] It is bodily resurrection that is at issue for Bowersock, which he argues is an idea that does not occur within Greco-Roman literature until the advent of Christianity.

In fact, Bowersock seeks to reverse the direction of influence in the interaction of novelistic literature and the Gospels. Whereas some New Testament scholars hold that Hellenistic novelistic literature influenced the literature of the early Christian communities such as the Gospel of Mark,[7] Bowersock argues that early Christian traditions inspired both the spread of novelistic literature as well as its recurrent theme of resurrection. At the end of a chapter on resurrection in ancient literature, he proposes his radical hypothesis:

> The question we must now ask is whether from a historical point of view we would be justified in explaining the extraordinary growth in fictional writing, and its characteristic and concomitant fascination with resurrection, as some kind of reflection of the remarkable stories that were coming out of Palestine precisely in the middle of the first century A.D. Already in the days of the emperor Claudius the name of Jesus Christ was known at Rome. The Gospels, as we have them, had not yet been written, but much of the story that they were to contain was obviously already in circulation. By the time of Claudius's successor, the emperor Nero, that great philhellenic patron of the arts, the claims of the Christians were being widely disseminated at Rome as a result of the residence of Paul in the city and the infamous immolation of many Christians in the aftermath of the fire that consumed it in 64. By this time it is possible that the earliest of the extant Gospels was actually being written .... It would be wise next to consider the possibility that

3. On p. 102 of *Fiction as History: Nero to Julian* (SCL, 58; Berkeley: University of California Press, 1994), Glen W. Bowersock cites Albrecht Oepke, 'Auferstehung II (des Menschen)' (in Klausner, et al. [eds], *RAC* 1.931): 'Die A., manchen alten Völkern bekannt, liegt griech.-röm. Denken im ganzen fern.'

4. Bowersock cites no specific texts here, referring to the traditions in general terms (*Fiction*, p. 101).

5. Bowersock, *Fiction*, p. 101.

6. Bowersock, *Fiction*, p. 101.

7. Frank Kermode, *The Genesis of Secrecy: On the Interpretation of Narrative* (CENL; Cambridge, Mass. and London: Harvard University Press, 1979); Tolbert, *Sowing*; Wills, *Quest*; and Pervo, *Profit*, among others.

the Gospel stories themselves provided the impetus for the emergence of that fiction in the first place.[8]

In the final chapter of his study, Bowersock works to support his theory through the analysis of a passage in *Leucippe and Clitophon* (second century C.E.) that exhibits close parallels to Gospel passages which describe the Christian eucharistic rite.[9] The result of this analysis – working in tandem with his perception of bodily resurrection as foreign to Greco-Roman culture – is Bowersock's conclusion that the genre of the novel seems 'to have come into being, to some degree, as a response to stories ... enshrined in the canonical Gospels'.[10] For Bowersock, Greco-Roman culture makes no contribution to the recurrent theme of bodily resurrection found in the Gospel of Mark.

However, Bowersock's attempt to reverse the order of influence is not convincing. His claims, like those of Munck and Cullmann before him, fail to take into consideration literary witnesses to a popular culture among the ancient Greeks in which the drama inherent in tales of resurrection accentuate significant points in a narrative. In this chapter I argue that although certain *elite* circles of Greco-Roman culture may have concluded that stories in which individuals physically die and later return to a bodily existence were ludicrous, certain resurrection narratives appealed to *popular* audiences in a time that pre-dates the advent of Christianity. This difference in conceptions of the afterlife is but one example of the relationship between popular and elite literature that Mary Ann Tolbert compares to a musical key change:

> Popular literature, as one aspect of popular culture, is related in theme and overall patterning to elite literature, but it is written in an entirely different key. Its vocabulary, plot development, rhetorical strategies, and characterization are simpler, more conventionalized, more homo-genized, and often more formulaic than the cultivated and self-conscious writings of the privileged classes.[11]

Within 'simpler, more conventionalized' novelistic literature, another conception of life after death arises which includes the possibility that certain individuals who have died may simply rise again in bodily form.

The vicissitudes of history during and since the days of the Greco-Roman world have clearly favored the preservation of writings of the elite.[12] However, as I have demonstrated in Chapter 1, novelistic literature

---

8. Bowersock, *Fiction*, p. 119.
9. Bowersock, *Fiction*, pp. 125–38. Bowersock cites Mt. 26.26, 28 as his point of comparison.
10. Bowersock, *Fiction*, p. 139.
11. Tolbert, *Sowing*, p. 61.
12. See Simon Swain, *Hellenism and Empire: Language, Classicism and Power in the Greek World, AD 50–250* (Oxford: Clarendon; New York: Oxford University Press, 1996).

of the lower-status and less-educated working classes of the Greco-Roman world has survived in several, often fragmentary forms. In addition to fragments of actual popular novelistic literature, the stories of popular culture are preserved in the writings of elite individuals such as Herodotus, Ovid, and Propertius, who were fascinated with popular mythography. In this chapter I examine several such narratives that witness to a belief in physical, bodily resurrection within the popular culture of the Greco-Roman world. These narratives date to the Classical period (Section 2.1) and to the pre-Christian Roman Imperial period (Section 2.2). Furthermore, contrary to Bowersock's suggestion that the theme of resurrection arose in response to the Christian Gospels, I will argue that Chariton's popular novel – in which resurrection narratives abound – was composed before the composition of the earliest Christian Gospel (Section 2.3). Finally, I will demonstrate how the inspiration behind Chariton's resurrection narratives does not even derive from pre-Markan Christian traditions, but rather from Homeric influences (Section 2.4). In my conclusion, I consider recent studies by scholars such as Dale B. Martin, Stanley E. Porter, and John P. Brown that also identify traditions of bodily resurrection within pre-Christian Greco-Roman culture.[13]

2.1 *Classical Witness to Resurrection as a Popular Theme*

Herodotus was a Greek historian who lived long before the advent of Christianity, in the middle of the fifth century B.C.E. (c. 485–420 B.C.E.).[14] The extensive prose narrative of his account of the Persian Wars and the tremendous influence of this narrative upon subsequent writers has led many scholars to refer to Herodotus as 'the father of history'.[15] However, unlike modern political science, Herodotus does not apply rationalistic standards as he investigates the past. In fact, the many popular fables and anecdotes of divine intervention and miraculous occurrences throughout his writing suggest that he had a fascination with popular folklore and

13. Dale B. Martin, *The Corinthian Body* (New Haven, Conn.: Yale University Press, 1995), Stanley E. Porter, 'Resurrection, the Greeks and the New Testament' (in Porter, Hayes and Tombs [eds], *Resurrection*, pp. 52–81), and John Pairman Brown, *Ancient Israel and Ancient Greece: Religion, Politics and Culture* (Minneapolis: Fortress, 2003).

14. David Sacks, *A Dictionary of the Ancient World* (OPR; New York, Oxford: Oxford University Press, 1995), s.v. 'Herodotus'; John P.A. Gould, 'Herodotus' (*OCD*, pp. 696–8); Rosalind Thomas, *Herodotus in Context: Ethnography, Science and the Arts of Persuasion* (New York and Cambridge, Engl.: Cambridge University Press, 2000).

15. As in the ancient world (Cicero, *Leg.* 1.5; Petrarch, *Rerum Memorandum* 4.25–26) and today (Momigliano, 'The Place of Herodotus in the History of Historiography', *History* 43 [1958], pp. 1–13 [3]).

religion.[16] The writings of Herodotus provide three ancient witnesses to the widespread circulation of resurrection narratives among the general population of the pre-Christian Mediterranean world (Section 2.1.1–3). Two other witnesses in texts of this period explicitly deny the idea of bodily resurrection (Section 2.1.4). The implication is that the theme is popular, but rejected by some elite members of society.

2.1.1 *The Aegean Resurrection Narrative of Aristeas*

In Book 4 of *The Persian Wars*, Herodotus retells a popular story about the poet Aristeas in which Aristeas is said to have risen from the dead:

> [4.14.1] I will tell the story that I heard about him [Aristeas] at Proconnesus and Cyzicus. It is said that this Aristeas, who was as well-born as any of his townsfolk, went into a fuller's shop at Proconnesus and there died; the fuller shut his shop and went away to tell the dead man's relatives, [2] and the report of Aristeas' death being spread about in the city was disputed by a man of Cyzicus, who had come from the town of Artace,[17] and said that he had met Aristeas going towards Cyzicus and spoken with him. While he argued vehemently, the relatives of the dead man came to the fuller's shop with all that was necessary for burial; [3] but when the place was opened, there was no Aristeas there, dead or alive. But in the seventh year after that, Aristeas appeared at Proconnesus and made that poem which the Greeks now call the *Arimaspeia*, after which he vanished once again. [4.15.1] Such is the tale told in these two towns.
>
> (Herodotus, *Hist.* 4.14.1–4.15.1 [Godley, LCL 118])

The story of Aristeas' resurrection is a story of a physical resurrection. The corporeal aspect of the risen Aristeas in the narrative is emphasized by the testimonial element of the man who had met him walking on the road and had spoken with him face-to-face, as if he had not died and been shut within the fuller's shop (*Hist.* 4.14.2).[18] The kinsfolk had come 'with all that was needful for burial; but ... there was no Aristeas there' (4.14.2–3). Despite the anticipated preparation of the physical body for burial, the body itself is gone.[19] Seven years later, Aristeas' body is such that he is able to write out a poem which the people still appreciate some time after his death (4.14.3). His is a corpse that appears alive in a variety of manifestations.

At the beginning and end of the narrative, Herodotus states that the tale

---

16. See ancient Cicero, *Div.* 2.116; and contemporary Thomas Harrison, *Divinity and History: The Religion of Herodotus* (OCM; Oxford: Clarendon; New York: Oxford University Press, 2000).

17. Artace is one of two harbor towns of Cyzicus.

18. Compare Lk. 24.13-32 and Plutarch, *Rom.* 28.

19. Compare Mk 16.1 and Lk. 23.56; 24.1.

is told in Proconnesus, an island in the Black Sea, and at Cyzicus in the northeast Aegean. Several indications suggest that the narrative also had a broad audience which extended to the general population of the Mediterranean world several centuries before the advent of Christianity. First of all, the specific towns that Herodotus describes as the provenance of the story are not remote settlements on the fringes of society. Proconnesus, which is now called Marmara, is the largest island in the Propontis.[20] Cyzicus, a Greek colony founded in the eighth century B.C.E. on the south side of the Propontis, had two harbor towns – one to the east and one to the west. This tale of resurrection circulates in the preeminent commercial center for trade passing between the region of the Aegean and the Black Sea.[21]

A second indication that this resurrection story was a popular tale along this trade-route is its conspicuous placement in Herodotus' own narrative. Herodotus does not include the account among other stories of death and rising, nor even among any other stories about individual Scythians. This particular narrative occurs in the midst of a much broader description of the region and culture of Scythia, suggesting that the story held a central place in the folklore of this ancient people group just north of ancient Greece. Specifically, the narrative context begins with a brief mention of an expedition by Darius into Scythia (*Hist.* 4.1.1), prompting Herodotus to describe the Scythians' 28-year hegemony in Upper Asia (4.1.2–6), a mass rebellion of their wives and slaves at that time (4.2–4), and four popular stories about the origin of the Scythian people, the last one sung by the poet Aristeas (4.4–13). The digression about the resurrection of Aristeas occurs at this point in the narrative (4.14–15). Herodotus then returns to his subject of the country of Scythia as an entire region: 'With regard to the regions which lie above the country whereof this portion of my history treats ....' (4.16.1). The story of the resurrection of Aristeas stands in the center of a description of Scythian culture as a whole and may very well have served as a primary tradition for that culture, enjoyed both by elite Greeks who came in contact with the culture as historians and writers such as Herodotus, and perhaps more frequently by average Greeks who came into contact with the culture as tradespeople.

Third, the close association of the narrative with the prominent historical figure, Aristeas, also suggests that this story had a substantial

---

20. This sea is located between the Aegean and the Black Sea.

21. Frederick W. Hasluck, *Cyzicus: Being Some Account of the History and Antiquities of That City* (CAES; New York and Cambridge, Engl.: Cambridge University Press, 1910). See also Walter Ruge, 'Kyzikos', in Pauly (ed.), *RE* 12, cols. 227–233 (232); Krystyna Bartol, 'From Cyzicus to Samothracians: On the Allusion to the Homeric Verse in *Anth. Pal.* 11.346 (= Automedon VIII Gow-Page)', *Eos* 82 (1994), pp. 31–6 (34).

impact on its culture and other people in contact with that culture. Herodotus' description of Aristeas gives the impression of a Scythian Homer: he sang poems of national origins which had a lasting impact upon the Scythian society (4.13.1; 4.16.1). Like Homer, his song tells of a journey to faraway lands in which Aristeas himself encounters typically epic characters such as 'men with one eye' and 'gold-guarding Griffins' (4.13.1).[22] As though held dear, the people remember the place of Aristeas' birth (4.14.1), and his resurrection story is told to Herodotus in two different commercial centers (4.14.1). Stories about the life and times of Aristeas may not have been as prevalent throughout the ancient Mediterranean as were stories of the life of the poet Homer, but Aristeas does seem to have been a poet who received significant attention from the people in the form of several circulating traditions, including the tradition of resurrection.

Finally, as Herodotus himself points out (4.15.1), the resurrection narrative of Aristeas was sufficiently popular to divorce itself from the specific province of Scythia and subsequently spread from the northeast Aegean – through ancient Greece – to the lands of ancient Italy, approximately 800 miles away.

2.1.2 *The Italian Resurrection Narrative of Aristeas*

The ancient resurrection narrative of Aristeas spawned other narratives throughout the eastern Mediterranean. Immediately following his retelling of the first resurrection narrative, Herodotus shares a second story told not only in Proconnesus but even in Metapontium, Italy. In this story, the deceased Aristeas reappears 240 years after his death to call for the erection of an altar and statue in his honor:

> [4.15.1] But this, I know, happened to the Metapontines in Italy, two hundred and forty years after the second disappearance of Aristeas, as reckoning made at Proconnesus and Metapontium shows me: [2] Aristeas, so the Metapontines say, appeared in their country and told them to set up an altar to Apollo, and set beside it a statue bearing the name of Aristeas the Proconnesian; for, he said, Apollo had come to their country alone of all Italian lands, and he – the man who was now Aristeas, but then when he followed the god had been a crow – had come with him. [3] After saying this, he vanished. The Metapontines, so they say, sent to Delphi and asked the god what the vision of the man could mean; and the Pythian priestess told them to obey the vision, saying that their fortune would be better. [4] They did as instructed. And now there stands beside the image of Apollo a statue bearing the name of Aristeas; a grove of bay trees surrounds it; the image is set in

---

22. Compare Homeric epic as described in Section 1.4.1.

the marketplace. Let it suffice that I have said this much about Aristeas.
(Herodotus, *Hist*. 4.15.1–4 [Godley, LCL 118])

Traditions about Aristeas' resurrection seem to be 'alive and well' even 240 years after the narratives began to circulate (*Hist*. 4.15.1). Perhaps in order to explain his travel across Greece and the intervening oceans, it is said that Aristeas was transformed into a crow when he followed Apollo to Italy (4.15.2). A legend of metamorphosis has apparently been joined to the resurrection tradition. However, the predominant narrative associated with Aristeas, like the first narrative, is that of bodily resurrection: Aristeas appears to the people in human form and communicates with them in human language (4.15.2). It is this physical form, in fact, which the Italians will place next to the form of Apollo as a memorial (4.15.4).

The spread of this resurrection narrative from the Black Sea to Italy suggests a broad field of influence. Over its centuries-long existence, the fabulous tale of the great poet Aristeas had made its way along trade-routes throughout the broad region that extends from Greece into Italy and very likely elsewhere as well. Such an extensive geographical and chronological span of influence may well indicate the popularity of the story among the people as a whole, as does the erection of Aristeas' resurrected image in the marketplace of the Metapontines (4.15.4).

Despite the energy which Herodotus invests in telling this entertaining story, he distances himself from ideas of resurrection. He repeatedly attributes the existence of the tale solely to the storytelling of groups of people, employing qualifiers throughout, such as 'it is said that' (4.14.1), 'such is the tale' (4.15.1), 'as reckoning made at Proconnesus and Metapontium shows' (4.15.1), and 'so the Metapontines say' (4.15.2, 3). That the elite Herodotus himself dismisses resurrection stories as popular nonsense becomes especially apparent when he tells about a third resurrection narrative in circulation in his day.

2.1.3 *The Resurrection Narrative of Salmoxis*

Following his general description of Scythia, Herodotus begins to narrate the northward march of King Darius and his troops toward that region, noting in some detail the specific locations that the company passes along the way (*Hist*. 4.16.1–4.92.1). While the troops are south of Scythia – not far from either the Propontis, Cyzicus, or Greece – they come to the region of the Hellespont in which, according to Herodotus, people believe that a deity known as Salmoxis[23] grants immortality to those who believe in an afterlife (4.93.1–4.94.1). Herodotus describes the human sacrifices which a Thracian group known as the Getae perform to this deity (4.94.2–3). Then he relates the history behind the worship of the god Salmoxis:

23. Also 'Zamolxis', 'Zalmoxis'.

[4.95.1] I understand from the Greeks who live beside the Hellespont and Pontus, that this Salmoxis was a man who was once a slave in Samos, his master being Pythagoras son of Mnesarchus; [2] then after being freed and gaining great wealth, he returned to his own country. Now the Thracians were a poor and backward people, but this Salmoxis knew Ionian ways and a more advanced way of life than the Thracian; for he had consorted with Greeks, and moreover with one of the greatest Greek teachers, Pythagoras; [3] therefore he made a hall where he entertained and fed the leaders among his countrymen, and taught them that neither he nor his guests nor any of their descendants would ever die, but that they would go to a place where they would live forever and have all good things. [4] While he was doing as I have said and teaching this doctrine, he was meanwhile making an underground chamber. When this was finished, he vanished from the sight of the Thracians, and went down into the underground chamber, where he lived for three years, [5] while the Thracians wished him back and mourned him for dead; then in the fourth year he appeared to the Thracians, and thus they came to believe what Salmoxis had told them. Such is the Greek story about him.

[4.96.1] Now I neither disbelieve nor entirely believe the tale about Salmoxis and his underground chamber; but I think that he lived many years before Pythagoras; [2] and as to whether there was a man called Salmoxis or this is some deity native to the Getae, let the question be dismissed. [4.97.1] Such were the ways of the Getae, who were subdued by the Persians and followed their army.

(Herodotus, *Hist.* 4.95.1–4.97.1 [Godley, LCL 118])

Salmoxis promises eternal life in their physical bodies (4.95.3) to the community of underprivileged citizens that he convenes (4.95.2). Just as he 'dies' for three years and then 'resurrects' (4.95.4–5), so they, he teaches, will physically resurrect.

Herodotus would paint this cultic community as a phenomenon that occurred among the Thracians (4.95.2). However, the text itself provides some sound indications that the group of people who held this belief in Salmoxis about bodily resurrection might not have been as defined as Herodotus suggests. The first indication is that the story has come to Herodotus from Greeks who live in the region and who must have interacted to a greater or lesser degree with the Thracians in order to appreciate the story in the detail that they do (4.95.1, 5). Secondly, the portrayal of Salmoxis himself demonstrates how interaction with a wider variety of people was certainly possible: he lived with great success among both Greeks, as a freedman of Pythagoras, and Thracians, as a leader in their community (4.95.2). Furthermore, the attention and honor afforded this dual citizenship both in the text as well as by the Thracian leaders and groups who gather to hear his teaching (4.95.3) suggests a value for intercultural exchange. In fact, such a value inspires Herodotus' ethnographic work.

Perhaps the adjectives 'poor and backward' rather than the name 'Thracians' should be considered the operative term in Herodotus' description (4.95.2). The popular audience of this story is indicated first and foremost in the description of the Thracians as poor, the economic condition of the masses in the ancient world. Interestingly, an independent ancient witness written six centuries later indicates that the story of Salmoxis was told among other popular audiences of a different place and time. Salmoxis receives mention in the popular novel by Antonius Diogenes of the second century C.E., who writes about 'how Astraeus met Salmoxis, who was already regarded as a god among the Getae, and of what Dercyllis and Mantinias asked Astraeus to say to him and ask him on their behalf' (Photius, *Bibliotheca* 110a [Sandy, *CAGN*]). Although Photius' summary does not afford us the opportunity of learning exactly what is said by the characters of Diogenes' novel, the tale of this resurrection apparently circulates throughout the popular culture of the Hellenistic world: Salmoxis is 'regarded as a god'. Even if Diogenes' tale derives directly from Diogenes' reading of Herodotus, his revival of the story suggests its survival beyond the community gathered by Salmoxis – perhaps as early as that of Pythagoras in the sixth century B.C.E. (4.96.1) – and beyond members of a local Greek community who share it with Herodotus in the fourth century B.C.E. (4.95.1) to the second century C.E. audience of Diogenes' popular novel.

2.1.4 *Explicit Denial of Resurrection*

Elsewhere in Herodotus, the historian notes an explicit denial of bodily resurrection on the part of a servant of the King of Persia. When King Cambyses asks his servant Prexaspes if he has killed a certain Smerdis who posed a threat to the King's security, Prexaspes declares:

> [Smerdis] cannot have any quarrel with you, small or great; I myself did as you instructed, and I buried him with my own hands. If the dead can rise, you may expect to see Astyages the Mede[24] rise up against you; but if things are as usual, assuredly no harm to you will arise from Smerdis.
> (Herodotus, *Hist.* 3.62.3–4 [Godley, LCL 118])

Such a reference to a dead body coming out of its burial place suggests that the idea of physical resurrection may circulate within the culture. Other elite authors throughout the Classical period also write to deny the belief of a physical resurrection. For example, in his play, *The Eumenides*, Aeschylus writes against the idea in quite strong terms:

---

24. Astyages had been deposed by King Cyrus for some time (Herodotus, *Hist.* 1.127–130).

Zeus could undo fetters, there is a remedy for that,
645 and many means of release.
But when the dust has drawn up the blood of a man,
once he is dead, there is no return to life.
For this, my father has made no magic spells,
although he arranges all other things, turning them up and down;
650 nor does his exercise of force cost him a breath.

(Aeschylus, *Eumen.* 644-50 [Smyth, LCL, 146])

Figure 5   Aeschylus, *Eumenides* 644–650

The text images a dead body drained of blood yet also portrays that body returning to life. Again, the image may very well have been employed because claims about physical resurrection circulated.[25]

2.1.5 *Conclusion*

In three anecdotes, Herodotus indicates that narratives of bodily resurrection circulated among people living between the Black Sea and ancient Italy from the eighth to the fifth century B.C.E. These stories are told among citizens and tradespeople throughout this vast region surrounding Greece as well as to elite travelers such as Herodotus. Other texts from the Classical period suggest an intentional attempt to negate this belief within elite society. However, despite disbelief on the part of some, the following texts from the early Imperial period indicate that ordinary people continued to disseminate resurrection narratives.

2.2 *Imperial Witness to Resurrection as a Popular Theme*

Two ancient collections of popular mythology from the early Imperial period indicate that narratives of bodily resurrection circulated in popular Greco-Roman myth and folklore before the advent of Christianity: a collection made by Ovid (Section 2.2.1) and another gathered by Propertius (Section 2.2.2). A third novelistic text from this period, a mockery of resurrection, also suggests that pre-Christian popular culture of the Greco-Roman world entertained certain conceptions of resurrection (Section 2.2.3).

2.2.1 *Ovid*

In his poetic exposition of the Roman festal calendar, *The Fasti*, Publius Ovidius Naso ('Ovid') recounts a popular narrative about the bodily resurrection of Hippolytus. The pre-Christian date of *The Fasti* is indicated in part by Ovid's letter of dedication to the emperor Augustus

---

25. See also Aeschylus *Electra* 137–139 ('never by weeping nor my prayer will you resurrect [ἀνστάσεις] your father from the pool' [Lloyd-Jones (LCL 20)]), and *Ag.* 1360.

737 Familiar is the tale of Phaedra's love, familiar, too, the wrong that Theseus did,
  when, too confiding, he did curse his son to death.
 Doomed by his piety, the youth was journeying to Troezen,
740 when a bull cleft with his breast the waters in his path.
 Fear seized the startled steeds; in vain their master held them back,
  they dragged him along the crags and flinty rocks.
 Hippolytus fell from the car, and, his limbs entangled by the reins,
  his mangled body was whirled along,
745 till he gave up the ghost, much to Diana's rage.
 "There is no need for grief," said the son of Coronis,
  "for I will restore the pious youth to life all unscathed,
  and to my leechcraft gloomy fate shall yield."
 Straightway he drew from an ivory casket simples
750 that before had stood Glaucus' ghost in good stead,
 what time the seer went down to pluck the herbs he had remarked,
  and the snake was succoured by a snake.
 Thrice he touched the youth's breast, thrice he spoke healing words;
  then Hippolytus lifted his head, low laid upon the ground.
755 He found a hiding place in a sacred grove and in the depths of Dictynna's own woodland;
  he became Virbius of the Arician Lake.
 But Clymenus and Clotho grieved, she that life's broken thread should be respun,
  he that his kingdom's rights should be infringed.
 Fearing the example thus set, Jupiter aimed a thunderbolt at him
760 who used the resources of a too potent art.
 Phoebus, thou didst complain. But Aesculapius is a god, be reconciled to thy parent:
  he did himself for thy sake what he forbids others to do.

         (Ovid, *Fasti* 6.737-62 [Frazer, LCL, 253])

Figure 6 Ovid, *Fasti* 6.737–62

written in 8 C.E.[26] Other indications in the work itself suggest that Ovid's recensions continued until his death around 18 C.E.[27] So the bodily resurrection recounted in Ovid's *Fasti* predates the ministry of Jesus and the rise of Christianity, having been written before 18 C.E.

 Hippolytus' death results from a curse. Considered a man of great piety, Hippolytus has repulsed the seductive advances of his father Theseus' wife, Phaedra. When the situation comes to the attention of Theseus, however, Phaedra accuses the young man Hippolytus of making the advances toward her.[28] Seeking a suitable punishment for Hippolytus, Theseus prays to his father, Poseidon, lord of the sea. In response, Poseidon sends a bull out of the sea just as Hippolytus drives his chariot along the shore, frightening his horses and causing them to drive his chariot into the rocks of the coastline. Hippolytus is killed . . . though only to be raised again (see Figure 6 above).

 The epanaphora[29] which opens the poetic narrative emphasizes that the

26. See Ovid's *Tristia* 2.549–52.

27. Frazer describes the *Fasti* as 'a work of Ovid's maturity' ('Introduction' to Ovid's *Fasti* [ed., trans. James G. Frazer; rev. by George P. Goold; LCL, 253; Cambridge, Mass. and London: Harvard University Press, 2nd edn, 1989]), p. xxiii.

28. On the influence of this story, see Wills, *Jewish Novel*, p. 164.

29. [Pseudo-]Cicero, *Rhet. Her.* 4.12.19 (Caplan [LCL 403]); Quintilian, *Inst.* 7.4.8.

Diana hid Hippolytus in secret,
775   then sent him to the nymph Egeria,
       the grove where all alone, unhonored, he
       lived out his life among Italian forests
       And changed his name to Virbius.
              (Virgil, *The Aeneid* 7.774-78 [Mandelbaum])

Figure 7   Virgil, *The Aeneid* 7.777–778

story to follow is indeed 'familiar' to the ancient world (*Fasti* 6.737).[30] As early as the fifth century B.C.E. Euripides wrote his tragedy, *Hippolytus*, on this subject, though there is no resurrection in his dramatization. Nor is there a resurrection scene in Lucius Annaeus Seneca's mid-first century C.E. dramatization in Latin, also entitled *Hippolytus*. However, the fact that Hippolytus' resurrection was known before the advent of Christianity is apparent both from this telling by Ovid as well as from another version by Ovid in a slightly different form at lines 497–529 of Book 15 of his *Metamorphosis*.[31]

The descriptions of both death and resurrection are graphic and physical – the text narrates a bodily resurrection. Hippolytus' body is 'mangled' (*Fasti* 6.744) as it is dragged by the speeding chariot over 'crags and flinty rocks' (6.742). Though he has 'given up the ghost' (6.745), Asklepius vows to 'restore the pious youth to life' (6.747). The promise includes a description of a restored physical body: Hippolytus will not only be alive, but he will be 'all unscathed' (6.747). Asklepius applies his magic herbs directly to the chest of the mangled body and that very body restores to its original glory (6.753–54). The head which lays 'low upon the ground' rises up again (6.754). Virgil's *Aeneid*, a pre-Christian epic written between 30 and 19 B.C.E., confirms this reading, describing the figure of 'Virbius'[32] not as a shade, but as a living man (see Figure 7 above).

Though in hiding, neither text portrays Virbius/Hippolytus as anything but a living man who – given a renewed body – 'lived out his life' (*Aeneid* 7.777).

Ovid's text points us to another pre-Christian resurrection narrative, that of Glaucus. Lines 6.749–750 of Ovid's *Fasti* indicate that the same herbs which raise Hippolytus from the dead have 'stood Glaucus' ghost in good stead'. There are no extant pre-Christian texts devoted to the narration of this tale. However, Glaucus' story is retold by two popular mythographers who wrote sometime around the second century C.E.[33] As a young boy, Glaucus drowns in a jar of honey. His father, Polyides, is desperate to restore the child to life. He happens to see a serpent using a

---

30.   Originally: '**Notus** amor Phaedrae, **nota** est iniuria Thesei.'
31.   See also Apollodorus (3.10.3), Pausanius (2.27.4).
32.   'Virbius' carries no apparent signification.
33.   See Apollodorus, *Bibl.* 3.3.1; Hyginus, *Poet. Astron.* 2.14.

magic herb to revive a fellow serpent who has died (*Fasti* 6.752). By applying this herb to his son, Polyides is able to restore Glaucus to life (6.749–754). Common elements of (1) following the example of the serpent, (2) the application of the herb, and (3) a dead person who resurrects clarify Ovid's allusion to the Glaucus story. Ovid was aware of at least two popular resurrection narratives in the early first century C.E.

2.2.2 *Propertius*

A third pre-Christian resurrection narrative with many similar elements occurs in the poetry of Propertius, who wrote in Italy slightly before the time of Ovid.[34] Propertius collected tales of popular mythology and represented them in a fancy, elegiac style. As he extols the powers of the medicine of his day, Propertius tells of the resurrection of Androgeon:

> Medicine can cure all human pains: only love loves not a doctor of its disease. Machaon healed the lame legs of Philoctetes, and Chiron, son of Phillyra, the blindness of Phoenix; and the god of Epidaurus[35] by his Cretan herbs restored the lifeless Androgeon to his father's hearth; and the Mysian prince who received his wound from the Thessalian's spear, from the selfsame spear received its cure ....
>
> (Propertius, *Elegies* 2.1.57–66 [Goold, LCL 18])

As in the tales of Hippolytus and Glaucus, so the 'lifeless' body of young Androgeon is restored through the application of herbs. In his commentary on *The Fasti*, the classical scholar James G. Frazer notes this particular tradition of bodily resurrection as dating from the pre-Christian Greco-Roman world.[36] He reviews several similar stories from different cultures and different times around the developing Western world. In his summary, Frazer suggests not Christianity, but pre-Christian, pre-Ovidian inspirations behind ancient Western stories of physical resurrection: 'We need not necessarily suppose that these modern tales are direct echoes of the old story of Polyidus and Glaucus; they may be so, but it is also possible that they are all drawn independently from a still older source, the perennial wellspring of popular fancy.'[37]

---

34. Propertius' *Elegies* (4.1.119–134); Ovid, *Am.* 764 (written in the year 2 B.C.E., in which Ovid implies that Propertius is dead); Guy Lee, Propertius' *Poems* (Oxford: Clarendon, 1994), pp. xxiv-xxv.

35. That is, Asklepius, to whom Epidaurus dedicated a major center for healing (an Asklepeion).

36. James G. Frazer, *Publii Ovidii Nasonis, Fastorum Libri Sex* (The Fasti *of Ovid*), *Edited with a Translation and Commentary in Five Volumes* (5 vols; London: Macmillan, 1929), pp. 4.326-7.

37. Frazer, *Publii Ovidii Nasonis*, pp. 4.326-7.

2.2.3 *The Mockery of Resurrection*

In a phenomenon analogous to the explicit denial of resurrection that I noted in the Classical period, the Neronian novelist Petronius overtly mocks the notion of resurrection. Encolpius, the narrator of his novel, *The Satyricon*, compares the *physical* restoration of his genitals, once severed and now miraculously restored in the flesh, to Protesilaus' visit from Hades[38] in a passing reference:

> The gods are greater, who have restored me to my full self. For Mercury, who conducts souls to and from Hades, by his kindness gave back to me what an angry hand had cut off, so be sure that I am more lucky than Protesilaus or any other of the ancients.
>
> (Petronius, *Satyr.* 140.12 [Conte, *Hidden Author*, 97])

The treatment of this reference is sufficiently oblique so as to suggest that the story of Protesilaus was known to general audiences at the time of the writing of the novel. Petronius' specific association of the physical restoration to the resurrection of Protesilaus suggests that the popular myth had an association with physical resurrection at that time. Bowersock rightly notes that during the reign of Nero – as Petronius composed his novel – the influence of the Christian community was likely beginning to spread.[39] Notice, however, that Petronius employs Protesilaus as the object of his mockery rather than Jesus, a figure who would be more fitting were Petronius mocking the adherents of a developing Christianity. He applies Protesilaus as a metaphor to mock, however, indicating a Greek tradition of resurrection as well as a physical interpretation of Protesilaus' return among some segments of the population in the early first century C.E.[40]

2.2.4 *Conclusion*

An examination of both Classical and Imperial texts has led to the same observation: the concept of resurrection was not 'altogether alien to Greco-Roman thought' before the advent of Christianity, but rather occurs in popular thinking.[41] Even though many elite texts scorn the notion of physical resurrection, textual witnesses to the circulation of the idea survive both in the popular mythography that a few writers among the elite have preserved, as well as in Petronius' mockery of the myths of physical resurrection.

---

38. Apollodorus 5.3.30.

39. Bowersock, *Fiction*, p. 119.

40. The myth of Protesilaus' return from the Underworld would need to be well established to allow mockery or mythomania (as Conte, *Hidden Author*, p. 97).

41. Bowersock, *Fiction*, p. 102.

2.3 *The Pre-Markan Date of the Composition of Callirhoë*

In addition to this fragmentary witness derived primarily from elite texts, the earliest, most complete popular novel, Chariton's *Callirhoë*, is replete with references to resurrection. Bowersock claims that the novelistic emphasis on resurrection derives from an exposure to either the Christian Gospels or developing Christian tradition.[42] In this section, I will argue that resurrection in novelistic literature is not a reaction to the Christian Gospels, because Chariton writes during the period of Nero's reign before the composition of the earliest Gospel, the Gospel of Mark, around 70 C.E. The evidence for a Neronian date for Chariton's composition is textual (Section 2.3.1), stylistic (Section 2.3.2), historiographical (Section 2.3.3), political (Section 2.3.4), and indicated by external witness (Section 2.3.5). In a final section of the chapter, I will take this argument one step further, demonstrating that Chariton was most likely not influenced even by the developing pre-Gospel traditions of the early Christian community (Section 2.4).

2.3.1 *Textual Witnesses to the Date of Chariton's Novel*

Specific though they may be, internal remarks about the identity and location of the author provide no assistance in identifying the date of the novel: 'I, Chariton of Aphrodisias, clerk of the lawyer Athenagoras, am going to relate a love story . . .' (*Callir.* 1.1.1). Aphrodisias has been the subject of extensive archaeological research since the middle of the twentieth century. In fact, inscriptions containing the name Chariton have been discovered there as well as other inscriptions mentioning individuals known as Athenagoras.[43] However, inscriptions uncovered to date provide us with no further information about who these people were or specifically when they might have lived.

Manuscript evidence, however, provides significant insights. Four manuscripts have been decisive in the development of complete modern editions of *Callirhoë* : one extensive medieval manuscript and three highly fragmentary ancient papyri. The medieval manuscript, dating from the thirteenth century, contains an extensive text of Chariton's novel with a few minor lacunae.[44] Working from this text alone in 1876 – the sole modern witness to the novel until the early twentieth century – Erwin Rohde assessed Chariton's work to be the latest of the five complete

---

42. Bowersock, *Fiction*, pp. 125–38.

43. Kenan T. Erim, *Aphrodisias: City of Venus Aphrodite* (London: Muller, Blond & White, 1986).

44. Seven letters, for example, are illegible at Chariton, *Callir.* 1.1.6. There is a lacuna of 21 lines at *Callir.* 6.4.6.

romance novels, 'scarcely to be placed before the beginning of the sixth century [C.E.], at the very earliest in the closing years of the fifth.'[45]

This position was determined to be untenable, however, during excavations in the Egyptian desert at the turn of the twentieth century.[46] Discoveries there would effectually topple Rohde's theory, revealing *Callirhoë* most likely to have been the *earliest* of the complete novels.[47] A team of archaeologists under the direction of Bernard Grenfell and Arthur Hunt discovered two papyrus fragments of Chariton's novel. Papyrus Fayûm I, containing fragments of the text from *Callir.* 4.2.5 – 4.3.2,[48] can be dated on palaeographical grounds to around 200 C.E., give or take a quarter of a century.[49] Papyrus Oxyrhynchus 1019 is written on papyrus different from that of Papyrus Fayûm I, yet dates to the same time period.[50] It contains fragments of Chariton's text between *Callir.* 2.3.5 and 2.4.2.

Yet another papyrus fragment from the novel was discovered in the 1950s as part of the private collection of G.A. Michaelidis.[51] The papyrus, dubbed 'Papyrus Michaelidis no. 1', was recognized as the earliest extant fragment of *Callirhoë* when both its editor, David S. Crawford, and an independent study by papyrologist Eric Turner assigned the papyrus to the middle of the second century C.E.[52] The surviving text, which extends from 2.11.5 to the end of Book 2, closes with an intriguing self-reference: 'The story of Chariton of Aphrodisias about Callirhoë, Book 2.'[53] Though modern editions often refer to the novel by the title *Chaereas and Callirhoë*, the ancient title was simply *Callirhoë*.[54] This is an appellation which, as I explore in Section 2.3.5, also occurs in ancient external witnesses.

In the early 1970s, further fragments of Papyrus Oxyrhynchus 1019

---

45.   Erwin Rohde, *Der griechische Roman und seine Vorläufer* (Leipzig: Breitkopf und Hartel, 1876), p. 489.

46.   See Christina Lucke, 'Zum Charitontext auf Papyrus', *ZPE* 58 (1985), pp. 21–33.

47.   See Reardon, 'General Introduction', in *CAGN*, p. 2; Lesky, 'Prose Romance', p. 857.

48.   Bernard P. Grenfell and Arthur S. Hunt (eds.), *Fayûm Towns and their Papyri* (EEFGRB, 3; London: Offices of the Egypt Exploration Fund, 1900).

49.   See Remy Petri, *Über den Roman des Chariton* (BKP, 9; Meisenheim an Glan: A. Hain, 1963), p. 47.

50.   Bernard P. Grenfell and Arthur S. Hunt (eds), *Oxyrhynchus Papyri* (EEFGRB, 8; London: Offices of the Egypt Exploration Fund, 1910).

51.   David S. Crawford, *Papyri Michaelidae, Being a Catalogue of the Greek and Latin Papyri, Tablets, and Ostraca in the Library of Mr. G.A. Michaelidis of Cairo* (Aberdeen: Aberdeen University Press, 1955).

52.   Petri, *Über den Roman*, p. 47.

53.   Crawford, *Papyri Michaelidae*, p. 1.

54.   See the introductory notes to Goold's 1995 translation of the text, entitled simply *Callirhoë*.

were identified and published as Papyrus Oxyrhynchus 2948.[55] Like Oxyrhynchus 1019, this remnant, which contains fragments extending from *Callir.* 2.4.5–2.5.1, also dates between 175–225 C.E.

In light of these discoveries, Wilhelm Schmid made significant modifications to Rohde's study in the form of supplemental notes appended to the third edition.[56] The early papyri indicate not only that Chariton wrote before the middle of the second century C.E., but also that the text of the romance had a fairly wide circulation by this time. Factoring in the requisite time for a novel written in Aphrodisias (*Callir.* 1.1.1) to find an audience in Egypt calls for an earlier date – 'perhaps much earlier' – than c. 150 C.E.[57] In fact, Schmid asserts that Chariton's novel is to be dated 'at the latest towards the end of the first century B.C.E.'[58]

However, determining the date of *Callirhoë* need not rely on papyrological evidence alone. Other, less objective criteria allow us to approximate the period in which the novel was written, with greater definition. Linguistic style, historiographical content, and sociological descriptions within the text – as well as extra-textual references to the novel itself – suggest that Chariton's novel was written during or before Nero's reign in 58–64 C.E.

2.3.2 *The Date of Chariton's Novel as Reflected in Its Language and Style*

Observations regarding the language and style of *Callirhoë* have played a primary role in defining the time period in which Chariton wrote. In and of itself, linguistic analysis is an admittedly fluid and imprecise basis for establishing the date of any text. Considerable variation exists even among writers who live in similar times and places. However, Chariton's literary style does provide one piece of substantiating evidence among several others that the work is written during or before the reign of Nero. In the period of dynamic literary criticism which extended from the early first century B.C.E. until the late first century C.E., writers of Greek typically emulated one of three competing literary tendencies: 'Asianic', 'Atticistic', or 'Koine' Greek. The strikingly Asianic and Koine style of the text of *Callirhoë* suggests a date of composition before the rise of Atticism which dominated Greek literature of the late first century C.E.

As early as the first century B.C.E., certain teachers and literary critics began to condemn a prominent style of oration referred to as 'Asian'

---

55. See vol. 57 of Grenfell and Hunt (eds), *Oxyrhynchus Papyri*, pp. 12–14.

56. Rohde's book, *Der griechische Roman und seine Vorläufer*, sustained four post-mortem editions (Leipzig: Breitkopf und Hartel, 2nd edn, 1900, 3rd edn, 1914; Darmstadt: Wissenschaftliche Buchgesellschaft, 4th edn, 1960; Hildesheim: Georg Olms, 5th edn, 1974). For Schmid's supplement, see the 2nd, 3rd and 4th edns.[4]

57. So Reardon, 'Chariton', *NAW*, p. 314.

58. Rohde, *Der griechische Roman* (1914), p. 610.

which they characterized as grossly ornate.[59] Texts labeled as Asian tended to embellish their language with an air of emotion, rhythm, wordplay, and diction disproportionate to the subject described.[60] In its place, teachers such as Caecilius of Caleacte, who flourished under the relative peace and stability of Caesar Augustus, espoused a Greek revival, an imitation of the classic fifth century B.C.E. Attic orators.[61] His influential treatises, perhaps known by titles such as 'On the Difference Between the Attic and Asianic Taste' and 'On the Style of the Ten [Attic] Orators', circulated early in the first century C.E.[62] Both essays condemned the florid Asian style in deference to a more natural yet erudite Atticism. Such stylistics rarely occur in texts dating after the middle of the first century C.E., perhaps as a result of teachers such as Caecilius. Thus Ulrich von Wilamowitz's identification of Asianic qualities in Chariton's text leads him to the conclusion that Chariton wrote 'in Nero's time, certainly not much later':

> Vielleicht noch in neronischer Zeit, sicherlich nicht viel später, hat Chariton von Aphrodisias die 'syrakusische Liebesgeschichte' geschrieben, die großen Beifall fand: wir haben Fetzen eines Exemplares aus einem Landstädtchen Ägyptens . . . . Sein Stil ist jener kommatische, den man vielleicht asiatisch nennen kann . . ., verziert noch ganz und gar mit den hellenistischen Rhythmen, für die Chariton in Wahrheit das leuchtendste (wenn auch bisher hier unbemerkte) Beispiel ist.[63]

Many of the teachers who shunned Asianism at the turn of the Common Era also sought to elevate the stylistics of their students above the syntactical and morphological simplicity of a Koine Greek (from Greek κοινή meaning 'common') that had developed throughout the Hellenistic period following the conquests of Alexander the Great. The spread of Koine Greek effected changes in verbal mood, tense, voice, and linguistic morphology.[64] Use of the optative mood had nearly disappeared. Distinctions between verb tenses such as the imperfect, aorist, and perfect had faded, as had the distinctiveness of the middle and dual voices. Furthermore, a simplification of morphology among speakers of Koine Greek favored the use of finite verbs in parataxis instead of participles and

---

59. See Cicero, *Brutus* 325.

60. Ulrich von Wilamowitz-Moellendorff, 'Asianismus und Atticismus', *Hermes* 35 (1900), pp. 1–52; Patricia Bizzell and Bruce Herzberg, *The Rhetorical Tradition: Readings from Classical Times to the Present* (Boston: Bedford, 2nd edn, 2001), pp. 284–5.

61. Pseudo-Longinus, 'On the Sublime'. See Malcolm Heath, 'Caecilius, Longinus, and Photius', *GRBS* 39 (1998), pp. 271–92.

62. *The Suda*, s.v. 'Caecilius' (k1165).

63. Wilamowitz-Moellendorff, 'Griechische Literatur', p. 184.

64. Robert Browning, *Medieval and Modern Greek* (Cambridge, Engl.: Cambridge University Press, 1983), pp. 19–52.

infinitival clauses structured within subordinated periods. In an effort to reverse this 'vulgarization' of the Greek language, teachers of the late first century C.E. trained their students to once again imitate the literary art which had flourished under the tutelage of the early sophists of Athens such as Gorgias and contemporaries. By the end of the first century C.E., a period of revivalist Atticism flourished, referred to as the 'Second Sophistic'.[65]

Chariton, however, writes predominately in a lackluster Koine which prevailed in the period before the Second Sophistic. The use of Koine Greek in Chariton's language has been analyzed extensively by Antonios D. Papanikolaou in his book, *Chariton-Studien*.[66] These studies consist almost entirely of specific examples from the text itself in which Chariton's use of particular words (ch. 2); verb forms (chs 3–5); cases (ch. 6); participles, infinitives, and conjunctions (chs 8–9); and other peculiarities (ch. 7) are shown to have characteristics of Koine. 'Er gehört in die vorattizistische Periode', Papanikolaou concludes, 'bzw. in die Zeit, in der die attizistischen Tendenzen erst ganz allmählich zu wirken begannen.'[67]

Certainly, literary Atticism did not replace Asianism overnight. Nor did the impetus toward Atticism affect all writers in a uniform fashion. To claim that Chariton's writing is completely free of the influences of Atticism would overstate the case.[68] Nevertheless, the subject matter, references, and structure of Chariton's text suggests an author who 'was more likely to learn of and follow the latest trends'.[69] The text clearly does not match the caliber of Atticism which predominates among writers of Greek by the end of the first century C.E. So Bryan Reardon concludes in a recent study, 'If [Chariton] had been writing at the end of the first century C.E ... ., he would have Atticized more than he does.'[70] For Reardon, 'it seems unlikely that Chariton wrote later than, say, the reign of Nero.'[71]

65. Philostratus, *Lives of the Sophists*, 19.

66. Antonios D. Papanikolaou, *Chariton-Studien: Untersuchungen zur Sprache und Chronologie der griechischen Romane* (Hypomnemata 57; Göttingen: Vandenhoeck & Ruprecht, 1973).

67. Papanikolaou, *Chariton-Studien*, p. 161.

68. Papanikolaou, *Chariton-Studien*, p. 162; Carl W. Müller, 'Chariton von Aphrodisias und die Theorie des Romans in der Antike', *A&A* 22 [1976], p. 118, n. 19.). Compare Consuelo Ruiz-Montero, 'Aspects of the Vocabulary of Chariton of Aphrodisias', *CQ* 41 (1991), pp. 484–9.

69. Perry, *Ancient Romances*, p. 344. See also Ben E. Perry, 'Chariton and His Romance from a Literary-Historical Point of View', *AJPh* 51 (1930), pp. 99–134, as well as Goold, 'Introduction', p. 2.

70. Reardon, 'Chariton', p. 325.

71. Reardon, 'Chariton', p. 319.

2.3.3 *The Date of Chariton's Novel as Reflected in Its Historiographical Content*

The extent to which Chariton incorporates history into his own story world is also helpful for determining the date of composition, suggesting a date of composition in the first century C.E. or earlier. By means of references that occur throughout the story, Chariton positions the narrative world of *Callirhoë* around the fourth century B.C.E. The hero and heroine of the novel are both children of real-life decorated war veterans, actual historical figures. Chaereas' father, Ariston, and Callirhoë's father, Hermocrates, were famed generals who helped to save Syracuse when the Athenians attacked toward the end of the fifth century B.C.E.[72] In his *Bibliotheca*, Diodorus Siculus mentions that Hermocrates had a daughter who 'had been slain' (just as Callirhoë is considered to be slain by Chaereas throughout the majority of the novel) as well as a 'son' named Dionysius (the name of Hermocrates' 'son-in-law' in the novel).[73] Chariton's King Artaxerxes probably represents Artaxerxes II Mnemon (404–358 B.C.E.) whose wife has the same name as the wife of the Persian king in Chariton's story, Statira.[74]

Despite this fourth-century setting, Chariton's literary style clearly does not date from the fourth century B.C.E. As I have shown in the previous subsection, the 'common' Greek form in which the novel is written is a development of the Hellenistic era. In fact, my research has encountered *no scholar* who argues for a date of composition before the first century B.C.E.[75] So these several allusions to the fourth century B.C.E are not indicative of the historical setting in which the book was written.

Yet the fact that Chariton's story does historicize as extensively as it does is informative, as Ben Perry notes, because 'historical persons and events are much more prominent in his book than in any extant romance known to have been written in the second century C.E or later'.[76] Although many ancient novels refer to history in one way or another, the early novels – those written before the first century C.E. – do so to a much greater degree. The *Ninus Romance* fragments for example, dating from the first century B.C.E., witness to a novel built around the historical figure of Ninus, premier king of Nineveh, and his wife Semiramis, a Babylonian princess who is fabled to have conquered Bactria and built

---

72. Regarding Ariston, see Thucydides *Hist.* 7.39; Plutarch, *Nic.* 25. On Hermocrates, clearly the more famous of the two, see Thucydides 4.58–65; 6.32–35, 72–81, 96, 99; 7.21, 73; 8.26, 29, 85; Xenophon, *Hell.* 1.1–3; Polybius, *Hist.* 12.25–26; Plutarch, *Nic.* 1, 16, 26, 28; Diodorus Siculus, *Bibl.* 13.4, 11, 18–19, 34, 39, 63, 75; 14.44.

73. Diodorus, *Bibl.* 13.91, 14.44; see also Xenophon, *Hell.* 2.2.

74. See Plutarch, *Artax.* 5.3; 6.5; 17.6; 18.4; et al.

75. See details at n. 98 of this chapter.

76. Perry, *Ancient Romances*, p. 343.

Babylon.[77] An even closer parallel to *Callirhoë* is found in the hero and heroine of the first century C.E. novel *Metiochus and Parthenope*: both are children of decorated war veterans. The father of Metiochus is none other than the famous Athenian general Miltiades,[78] and the father of Parthenope is Polycrates, the unrivalled tyrant who seized power in Samos in the sixth century B.C.E. and attempted to establish a thessalocracy.[79] Both Metiochus and Parthenope also appear in Herodotus' history, though – as Callirhoë and Dionysius – to a much lesser extent.[80] The fragments of a third novel 'which could be as old as *Ninos* …',[81] also focus on a historical national hero: the Egyptian king Sesonchosis/Sesostris.[82]

The Hellenistic Jewish novels manifest a similar phenomenon: only those written in the first century C.E. or earlier incorporate historical figures into their respective narrative worlds. The Greek edition of Esther, for example, was complete with six additions in the second or early first century B.C.E. Its narrative is situated in the court of King Artaxerxes (Esth. 1.1; 2.16-17; 4.6).[83] Like the Greek novels, the story of Esther can be traced in part to Herodotus' *Histories*, which describes Xerxes (Ἀσσουήρος in Greek), king of the Persian Empire from 485–465 B.C.E., with characteristics strikingly similar to Esther's Ahasuerus. For example, both Esther's and Herodotus' Ἀσσουήρος are philanderers. In Esther, the king disowns Queen Vashti for failing to appear before the people and seeks out another virgin to take her place in his harem (1.1–2.4). In Herodotus, he tries unsuccessfully to have an affair with his brother's wife, but succeeds in his efforts with her daughter (*Hist.* 9.108–13). Also, both Herodotus and the Jewish novel are surprisingly unflattering in their portrayal of this king: he is choleric and restive.[84] Such similarities in name and character lead most scholars to conclude that the story of Esther is set in Xerxes' Persian court in the fifth century B.C.E.[85]

The Greek version of the book of Daniel probably arrives at the form

77. Veysel Donbaz, 'Two Neo-Assyrian Stelae in the Antakya and Kahramanmaras Museums', *ARRIM* 8 (1990), pp. 4–24; Perry, *Ancient Romances*, 153–66; Stephens and Winkler (ed), *Fragments*, pp. 23–71.

78. See Herodotus, *Hist.* 4.137; 6.41, 132–6; Pausanias, *Descr.* 1.15; and the first biography of Cornelius Nepos' *De excellentibus ducibus* (first century B.C.E.).

79. See Herodotus, *Hist.* 3.39–60, 120–5, 140–51 and Thucydides, *Hist.* 1.13, 3.104, among others.

80. Metiochus: Herodotus, *Hist.* 6.41. Parthenope: Herodotus, *Hist.* 6.23 and 7.165.

81. Stephens and Winkler (eds), *Fragments*, p. 248.

82. 'Sesonchosis' in Josephus, *In Ap.* 1.15 and *Ant.* 8.246; 'Sesostris' in Herodotus, *Hist.* 2.102–10; Aristotle, *Pol.* 1329b; Strabo, *Geogr.* 3.54; and Plutarch, *Mor.* 24; 'Sesoosis' in Diodorus Siculus, *Bibl.* 1.53–9.

83. See Wills, *AJN*, 27–30.

84. Cf. Esther 1.12; 2.1; 7.7-8; Herodotus, *Hist.* 9.111.5; 9.113.2.

85. Carey A. Moore, *Esther*; (AB, 7B; New York: Doubleday, 1971), p. 69.

found in the Septuagint around the first century B.C.E.[86] Its narrative setting, however, is the period around the time of the Babylonian deportation of the Jews in the sixth century B.C.E.[87] Other Hellenistic Jewish writings which participate in this early, historicizing phase of the novel include:[88]

- Artapanus' *On Moses* – a novel of the third to second century B.C.E. which narrates stories of the central figure of Hebrew tradition;
- Tobit – a novel written in the early second century B.C.E. that is set in the period of Assyrian exile in the eighth century B.C.E.;
- Judith – written around the second century B.C.E. and set in a historically confused period when the Assyrians invaded the Levant (eighth century B.C.E.) under the direction of Nebuchadnezzar (a Neo-Babylonian king [605–562 B.C.E.]);
- *Joseph and Asenath* – written around the turn of the Common Era, set in the ancient lifetime of the Jewish figure Joseph;
- *Third Maccabees* – written around the turn of the Common Era, but set in the reign of the Hellenistic king Ptolemy IV Philopater (222–203 B.C.E.);
- *The Tobiad Romance* – written by Josephus in the first century C.E. based upon an older account of the story written in the second century B.C.E. concerning events of the third century B.C.E.; and
- *The Royal Family of Adiabene* – written by Josephus in the first century C.E. based upon an older account of uncertain date concerning an event that is also mentioned in Pausanias' *Desc.* 8.16.5 and twice in the Mishnah (*Nazir* 3.6; *Yoma* 3.10).

Novels of the second century C.E. and later are not as self-consciously historical as these early novels. The setting and characters of Achilles Tatius' *Leucippe and Clitophon* and Longus' *Daphnis and Chloë* do not attempt to dress themselves in the accoutrements of history.[89] Indeed, not until the advent of Heliodorus' voluminous fourth century C.E. novel, *Aethiopica*, is there a return to such historical décor. Furthermore, even though this story takes place in the pre-civilized Alexandria of the late sixth or early fifth century B.C.E., the historic allusions are much weaker than in the earlier historicizing novels.

Chariton's extensive use of history is much more in line with the historicizing novels of the first century C.E. and before, rather than the novels of the second century C.E. and after. The fact that Chariton places

---

86. Wills, *AJN*, pp. 51–4.
87. See John J. Collins, *Daniel* (ed. Frank M. Cross; Hermeneia; Minneapolis: Fortress, 1993), pp. 29–38.
88. Wills, *AJN*.
89. Achilles Tatius' *Leucippe and Clitophon* is a first-person, autobiographic narrative; Longus' *Daphnis and Chloë* presents an ecphrasis of a rustic painting.

his narrative world within a specific historical setting suggests that he writes in the first century C.E. or earlier.

2.3.4 *The Date of Chariton's Novel as Reflected in Its Politics*

In his book, *Der Antike Roman*, Niklas Holzberg appeals to the political situation reflected in Chariton's writing to argue for an early first-century C.E. date of *Callirhoë*. Holzberg suggests that the emphasis upon the cult of Venus/Aphrodite in the work is part of a larger, politically motivated program within the *polis* of Aphrodisias. In order to garner favor with the Julio-Claudian dynasty (27 B.C.E.–68 C.E.) – which frequently sought to legitimize its rule by claiming Aphrodite as a direct ancestor (Venus Genetrix) – *poleis* such as Aphrodisias venerated Aphrodite.[90] By sculpting her image or writing pious novels in which she figured prominently, a city might acquire the increased security and financial favors that alliance with Rome often afforded.[91] Holzberg points out how Chariton's emphasis on the goddess could serve this purpose: 'Der Kult der Aphrodite in dieser Stadt war offenbar mit dem Venus-Kult des julisch-claudischen Kaiserhauses verbunden und garantierte so entsprechend gute Verbindungen zwischen der Oberschicht der Polis und Rom.'[92] The centrality of Aphrodite in the novel suggests that the text was written before the end of the decline of the Julio-Claudian dynasty during the reign of the Emperor Nero.

2.3.5 *The Date of Chariton's Novel as Reflected in an External Reference to the Novel*

One final piece of evidence serves as a 'capstone' to my argumentation that – contrary to the assertion of some biblical and classical scholars – Greco-Roman conceptions of bodily resurrection, particularly those expressed in *Callirhoë*, predate the end of Nero's reign and the writing of the Christian Gospels. Before his death in 62 C.E., the Roman satiric poet Persius refers to an unspecified form of literary production using the title *Callirhoë*:

> [123] O all ye that have caught the bold breath of Cratinus – [124] ye who have grown pale over the blasts of Eupolis or of the Grand Old Man – [125] look here too, if you have an ear for anything of the finer sort. [126] Let my reader be one whose ear has been cleansed and kindled by such strains, [127] not one of the baser sort who loves to

---

90. See Pliny, *Nat.* 2.93–4; Clifford Ando, *Imperial Ideology and Provincial Loyalty in the Roman Empire* (CCT, 6; Berkeley: University of California Press, 2000), p. 288.

91. Ando, *Imperial Ideology*, pp. 189–90, 288.

92. Niklas Holzberg, *Antike Roman: Eine Einführung* (Dusseldorf: Artemis & Winkler, 2nd edn, 2001), 63.

poke fun at the slippers of the Greeks, [128] and who could cry out 'Old one-eye!' to a one-eyed man; [129] nor yet one lazy in his dignity as a provincial aedile who deems himself somebody [130] because he has broken up short pint measures at Arretium. [131] Nor do I want a man who knows how to laugh slyly [132] at numbers on a counting-board, or cones traced in the sand, [133] and is ready to scream with joy if some saucy wench plucks a Cynic by the beard. [134] To such gentlemen I would commend the playbill in the morning, for the afternoon, Callirhoë.

(Persius, *Sat.* 1.123–34 [Ramsey, LCL 91];
the approximate line divisions in the English text are mine)

In the context of Persius' *Satires*, the reference to 'such gentlemen' (*Sat.* 1.134) is one of condescension. They are people who are 'ready to scream with joy if some saucy wench plucks a Cynic by the beard' (1.132–3). Unable to appreciate Persius' own satire 'of the finer sort' (1.125), 'such gentlemen' are fit only for things popular such as 'the playbill in the morning' (*edictum* in Latin – an offering of entertainment for general, popular consumption[93]) or a piece known as 'Callirhoë' (1.134). As I have noted at the outset of this section, Papyrus Michaelidae no. 1 also refers to its own contents as 'the story of Chariton of Aphrodisias about Callirhoë', placing an emphasis on the heroine that is consonant with the narrative itself.[94] Persius' reference to 'Callirhoë' fits the self-designation and character of the ancient text of Chariton's novel.

Whether or not Persius is referring specifically to Chariton's novel is uncertain. He may be referring to another piece by someone else, utilizing the same character or perhaps an entirely different character with a similar name. He may be referring to a mime, scripted drama, or another literary work.[95] However, (1) the context of Persius' comment which alludes to popular entertainment, (2) the timing of the comment toward the end of the Julio-Claudian dynasty, and (3) the specific reference of the same title *Callirhoë* as is found on an ancient manuscript of the novel itself indicate that Persius is indeed referring to Chariton's novel. 'It seems hard to come to any other conclusion.'[96] In fact, 'it would be a fantastic coincidence if the satirist were not referring to Chariton's *Callirhoë*.'[97]

2.3.6 Conclusion

Textual witnesses, language and style, historiographical context, the political context, and an external witness predating 62 C.E. suggest that

---

93.   See Reardon, 'Introduction' to Chariton, *Callirhoë*, in *CAGN*, p. 18.
94.   Crawford, *Papyri Michaelidae*, p. 94; see also n. 3 of the Introduction of this study.
95.   George G. Ramsay, Persius' *Satires*, p. 331, n. 1.
96.   Reardon, *NAW*, pp. 315–16.
97.   Goold, introduction to *Callirhoë*, p. 5.

Chariton wrote his novel before the end of Nero's reign. Indeed, a significant core of scholars who have studied Chariton's novel since the 1970s assert that the work was written in the middle of the first century C.E. or earlier.[98] Toward the end of a lifetime studying novelistic literature, Bryan P. Reardon, a leading scholar of the Greek novel, concludes that is it unlikely 'that Chariton wrote later than, say, the reign of Nero'.[99]

The composition of *Callirhoë* before 62 C.E. or even in the first century B.C.E. is quite plausible, given the existence of Petronius' *Satyricon*, an extensive parody of the same genre also from the Neronian period. In his novel, Petronius parodies both the substance and style of the ancient Greek novel, indicating that 'the idealized novel (especially in its original, rather unsophisticated forms) must itself have constituted an easily recognizable paradigm'.[100] Most of the early works of this paradigm, however, are lost to us or survive only in fragmentary form. But *Callirhoë*, written before 62 C.E., is one pre-Petronian romantic novel that survives in complete form. As such, its resurrection narratives were not influenced by the Gospel of Mark, the earliest of the Christian Gospels, written around 70 C.E. In fact, Christian tradition as a whole was not a primary influence upon the Aphrodisian, as I will demonstrate in the following section.

2.4 *Chariton's Witness to Resurrection as a Popular Theme*

Although an appreciation of the placement of *Callirhoë* in the mid-first century or earlier weakens Bowersock's assertion that fictional writing and its emphasis on resurrection grew out of the Gospels or Christian ideas, his argument is not aimed exclusively at the written Gospels. He affirms that ancient novels may have developed even before the Gospels, in reaction to 'the story that they [the Gospels] were to contain', a story which 'was obviously already in circulation'.[101] In this final section, I will

---

98.   Ewen L. Bowie, 'Greek Novel', in Patricia E. Easterling and Bernard M.W. Knox (eds) *Greek Literature* (CHCL, 1; Cambridge: Cambridge University Press, 1985), p. 684: 'mid-first century B.C./A.D.?'; George P. Goold, introduction to *Callirhoë*, p. 2: 25 B.C. – A.D. 50; Niklas Holzberg, *Antike Roman*, p. 63: 'die Mitte des 1. Jahrhunderts n. Chr. oder etwas früher'; Carl W. Müller, 'Chariton von Aphrodisias', p. 118, n. 19: first century B.C.E.; Ben E. Perry, *Ancient Romances*, p. 344: 'the early part of the first century [C.E.] rather than later ...'; Karl Plepelits, 'Einleitung', in *Chariton von Aphrodisias: Kallirhoë. Eingeleitet, Übersetzt und Erläuter* (BGL, 6; Stuttgart: Anton Hiersemann, 1976), p. 8: 'am ehesten die Mitte des 1 Jahrhundert nachchristus'.

99.   B.P. Reardon, 'Chariton', in *NAW*, p. 319.

100.   Conte, *Hidden Author*, p. 33, n. 40; see Richard Heinze ('Petron und der griechische Roman', *Hermes* 34 [1899], pp. 494–519; Bryan P. Reardon, *Courants littéraires grecs des IIe et IIIe siècles après J.-C.* (ALUN, 3; Paris: Les Belles Lettres, 1971), pp. 322–38; Michael Coffey, *Roman Satire* (Bristol: Bristol Classical, 2nd edn, 1989), pp. 183–4.

101.   Bowersock, *Fiction as History*, 101.

argue that Chariton was not influenced by the developing Christian community. My argument does not depend primarily upon the fact that Chariton lived in Aphrodisias, a location without a known Christian community. Rather, I will review literary parallels which suggest that Chariton develops Homeric rather than Christian traditions.[102] These parallels witness to a tradition of resurrection narratives that may have circulated throughout the Greco-Roman world distinct from the traditions of Christianity.

The influence of a Homeric patterning of resurrection narratives is perhaps best illustrated by example. In this section I will analyze a resurrection narrative at the beginning of Chariton's novel which closely imitates the narration of a resurrection experience that Hector's wife, Andromache, suffers in *The Iliad*.[103] The observation of this patterning not only counters Bowersock's theory, but also initiates several new ideas about the nature of patterns within resurrection narratives of the Greco-Roman world. These narratives function as a kind of recognition scene, yet intensified in that the characters progress not simply from ignorance, but from an extreme 'confusion' that manifests itself physically with such force as to evoke terms related to death and a resurrection in which a deepened knowledge or awareness akin to enlightenment is obtained.[104]

In Table 3, overleaf, I have juxtaposed the two narratives to illustrate their close relationship. I have emboldened references in the two texts that are particularly similar to each other.

Although the Greek words describing the resurrection of Andromache are not an exact parallel of Callirhoë's first resurrection,[105] specific concepts and themes do correlate closely.[106] Not only are the motifs similar, but they follow a similar overall pattern so that the progressions of the two texts run a parallel course. In both Chariton and Homer, motifs of confusion (Sections 2.4.1–2), death (Sections 2.4.3–4), resurrection (Sections 2.4.5–6), enlightenment (Sections 2.4.7–8), and the crowd (Sections 2.4.9–10) are present and parallel.

2.4.1 *Confusion in Chariton's Text*
Chariton follows his narrative of a happy, purposeful processional intent upon a wedding ceremony (*Callir.* 1.1.12–13) with a contrasting portrait

---

102. This study of the Hellenistic period does not concern itself with theories about the Indic influence upon conceptions of an afterlife as scholars Gregory Nagy and his student, Douglas Frame.

103. Her name occurs in *Il.* 6.390–502.

104. Aristotle acknowledges many 'kinds of recognition' (*Poet.* 1452a33).

105. George P. Goold makes this identification. See Goold, *Callirhoë*, p. 57, note b.

106. Such John Miles Foley, *The Singer of Tales in Performance* (VPT; Bloomington and Indianapolis: Indiana University Press, 1996), p. 2.

TABLE 3: Two Comparable Resurrections in Homer and Chariton	
A Resurrection of Andromache *The Iliad* 22.437-515	**Callirhoë Resurrects** *Callirhoë* 1.1.14-16
The wife **knew nothing as yet** (οὔ πώ τι πέπυστο) – the wife of Hector – for no true messenger had come to tell her that her husband remained outside the gates; [440] but she was weaving a tapestry in the innermost part of the lofty house, a purple tapestry of double fold, and in it she was weaving flowers of varied hue. And she called to her fair-tressed handmaids through the house to set a great tripod on the fire so that there should be a hot bath for Hector when he returned from the battle [445] – **unwitting one** (νηπίη), **nor did she know** (οὐδ᾽ ἐνόησεν) that far from all baths flashing-eyed Athena had vanquished him at the hands of Achilles.	[1.1.14] **Knowing nothing of this** (οὐδὲν εἰδυῖα τούτων) the girl had flung herself on her bed, buried her head, and was silently weeping.
But **she heard the shrieks and the groans from the wall**, and her limbs reeled, and from her hand the shuttle fell to the floor. Then she spoke again among her fair-tressed handmaids: [450] "Come here two of you, and follow me, let me see what deeds have been done. It was the voice of my husband's honored mother that I heard,	**Her nurse came to her bed** and said, "Get up, my child. The day we have all been looking forward to has arrived. **The city is here** to attend your wedding."
and in my own breast **my heart leaps to my mouth** (πάλλεται ἦτορ ἀνὰ στόμα), and **beneath me my knees are numbed** (νέρθε δὲ γοῦνα πήγνυται);	At this **her knees collapsed** and **the heart within her** (λύτο γούνατα καὶ φίλον ἦτορ), for **she had no idea** to whom she was being married.
surely near at hand is some evil thing for the children of Priam. Far from my ear be the word, but [455] I am dreadfully afraid lest to my sorrow noble Achilles may have cut off bold Hector by himself alone, and has driven him from the city to the plain, and has by now made him cease from the baneful valor that possessed him; since he would never remain in the mass of men, but would even charge far to the front, yielding to no man in his might. [460] So saying, she rushed through the hall with throbbing heart like one beside herself, and with her went her handmaids. But when she came to the wall and the throng of men, then on the wall she stopped and looked, and caught sight of him as he was dragged before the city, and swift horses were [465] dragging him ruthlessly toward the hollow ships of the Achaeans. Then	At once she was unable to speak,
down over her eyes came the darkness of night and enfolded her (τὴν δὲ κατ᾽ ὀφθαλμῶν ἐρεβεννὴ νὺξ ἐκάλυψε) and she fell backward	**darkness covered her eyes** (σκότος αὐτῆς τῶν ὀφθαλμῶν κατεχύθη),
and **gasped out her spirit** (ἀπὸ δὲ ψυχὴν ἐκάπυσσε). Far from her head she cast her bright headbands, the frontlet and net and plaited clasp, [470] and the veil that golden Aphrodite had given her on the day when Hector of the flashing helmet led her as his bride from the house of Eëtion, after he had brought countless brideprice.	and **she nearly expired** (ἐξέπευσεν – which those who saw her thought just modesty.
And round about her **thronged her husband's sisters and his brother's wives**, who held her up in their midst,	[15] As soon as her maids had dressed her, **the crowd** at the door made way, and **his parents** brought **the bridegroom** to the girl. Then Chaereas ran forward and kissed her; recognizing the man she loved, Callirhoë,
distraught even to death (ἀτυζομένην ἀπολέσθαι).	**like a dying lamp** (λύχνον φῶς ἤδη σβεννύμενον) once it is replenished with oil,
[475] But when **she revived** (ἡ δ᾽ ἐπεὶ οὖν ἔμπνυτο), and **her spirit returned into her breast** (καὶ ἐς φρένα θυμὸς ἀγέρθη),	**flamed into life again** [ἀνέλαμψε], and **became taller and stronger**.
then **she lifted up her voice in wailing and spoke among the women of Troy**: "Ah Hector, how wretched I am! To one fate, it seems, were we born, both of us, you in Troy in the house of Priam, and I in Thebes beneath wooded Placus [480] in the house of Eëtion, who reared me when I was a babe, unlucky father of a cruel-fated child; how I wish he had never begotten me! (*Her lament next reviews the major events of her and Hector's life, and concludes 30 lines later [515].*)	[16] When **she came out into the open**, all were astounded, as when Artemis appears to hunters in lonely places. Many of the onlookers even knelt in homage. All were entranced by Callirhoë and congratulated Chaereas.

of an intensely confused Callirhoë (1.1.14). She knows nothing of the wedding heading her way in which she will participate as the bride. Too confused to proceed with the activities of everyday life – let alone process what is going on around her – Callirhoë has flung herself onto her bed, has buried her head, and weeps silently. When her nurse tells her that she is to be married, the description of Callirhoë's response suggests that a concern other than realism guides Chariton's narrative. For even though she is lying on a bed, 'her knees collapsed and her heart within her' (1.1.14). Would not this statement better apply to someone who is standing up? Why does Chariton use this seemingly inappropriate description? It is not the *fact* of her collapse that is important, but the *function in the narrative*. Chariton's focus is an allusion to Homeric tradition. The line 'her knees collapsed and her heart within her' is the very first of many lines Chariton will draw from Homer throughout his story.[107] In Homer, the phrase describes a variety of responses made by a major character to an unexpected or unfortunate event, occurring no less than seven times in *The Odyssey* and twice in *The Iliad*.[108] Although unsuited to her physical situation, this line is an apt expression of Callirhoë's confused emotional response to the sudden announcement of her own, unanticipated wedding.

Chariton's use of this line may also serve to prepare his audience for the significant allusions to Homer that follow. A full appreciation of the death that Callirhoë next undergoes requires attention to Homeric phraseology.

2.4.2 *Confusion in Homer's Text*
At the outset of the narrative that will develop into Andromache's resurrection, she also is in a state of confusion. The Homeric text makes three specific references to this confusion: (1) the 'unwitting one' (*Il.* 22.445) (2) 'knows nothing' of her husband's fate (22.437), (3) 'nor did she know' that he had been overpowered and killed by Athena (22.445). Like Callirhoë, her ignorance concerns the state of her relationship with a man with whom she hopes to soon be reunited. Andromache's confusion, however, does not manifest itself in inactivity and weeping. Rather, she weaves a tapestry and prepares a bath for her husband, despite the situation that Hector is 'far from all baths' and will not return (22.445).

2.4.3 *Death in Chariton's Text*
Chariton continues to describe Callirhoë's response using three phrases: 'she was unable to speak, darkness covered her eyes, and she nearly expired' (*Callir.* 1.1.14). The fact that the motif of death has entered the scene is apparent not only in the forthright statement that Callirhoë 'nearly expired', but also in the reference to darkness covering her eyes. Again, Homeric allusion informs the ancient audience's appreciation of Callirhoë's first resurrection, for the expression 'darkness covered her eyes' (σκότος αὐτῆς τῶν ὀφθαλμῶν κατεχύθη; 1.1.14) mimics a phrase

---

107. The first Homeric quotation cited in the story.
108. *The Odyssey* 4.703; 5.297, 406; 22.68, 147; 23.205; 24.345; *The Iliad* 21.114, 425.

TABLE 4: DEATH AS "DARKNESS OVER THE EYES" IN HOMERIC LITERATURE			
Homeric Phrase	Occurrence	Subsequent Rising?	Context
"…and darkness enfolded his/her eyes" (τὸν δὲ σκότος ὄσσε κάλυψεν)	*Il.* 4.461	No	Echepolus receives a spear in the forehead…
	Il. 4.503	No	Democoön receives a spear through the temples…
	Il. 4.526	No	Peiros spears Diores beside the navel…
	Il. 6.11	No	Acamas receives a spear in the forehead…
	Il. 13.575	No	Meriones spears Antilochus between the genitals and navel…
	Il. 14.519	No	Agamemnon's bronze cuts through Hyperenor's bowels…
	Il. 16.316	No	The son of Phyleus spears through Amphiclus' thigh…
	Il. 16.325[334]	No	Thrasymedes' spear takes off Maris' arm below the elbow…
	Il. 20.393	No	Achilles "slays" Iphition…
	Il. 20.471	No	Achilles excises Tros' liver…
	Il. 21.181	No	Achilles excises Asteropaeus' intestines…
	To Apollo 370[335]	No	Apollo kills the serpent at Delphi…
	Frogs and Mice 231	No	Sludgecouch "slays" Lickplatter…

that recurs no less than 13 times in Homeric writings: 'and darkness enfolded his eyes' (τὸν δὲ σκότος ὄσσε κάλυψε[ν]). In Homer the phrase connotes the finality of death; there is no subsequent rising.

Each occurrence of the phrase follows a grisly wound. A spear travels through the temples of Echepolus (*Il.* 4.461), Maris' arm is hacked off (16.325), Tros' liver is excised (20.471) … 'and darkness enfolded his eyes'. In each case, there is no resurrection. A reader unfamiliar with Homer might pass over Callirhoë's experience of darkness over the eyes as a mere fainting spell. Yet for an audience versed in Homer, the darkness which covers Callirhoë's eyes suggests death. This interpretation is confirmed in the final phrase of the three: 'she nearly expired'. A few lines later, the text describes Callirhoë as a 'dying lamp' and 'a light which has already been extinguished' (φῶς ἤδη σβεννύμενον; *Callir.* 1.1.15). So Chariton highlights this significant point in the narrative by evoking the theme of death.

Note also the qualified nature of this theme in the text. Nowhere does the narrator state unqualifiedly that she expired. Rather, he alludes to a Homeric expression of death and comments that Callirhoë 'nearly expired' (*Callir.* 1.1.14), a statement that is thrown into further debate by observations of the crowd, many of whom attribute the event to her 'modesty' (1.1.14). Furthermore, the phrase 'light already extinguished' (1.1.15) suggests the finality of death, yet the metaphoric nature of the expression – using 'light' rather than 'life' – allows some room for the possibility that the death theme will not be final.

2.4.4 *Death in Homer's Text*

Andromache's confusion increases not as a result of an announcement of marriage, but rather by the groans of those who lament her husband's death. Yet just as Callirhoë 'had no idea to whom she was being married' after the initial announcement and becomes weak in her knees and heart

TABLE 5: DEATH AS "DARK NIGHT OVER EYES"			
Homeric Phrase	**Occurrence**	**Subsequent Rising?**	**Context**
a. "…and dark night enfolded his/her eyes" (τὸν δὲ κατ' ὀφθαλμῶν ἐρεβεννὴ νύξ ἐκάλυψε)	*Il.* 5.659	No	Sarpedon strikes Tlelpolemus square on the neck…
	Il. 13.580	No	Helenus strikes Deipyrus on the temple with a great sword…
	Il. 22.466	Yes	Andromache learns of Hector's death…
b. "…and dark night enfolded his eyes" (ἀμφὶ δὲ ὄσσε κελαινὴ νύξ ἐκάλυψε)	*Il.* 5.310	Yes	Diomedes strikes Aeneas on the hip with a large stone…
	Il. 11.356	Yes	Diomedes strikes Hector on the helmet with a bronze spear…
c. "…and black night enfolded both his eyes" (τὼ δὲ οἱ ὄσσε νύξ ἐκάλυψε μέλαινα)	*Il.* 14.438-39	Yes	Aias strikes Hector on the neck with a stone; he vomits out black blood…

as she struggle to process what could very well be unfavorable (*Callir.* 1.1.14), so Andromache hears the groans outside, remains uncertain as to their cause, yet begins to fear that the pending news will not be favorable for her. 'Some evil thing' is at hand (*Il.* 22.453). Not knowing exactly what that is leads Andromache, like Callirhoë, to become weak in her knees and heart (22.452).[109] Then the news comes with greater certainty. As Andromache catches sight of the horses that drag Hector's dead body around the city walls below (22.463–4), an intense emotion strikes that manifests itself in terms of death.

In a sequence similar to that of Callirhoë, darkness overcomes Andromache, and she nearly expires (*Il.* 22.466–7; cf. *Callir.* 1.1.14). The description of their experiences differs slightly. Homer states that 'dark night' enfolded Andromache's eyes (*Il.* 22.466), while Chariton uses the word 'darkness' for Callirhoë (*Callir.* 1.1.14).[110] Yet the phrase Homer applies to Andromache is used throughout *The Iliad* to connote death, as illustrated in the occurrences charted in Table 5, above.

Section 'a' of this table illustrates how two earlier uses of this same phrase in *The Iliad* are used to communicate actual, final death in the narratives of Tlelpolemus and Deipyrus. Andromache, on the other hand, eventually moves from this same fatal description back into an experience of life. As sections 'b' and 'c' of the table indicate, there are two other

109. Chariton's imitation is not slavish.
110. See Table 4.

characters in *The Iliad* who enter this stage and experience a return to life: Aeneas and Hector. I will explore these resurrection narratives in the next chapter of this study.

In Andromache's narrative, the verse next magnifies the presence of the theme of death as she falls backward, 'gasping out her spirit' (*Il.* 22.467). The description parallels the meaning behind the Greek word Chariton uses to convey Callirhoë's experience: *ekpneo* (ἐκπνέω; *Callir.* 1.1.14), the basic meaning of which is to breath out (*ek*, ἐκ-) one's spirit (*pneuma*, πνεῦμα). Both Andromache and Callirhoë give up their spirits in experiences described to convey a sense of death. As Andromache's distress produces symptoms of death, the women of the family gather around as though to pay their last respects (*Il.* 22.473–4).

Lastly, both narratives make an additional, succinct reference to death immediately before alluding to resurrection. Whereas Chariton's text likens Callirhoë to a 'dying lamp' which then flames to life (*Callir.* 1.1.15), the Homeric text reasserts that Andromache was 'distraught even to death' (*Il.* 22.474) before she 'revives' (22.475). The parallels in content and arrangement are indeed striking.

Like Chariton, the Homeric text qualifies its presentation of death through allusion and suggestion. Although the expressions 'dark night' over the eyes (22.466) and 'gasping out her spirit' (22.467) allude to death, an experience as absolute as actual death is in no way necessitated. The only use of the word 'death' in the narrative occurs within a phrase that may be taken to be metaphorical: Andromache is 'distraught *even to* death' (22.474). In each instance, the suggestion of death is softened to avoid an absolute portrayal of death.

2.4.5 *Resurrection in Chariton's Text*
Immediately following this near-death experience, Chaereas rushes into Callirhoë's chambers. His kiss produces the effect of resurrection on her. Although she was once 'a light which has already been extinguished', she now 'flames to life again' (ἀνέλαμψε; *Callir.* 1.1.15). This is her first resurrection (cf. 1.8.1).

2.4.6 *Resurrection in Homer's Text*
As in Chariton's narrative, Homer's description of Andromache's resurrection is dramatic. Callirhoë 'flames to life again' (1.1.15), and Andromache 'revives' (*Il.* 22.475). Furthermore, both characters experience a type of physical revitalization as they return to life. Chariton's description of Callirhoë growing 'taller and stronger' (*Callir.* 1.1.15) occurs at a position parallel to that in which Homer describes Andromache's spirit as 'returning into her breast' (*Il.* 22.475).

2.4.7 *Enlightenment in Chariton's Text*

Chariton describes the final outcome of Callirhoë's resurrection as enlightenment, the reversal of her confused situation. No longer is she unaware of whom she will marry (*Callir.* 1.1.14); rather she recognizes Chaereas (1.1.15). No longer is she flung upon her bed (1.1.14); rather, she stands 'taller and stronger' than ever before (1.1.15). No longer is she locked in her chamber where a representative fraction of the crowd throngs at the door (1.1.15); rather, she comes 'out into the open' to be received by the crowd (1.1.16). Most significant of all, however, is the fact that Callirhoë no longer pines for her beloved Chaereas (1.1.14); rather she stands with 'the man she loved' (1.1.15).

2.4.8 *Enlightenment in Homer's Text*

Whereas Callirhoë's enlightenment is visual, Andromache's enlightenment is manifest through verbal expression. She no longer calls for a hot bath to be prepared for a body that the gods know to be 'far from all baths' (*Il.* 22.445). Instead she shares in the enlightenment of the gods and speaks forth a wisdom which perceives the fate ordained both for herself and Hector – even since the moment they were born – in an eloquent speech of more than 30 lines (22.477–515). Her situation has reversed from a position of bliss and ignorance to one of intense mourning in full knowledge that her husband is dead. Her mindless productivity has changed into an awareness of a reality into which she wishes she had never been born (22.481).

2.4.9 *The Crowd in Chariton's Text*

In my treatment of crowds in Section 1.3.2, I demonstrated the fact that in ancient novelistic literature crowds serve a variety of functions. Crowds intensify the powerful emotions that the author would associate with the event. Just as this resurrection narrative highlights the significant point in Chariton's text at which Callirhoë and Chaereas will be married, the image of the crowds making way for the bride instills a sense of bustling excitement (*Callir.* 1.1.14). After the resurrection, Chariton is able to induce a variety of emotions through the diverse reactions of the crowd: some are astounded, others kneel in homage, and all are entranced (1.1.16).

2.4.10 *The Crowd in Homer's Text*

In this particular Homeric text, the emotions are also intense as in the Hellenistic novel. The wailing of the crowd disturbs the secluded, domestic habitation of Andromache (*Il.* 22.447). A throng of Andromache's family gathers around her spiritless body, holding her up in the midst of the crowd (22.473–4). Though crowds are present in Homeric resurrection narratives, they typically do not serve an emotive function. Rather, their presence typically relates to an individual's separation and/or reintegration into society after their experience of death. So this text concludes with Andromache 'among the women of Troy' (22.476).[111]

2.4.11 *Conclusion*

The similar word choice and highly parallel relationship that Chariton's text bears to its Homeric antecedent suggests that Chariton patterns his account of Callirhoë's first resurrection after Homeric rather than Christian tradition. Used for an intensified kind of recognition, these narratives move characters from a position of ignorance manifest as an extreme, oppressive 'confusion' to a type of death and resurrection before enlightenment arrives.

Literary critics who trace the use and reuse of patterns such as the one I identify in these parallel narratives refer to them as *topoi*, 'commonplaces'. A topos is a constellation of motifs, themes, images, or even arguments that occurs frequently within the texts of a particular discourse (e.g. novelistic literature) or of a particular place and age (e.g. the Mediterranean basin during the Hellenistic period).[112] Based on my observations, I suggest the existence of a topos within epic literature that influenced novelistic Hellenistic literature: an Epic resurrection topos.

2.5 *Conclusion*

Despite the claims of biblical and classical scholars such as Oscar Cullmann and Glen Bowersock, resurrection narratives have not 'come into being ... as a response to stories ... enshrined in the canonical Gospels'.[113] Rather, the ancient texts of Herodotus, Ovid, Propertius, and Chariton – among others[114] – suggest that resurrection narratives were

---

111. Callirhoë attracts more attention than even the resurrected Chaereas, another indication that she is the main character of the novel.

112. Over the last 50 years, literary critics have traced *topoi* from the writings of the Neo-Sumerians (Jacob Klein, 'The Birth of a Crown Prince in the Temple: A Neo-Sumerian Literary Topos', *La femme dans le Proche-Orient Antique* [RAI 33; Paris: Editions Recherche sur les Civilisations, 1987], pp. 97–106) through the eighteenth century (Ernst Robert Curtius, *European Literature and the Latin Middle Ages* [trans. Willard R. Trask; Bollingen Series, 36; Princeton, N.J.: Princeton University Press, 1953]).

113. Bowersock, *Fiction as History*, 139.

114. As Theophrastus, fragment 77; Stanley E. Porter, 'Resurrection', pp. 77–80; and Daniel I. Block, *The Book of Ezekiel: Chapters 25–48* (NICOT; Grand Rapids, Mich. and Cambridge, Engl.: Eerdmans, 1997), p. 385.

known within the popular culture of the Greco-Roman world before the advent of Christianity.

Studies by three other biblical scholars arrive at similar conclusions, though each study is appreciative of the nature of Greek influence upon Christian tradition in a slightly different way. In the fifth chapter of his book, *The Corinthian Body*, Dale B. Martin marshals an impressive body of Greco-Roman texts – including some that I have reviewed in this chapter – which demonstrate that a view of the Greco-Roman conception of the afterlife determined solely by a body/soul dichotomy is 'oversimplified and ultimately misleading'.[115] He offers a description of resurrection in the Greco-Roman world that is more nuanced than the biblical and classical scholars who preceded him, taking into consideration 'popular conceptions of the state of the dead'.[116] 'Greek myth and folklore knew many stories of people returning from the dead,' Martin writes.[117] This assertion recalls the 'perennial wellspring of popular fancy' that James G. Frazer identified as the home of resurrection narratives 75 years earlier.[118] However, Martin maintains that Jewish, rather than Greek influences affected the notion of resurrection in early Christianity: 'the early Christian notion of the resurrection of body as primary form of afterlife came from Jewish eschatology, not Greek mythology.'[119]

Stanley Porter also argues, contra F.F. Bruce in particular, that 'the Greeks did have a significant tradition of bodily resurrection that has been neglected in discussion of the resurrection in the New Testament'.[120] Acknowledging that his conclusions may seem 'unorthodox',[121] Porter describes Greco-Roman traditions as the primary influence upon early Jewish and Christian beliefs in resurrection:

> The tenor of Jewish thought until the Hellenistic period seemed to accept a high degree of finality to death …. It was not until the Hellenistic period that there was any thought of a bodily resurrection, and even here the evidence was never particularly strong. Greek thought, however, much earlier engaged in serious discussion about the afterlife …. It appears that both Jewish thought and then, inevitably, Christian thought came under the influence of Greek and then Graeco-Roman assumptions regarding resurrection.[122]

---

115. Dale B. Martin, *Corinthian Body*, p. 110–14.
116. Martin, *Corinthian Body*, p. 110.
117. Martin, *Corinthian Body*, p. 111.
118. James G. Frazer, *Fastorum Libri Sex*, p. 327, n. 263.
119. Martin, *Corinthian Body*, p. 110.
120. Porter, 'Resurrection', p. 53.
121. Porter, 'Resurrection', p. 53.
122. Porter, 'Resurrection', p. 80.

Porter describes a scenario in which Greek influence seems to eclipse earlier Jewish thought which, in the Hellenistic period, has 'come under the influence' of Greek assumptions.

John Pairman Brown's study of the ancient context of the Gospels has led him also to understand the influence of Greek ideas of the afterlife as formative upon Jewish and Christian conceptions of resurrection:

> The prospect of going down to Hades monopolized Greek attention more strongly than Sheol for the Hebrews. And so the lively imagination of the Greeks more strongly than with the Hebrews constructed hopes of blessedness in better land, first for military heroes, then for the morally virtuous. Perhaps the Hellenization of the Near East then assisted the rabbis in constructing the doctrine of the 'raising of the dead' out of the ambiguous hints in the Psalms.[123]

Like Porter, Brown identifies an attentiveness to the afterlife in Greek culture that he deems significant. However, his lively reconstruction describes a Greek influence that is perhaps more limited than Porter's: the Greeks 'assisted the rabbis'.

In Part II of this study, my own readings of several ancient texts identify the influence of a resurrection topos in Homeric literature and thereafter in novelistic literature, including the Gospel of Mark.[124] Christianity, in turn, also has an influence on the tradition, further popularizing the theme. For the early Christians, resurrection could not only be experienced by unique individuals such as Salmoxis and Hippolytus, but also by ordinary individuals from among the crowds (as Mk 9.14-29). Moreover, Christian resurrection is not simply a return to normal life, but a progression to an eternal life comparable to the existence of 'angels in heaven' (12.25).

---

123. John P. Brown, *Ancient Israel and Ancient Greece*, p. 24.

124. Contrary to MacDonald, *Homeric Epics*, my thesis does not assert the direct or primary influence of Homeric literature. See n. 8 of the Introduction of this study, as well as Section 6.1.2.

Part II Texts: Resurrection in Mark's Literary-Historical Context

PREFACE TO PART II

Throughout ancient literature, expressions of resurrection convey hope for the return of spring, for national recovery, for justice in a new world ....[1] In Part II of this study, I examine *themes of death followed by themes of a return to life on earth* in ancient texts that bear a close literary-historical relationship to the Gospel of Mark. My starting point is Hellenistic novelistic literature (Section 3.1) and its progenitor, Homeric epic (Section 3.2). In several passages of these writings, I trace a recurring constellation of motifs – an Epic resurrection topos – related to themes of death and resurrection. Like the parallel texts I examined at the end of the last chapter (Section 2.4), the resurrection narratives I will examine in Chapter 3 begin in a sense of confusion, proceed through death and resurrection, and ultimately arrive at a place of enlightenment. In essence, the narratives are another example of the several kinds of recognition considered by Aristotle, akin to recognitions that occur with reversals and at the close of a story.[2] As I will note throughout my reading of these texts, the element of death is consistently qualified. Nevertheless, the theme is one of 'resurrection' (*Callir.* 1.8.1). The survey of texts also suggests the function of these narratives: they accentuate strategic points within a narrative.

In addition to Hellenistic novelistic literature, the ancient biblical writings that constitute the modern Hebrew Canon also bear a close literary-historical relationship to the Gospel of Mark. As I will demonstrate in Chapter 4, the author of Mark frequently draws upon these texts in both citation and allusion. Themes of death and revival within the Hebrew Canon occur in prophetic traditions for the most part, often as part of a recurring constellation of motifs. I will identify a Prophetic resurrection topos with roots extending back to a time and text comparable to the Epic resurrection topos within the oracles of the 'classic' eighth-century prophet

---

1. See especially Odette Mainville and Daniel Marguerat, eds, *Résurrection: L'après-mort dans le monde ancien et le Nouveau Testament* (MB, 45; Montreal: Médiaspaul; Geneva: Éditions Labor et Fides; 2001) and Aimo T. Nikolainen's three-volume study, *Der Auferstehungsglauben in der Bibel und ihrer Umwelt* (AASF, B49.3, B59.3; 266; Helsinki: Finnischen Akademie der Wissenschaften, Suomalainen Tiedeakatemia, 1944–92).

2. See Section 1.5.3.

Hosea.[3] A reading of several prophetic biblical texts from the eighth through the fourth century B.C.E. reveals how the Prophetic topos begins with a complaint regarding a divine breach of trust, proceeds through death and resurrection, and arrives at a reestablishment of communion (Section 4.1). However, unlike the treatment of resurrection in the Epic topos, themes of death and a return to life in the Prophetic topos do not typically highlight strategic points in a literary composition. Neither is the element of death qualified. Rather, death in the Prophetic topos is stark and vivid, so that the narratives function to convey a triumphant divine power that prevails in the direst of circumstances.

Following the conquests of Alexander the Great, a complex assimilation of cultures began under the Greek empire and continued throughout much of the period of Roman rule. The sweeping social changes brought about by this 'Hellenization' inspired, in part, new literary forms among which popular novelistic techniques were prominent.[4] The Epic and Prophetic topoi merge within novelistic Jewish texts of the Hellenistic period, as a reading of five resurrection narratives from the period demonstrates (Section 4.2).[5] A striking hybridity of Epic and Prophetic topoi characterizes these novelistic texts, though certain elements of each topos may be discerned.

Part II culminates in a reading in Chapter 5 of expressions of death and resurrection within the Gospel of Mark. In light of the observations of Chapters 3 and 4, the presentation of resurrection narratives in Mark's Gospel reveals a thorough-going hybridity. Like other Hellenistic novelistic texts, in this Gospel both Epic and Prophetic influences are apparent. However, certain characteristics of resurrection narratives within the Gospel indicate that the Epic topos plays the dominant role. For example, as in the Epic topos, the resurrection motif occurs at significant points throughout Mark's story, highlighting not only the power of Jesus' ministry but also the subsequent failure of his disciples as that failure is both assured and realized. Also particularly noteworthy is the presence of a crowd and the qualified nature of the elements of death in Markan resurrection narratives.

---

3. See Grace I. Emmerson, *Hosea: An Israelite Prophet in Judean Perspective* (JSOTSup, 28; Sheffield, Engl.: JSOT, 1984), Gale A. Yee, *Composition and Tradition in the Book of Hosea: A Redaction Critical Investigation* (SBLDS, 102; Altanta: Scholars, 1987), Andreas Weider, *Ehemetaphorik in prophetischer Verkündigung: Hos 1–3 und seine Wirkungsgeschichte im Jeremiabuch* (FZB, 71; Würzburg: Echter, 1993), Martin Schulz-Rauch, *Hosea und Jeremia: Zur Wirkungsgeschichte des Hoseabuches* (CTM, A16; Stuttgart: Calwer, 1996), and Richtsje Abma, *Bonds of Love: Studies of Prophetic Texts with Marriage Imagery* (SSN, 40; Assen: Van Gorcum, 1999).

4. See Wills, *Jewish Novel*, 23–6.

5. Daniel Boyarin has rightly problematized the appropriateness of deeming any work of literature from the early Hellenistic period as 'Jewish' (*Border Lines*). See also Buell and Johnson Hodge, 'Politics of Interpretation'.

Chapter 3

RESURRECTION IN NOVELISTIC HELLENISTIC & HOMERIC LITERATURE

In Book 1 of Chariton's *Callirhoë*, the heroine experiences a return to life that the narrator designates to be a 'resurrection' (παλιγγενεσία; *Callir.* 1.8.1). Although Callirhoë has 'presented to all the appearance of death' (1.5.1), the narrator explains how Callirhoë's 'blocked respiration' (1.8.1) loosens, enabling her both to 'breathe once more' (ἀνέπνευσεν; 1.8.1) and to 'regain consciousness as though waking from sleep' (ἐγειρομένη ἐξ ὕπνου; 1.8.1). Albeit with difficulty, Callirhoë simply 'comes to her senses' (μόλις δὲ ἀνεγειρομένη; 1.8.2).

The context of Chariton's designation suggests that his ancient Hellenistic definition of 'resurrection' is broader than concepts associated with this term in modern, Western civilization. Nothing particularly miraculous characterizes the narrative. Rather, the text describes Callirhoë's resurrection as fully attributable to natural causes. Categorizing this text as a narration of a 'resuscitation' rather than a 'resurrection' is perhaps preferable in a context that values highly specific, scientifically verifiable categorizations. For Chariton, however, the mere presence of *themes* of death and a return to life constitute a resurrection, regardless of whether or not the death of the individual has undergone scientific verification. This appreciation of resurrection derives not from Christian tradition but from Homeric epic in which these themes are recurrent.[1] Rather than serving as a model *for* novelistic literature, the Gospel of Mark provides another example *of* novelistic literature and, as such, is also very likely influenced in part by Homeric literature. Indeed, as this study will demonstrate, an examination of resurrection in the works of Chariton and Homer ultimately informs our appreciation of Mark's Gospel.

In this chapter, I examine narratives of resurrection in which *themes of death applied to an individual precede themes of that individual's return to life on earth* both in novelistic Hellenistic literature (Section 3.1) and a prominent standard of the Hellenistic world, Homeric literature (Section 3.2). My analysis of several texts builds upon the work I initiated in my

---

1. A consideration of arguments for this restructuring of Bowersock's notions of literary relationships constitutes the work of Chapter 2.

comparison of two resurrection narratives at the end of Chapter 2, returning again to Chariton's *Callirhoë*.[2] The readings of the present chapter observe a recurring constellation of motifs, suggesting an Epic resurrection topos within novelistic writings of the Hellenistic period. Four primary characteristics mark this topos. First, these narratives begin with a theme of confusion that proceeds through death and resurrection to arrive at a place of enlightenment. Second, an emotive crowd is present, perhaps to guide the responses of the audience. Third, the presentation of death is highly qualified. And, finally, these narratives mark strategic points in the course of the story overall.

3.1 *Resurrection Themes in Novelistic Hellenistic Literature*

As early as the outset of his novel, Chariton introduces both Callirhoë and Chaereas in a series of activities that elicits themes of death and culminates in themes of resurrection (Section 3.1.1). After the introductions, these themes recur at strategic points throughout the narrative of the story (Section 3.1.2). And at its close, the story climaxes with a dramatic series of deaths and resurrections (Section 3.1.3). Each of these resurrection narratives progresses from confusion to enlightenment, with an emotive crowd present to prompt the responses of the audience. I have chosen to focus my analysis of resurrection in novelistic Hellenistic literature upon one ancient novel, Chariton's *Callirhoë*, in order to appreciate the operation of the themes in detail. However, as I mention in several footnotes throughout my treatment, other works of novelistic literature manifest similar patterns as well.

3.1.1 *Resurrection Themes in the Introduction of Key Characters*

Both of the main characters in Chariton's novel, the divinely beautiful Callirhoë (Section 3.1.1.1) and her beloved Chaereas (Section 3.1.1.2), experience a type of a death and resurrection as they first enter the plot. Though initially confused about the nature of their relationship, they become enlightened to the fact that they are to be married. As each character awakens to this realization, a crowd of onlookers is present, expressing histrionic emotions along the way. These resurrection experiences highlight a strategic point in the narrative: the introduction of the heroes.

3.1.1.1 *An Introductory Resurrection of Callirhoë*

In the first sentences of his narrative, Chariton introduces Callirhoë as the most beautiful of women on the Balkan Peninsula (*Callir.* 1.1.1–3). Divine

---

2.   Compare *Callir.* 1.1.14–16 and *Il.* 22.437–515 in Section 2.4.

beauty is soon coupled with passionate romance as she meets Chaereas, 'whose handsomeness surpassed all' (1.1.3). After literally walking into each other in a narrow intersection, the two fall 'in love at first sight' (1.1.6). A mere passing glance is all that is needed for passion to infect both characters. They exchange no confessions of love – not even a single word – yet soon the silence turns deadly. Both characters suffer intensely when their brief encounter has ended. Eventually, crowds of people who are concerned for the well-being of this couple request that Hermocrates, famed leader and father of Callirhoë, grant her hand to Chaereas in marriage (1.1.7–12). Although the wedding is sanctioned and even initiated, Callirhoë remains in confusion, sequestered in her room in mourning (1.1.12–13). At length, the confusion culminates in a death and return to life that constitute Callirhoë's first resurrection. This resurrection narrative provides the basis of my argument that resurrections in *Callirhoë* manifest the influence of Homeric, rather than Christian, traditions. In Section 2.4 of this study I have examined the motifs of confusion, death, resurrection, enlightenment, and the crowd in this introductory resurrection.

3.1.1.2 *An Introductory Resurrection of Chaereas*

Chaereas also experiences death and resurrection in his passionate anguish and its eventual relief. This process begins immediately after the two characters bump into each other and fall madly in love (*Callir.* 1.1.5–6). Initially, Chaereas can barely walk:

> [1.1.7] So smitten, Chaereas could barely make his way home; like a hero mortally wounded in battle, he was too proud to fall but too weak to stand .... [8] But when Chaereas, a well-bred and spirited youth, began to waste away, he had the courage to tell his parents that he was in love and could not live without Callirhoë as his wife. [9] At this his father groaned and said, 'I fear you are done for, my son. Hermocrates will surely never give you his daughter when he has so many rich and royal suitors for her. You must not even make the attempt, in case we suffer a public humiliation.' His father then tried to comfort the boy, but the latter's malady grew worse, and he no longer went out even to his usual pastimes. [10] The gymnasium missed Chaereas and was virtually deserted, for the young people loved him. Their curiosity found out the cause of his sickness, and all felt a pity for a handsome youth who seemed likely to die from the passion of an honest heart. [11] A regular assembly occurred. When the people had taken their seats, their first and only cry was this, 'Excellent Hermocrates, mighty leader, save Chaereas! This will be your greatest triumph. The city petitions for the marriage today of a couple worthy of each other.' [12] Who could describe that assembly, at which Love was the spokesperson? The patriotic Hermocrates was unable to refuse the appeals of the city.

When he gave his consent, the people all rushed from the theater ....
(Chariton, *Callir.* 1.1.7–12 [Goold, LCL 481])

Following the assembly, the young men of Syracuse find the ailing Chaereas at home. They carry him to Callirhoë's estate. Then, when the crowd reaches Callirhoë's chambers, Chaereas resurrects:

[1.1.15] The crowd at the door made way, and his parents brought the bridegroom to the girl. Then Chaereas ran forward and kissed her ....
[16] All were entranced by Callirhoë and congratulated Chaereas.
(Chariton, *Callir.* 1.1.15–16 [Goold, LCL 481])

Within this narrative there are identifiable elements of confusion, death, resurrection, enlightenment, and the crowd.

CONFUSION. Chariton's text portrays Chaereas' confusion with an amusing physical description: he does not even know whether to fall or stand (1.1.7). Such an ambivalent image of a body neither falling nor standing results in a visual paradox. Audience members who attempt to envision Chaereas' situation at this point in the story may find that they participate in his confusion! Even though Chaereas is eventually able to return home, his confusion only magnifies. Despite much reluctance, he must look to his father for advice (1.1.8–9). Yet there is still no relief. The confusion grows to the extent that Chaereas' 'usual pastimes' are no longer manageable (1.1.9).

DEATH. Allusions to death are abundant and emphatic in this narrative. A sequence of no less than four references asserts the motif. First, Chariton describes Chaereas' wound as mortal: he is 'like a hero mortally wounded in battle' (1.1.7). Second, as Chaereas suffers from an intense passion for Callirhoë, he begins to 'waste away' physically (1.1.8), raising concerns about his ability to survive the ordeal. The life-threatening nature of the atrophy is confirmed by the subsequent response of his father, Ariston, whose statement of concern constitutes a third allusion to death: 'I fear you are done for, my son,' Ariston laments (1.1.9). In Greek, this statement is a colloquial expression that often serves as a euphemism for death (οἴχῃ δή μοι, τέκνον; literally, 'you are indeed gone to me, my son').[3] And fourth, the entire community considers Chaereas to be one who 'seemed likely to die' (1.1.10). They cry for Hermocrates, leader of Syracuse, to save the lifeless young boy.

Notice that every expression of Chaereas' death experience is stated in qualified terms. The narrator describes Chaereas not as mortally wounded, but '*like* a hero mortally wounded' (1.1.7; ital. mine). Chaereas' father 'fears he is done for' but never says outright that Chaereas will, in fact, die (1.1.9). The text presents the crowd as believing

---

3. Cf. LSJ, s.v. οἴχομαι II.1.: 'of persons, euphem. for θνῄσκω, to have departed, be gone hence, εἰς Ἀΐδαο.'

that Chaereas is '*likely* to die' rather than as asserting that he is certain to die (1.1.10). Though the theme of death is clearly present, its expression is not absolute.

RESURRECTION. The young man soon reenters the plot not as a terminal invalid, but as a renewed hero, energetically 'running forward' to kiss his beloved bride (1.1.15). The pleading of the crowd for Hermocrates to 'save' the boy has resulted in his return to life (1.1.11). This outcome is not entirely unexpected, for the crowd's proclamation that Hermocrates' intervention would be his 'greatest triumph' (1.1.11) suggests an event even more notable than an earlier triumph in which he saved all of Syracuse from an invasion of the Athenians.[4] As significant as this battle was, Hermocrates here does something even more remarkable: he saves a beloved youth from intense confusion and the threat of death. By granting Chaereas the hand of his daughter, Hermocrates performs a resurrection.

ENLIGHTENMENT. Although the dying Chaereas was uncertain as to whether or not he could obtain Callirhoë as a wife, the revitalized Chaereas knows that he will. Thus enlightened, Chaereas neither waivers between falling or standing, nor does he manifest confusion about what he should do. Rather he runs ahead (προστρέχω), directly to Callirhoë (1.1.15). Following the wedding, Chaereas no longer receives pity, but instead congratulations from the Syracusan crowd (1.1.16).

THE CROWD. Throughout this narrative, a passionate crowd enhances the emotion surrounding Chaereas' death and resurrection. Certainly, the interaction between Ariston and his dying son is extremely poignant. Yet Chariton is able to further intensify the emotional impact of the episode by attributing an arsenal of strong feelings to the crowd: 'the gymnasium missed Chaereas . . . the young people loved him . . ., and all felt a pity' for the young man (1.1.10). These emotions quickly escalate as Chariton presents a rioting mass who clamor on Chaereas' behalf (1.1.11). When Hermocrates agrees to their wishes, the crowd excitedly 'rushes' forth to participate in the wedding (1.1.12). In a grand crescendo following the ceremony, the amazement and elation of the crowd round off the scene (1.1.16).

3.1.1.3 *Callirhoë and Chaereas: Interwoven Resurrections*
Chaereas' resurrection is closely related to Callirhoë's first resurrection in both textual position and function. Chariton weaves the two introductions into one tapestry, culminating in a dual resurrection scene. Chaereas suffers as though from a 'mortal wound' (1.1.7), although 'the girl's suffering was worse' (1.1.8). Chaereas 'began to waste away' and 'seemed likely to die' (1.1.8, 10) as 'darkness covered Callirhoë's eyes' and 'she

---

4. See *Callir*. 1.1.1; 1.1.13; 1.11.2; et al., as well as the references to ancient historiography in Section 2.3.3.

nearly expired' (1.1.14). It is not until the resurrected Chaereas runs forward to kiss Callirhoë that she also 'flames to life again' (1.1.15).

Both narratives share an association of each primary character with the divine, though, unlike Homer, a specific divine sponsor is not identified. Chariton's portrayal of Chaereas 'like a hero mortally wounded in battle' (1.1.7) places Chaereas among the ranks of Homeric heroes such as Diomedes, Aeneas, and Sarpedon of *The Iliad*, each of whom is mortally wounded in battle, has an experience of death, and yet resurrects at the hand of a sponsoring deity as he is introduced into the Homeric epic.[5] Callirhoë's resurrection narrative includes four indications that she is special to the gods.[6] First, her resurrected state is typical of resurrections that the goddess Athena presides over: she 'became taller and stronger' (*Callir.* 1.1.15, cf. *Il.* 5.136–45 and *Od.* 6.229–43). Second, Chariton explicitly likens the appearance of Callirhoë to the appearance of the goddess 'Artemis ... to hunters in lonely places' (*Callir.* 1.1.16). Third, Chariton describes the 'astounded' people as kneeling before her in reverential homage, 'entranced by Callirhoë' (1.1.16). Finally, Chariton declares that the wedding of divine Thetis, the sea-nymph who marries the mortal Peleus, is comparable to this wedding in which the divine Callirhoë marries Chaereas.[7]

3.1.1.4 *Conclusion*

Both of the main characters of Chariton's story, Callirhoë and Chaereas, enter the narrative in a sequence of events marked by confusion and death, yet culminating in resurrection and enlightenment.[8] Through these resurrection narratives, as well as through the emotive presence of the crowd, the author portrays his lead characters as possessing powers associated with the divine.[9]

3.1.2 *Resurrection Themes at Key Turning Points*

Resurrection narratives in novelistic literature do not cease once the major characters have been introduced. One need not read far past the wedding of Callirhoë and Chaereas in Book 1 of Chariton's novel before confusion again initiates an encounter with death that is followed by a resurrection,

5. See Section 3.2.1.1.

6. More indicators of divine association apply to Callirhoë than to Chaereas; see Ch. 2, n. 111.

7. See Ovid, *Met.* 11.221–65.

8. Chariton employs this same technique in the introduction of King Mithridates (*Callir.* 4.1.9, 4.2.4–5).

9. Xenophon of Ephesus is also aware of this 'tool' (*Eph. Tale* 1.5–9). The practice of immediately associating primary characters with the divine is also apparent in *Callir.* 2.1.2–3. In Section 3.2.1 I will identify this practice within Homeric traditions as well.

culminating in enlightenment. Chariton routinely employs resurrection narratives to highlight strategic points in the narrative structure of his popular novel. As with their first resurrections, additional resurrections of both Callirhoë (Section 3.1.2.1) and Chaereas (Section 3.1.2.2) occur at prominent *peripeteiai* in the novel.[10]

3.1.2.1 *Callirhoë Is Resurrected at the Initial Peripeteia of the Story*
The events that lead up to what Chariton refers to as Callirhoë's 'second resurrection' (*Callir.* 1.8.1) commence soon after her first resurrection on her wedding day (1.1.14–16). A group of angry suitors, jilted by her marriage to Chaereas, convinces the hero that his new bride is already cheating on him (1.2.1–1.3.7). In fact, the suitors claim that they can show Chaereas this infidelity in action. Their plans operate on several layers. First, Chaereas will pretend to leave town, allowing Callirhoë an opportunity to meet with her new lover. Then, unbeknownst to Callirhoë, Chaereas will hide by the house the night after his supposed departure in order to espy her infidelity. At the same time, unbeknownst to Chaereas, one of the former suitors disguised as a lover will enter the house for a late-night rendezvous, not with Callirhoë, but with her personal handmaid (1.4.1–8).

Evening falls, and everything goes according to plan. After Chaereas spies the suitor entering the house at the hand of Callirhoë's personal servant, he himself rushes in 'to kill the lover in the act' (1.4.10). The unctuous suitor slips out another door, however, leaving only a faithful Callirhoë in the house where she sits, pining for Chaereas in utter darkness:

> [1.4.11] Callirhoë was sitting on her couch longing for Chaereas and in her unhappiness had not even lighted a lamp. At the sound of footsteps she was the first to recognize her husband by his breathing; joyfully she ran to greet him. [12] He could find no voice with which to reproach her; but overcome by anger, he kicked at her as she ran forward. His foot struck the girl squarely in the diaphragm and stopped her breath. She collapsed, and her maidservants, picking her up, laid her on the bed. [1.5.1] Thus Callirhoë lay without speech or breath, presenting to all the appearance of death. Rumor ran throughout the city reporting the tragedy and arousing cries of grief through the streets down to the sea. On every side lamentation could be heard, and the scene resembled a captured city.
>
> (Chariton, *Callir.* 1.4.11–1.5.1 [Goold, LCL 481])

Chaereas' impetuous kick injures Callirhoë to such an extent that she 'presents to all the appearance of death' (1.5.1). Her handmaidens, her

---

10. For a definition of *peripeteia*, see Section 1.5.2.

family members, indeed all the citizens of Syracuse consider her dead. Representatives from every level of public life come from throughout the region to acknowledge this death in an elaborate funeral procession (1.6.2–6). So elaborate is the procession, in fact, that it attracts a pirate captain named Theron and a host of cronies who plan to rob the tomb shortly after the funeral is over (1.7.1–6).

However, Callirhoë has not died. Rather, she merely suffers from a temporary blockage of her respiration:

> [1.8.1] Thus they [the tomb robbers] were occupied, but as for Callirhoë, she experienced a second resurrection (δευτέραν ... παλιγγενεσία). When lack of food had led to some loosening of her blocked respiration, she slowly and gradually regained her breath. Then she began to stir, limb by limb, and opening her eyes she regained consciousness as though waking from sleep, and called Chaereas, thinking he was asleep at her side. [2] But when neither husband nor servants answered, and all was dark and lonely, she began to shiver and tremble, unable by reasoning to guess at the truth. As she slowly came to her senses, she touched the funeral wreaths and ribbons, and caused the gold and silver to clink. There was a prevalent odor of spices. [3] She next remembered the kick and the ensuing fall and eventually realized that as a result of her unconsciousness she had been buried. Then she screamed at the top of her voice, crying out 'I am alive!' and 'Help!' When after much shouting nothing happened, she gave up all hope of rescue, and bending her head on her knees she sobbed: 'Oh how dreadful! I have been buried alive though I did no wrong, and I am to die a lingering death. They mourn me as dead, though I am well. Who can be found to take a message? [4] Cruel Chaereas, I blame you, not for killing me, but for being so quick to remove me from the house. You should not have buried Callirhoë with such speed, not even if she were really dead. But perhaps you are already thinking of another marriage!' [1.9.1] Thus she was bewailing her several sorrows ....
>
> (Chariton, *Callir.* 1.8.1–1.9.1 [Goold, LCL 481])

Callirhoë's death and resurrection is a major *peripeteia* that prompts a change 'from one state of things to its opposite' because as a result of these events the happy couple are separated.[11] Hopes for reunion consume the remainder of the novel. Even though the resurrection narrative functions at a turning point rather than at the introduction of a main character, Chariton relates the resurrection in a comparable mode. Callirhoë's second resurrection manifests the same elements of the Epic resurrection topos – confusion, death, resurrection, enlightenment, and

---

11. The quote is from Aristotle's definition of *peripeteia*. See Section 1.5.2.

the crowd – that I have observed in Callirhoë's and Chaereas' first resurrection narratives.[12]

CONFUSION. At the beginning of the narrative sequence, Callirhoë sits alone in utter darkness. She is completely unable to see Chaereas as he enters the room (1.4.11). Ironically, even though Callirhoë accurately recognizes that the footsteps and breathing are those of Chaereas, a fundamental confusion prevails because she fails to comprehend that the passion behind the footsteps and breathing is not love, but anger (1.4.11). In a state of complete misunderstanding, she joyfully runs to greet an angry man bent on revenge for the pangs of betrayal he feels (1.4.11). As a result, she encounters extreme violence in return for her misguided offer of love.

DEATH. Unlike the emotional impetus behind Callirhoë's first death, this second death experience has a blatant physical cause. Chaereas rushes at Callirhoë and kicks her in the diaphragm (1.4.12). The motif of death is clearly present, asserting itself (1) in the portrayal of Callirhoë *sans* speech, breath, and the ability to stand (1.4.12–1.5.1); (2) in the explicit references to 'death' made by the narrator (1.5.1); and (3) in the extended presentation of her funeral procession (1.6.2–6). However, as in the introductory resurrection narratives, wherever the narrator mentions death in this passage, the narrator also qualifies the nature of the death. Callirhoë 'presents to all the *appearance* of death' (1.5.1), she is compared to '*sleeping* Ariadne' (1.6.2), and she receives gifts '*intended* to honor the dead girl' (1.6.5). Although the theme of death is prominent, nowhere does the text assert outright that Callirhoë is dead.

RESURRECTION. Though the reference to death is not absolute, the narrator identifies Callirhoë's subsequent return to life as a 'resurrection' (παλιγγενεσία; 1.8.1) which – as I note at the outset of this chapter – is fully attributable to natural causes.[13] For Chariton, it is the presence of *themes* of death and a return to life that constitute a resurrection, regardless of whether or not the death of the individual has undergone scientific verification.

Of particular importance for this study is the designation of the narrative as Callirhoë's second resurrection, for such numbering suggests an intentionality in the relationship between the novel and the motif. Furthermore, mention of a second resurrection actively engages the audience in the literary theme, prompting the reader/hearer to review, compare, and track resurrection narratives. 'When was Callirhoë's first resurrection?' the audience wonders, and reviews the narrative past. The

---

12. See Sections 2.4 and 3.1.1.2.

13. According to Friedrich Büchsel, '[i]n the first century B.C. ... παλιγγενεσία is *in general use* in educated circles' (*TDNT* 1: 687, s.v. γίνομαι, γένεσις, γένος, γένημα, ἀπογίνομαι, παλιγγενεσία; italics mine).

reference to a second resurrection also calls the audience to the action of comparison. An explicit counting of two resurrection accounts suggests that they somehow belong together. More questions flood the mind: 'What is the significance of this categorization? Why is the narrator counting resurrections? How do these resurrections of Callirhoë compare to experiences of resurrection of other characters?' Finally, the reference summons the audience to track the events that follow, looking ahead.[14] 'Will Callirhoë have a third resurrection?' Since the narrator considers resurrections to be important enough to be tracked and counted, the audience also begins to keep track of the literary theme as well. Indeed, the attention is warranted, because Chariton's novel employs resurrection narratives at several major turning points.

ENLIGHTENMENT. Although the narrative begins with an element of confusion, it ends with an element of enlightenment. However, this enlightenment does not occur until the final reunion of the lovers in Book 8. Such an extension of the resurrection of an individual is not an unusual application of the resurrection theme, as will become apparent in the course of this study. Homer's *Iliad* presents a narrative in which Hector experiences death and resurrection that extends across several episodes (*Il.* 14.438–15.239).[15] Also, as I will demonstrate in Chapter 4, the author of the Jewish novel *Joseph and Aseneth* extends the resurrection motifs across much of his story (*Jos. Asen.* 9.1–17.6).[16] The elements of Callirhoë's second resurrection extend through the remainder of the story. In Book 1 Callirhoë returns to life in seclusion, but public acknowledgement of the resurrection does not occur until Book 3. As the Syracusans gather around her empty tomb, Callirhoë's resurrection is rehearsed once more (*Callir.* 3.3.1–10). However, Chariton is able to sustain the anticipation until Book 8, because Callirhoë's body is still unavailable to the people due to her kidnap by Theron.

The delay allows Chariton to continue his masterful play with the theme. For example, there is frequent reference to Callirhoë's life in the tomb (1.11.3; 1.14.6; 6.1.3; 6.1.5), her experiences 'since burial' (3.2.16), and her experience as a corpse (1.13.11). Also, an ironic juxtaposition of life and death possesses great shock value, as when Chaereas finds

---

14. 'The [ancient] author not only presupposes the reader's literary "competence" – knowledge of the conventions of a given genre – but also creates that competence in the reader who both uses and modifies the code. The poet's task, like that of any writer, is to invent a reader' (Gian Biagio Conte, *The Rhetoric of Imitation: Genre and Poetic Memory in Virgil and Other Latin Poets* [ed. Charles Segal; CSCP, 44; Ithaca, N.Y. and London: Cornell University Press, 2nd edn, 1996], p. 10). See also Walter J. Ong, *Interfaces of the Word: Studies in the Evolution of Consciousness and Culture* (Ithaca, N.Y. and London: Cornell University Press, 1977), p. 76.

15. See Section 3.2.2.

16. See Section 4.2.5.

Callirhoë's 'empty tomb' (3.3.1–7; 3.3.14), when Theron tells of finding a 'living corpse' (3.4.13), or when Callirhoë threatens to *kill* her yet *unborn* baby who has already been *saved from the tomb* (2.8.6; cf. 2.9.5). 'We have buried each other', Callirhoë bemoans as she speaks to the image of Chaereas at his tomb, 'yet neither of us possess even the other's dead body' (4.1.11). Chariton revels in the humor and shock value of Callirhoë's extended second resurrection.[17]

When enlightenment does occur in Book 8, Callirhoë receives a full report of Chaereas' whereabouts since their separation: Chaereas 'gave her an exact account of it all ...' (8.1.17).[18] Employing the full force of his craft, Chariton emphasizes the light of this enlightenment in direct contrast to the night of the initial confusion by explicitly stating that the couple enlighten one another during daylight hours. Chaereas 'did not even wait until evening before coming to the royal chamber', the text begins (8.1.13).

THE CROWD. Once again, crowds throughout Callirhoë's progressive second resurrection draw out the powerful emotions the author would associate with the event. Following Callirhoë's seeming death, the crowd raises 'cries of grief through the streets down to the sea' (1.5.1) – so intense is the emotion that 'on every side lamentation could be heard, and the scene resembled a captured city' (1.5.1). When Chaereas discovers the empty tomb, 'rumor swiftly [brings] the shocking news to Syracuse, and everyone hasten[s] to the tomb' (3.3.2). There, Chaereas' fervent prayer for the recovery of the body elicits more emotional reactions on the part of the crowd that serve to reassert the theme of death: 'the crowd broke into lamentation and all began to mourn for Callirhoë as though she had just died' (3.3.7). Finally, when a living Callirhoë returns to Syracuse in embodied form, the enthusiastic 'shout' of the crowd imbues the scene with an emotional intensity that prepares for the dramatic reunion of father and daughter (8.6.8). Albeit brief, the interchange that the two share transpires in terms of death and resurrection, recalling the extensive theme:

> [7] All [the Syracusan people] were puzzled and straining their eyes when suddenly the tapestries were drawn aside, and Callirhoë was to be seen, clothed in Tyrian purple and reclining on a couch of beaten gold, with

---

17. See also *Callir.* 1.8.4; 1.13.8; 5.8.5; 6.6.2. Furthermore, Chariton highlights Callirhoë's return to life in the many summaries that frequent the novel (5.1.1–2; 8.1.14; 8.7.5; cf. 3.2.7). Resurrection also repeatedly tops Callirhoë's many *peristaseis* (2.5.10; 3.8.9; 5.1.4; 5.5.2–3; 6.6.4; 6.7.9). All told, Chariton refers to this resurrection experience an impressive 26 times (*Callir.* 1.8.4; 1.11.3; 1.13.11; 1.14.6; 2.5.10; 2.8.6; 2.9.5; 3.2.7; 3.2.16; 3.3.1–7; 3.3.14; 3.4.13; 3.8.9; 4.1.11; 5.1.1–2; 5.1.4; 5.5.2–3; 6.1.3; 6.1.5; 6.6.4; 6.7.9; 8.1.14; and 8.7.5).

18. Although Callirhoë begins her story, she will not narrate it in its entirety. At an early point in her story, 'Callirhoë fell silent' (8.1.15). Because this is her resurrection narrative, she is the one who is enlightened.

Chaereas sitting beside her in the uniform of a general. [8] Never did thunder and lightning so startle the ears and eyes of witnesses! Never did anyone who had discovered a treasure of gold shout so loudly as the crowd did then at this unexpected sight too marvelous for words. Hermocrates leaped on board and rushed to the tent; embracing his daughter he cried, 'My child, are you really alive [ζῆς] or am I deceived in this, too?' 'Yes, father, I live [ζῶ], and really so now I have seen you.' Everybody wept for joy.

(Chariton, Callir. 8.6.7–8 [Goold, LCL 481])

Hermocrates' pointed question reasserts the assumption that Callirhoë was perceived as dead, to which she declares with finality 'I live' (8.6.8). At the end of this narrative, in a type of affective exclamation point, Chariton accentuates the emotion of the interaction through the element of the crowd: everybody weeps for joy (8.6.8).

CONCLUSION. Two prominent motifs at the initial *peripeteia* of Chariton's novel, death and return to life, signal the influence of the resurrection topos. Three other motifs – confusion, enlightenment, and the crowd – accompany these themes of death and resurrection, but unlike the other narratives considered so far, Callirhoë's second resurrection extends throughout the course of the novel. The extension allows Chariton not only to remind the audience of the need for reunion that sustains the narrative but also to play masterfully with the irony afforded by resurrection as a literary theme.

3.1.2.2 *Chaereas Resurrects at the Central Peripeteia of the Story*

The courtroom scene in Book 5 of Chariton's novel functions as the central *peripeteia* of the novel as a whole.[19] Dionysius, Callirhoë's second husband, has intercepted a letter that Chaereas, Callirhoë's first husband, has written to her (*Callir.* 4.5.8). In the letter, Chaereas begs Callirhoë to annul her marriage with Dionysius so that Callirhoë and Chaereas might be reunited. However, Dionysius believes that Chaereas is dead (4.5.10). He suspects that the letter is the handiwork of Mithridates who, after being a guest in Dionysius' household, is now attempting to seduce his wife (4.5.10). Dionysius calls Mithridates to court on charges of seduction (4.6). So all of the main characters in the novel travel to Babylon and await the beginning of the trial (5.1–5). The opening statements by Dionysius and Mithridates are substantial, each consuming what is now a complete section of the novel (Sections 5.6 and 5.7, respectively). In Mithridates' opening statement, the elements of a resurrection narrative begin to assert themselves in preparation for the *peripeteia* in Section 8.

CONFUSION. Toward the end of his opening statement, Mithridates refers to Chaereas in terms of confusion: 'It is Chaereas who is looking for

---

19. See Section 1.5.2 for supporting argumentation.

Callirhoë', he states. 'Try him therefore for adultery' (5.7.6). Mithridates does not identify Chaereas as Callirhoë's first husband or as his former slave.[20] Rather, this very limited description focuses on Chaereas' angst: he is seeking his beloved Callirhoë.[21] Through this description, the author introduces an image of Chaereas in confusion. Mithridates then calls upon Dionysius to try Chaereas for adultery, even though – as far as Dionysius is concerned – Chaereas is dead. The ironic call accentuates Chaereas' utter inability to debate the issue on his own behalf with mental clarity, at least until his resurrection and subsequent enlightenment.

DEATH. Two references to death directly follow this portrayal of Chaereas in confusion. First, Mithridates describes the situation from Dionysius' perspective: '"Yes," he [Dionysius] will say, "but Chaereas is dead, and you tried to seduce my wife in the name of a dead man"' (5.7.6). Second, the narrator asserts that Dionysius 'never dreamed that Chaereas was still alive' (5.7.8). Immediately before Chaereas presents himself alive, a dramatic summoning of the hero from the dead concludes Mithridates' opening statement. 'Under divine inspiration' he conjures up otherworldly gods of the afterlife, the deities of 'Heaven and Hell' (ἐπουράνιοί τε καὶ ὑποχθόνιοι; 5.7.10). Sacred sacrifices provide the justification for his incantation of no less than five imperatives directed to these deities ('render', 'grant', 'appear', 'take your stand', 'tell'; 5.7.10): Mithridates would raise the dead.

However, just before Chaereas steps out into the crowd, the narrator asserts that the entire event 'had been arranged' (5.8.1). This knowledge qualifies the nature of the death experience in this text. Some of the characters present in the courtroom that day would debate that the nature of the death and resurrection was authentic. Chariton's audience, however, would argue that the resurrection was a sham. Regardless, the event provides a dramatic central *peripeteia*.

RESURRECTION. The resurrection element presents itself as Chaereas, who is assumed to be dead, steps forward:

> [1] While he [Mithridates] was still speaking (for so it had been arranged) Chaereas himself stepped forward. Callirhoë, on seeing him, cried out, 'Chaereas, are you alive?' and started to run to him. But Dionysius stopped her and, standing between them, would not allow them to embrace. [2] What reporter could do justice to the scene in that courtroom? What dramatist ever staged such an extraordinary situation?

---

20. Mithridates learns that Chaereas is Callirhoë's first husband in Section 4.3 of the novel. Regarding Chaereas as Mithridates' former slave, see *Callir.* 3.7; 4.2.

21. In romantic novels, the element of confusion often expresses itself as a lack of clarity as to how separated lovers will be reunited. Confusion in the resurrection narratives at the introduction of the heroes, for example, results from the separation of the lovers (see *Callir.* 1.1.7).

> Audience members would have thought themselves to be in a theater filled
> with every conceivable emotion. All were there at once – tears, joy,
> astonishment, pity, disbelief, prayer. [3] They blessed Chaereas and
> rejoiced with Mithridates; they grieved with Dionysius; about Callirhoë
> they were baffled. She herself was totally confused and stood there
> speechless, gazing with eyes wide open only at Chaereas: I think that on
> that occasion even the king would have wished to be Chaereas ....
>
> (Chariton, *Callir.* 5.8.1–5.8.3 [Goold, LCL 481])

Callirhoë punctuates the event with her cry: 'Chaereas, are you alive?'
(5.8.1) Both she and Dionysius receive Chaereas' appearance as a return
to life.

At this point in his narrative, Chariton halts the progress of the story so
that he might explicitly praise the effects of the resurrection theme: 'What
reporter could do justice to the scene in that courtroom? What dramatist
ever staged such an extraordinary situation?' (5.8.2) The dramatic power
of Chaereas' resurrection is far-reaching, and Chariton is so pleased that
he cannot help but stop to praise his own artistry.[22] This is an unusual
move for Chariton. He interrupts the narrative flow very infrequently; so
these explanations provide a rare and explicit witness to the unique ability
of resurrection narratives to accentuate a significant point in a narrative.[23]

ENLIGHTENMENT. Chaereas' newfound enlightenment manifests itself as
extreme mental clarity in a debate with Dionysius that closes the
courtroom drama for the day:

> [5.8.5] 'I am her first husband', said Chaereas. 'But I am the more
> constant', retorted Dionysius. 'Did I divorce my wife?' 'No, but you
> buried her.' 'Show the divorce papers!' 'You can see her tomb!' 'Her
> father gave her to me.' 'Yes, but she gave herself to me.' 'You are
> unworthy of Hermocrates' daughter.' 'More so you, who were a slave of
> Mithridates.' 'I demand Callirhoë back.' 'And I am keeping her.' 'You
> are detaining another man's wife.' 'You killed your own.' 'Adulterer!'
> 'Murderer!' [6] Such was their thrust and parry, and the audience
> listened with no small pleasure.
>
> (Chariton, *Callir.* 5.8.5–6 [Goold, LCL 481])

The narrator describes the fight as one 'confined to words' (5.8.5). It is a
mental game in which Chaereas, contrary to his previous state, is both
present and sufficiently enlightened to debate on his own behalf.[24]

---

22. On editorial intrusion in novelistic literature see Claude Calame *Le Récit en Grèce
Antique* (Semiotique; Paris: Klincksieck, 1986), pp. 71–7.

23. For other instances of explicit commentary by the narrator, see *Callir.* 3.2.17; 5.4.4;
6.9.4; and 8.1.4.

24. Although both heroine and hero see one another after Chaereas' resurrection, only
Callirhoë remains 'totally confused' (5.8.3). One might expect Chaereas as husband to react
in a corresponding fashion. However, his role here as resurrected one predominates.

In addition to accentuating this central turning point, the resurrection theme also affords Chariton the opportunity to introduce humor into the debate. Dionysius argues that Chariton does not deserve Callirhoë as a wife because 'he buried her' (5.8.5). Although Chaereas can accuse Dionysius of detaining Callirhoë, Dionysius can accuse Chaereas of killing the living person about whom they quarrel (5.8.5). Here again the text reveals that as an ancient storyteller, Chariton is attentive to the resurrection theme and gets much mileage from its application.

THE CROWD. Immediately following Chaereas' resurrection, Chariton widens the lens of his narration beyond the primary characters, attributing the astonishment explicitly stated by Callirhoë to every single person present in the courtroom (5.8.2). In the broadest of strokes and the brightest of colors, Chariton portrays the boisterous crowd as exuding a variety of emotions: 'All were there at once – tears, joy, astonishment, pity, disbelief, prayer' (5.8.2). The extreme awe of the crowd adds to the emotional force of the event. They 'bless' Chaereas as one who is a 'privileged recipient of divine favor' (5.8.3).[25] The scene ends with yet another emotive 'exclamation point' made possible by the crowd: 'the audience listened with no small pleasure' (5.8.6).[26]

CONCLUSION. At a major *peripeteia* in Chariton's novel, I have identified five themes which occur in many Hellenistic treatments of death and a return to life. Two additional observations suggest that the author does not treat these themes haphazardly, but is quite cognizant of their potential: (1) Chariton's explicit praise of the device (5.8.2) and (2) the centrality of resurrection themes in the witty retorts between Chaereas and Dionysius (5.8.5–6).

3.1.3 *Resurrection Themes at the Climax of the Story*

There is little question that the climax of Chariton's novel is the reunion of Callirhoë and Chaereas. As I have noted, the separation effected early on by Callirhoë's apparent death in Book 1 introduces a dramatic tension that extends through the narrative.[27] Following her second resurrection, a variety of obstacles sustain this separation, including slavery, competing love interests, the demands of war, and so forth. The lovers hope and yearn for their reunion throughout the novel. When they finally do reunite, Chariton employs themes of resurrection to narrate the climactic event.

This final recognition occurs on the island of Aradus. Chaereas,

---

25. Chariton's verb is μακαρίζω. The customary connotation of divine favor quoted here is noted in BDAG, s.v. μακάριος.

26. This final, punctilial expression of emotion via the reaction of the crowd occurs also in *Callir.* 1.1.16 (see Section 2.4); 1.5.1; and 8.6.8 (see Section 3.1.2.1).

27. See Section 3.1.2.1.

temporarily serving as naval captain over a fleet of Egyptian ships, has encircled and conquered the island (7.6.1–8.1.4). Just as he prepares to sail on, he finds his beloved Callirhoë among the spoils of war:

[8.1.5] Evening had fallen, but much of the captured material was still left on shore. Wearily Chaereas got up to give orders for embarkation. [6] As he passed through the marketplace, the Egyptian [soldier] said to him, 'Sir, here is that woman who would not come to you, but is bent on suicide. Perhaps you can persuade her to get up, for you ought not to leave behind the most beautiful of the spoils.' Polycharmus also supported the suggestion, since he wished, if possible, to involve Chaereas in a new love which might console him for the loss of Callirhoë. 'Let us go in, Chaereas', he said. [7] So he crossed the threshold into the room. The moment he saw her, lying down and wrapped up though she was, his heart was stirred by the way she breathed and looked, and he was seized with excitement. He would certainly have recognized her, had he not been utterly convinced that Dionysius had recovered Callirhoë. [8] Quietly going to her, he said, 'Courage, my dear, whoever you are! We are not going to use force on you. You shall have the husband you want.' While he [Chaereas] was still speaking, Callirhoë recognized his voice and uncovered her face. At the same instant they both cried out: 'Chaereas!' 'Callirhoë!' As they rushed into each other's arms they fainted and fell to the floor. [9] At first Polycharmus, too, stood speechless at this miracle, but after a while he said, 'Stand up! You have recovered each other; the gods have granted the prayers of you both. But remember, you are not at home, but in an enemy country, and first you must take good care that no one separates you again.' [10] He had to shout: they were like people plunged in a deep well barely able to hear a voice from above. Gradually they recovered; then after gazing at each other and kissing, they swooned again and this happened a second and a third time. The only thing they could say was, 'Are you really Callirhoë whom I hold in my arms?' and 'Are you really Chaereas?' [11] The rumor swiftly spread that the admiral had found his wife. No soldier remained in his tent, no sailor on his ship, no janitor at his door, but from all sides they flocked together exclaiming, 'What a lucky woman to have gained so handsome a husband!' Nevertheless when Callirhoë appeared, no one praised Chaereas any more, but all turned their gaze on her, as though only she were there. [12] She moved with dignity, escorted by Chaereas and Polycharmus on either side. Flowers and wreaths were showered upon them; wine and myrrh were poured at their feet, and the sweetest fruits of war and peace, the triumph and the wedding, were there combined.

(Chariton, *Callir.* 8.1.5–12 [Goold, LCL 481])

Chariton finishes his novel with a flurry of resurrections that is comparable to the grand finale of a fireworks display. Three resurrection events are encompassed within the one resurrection narrative that

Chariton has strategically placed at the final recognition of his novel. The five motifs of an Epic resurrection topos mark the presentation.

CONFUSION. Both of the lovers exhibit substantial confusion at the onset of the scene. Callirhoë, crying out and tearing her hair in grievous response to her capture on Aradus, has cast herself face-down on the ground and covered her head (7.6.8–9). She remains there – a disheveled bundle of hair and clothes – until Chaereas comes to assess her value as booty (8.1.7). Chaereas, also, suffers from confusion. The 'weary' captain (8.1.5) requires the guidance of one of his soldiers so that he does not 'leave behind the most beautiful of the spoils' (8.1.6). Although he has the better vantage point, he fails to fully recognize the beloved for whom he seeks. 'Courage, my dear, *whoever you are* … you shall have the husband you want', he quietly assures her in a delightfully ironic statement that highlights the utter extent of Chaereas' confusion (8.1.8, ital. mine): though he is so close, in his confusion he fails to see that the woman is Callirhoë and he himself is the husband she wants.

DEATH. Callirhoë, who accurately identifies Chaereas' breathing in Book 1 (1.4.11; contra Chaereas at 8.1.7), recognizes his voice here, effecting the reunion of the two lovers. Yet in a somewhat surprising move, Chariton presents this climactic reunion not with images of lively rejoicing, but rather with intimations of death: intertwined in each other's arms, Callirhoë and Chaereas both lay unconscious on the floor (8.1.8).

Note that Chariton's use of temporal adverbs qualifies the death-like state of the reunited lovers. They lie motionless on the floor intertwined in each other's arms for 'a while', with Polycharmus standing over them 'speechless' (8.1.9). Imagery akin to burial in a tomb follows: 'they were like people plunged in a deep well barely able to hear a voice from above' (8.1.10). 'Have they died?' the audience may wonder. Chariton's fondness for stories of resurrection and the presence of the element of confusion which pervade the previous significant points in his narration suggest the possibility. 'Gradually' they recover (8.1.10). On the level of the plot, the two lovers have not died. Yet the audience may well recognize the resurrection motif at work accentuating this significant point in the narrative.

RESURRECTION. At length Polycharmus attempts to revive the two lovers; however, he must resort to shouting. Once they do revive, the lovers repeat a cycle of confusion, death, and resurrection three times.[28] 'The *only* thing they could say' consists of repeated attempts to gain clarity in the midst of their confusion: 'Are you really Callirhoë …? Are you really Chaereas?' (8.1.10; ital. mine) They reenter their lifeless swoon before resurrecting again and again ('a second and a third time'; 8.1.10).

28. See Ch. 1, n. 39.

ENLIGHTENMENT. The narrative sequence concludes with a sense of enlightenment that counters the opening portrayal of the heroes in disheveled confusion. Chaereas is handsome, yes, but Callirhoë's beauty garners even more praise despite all that she has been through (8.1.11). No longer cast upon the ground, she 'moves with dignity' (8.1.12). Neither is Chaereas in need of a guide any longer: he himself serves as a guide to Callirhoë (8.1.12).[29] Chariton's description of flowers, wreaths, wine, and myrrh (8.1.12) recall the initial union of the lovers in Book 1, for these very objects decorate the initial resurrection narrative in which both Callirhoë and Chaereas resurrect and wed (1.1.13). The symbols signify an enlightenment that not only ends the confusion represented in Section 8.1 but also the confusion of the separated lovers that begins in Book 1.

THE CROWD. Chariton intensifies the emotional impact of the scene through his deployment of the crowd, every member of which is excited by the event: 'no soldier ... no sailor ...., no janitor ...' fails to attend (8.1.11). As they gather, they exclaim praises and gawk at the bride (8.1.11). Their enthusiasm is irrepressible, manifesting itself in the outpouring of flowers, wreaths, wine, myrrh, and fruits (8.1.12). With the reunion accomplished, this excitement now sustains the remainder of Book 8. After retelling their adventures to an inquisitive audience, Callirhoë and Chaereas return to Syracuse where other massive crowds celebrate their return to life with great emotion (8.6.7–8).

CONCLUSION. The great pleasure this author takes in narrating resurrection is as apparent here at the final recognition as in the introduction of the heroes and in the praises of the central turning point: his primary characters each resurrect three times. The audience also may enjoy the creative repetition of a theme with which they have now become familiar. Certainly, Chariton's consistent mode of presentation from confusion and death to resurrection and enlightenment fosters recognition of resurrection narratives.

3.1.4 Conclusion

In their progression from confusion to enlightenment, resurrection narratives serve as recognition scenes which occur throughout Chariton's novel at strategic points in the narrative structure such as the introduction of a central character or the climax of the story. Other ancient novels manifest a similar phenomenon. Xenophon of Ephesus imitates many of Chariton's resurrection scenes and employs them at strategic points in his own story.[30] Like Callirhoë, the lead character

---

29. The description here suggests once again that the primary character of the novel is not Chaereas, but Callirhoë.

30. On the relationship of Xenophon of Ephesus to Chariton, see Ch. 1, n. 191.

Anthia experiences an apparent death after her long-anticipated wedding, is the subject of a funeral, and awakens in a tomb to be stolen by pirates (Xenophon, *Eph. Tale* 3.6–8). A resurrection narrative in Apuleius' *Golden Ass* marks the end of a series of tales about a certain unusual household (*Golden Ass* 10.12). Three resurrection narratives in Achilles Tatius' novel are distributed throughout the story (*Leuc. Clit.* 3.15–17; 5.7.4; and 7.16.3). In Section 4.2, I will consider several other resurrection narratives that occur at strategic points in the novelistic literature of Judaism.

3.2 *Resurrection Themes in Homeric Literature*

The use of resurrection narratives at strategic points in *Callirhoë* and other novelistic literature is not simply novelistic but derives, in large part, from Homeric literature. Certainly, traditions associated with Homer had an inestimable impact upon education in the Hellenistic era.[31] As I have already noted, Chariton's dependence upon Homeric literature is both overt and covert.[32] In order to further reveal the Homeric roots behind the Hellenistic mode of resurrection themes, in this section I will demonstrate how resurrection narratives accentuate the introductions of several primary characters in *The Iliad* and *The Odyssey* in a manner that is comparable to the resurrection narratives at the introductions of Callirhoë and Chaereas in Chariton's novel. In the Homeric texts I will analyze, each introductory resurrection narrative accentuates the divine sponsorship of the primary character, asserting her or his relationship with a particular deity who performs the work of resurrection in a manner specifically characteristic of that deity (Section 3.2.1). Also like Chariton after him, the Homeric bard employs resurrection narratives at key turning points in the narrative structure (Section 3.2.2) and at the climax (Section 3.2.3) of each epic. Note in particular that each narrative includes clear indications of the presence of the theme of death, yet in each case the theme is somehow qualified.

Although my treatment of Homeric texts in this section is illustrative, and therefore selective and brief, a concluding table of similar narratives summarizes further evidence of the function and elements of several Homeric resurrections (Section 3.3).

3.2.1 *Resurrection Themes in the Introduction of Key Characters*
The Homeric episodes very likely influence Chariton's opening resurrection of Chaereas, in which he becomes 'like a hero mortally wounded'

31. See Ch. 1, n. 116.
32. See Tables 3–5.

(*Callir.* 1.1.7), before experiencing a return to life. Indeed, the introductions of several central warriors in Homeric literature involve their own death and return to life on the battlefield. In this section I will analyze one representative text from *The Iliad* (Section 3.2.1.1) and another from *The Odyssey* (Section 3.2.1.2).[33] The process reveals that not only the function, but also the mode of resurrection from confusion and death to resurrection and enlightenment may very well derive from Homeric precedent.

3.2.1.1 *The Iliad: Zeus Resurrects Sarpedon*

Homer employs the theme of death followed by a return to life in the introduction of three major characters shortly after the battle described in *The Iliad* commences in Book 4. The warrior Diomedes experiences death and revival as he is introduced to the story (*Il.* 5.95–145). Homeric tradition shapes this narrative in accordance with the sponsorship of the warrior goddess Athena: Diomedes is afforded mental clarity throughout the experience and rises as a stultifying force in battle.[34] Shortly afterward another warrior, Aeneas, also experiences a death and resurrection (5.302–18). Homer shapes this narrative in accordance with Aeneas' sponsorship by the 'weakling goddess' Aphrodite (5.331): the resurrection is aborted and resumed by the god of enlightenment, Apollo (5.335–46, 445–8).[35] In this section, I will read a third episode of resurrection in Book 5 that occurs at the introduction of Sarpedon. Although Sarpedon may not be as familiar to a modern reader of Classical literature as Diomedes or Aeneas, he is truly a central figure in *The Iliad* due to his status as progeny of the divine. In fact, he is the son of none other than the main divinity of the Greek pantheon, Zeus (15.67), and repeatedly receives the title 'godlike' (cf. 5.629 below; also 6.198–9). As leader of the Lycians, the closest allies of the Trojans, his role in *The Iliad* is central: 'He is one of the strongest warriors on the Trojan side and takes a prominent part in the fighting, killing Heracles' son, Tlepolemus (5.628–62), leading an assaulting group of the allies on to the Greek wall (12.101), and making the first breach in that wall (12.290). The story of his death at the hands of Patroclus is narrated in detail (16.419–683) ….'[36] It is his resurrection

---

33. See the conclusion to this section for references to further examples.

34. Contrary to expectations of confusion, Diomedes maintains a heightened lucidity throughout the entire narrative process of death and resurrection. Such ironic clarity in a man so wounded is appropriate for one sponsored by Athene, the goddess of wisdom who gives those whom she loves 'presence of mind' (cf. e.g. *Od.* 5.437). Far from being in confusion, it is Diomedes who in fact confuses others (κλονέοντα, *Il.* 5.135) as he is shot down. See LSJ, s.v. κλονέω: 'to drive tumultuously or in confusion'. See also Table 7.

35. See Table 7.

36. Jennifer R. March, 'Sarpedon' *OCD*, 1357.

> Tlepolemus, son of Heracles, a powerful man and tall,
> was roused by resistless fate against godlike Sarpedon.
> 630 And when they had come near as they advanced against each other,
> the one the son, the other the grandson of Zeus the cloud-gatherer,
> then Tlepolemus was first to speak, saying:
> "Sarpedon, leading counselor of the Lycians, why must you
> be skulking here, you who are a man unskilled in battle?
> 635 They lie when they say you are sprung from Zeus who bears the aegis,
> since you are inferior far to those warriors
> who were sprung from Zeus in the days of men of old...."
>
> 655   And raised high his ashen spear
> Tlepolemus, and the long spears sped
> from the hands of both at the same instant. Struck him square on the neck
> did Sarpedon, and the grievous point passed clean through,
> and down on his eyes the darkness of night enfolded him.
> 660 Tlepolemus had struck Sarpedon on the left thigh with his long spear,
> and the point sped through furiously
> and grazed the bone; but his father as yet warded off destruction....
>
> Then his noble comrades had godlike Sarpedon
> sit beneath a beautiful oak of Zeus who bears the aegis,
> and out from his thigh thrust the spear of ash
> 695 mighty Pelagon, who was his dear comrade,
> and his spirit left him, and down over his eyes a mist was shed.
> But he caught his breath again, and the breath of the North Wind
> as it blew on him made him live again after he had painfully breathed out his spirit.
>
> But the Argives, pressed by Ares and Hector clad in bronze,
> 700 neither turned to make for the black ships,
> nor yet could they hold out in fight,
> but they constantly gave ground backward,
> having become aware that Ares was among the Trojans.
>   (Homer, *Il.* 5.628-37, 655-62, 692-703 [Murray and Wyatt, LCL ,170])

Figure 8   Homer, *Il.* 5.628–37, 655–62, 692–703

before this death, however, that firmly introduces his character to the text, accentuating his association with his father, Zeus (see Figure 8, above).

The close fighting between Sarpedon and Tlepolemus is prompted by a brazen attack upon Sarpedon's association with Zeus. 'They lie when they say you are sprung from Zeus,' Tlepolemus taunts in line 635 of Book 5, 'you are inferior far to those ... who were.' One might expect a strong show of divine power in response to such a strong assault on the honor of the son of the head of the pantheon. Indeed, this expression of death followed by a return to life possesses very dramatic components.

CONFUSION. Tlepolemus' taunt portrays the warrior Sarpedon as someone who is confused in battle, 'skulking' on the battlefield (*Il.* 5.634). In Homeric literature, this verb describes not only those who 'gaze at the battle' from afar as if confused as to how to proceed (4.370), but also those who aimlessly cower about, roaming the country as a beggar (*Od.* 17.226; 18.362).[37]

---

37. See LSJ, s.v. πτώσσω. See also *Od.* 22.304 and *Il.* 7.129; 20.426; 21.13, 25.

DEATH. Given the context of a battle, an intense wound rather than an intense emotion initiates this resurrection narrative. The one who hurled the insult has received in return a spear through the neck, 'and down on his eyes the darkness of night enfolded him' (*Il.* 5.659).[38] Before Sarpedon strikes Tlepolemus, however, Tlepolemus spears Sarpedon with a wound that runs clear through the thigh (5.660–2). Death finds Sarpedon as he sits under an 'oak of Zeus' after Pelagon forcibly removes the wooden spear from his thigh. The words describing death's work are familiar to the ancient audience because there are variations on this phrase in the death of several Homeric figures (Tables 4–5) as well as in the resurrection narratives of Andromache and Callirhoë: 'his spirit left him, and down over his eyes a mist was shed' (5.696; τὸν δὲ λίπε ψυχή, κατὰ δ' ὀφθαλμῶν κέχυτ' ἀχλύς).[39]

RESURRECTION. Despite the death, Zeus the cloud-gatherer (5.631), god of the weather, is able to call upon his servant the North Wind and effect a resurrection for his son, Sarpedon.[40] Homer describes this resurrection in vivid detail. Sarpedon first receives his spirit again. The verb which describes this activity contains the Greek root *pne-*, meaning spirit or breath (ἀμπνέω; 5.697 above). Homer uses this same verb root in describing the resurrection of Hector's wife after she gasps out her spirit (ἐμπνέω; 22.475). The second stage of this detailed resurrection account continues as the breath of the North Wind 'blew on him' (ἐπιπνέω; 5.698 above), which also translates as 'breathed upon him' or 'inspired him'. The work of the North Wind returns his spirit, *pneuma* (πνεῦμα) unto Sarpedon. This work makes him live again (ζώγρει; 5.698), even after he has painfully breathed out his soul (κακῶς κεκαφηότα θυμόν; 5.698). Homer seems to spare no expense in explicitly communicating that the situation was one of death and revival. Sarpedon's spirit leaves him, he has painfully breathed it out, and the mist of death covers his eyes. However, the North Wind inspires him once again and makes him live.

ENLIGHTENMENT. Following this resurrection, Sarpedon is no longer portrayed – even tauntingly – as a confused and cowering warrior. At his next foray into the plot, he is 'leading' the Trojans 'making straight for the Danaans, full eagerly' (12.101–9).

THE CROWD. As I point out in the resurrection narrative of Andromache, the Homeric mention of the crowd relates not to any emotional reaction as novelistic literature would emphasize, but rather to the reintegration of the resurrected one into society.[41] In this regard, the explicit presence of

---

38. See Table 6.
39. See *Od.* 22.88; *Il.* 5.127; 15.668; 16.344; 20.321, 341, 420.
40. Konrad Wernicke, 'Boreas' (*RE* 3, col. 723): the North Wind 'steht im Dienste ... des Zeus' (line 40).
41. See Section 1.3.1; 2.4.10.

'the noble comrades' in line 692 is striking. They may appear in part for the practical purpose of moving a man with a spear impaled in his thigh. However, they may also function as the community which witnesses both the death and the subsequent resurrection.

THE FUNCTION OF THE RESURRECTION THEME. The resurrection effectively introduces this significant character into the plot of *The Iliad*. Before this resurrection narrative, the name Sarpedon occurs only in the list of Trojans who assemble at Priam found at the end of Book 2. Sarpedon and his companion Glaucus are the last two figures listed in the book (2.876–7). In Book 5, however, Sarpedon enters the action of the plot, proclaiming that he has come to help the Trojans, in lines 471–92. His comments encourage Hector and the other Trojans with the result that they gain ground against the Achaeans for the first time since the battles began (5.493–630).

The narrative also serves to assert Zeus' sponsorship of Sarpedon. Pandarus claims that Sarpedon is not beloved by Zeus (5.635). But the narrated actions prove quite the opposite, for Pandarus receives a spear in the mouth, and Zeus resurrects his son Sarpedon. The implication is that anyone who says that Sarpedon is not a son of Zeus is clearly in the wrong. The sponsorship of Zeus is also communicated in the nature of the resurrection, the power of which is characteristic of the lord of lords rather than the warrior Athene, who effects Diomedes' return to battle (5.95–145), or 'weakling' Aphrodite (5.331), who only partially raises Aeneas (5.302–18, 335–46, 445–8).[42] The mightiest of the gods produces the final and most vivid of the resurrections in Book 5 of *The Iliad* in which a mortal is made to 'live again even after he had painfully breathed out his spirit' (5.598).

Finally, the resurrection functions as a marker for a significant turning point in *The Iliad*. Immediately after the resurrection of Sarpedon, the Achaeans (a.k.a. Argives) 'constantly give ground backward' in the first retreat they must make since the battle began (line 701; see lines 699–703). This newfound success on the part of the Trojans produces great concern among the gods, to whom the narrative turns (5.711–77).

3.2.1.2 *The Odyssey: Athena Resurrects Odysseus*

The examination of a Homeric resurrection within the other Homeric epic, *The Odyssey*, will strengthen my assertion that themes of death and a return to life serve as part of the introduction of a hero. Furthermore, significant insights into the patterns of Homeric resurrection will be gained through this text because the narrative I will analyze, Athena's resurrection of Odysseus, has particularly close parallels to Athena's

---

42. See n. 34 of this chapter.

resurrection of Diomedes[43] as well as to the resurrection narrative involving Andromache.[44]

Odysseus' resurrection occurs at the introduction of this central character, who does not enter the action of the narrative until Book 5. This book opens on Mount Olympus, as the gods confer about the fate of the sojourner. Athena pleads with Zeus and the pantheon to take pity on Odysseus, who has spent almost 20 years trying to return home from the Trojan War without avail (*Od.* 5.1–20). Zeus heeds her plea and ordains that Odysseus shall return home (5.21–42). The next leg of Odysseus' journey, Zeus decrees, shall be a voyage via raft to Scheria, land of the Phaeacians. The god Hermes then brings the news of the decree to the island, where the beautiful goddess Calypso holds Odysseus captive (5.43–115). Although Calypso is reluctant to give up her mortal love interest, she obeys the order of Zeus (5.116–46). Homer first introduces Odysseus into the action as Calypso goes to him to share this news (5.147-91).

The two spend a final night together (5.192–227), then Odysseus builds a raft (5.228–61; cf. 5.229) and sails for 17 days before approaching land (5.262–81). Tension envelops the narrative as Poseidon, who is distinctive among the gods in his great dislike of Odysseus, spies the sojourner on the sea and stirs the winds against him (5.282–96; cf. 1.19–21). Homer describes Odysseus' reaction to this unexpected development with a phrase I have noted in my analysis of Callirhoë's first resurrection: 'his knees collapsed and the heart within him' (5.297).[45] This intensity mounts when a great wave tosses Odysseus from his raft (5.313–32). The goddess Ino appears with a veil of immortality to protect him against an encounter with death (5.333–64). Another great wave dashes Odysseus' vessel to pieces (5.365–81), after which Athena causes a lull in the storm, leaving Odysseus clinging to a plank of the craft for two days and two nights before he spots land once again (5.382–403). The sea thrusts exhausted Odysseus toward sharp reefs and cliffs, and once again 'the knees of Odysseus collapsed and the heart within him' (5.406). Now more than ever, death threatens the weary Odysseus, who ponders whether to (1) swim into the jagged rock before him or (2) try to keep on swimming 'in hope of finding shelving beaches' (5.404–18) (see Figure 9, overleaf).

Homer expresses the themes of death and a return to life in this introduction in a manner that accentuates the sponsorship of the goddess Athena. As a result, the employment of the motifs in this resurrection

43. *Il.* 5.95–145. I introduce this narrative in Section 3.2.1.1.
44. See Section 2.4.
45. See Section 2.4 as well as Ch. 2, n. 108.

While he pondered these things in mind and heart,
a great wave bore him against the rugged shore.
425   There would his skin have been stripped off and his bones broken,
had not the goddess, flashing-eyes Athena, put a thought in his mind.
On he rushed and seized the rock with both hands,
and clung to it, groaning, until the great wave went by.
Thus he escaped this wave, but in its backward flow it once more
430   rushed upon him and struck him, and flung him far out in the sea....

From his valiant hands were bits of skin stripped off
435   against the rocks; and the great wave covered him.
Then surely would unfortunate Odysseus have perished beyond his fate
had not flashing-eyed Athena given him presence of mind.
Making his way out of the surge where it belched upon the shore,
he swam outside, looking continually toward the land in hope of finding
441   shelving beaches and harbors of the sea.
But when, as he swam, he came to the mouth of a fair-flowing river...

444   he knew the river as he flowed forth and prayed to him in his heart:...

450   "Pity me, king [river]; I declare myself your suppliant."
So he spoke, and the god at once made his current cease, and checked the waves,
and made a calm before him, and brought him safely
to the mouth of the river. And he let his two knees bend
and his strong hands fall, for the heart within him was crushed by the sea.
455   And all his flesh was swollen, and seawater oozed in streams up
through his mouth and nostrils. So he lay breathless and speechless,
with hardly strength to move; for terrible weariness had come upon him.
But when he revived and his spirit returned again into his breast,
then he unbound from him the veil of the goddess
460   and let it fall into the seaward-flowing river;
and the great wave bore it back down the stream,
and Ino quickly received it in her hands. Odysseus, going back from the river,
sank down in the reeds and kissed the earth, the giver of grain;
and deeply shaken he spoke to his own great-hearted spirit:

465   "Ah me, what will become of me? What in the end will befall me?
If here in the river bed I keep watch throughout the weary night,
I fear that together the bitter frost and fresh dew
in my feebleness may overcome me breathing forth my life;
and the breeze from the river blows cold in the early morning.
470   But if I climb up the slope to the shady wood
and lie down to rest in the thick bushes, in the hope that
the cold and the weariness might leave me, and if sweet sleep comes over me,
I fear I may become a prey and spoil to wild beasts."

Then, as he pondered, this thing seemed to him the better:
475   he set out for the wood, and he found his spot near the water
beside a clearing; there he crept beneath two bushes
which grew from the same place, one of thorn and one of olive....

491   So Odysseus covered himself with leaves, and Athena
shed sleep upon his eyes, that it might enfold his lids and speedily
free him from toilsome weariness.
        (Homer, *Od.* 5.423-30, 434-41, 444, 450-77, 491-93 [Murray and Wyatt, LCL, 170])

Figure 9   Homer, *Od.* 5.423–30, 434–41, 444, 450–77, 491–93

narrative is comparable to the narrative of Diomedes' resurrection (*Il.* 5.95–145).

CONFUSION. Contrary to expectations of confusion, Odysseus maintains a heightened lucidity throughout the narrative process of death and resurrection. The intentionality of this move is manifest in the extensive amount of text dedicated to Odysseus' coherence. As with Diomedes' resurrection (*Il.* 5.110–20; see Table 7), an overt attentiveness to displays of clarity attributable to Athena actively counters an expectation of confusion. Despite the harrowing events of the sea storm, Athena grants Odysseus lucidity (*Od.* 5.426) and 'presence of mind' (5.437).

DEATH AND RESURRECTION. The threat of death permeates the scene. At line 425, Odysseus' skin is nearly stripped off and his bones broken. In line 436 the narrator exclaims that Odysseus surely would have perished except for the saving work of Athena. Lines 455–7 present the clearest picture of death, however. His flesh is swollen; his mouth and nostrils are filled with fluids; he does not breathe or speak or move . . .. Yet despite this vivid portrayal, death is nowhere asserted unequivocally. Soon Odysseus revives and his spirit returns again into his breast (5.458). He is finally back on land and kisses the earth in celebration (5.463). However, the tension of this narrative is not yet released: two potential experiences of death remain to be averted in this dramatic introduction.

The first threat to the hero is the possibility of freezing to death on the cold earth as he lies down by the river in his exhaustion (5.466–9). Here death is described by a unique phrase commonly translated 'having breathed out life' (κεκαφηότα θυμόν; 5.468). In all of Homeric literature this phrase occurs only twice: here in the introduction of Odysseus and in the introduction of Sarpedon in Book 5 of *The Iliad* (*Il.* 5.697; see Section 3.2.1.1 above). The recurrence of such a rare phrase in two introductory resurrection narratives provides further evidence that the poet associated the two narratives with one another as part of a larger family: an Epic topos of resurrection narratives.

The second potential death scenario that extends the resurrection of Odysseus is the threat of a lethal attack by wild animals. Both of these threats are expressed in phrases that are overtly qualified: 'bitter frost may overcome' Odysseus (*Od.* 5.468), or he 'may become prey' (5.473). Eventually Odysseus finds lasting protection from his sponsor: 'Athena shed sleep upon his eyes' (5.491–2).

ENLIGHTENMENT. The element of enlightenment typically functions to express the renewed insight of the confused one. The situation is a *reversal* from confusion to insight. For those under the sponsorship of the 'bright-eyed' warrior Athena, however, there is no confusion to reverse. Instead, the renewal of the resurrected one is manifest *causally* – the resurrected one demonstrates an ability to cause confusion in others, particularly in battle. Just as Diomedes' enlightenment under Athena expresses itself in the capability to confuse others (*Il.* 5.135–6), so Odysseus' enlightenment under Athena serves to confound the maidens (*Od.* 6.129–34).[46] The texts even employ the same simile: as the risen Diomedes (*Il.* 5.136–43, esp. 141), so the risen Odysseus is like a lion on a hunt among flocks of sheep (*Od.* 6.130–4).

THE CROWD. Once again, the introduction of a crowd relates to the reintegration of the resurrected one into society. As Odysseus recuperates, Athena prepares the way for Odysseus' welcome among the Phaeacians by means of a crowd. The goddess directs a group of Phaeacian maidens to the spot where Odysseus lies (6.1–117). When he hears them playing, he wonders if he will be accepted or rejected by this society (6.117–26). A series of misconceptions and intense moments extenuates the uncertainty of reintegration for some time (6.127–85). In the end, however, it is none other than the daughter of the Phaeacian king and her maidservants whose welcome facilitates the revenant's return to civilization (cf. 6.186–7.171).

CONCLUSION. At the introduction of the major character in *The Odyssey*, a constellation of motifs portrays Odysseus as experiencing death then returning to life as the result of the sponsorship of Athena. The expression of these motifs emphasizes this sponsorship.

As I demonstrate in Table 6, the death and resurrection experience of Odysseus parallels the resurrection narrative involving Andromache in several respects, even though the narratives occur in different epic poems.

In both narratives, the description of the initial reaction affects the heart and knees, an experience of death ensues, then a resurrection takes place expressed in identical constructions (καὶ ἐς φρένα θυμὸς ἀγέρθη). Moreover, parallel conditional temporal clauses that introduce the resurrection ('when she/he revived and her/his spirit returned into her/his breast ...') are each followed by a result clause that allows for the introduction of a new narrative element ('then ...').

Among the differences in these narratives, there is one to be noted in particular. The narrative involving Odysseus functions as part of his introduction (Book 5 of *The Odyssey*), but the resurrection of Andromache occurs at one of the significant turning points in the story, immediately following the beginning of the end of the Trojan War (Book 22 of *The Iliad*).

3.2.1.3 *Conclusion: Homeric Resurrection Themes and the Introduction of Key Characters*

My analysis suggests that Homeric epic often employs a constellation of motifs involving death and a return to life in the introduction of a central character. The resurrection serves to align the new character with the

---

46. See n. 34 of this chapter as well as Table 7.

TABLE 6: THE RESURRECTIONS OF ANDROMACHE AND ODYSSEUS	
The Resurrection of Andromache *The Iliad* 22.437-515	**The Resurrection of Odysseus** *The Odyssey* 5.453-59
"It was the voice of my husband's honored mother that I heard,	The god brought him safely to the mouth of the river,
and **in my own breast my heart** leaps to my mouth, and beneath me my **knees** are numbed;…."	and he let his two **knees** bend and his strong hands fall, for **the heart within him** was crushed by the sea.
Then **down over her eyes came the darkness of night and enfolded her** (τὴν δὲ κατ' ὀφθαλμῶν ἐρεβεννὴ νὺξ ἐκάλυψε) and **she fell backward** and **gasped out her spirit** …. And round about her thronged her husband's sisters and his brother's wives, who held her up in their midst, **distraught even to death.**	And **all his flesh was swollen,** and **seawater oozed in streams up through his mouth and nostrils.** So **he lay breathless and speechless,** with **hardly strength to move;** for **terrible weariness had come upon him.**
But when she revived (ἡ δ' ἐπεὶ οὖν ἔμπνυτο), **and her spirit returned into her breast** (καὶ ἐς φρένα θυμὸς ἀγέρθη),	**But when he revived** (ἀλλ' ὅτε δή ῥ' ἄμπνυτο) **and his spirit returned again into his breast** (καὶ ἐς φρένα θυμὸς ἀγέρθη),
then she lifted up her voice in wailing and spoke among the women of Troy….	**then** he unbound from him the veil of the goddess….

sponsorship of a particular deity and to draw attention to a character whom the audience may not yet recognize as primary. Three specific observations suggest that some degree of intentionality accompanies the employment of this constellation, even as early as the Homeric period. First, I have identified texts with multiple, consecutive parallels in the resurrection narratives of Andromache and Callirhoë (Table 3) as well as Andromache and Odysseus (Table 6). Second, several phrases recur repeatedly throughout introductory resurrection narratives, one of which is unique to resurrection narratives (κεκαφηότα θυμόν; *Od.* 5.468; *Il.* 5.697).[47] Third, the manipulation of individual motifs in particular expressions indicates intentionality, such as when an author (1) expresses resurrection with spectacular force when Zeus is involved (cf. the resurrection of Sarpedon; *Il.* 5.697–8) or (2) replaces confusion with explicit clarity in resurrections sponsored by Athena (*Il.* 5.110, 115–20; *Od.* 5.426, 437). Furthermore, an awareness of this resurrection topos seems to extend into the Hellenistic period, for Chariton likens Chaereas to a 'hero mortally wounded in battle' (*Callir.* 1.1.7) as he narrates his introductory resurrection and Chariton models Callirhoë's first resurrection upon the resurrection of Andromache.[48]

---

47. See also Tables 4 and 5; λύτο γούνατα καὶ φίλον ἦτορ (e.g. *Od.* 5.297, 406; 24.345; *Callir.* 1.1.14); and καὶ ἐς φρένα θυμὸς ἀγέρθη (e.g. *Il.* 24.349; *Od.* 5.458; 24.349), among others.

48. See Section 2.4.

3.2.2 Resurrection Themes at Key Turning Points

In addition to their occurrence in the introduction of main characters, resurrection narratives in Homeric literature accentuate other key turning points in the epics, as they do in later Hellenistic literature. In this section I will analyze a representative text from *The Iliad* in order to establish my point: Apollo resurrects Hector during the divine debate regarding the outcome of the Trojan War.

In lines 14–77 of Book 15 of *The Iliad*, the outcome of the war is determined by a divine assembly. In his commentary on Books 13–16 of *The Iliad*, Richard Janko describes the divine dialogue on lines 14–77 of Book 15 as 'climactic for the whole *Iliad* .... Zeus ... reveals that his support for the Trojans is a temporary stage in their eventual ruin ....'[49] Although the Trojans are superior at the moment, Zeus proclaims that the Achaeans will triumph and Troy will fall (*Il.* 15.69–71). A constellation of motifs involving death and a return to life frame this divine assembly, accentuating the significance of this point in the narrative. Just before the divine assembly, the great Trojan warrior Hector receives a mortal blow from an Achaean combatant, the warrior Aias. Following the assembly, Hector returns to life (see Figure 10).

Like Callirhoë's second resurrection, the narration of Apollo's resurrection of Hector is distributed over an extended portion of text. The expression of themes associated with resurrection traverse the end of Book 14 and continue through the middle of Book 15.[50]

CONFUSION. The confusion that typically occurs early in a resurrection narrative takes on a powerful visual expression in this text. The great force of the large projectile causes Hector to physically 'whirl' 'like a top' 'round and round' after being struck on the neck (*Il.* 14.413). As Hector falls (14.418), so does his armor around him and on top of him (14.419–20); its audible ringing adds to the turmoil (14.421).

DEATH. 'Is he dead?' the audience may wonder as his comrades pick up the body and carry it away (14.432). He groans, has water poured over him, and then 'revives' (14.432–5). However, death reasserts itself by means of three powerful indicators: (1) Hector vomits 'black blood' (14.437), (2) darkness covers his eyes (14.439; see Tables 4 and 5), and (3) his spirit is overwhelmed (14.439). This experience of death threatens to become irreversible, extending throughout the end of Book 14 and into the beginning of Book 15, producing great suspense.

The qualified nature of the effects of death so often characteristic of

---

49. Richard Janko, *The Iliad, a Commentary: Volume 4 (Books 13–16)* (ed. Geoffrey S. Kirk; New York and Cambridge, Engl.: Cambridge University Press, 1992), pp. 228–9.

50. The narrative need not be confined to any one particular book of Homer (Martin L. West, *Studies in the Text and Transmission of the Iliad* [Munich and Leipzig: K.G. Saur, 2001], pp. 3, 18–19).

14.412 He [Aias] struck Hector on the chest over the shield rim, hard by the neck,
and set him whirling like a top with the blow; and he spun round and round....

418 So fell mighty Hector quickly to the ground in the dust.
And the spear dropped from his hand, and the shield fell on him,
and the helmet, and round about him rang his armor inlaid with bronze....

[His comrades] "carried him toward the city, groaning heavily.
But when they had come to the ford of the fair-flowing river,
eddying Xanthus, that immortal Zeus begot,
435 there they lifted him from the chariot to the ground and poured water over him.
And he revived (ἐμπνύνθη), and looked up with his eyes,
and kneeling on his knees he vomited out black blood.
Then again he sank back on the ground, and both eyes
were enfolded in black night (τὼ δέ οἱ ὄσσε νύξ ἐκάλυψε μέλαινα);
        and the blow still overwhelmed his spirit (θυμόν ἐδάμνα)...."

[Zeus declares the ultimate victory of the Achaeans to the Olympian deities:]
"Let Phoebus Apollo rouse Hector to the fight (Ἕκτορα δ᾽ ὀτρύνῃσι μάχην),
15.60 and breathe strength into him again (αὖτις δ᾽ ἐμπνεύσῃσι μένος), and make him forget
        the pains
that now distress his heart; and let him drive the Achaeans back...
        among the many-benched ships
of Achilles, son of Peleus; and he will send out his comrade
65 Patroclus, but him will glorious Hector slay with the spear
before the walls of Ilios after he himself has slain
many other youths, and among them my son, noble Sarpedon.
And in wrath for Patroclus will noble Achilles slay Hector.
Then from that time on will I cause a driving back from the ships
70 constant and continuous until the Achaeans
take steep Ilion through the counsels of Athena."

[At 15.220, the divine assembly adjourns. Zeus calls Apollo to rouse Hector:]
"Take in your hands the tasseled aegis,
230 and shake it fiercely over the Achaean warriors to frighten them.
And for you yourself, god who strikes from afar, let glorious Hector be your care,
and rouse in him great might (οἱ ἔγειρε μένος μέγα) until the time that the Achaeans
will come in flight to their ships and the Hellespont...."

He [Apollo] found the son of battle-minded Priam, noble Hector,
240 sitting up, for he lay not longer, and he was just now gathering back his spirit (ἐσαγείρετο
        θυμόν),
and recognized his comrades around him, and his gasping and his sweat
had ceased, for the mind of Zeus, who bears the aegis, revived (ἔγειρε) him.
And Apollo, who works from afar, came up to him and said:
"Hector, son of Priam, why is it that apart from the rest
245 you sit here fainting?..."

[Hector:] "I really thought that on the dead (νέκυας) and the house of Hades
I should look on this day when I had gasped out my life."
Then spoke to him again the lord Apollo, who works from afar:
"Now be of good cheer, so mighty a helper has the son of Cronos
255 sent out from Ida to stand by your side and protect you,
Phoebus Apollo of the golden sword, who has long protected you,
yourself and the steep citadel alike....

260 I [Apollo] will go before and make smooth all the way for the chariots

and will turn in flight the Achaean warriors."
So saying, he breathed great might (ἔμπνευσε μένος μέγα) into the shepherd of man.
And just as a stabled horse that has fed his fill at the manger
breaks his halter and runs stamping over the plain –
265 being accustomed to bathe in the fair-flowing river –
and exults; on high he holds his head and about his shoulders
his mane floats streaming, and as he glories in his splendor
his legs nimbly bring him to the haunts and pastures of mares;
so swiftly plied Hector his feet and legs,
270 urging on his charioteers, since he had heard the voice of the god....

[The Achaeans fear, and Thoas speaks:]
"Well now surely a great marvel is this that my eyes look upon,
that now Hector has recovered (ἀνέστη) and has avoided the fates.
The heart of each man of us hoped that he
had died at the hands of Aias, son of Telamon.
290 But some one of the gods has again delivered and saved
Hector, who has loosed the knees (ὑπὸ γούνατ᾽ ἔλυσεν) of many Danaans
indeed, as, I think, will happen even now; for not without
the will of loud-thundering Zeus does he stand forth so eagerly as a champion.
(Homer, *Il.* 14.412-13, 418-20, 432-39; 15.59-61, 63-71, 229-33, 239-45, 251-57,
260-70, 286-93 [Murray and Wyatt, LCL, 171])

Figure 10   Homer, *Il*. 14.412–13, 418–20, 432–9, 15.59–61, 63–71, 229–33, 239–45, 251–7, 260–70, 286–93

resurrection narratives is manifest in the reflections of two characters in the text. The subject of the narrative, Hector himself, refers to his own experience of death in tandem with the possibility of a misperception: 'I really *thought* that on the dead (νέκυας) and the house of Hades I should look on this day when *I had gasped out my life*' (15.251–2; ital. mine). Moreover, the Achaeans had wrongly concluded that Hector was dead (15.288–9). 'But,' Thoas proclaims, 'one of the gods has again delivered and saved' (15.290).

RESURRECTION. When the lord of lords, Zeus, commands that Hector's breath be restored (15.60), the warrior resurrects. The narrative reasserts this resurrection four times. First, Zeus instructs Apollo to 'rouse in him [Hector] great might' (οἱ ἔγειρε μένος μέγα; 15.232). By the time Apollo arrives at Hector's side, 'his gasping and his sweat had ceased, for the mind of Zeus, who bears the aegis, revived (ἔγειρε) him' (15.241–2), a second reference to resurrection. Nevertheless, Apollo furthers the process by breathing great strength into the man (ἔμπνευσε μένος μέγα; 15.262). Finally, the Achaeans later 'marvel' at the way in which 'Hector has recovered (ἀνέστη) and has avoided the fates' (15.287).

ENLIGHTENMENT. The description of Hector's enlightenment comple-ments his initial confusion: the enlightenment is both vivid and physical in its expression. Far from a spinning top, the warrior now demonstrates the competence of a stabled horse who has broken free from his reins and runs powerfully free (15.263–9).

THE CROWD. Thoas' speech before the crowd repeatedly references emotions. However, they are all emotions of the past rather than the vividly present emotions that the crowds of Hellenistic novelistic literature experience: he had marveled (15.286), the crowd had hoped (15.288), and Hector had in the past 'loosed the knees' of the Achaeans (15.291). Rather than emotions, the final exclamation of the narrative calls attention to Hector's reintegration into the society. Although Hector is 'apart from the rest' (15.244) in his experience of death, Thoas' post-resurrection speech to the crowd serves to acknowledge his reintegration into society (15.286–93). Each person in that crowd had hoped that Hector would never again return to their midst (15.288–9). Nevertheless, he now stands among them once again, even more of a champion than before his death and return to life (15.293).

CONCLUSION. Homer accentuates the divine decision to favor the Achaeans in the war with a resurrection narrative that involves much divine activity. Perhaps it is the agency of Zeus (15.241–2) that prompts the strong presentation of an Epic resurrection topos: overt signs of confusion and death lead to multiple references of resurrection. The fact that Apollo is also involved may contribute to the vivid portrayal of enlightenment in the narrative. In several other significant points in the story of *The Iliad*, themes of death and a return to life are present as well. Other examples include the end of Diomedes' involvement in the War (11.345–67), Achilles' decision to enter the fray (18.22–98, 203–27), and the moment in which Achilles actually begins to fight (20.153–350).[51]

3.2.3 *Resurrection Themes at the Climax of the Epics*
Finally, as in certain novelistic texts of the Hellenistic era, themes of death and a return to life accentuate the climax of Homeric plot.[52] At the end of Chapter 2 of this study I have analyzed the Homeric narrative in which Hector's wife experiences a return to life. This narrative occurs at the climax of *The Iliad*, marking the beginning of the fall of Troy in Book 22. Homer's *Odyssey* also positions a resurrection narrative at the climax of the plot: Odysseus' father, Laertes, experiences a death and return to life when Odysseus returns after an absence of 20 years. The scene is the third recognition within a series of three final recognitions in which Odysseus' nurse (*Od.* 19.392–4), his wife (23.205–46), and, climactically, his father recognize the hero[53] (see Figure 11).

---

51. In *Il.* 11.345–67, Apollo resurrects Hector at the culmination of Diomedes' reign of terror. The battle is the last to feature Diomedes, the dominant warrior from Book 5 through Book 11. Furthermore, the battle marks the climax of Achaean rule: following this battle, the Trojans have an advantage for some time under the leadership of the newly resurrected Hector.

52. See Section 3.1.3.

53. See Section 1.5.3.

24.302 Then resourceful Odysseus [disguised as Eperitus] answered him [his father, Laertes] and said:

309   "...But as for Odysseus, it is now the fifth year
       since he left there, and departed from my country.
       Ill-fated man! Yet he had birds of good omen, when he set out...."

315   So he spoke, and a black cloud of grief enfolded Laertes,
                      (τὸν δ' ἄχεος νεφέλη ἐκάλυψε μέλαινα)
       and with both his hands he took the sooty dust
       and poured it over his gray head, groaning without pause.
       And Odysseus' heart was stricken, and up through his nostrils
       shot a keen pang, as he beheld his dear father. And he sprang toward him,
320   and clasped him in his arms, and kissed him, saying:
       "That man am I, father, myself, standing here, of whom you ask,
       come back in the twentieth year to the land of my fathers.
       But cease from your grief and tearful lamenting, for I will explain...."

345   So he spoke, and his father's knees were loosened where he stood, and his heart melted,
                      (λύτο γούνατα καὶ φίλον ἦτορ)
       as he recognized the tokens which Odysseus showed him without error.
       About his dear son he flung both his arms, and the much-enduring noble Odysseus
       caught him, fainting (ἀποψύχοντα), to himself.
       But when he revived, and his spirit returned again into his breast,
       (αὐτὰρ ἐπεί ῥ' ἄμπνυτο καὶ ἐς φρένα θυμὸς ἀγέρθη)
350   once more he made answer and spoke, saying:
       "Father Zeus, truly you gods still hold sway on high Olympus,
       if indeed the suitors have paid the price of their wanton outrage.
       But now I have a terrible fear at heart, that immediately all
       the men of Ithaca will come here against us, and send messengers everywhere
355   to the cities of the Cephallenians."
                      (Homer, *Od.* 24.302, 309–11, 315–22, 345–55 [Murray and Wyatt, LCL, 105])

Figure 11   Homer, *Od.* 24.302, 309–11, 315–22, 345–55

The mere mention of Odysseus in lines 309–14 triggers an experience of death and resurrection for Laertes. The typical elements are not all present, but they are all operative – even in their absence.

CONFUSION. Confusion manifests itself when Odysseus, disguised as a certain 'Eperitus', mentions the long-lost son of Laertes (24.309–11). A 'black cloud of grief' enfolds Laertes, drawing him into all-consuming grief (24.315). Laertes is no longer able to continue an intelligible conversation with 'Eperitus', but now only groans incessantly (24.315–17).

DEATH. References to the motif of death commence as early as Laertes' confusion. The pouring of dust over his 'gray' head suggests both intense mourning as well as the customary burning of the corpse after death (24.316–17).[54] As often occurs in resurrection narratives, the death experience develops by means of a reference to the weakening of the knees and/or heart: 'his father's knees were loosened ..., and his heart melted' (24.345; cf. 5.297, 406, 454; *Il.* 14.437; 22.452–3; *Callir.* 1.1.14). Ultimately, the description of Laertes' death experience culminates with a Greek word often translated as 'fainting' (ἀποψύχοντα; *Od.* 24.348),

54.   See Nagy, *Greek Mythology*, pp. 85–121.

though a literal rendering of the word suggests a '[breathing] out (ἀπό) of his being/soul (ψυχή)'.[55] The theme of death is present, and the presentation is again qualified.

RESURRECTION. The experience of death reverses when Laertes 'revive[s], and his spirit return[s] again into his breast' (24.349). Like the terminology regarding Laertes' confusion (black cloud enfolding him) and death (knees and heart weakening), the 'revival' terminology in this resurrection is also commonplace among resurrection narratives (5.458; *Il.* 5.697; 11.359; 14.436; 15.232; 22.475).

ENLIGHTENMENT. In his enlightenment, the man who was reduced to pitiable groaning now proclaims an eloquent prayer of thanksgiving to Zeus, the lord of all gods. His clarity allows him to identify not only the source of his fear, but also the tactics of his enemies, the suitors (*Od.* 24.354). Furthermore, he keenly discerns the pending threat of conspiracy (24.355).

THE CROWD. Throughout this resurrection narrative, Homer's presentation emphasizes the intimacy of the exchange. Odysseus' emotional reaction to his father's grief and confusion is expressed in remarkably personal terms: a pang shoots up from his heart and through his nostrils (24.318–19). He embraces and kisses his father (24.320) who, in turn, embraces Odysseus (24.347). As a result of this emphasis, the crowd element is not present until the resurrection is complete. Just as the enlightened Laertes considers his own reintegration into society, a crowd of suitors enters the narrative (24.352–5). Because of their presence, reintegration will not be easy.

CONCLUSION. This resurrection is distinct in the intimacy it portrays, and the element of the crowd is particularly muted. Nevertheless, themes of resurrection mark the final, climactic recognitions of *The Odyssey* as a whole, just as the resurrection of Andromache in *The Iliad* provides a narrative highlight at the climax of that story, accentuating the beginning of the fall of Troy.[56]

3.3 *Conclusion*

A reading of themes of death followed by themes of a return to life in Homeric literature reveals that these themes are routinely associated with themes of confusion and enlightenment: an Epic topos of resurrection emerges. Furthermore, in Homeric literature these themes typically mark strategic points in the narrative structure of the epics. In imitation of this Homeric model, Hellenistic literature often deploys the same themes in a

---

55. See also Section 2.4.4.
56. See Section 2.4.

TABLE 7: Resurrection Motifs in Chariton and Homer						
Function	Text	Confusion	Death...	...Qualified	Resurrection	Enlightenment	Crowd

Function	Text	Confusion	Death...	...Qualified	Resurrection	Enlightenment	Crowd
Introduction	Callirhoë's First Resurrection	"no idea to whom she was being married" (*Callir.* 1.1.14)	"unable to speak", "darkness over eyes", "nearly expired" (1.1.14)	"*nearly* expired", etc. (1.1.14)	"flames to life" again (1.1.15)	aware of Chaereas, "taller & stronger" (1.1.16)	"city present", crowd at the door (1.1.15)
	Chaereas' First Resurrection	fall or stand? (*Callir.* 1.1.7), depends upon father (1.1.8-9)	"likely to die", etc. (1.1.7, 8, 9, 10)	"*like* a hero mortally wounded", etc. (1.1.7)	"running forward" (1.1.15)	running forward (1.1.15), congratulated (1.1.16)	assembly calls for help (1.1.12), crowd at the door (1.1.15)
	Athena Resurrects Diomedes	No: *lucidity* of Athena (*Il.* 5.110, 115-20)	"mist before eyes" (5.127)	Pandarus: "I *should* send him off to Aïdoneus, yet *I subdued him not.*" (5.184-91)	"put force back into breast" (5.125-26)	"force three times as great took hold", confuses others (5.135-36)	Trojans (5.103-05), foremost fighters (5.134)
	Aphrodite and Apollo Resurrect Aeneas	falls and remains, "leans on the earth" (*Il.* 5.309-10)	"dark night enfolded his eyes" (5.310)	Diomedes *eager* to slay, but unable (5.335-42, 347-51, 432-44)	swept out of human realm (5.314-46)	swept up to heavenly temple of illumination (5.448)	divine crowds (5.312, 344), Danaans (5.316, 345), throngs (5.346)
	Zeus Resurrects Sarpedon	depends on comrades (*Il.* 5.692-93)	spirit leaves; mist over eyes (5.696), breathes out soul (5.698)	*absolute power* of Zeus (5.877-78)	"revives" (5.697), "lives again" (5.698)	*absolute power* of Zeus (5.877-78)	"noble comrades" (5.692)
	Athena Resurrects Odysseus	No: *lucidity* of Athena (*Od.* 5.426, 437)	does not speak, breathe, move (5.455-57), breathes out soul (5.460)	"bitter frost *may* overcome" (5.468), "*may* become prey" (5.473)	"revives"; "spirit returns to breast" (5.458), comes forth from bushes (6.127-28)	*confuses others* (6.129-34)	Phaeacian maidens (6.127-28)
Significant Point in the Narrative	Callirhoë's Second Resurrection	sits in darkness (*Callir.* 1.4.11), oblivious to anger (1.4.12)	unable to speak, breathe, stand (1.4.12-1.5.1)	"*appearance* of death" (1.5.1; cf. 1.6.2, 5)	experiences "*palingenesia*" (1.8.1)	receives a full report (8.1.15-17)	--- (1.8.1), Chaereas & public witness (3.3.1-10), Syracusan witness (8.6.7-8)
	Chaereas' Second Resurrection	"looking for Callirhoë" (*Callir.* 5.7.6)	assumptions reasserted (5.7.6, 8), otherworldly "summons" (5.7.10)	death *assumed* by courtroom, but sham "had been arranged" (5.8.1)	Chaereas steps forward, Callirhoë: "You're alive!" (5.8.1)	apt mental debate arguing for Callirhoë (5.6.5-6)	awe throughout courtroom (5.8.2)
	Chaereas and Callirhoë Resurrect	Callirhoë despondent (*Callir.* 7.6.8-9), Chaereas relies on soldier (8.1.6)	both lay unconscious (8.1.8)	lay as if dead "*for a while*" (8.1.9)	they revive three times (8.1.10)	Callirhoë "moves with dignity", guided by Chaereas (8.1.12)	"no soldier, no sailor, no janitor" failed to see (8.1.11)
	Apollo Resurrects Hector	"whirls" "like a top" "round and round" (*Il.* 14.413)	vomits black blood, darkness over eyes, spirit overwhelmed (14.437-39)	even Hector *thought* he had died (15.251-52)	breath restored (15.60, 232, 242, 262, 287)	Hector has the control of a stable-trained horse (15.263-69)	comrades (14.432; 15.242), the Achaeans (15.286-93)
	Andromache Resurrects	"unwitting one" "knows nothing" (*Il.* 22.437, 445)	"dark night over eyes"; "gasped out spirit" (22.466-67)	"distraught *even to death*" (22.474)	"revives" (22.475)	eloquent, informed speech (22.477-515)	held up in midst of crowd (22.474)
	Laertes Resurrects	fails to recognize son; groans without pause, etc. (*Od.* 24.315-16)	breathes out soul (24.348)	No: emphasis on *intimacy* (24.318-20, 347)	"revives"; spirit returns to breast (24.349)	eloquent prayer (24.351-55)	No: emphasis on *intimacy* (24.318-20, 347)

similar manner. I have summarized my findings in Table 7 for further consideration.

The Table, which includes all of the resurrection narratives I have analyzed as well as the introductions of Diomedes and Aeneas in *The Iliad*, allows for a reassertion of the four primary characteristics that I suggest mark an Epic topos of resurrection narration. First, in each expression of the topos, some element of confusion is present as a prelude to the theme of death. Representations of resurrection may be appreciated as a kind of recognition – 'a change from ignorance to knowledge' – because the resurrection experience typically results in a reversal of the original state of confusion to enlightenment.[57] Second, death as a motif is often expressed as darkness over the eyes and a gasping out of life, though the absolute nature of this motif is repeatedly qualified. Third, the element of a crowd is manifest, but for significantly different reasons in the Hellenistic texts when compared to Homeric literature. Hellenistic texts employ the theme of the crowd as the means of expressing emotions. Homeric texts, on the other hand, utilize crowds to bring closure to the event of death and return: the presence of the crowd allows for a full reintegration into the social realm of life. Fourth and finally, this constellation of motifs that constitute the Epic resurrection topos finds expression at strategic points in the narrative structure, whether that point be at the introduction of a primary character, a significant turning point in the middle of the story, or at the climax of the story overall.

Several other specific textual observations I have made regarding Hellenistic novelistic literature in this analysis suggest that as Homeric literature was told and retold within educational and recreational gatherings, the Epic resurrection pattern of storytelling developed as one tool among many within the storytellers' 'box of tricks' for accentuating a key point in a narrative structure.[58] I have noted how storytellers of the eastern Mediterranean employ the constellation of motifs with a certain degree of consistency. Texts have multiple, consecutive parallels. Certain phrases recur repeatedly in the same situations throughout texts attributed to several different authors. The absence or alteration of any given motif within the overall constellation produces a reasonable justification. At times, the authors explicitly comment upon the effect achieved by the themes. Such consistency in the constellation suggests the existence of an Epic topos, which may have been quite well-established, though more likely is a product of a known and learned general mimesis prominent within ancient society.

Although I have assigned specific 'labels' to each of the five suggested motifs and placed them within the lines of a table, I do not make a claim of ultimate determinacy regarding the motifs. However, more importantly, my identification of these five motifs and their recurring function suggests one topos of narration associated with resurrection in epic and

57. Aristotle, *Poet.* 1452a31; see also Section 1.5.3.
58. Conte's studies identify such an ancient literary 'box of tricks' which he likens to a dictionary: 'Do you need a sensational suicide? . . . cast yourself from a cliff, cut your throat, hang yourself from a bedstead . . .' (Conte, *Hidden Author*, pp. 87, 94).

novelistic literature, an Epic resurrection topos, that will allow for a comparison of the themes of death and return to life to another form of the resurrection theme present in literature of the Ancient Near East: a Prophetic resurrection topos.

Chapter 4

RESURRECTION IN THE PROPHETIC AND HELLENISTIC LITERATURE OF JUDAISM

As early as its opening lines, the Gospel of Mark establishes a close literary relationship with the Hebrew Canon that is sustained throughout its text and heightened at its close. A recent work by Joel Marcus aptly summarizes this relationship:

> In a programmatic statement at the very beginning of his Gospel, the author of Mark announces his conviction that his story about the good news of Jesus Christ takes place 'as it has been written in Isaiah the prophet.' He then goes on to buttress this claim with a conflated citation from Exodus, Malachi, and Isaiah (Mk 1.1–3). A few verses later, at the climactic moment in Jesus' baptism, a divine voice comes forth from heaven to hail Jesus with words drawn from Psalm 2, Isaiah 42, and perhaps Genesis 22 (Mk 1.11). The situation is similar at the end of the Gospel: citations of the Old Testament occupy positions of extraordinary prominence …. In between this scriptural beginning and this scriptural ending, citations of and allusions to the Old Testament continually pop up in the Markan narrative ….[1]

Given such close literary ties, an examination of themes of death and revival in the Hebrew Bible will be crucial for an appreciation of resurrection in Mark's literary context. This chapter conducts an examination of four Hebrew Bible texts, beginning with the 'Classical prophet' Hosea, whose treatment of resurrection themes in Hos. 6.1-3 may very well have provided a type of 'standard for … later Jews and Christians'.[2] I demonstrate how this text as well as prophetic texts in Ezek. 37.1-14, 1 Kgs 17.17-24, and 2 Kgs 4.18-37 participate in a Prophetic topos of resurrection that is identifiably different from the Epic resurrection topos.[3] In each text, a constellation of motifs asserts a breach of

---

1. Marcus, *Way of the Lord*, p. 1.

2. Boadt, *Reading the Old Testament: An Introduction* (Mahwah, N.J.; New York: Paulist, 1984), p. 313.

3. Compare George W.E. Nickelsburg, *Resurrection, Immortality, and Eternal Life in Intertestamental Judaism*, whose project mentions Hosea 6 and Ezekiel 37 only in passing (p. 18) and makes no mention whatsoever of the resurrection traditions of Elijah (1 Kgs 17.17-24) and Elisha (2 Kgs 4.18-37).

divine trust, progresses through death and resurrection, and culminates in a reestablishment of communion.[4] Unlike the Epic resurrection topos, narratives of the Prophetic resurrection topos do not typically highlight strategic points in the structure of a literary work. Furthermore, crowds are not an integral component and – perhaps most significant – the element of death is stark and vivid rather than tempered by qualifiers.

In Section 2 of this chapter, I consider various non-canonical writings which circulated among Jewish communities at the time of the writing of Mark's Gospel. Themes of death and revival occur within two sets of such literature: (1) apocalyptic literature, which occasionally mentions resurrection; and (2) novelistic Jewish literature, which employs the themes with a surprising frequency. Within writings that date from the Hellenistic period – texts from the third century B.C.E. to the first century C.E. – the Epic and Prophetic topoi merge. A striking hybridity of Epic and Prophetic topoi characterize these Hellenistic texts. I demonstrate this confluence in a reading of five resurrection narratives from this period. By enhancing an appreciation of these topoi, this chapter prepares for the comparative analysis of resurrection narratives in the Gospel of Mark undertaken in Chapter 5.

4.1 *Resurrection Themes in Prophetic Literature*

References to bodily resurrection in Hebrew Bible texts are 'rare and dissimilar'.[5] The primary conceptions of life after death in this Canon are annihilation and immortality.[6] Psalm 90, for example, associates the afterlife with annihilation rather than bodily resurrection (see Figure 12).

Verses 1 and 2 locate the context of the poem within an extensive time span that encompasses not only 'all generations' (v. 1), but even the formation of the earth (v. 2). Throughout this time, individuals formed from the dust turn 'back to dust' (v. 3).[7] They are simply 'swept away' 'like a dream' (v. 5a). The four verbs of v. 6 'focus on the transitory plant which flourishes, is renewed, fades, and withers'.[8] Set in this time span, human life seems as fleeting as grass, only 70 or 80 years of existence that 'come to an end like a sigh' (vv. 9–10). The only means of life beyond

4. See William R. Millar, *Isaiah 24–27 and the Origin of Apocalyptic* (Missoula, Mont.: Scholars, 1976) and Wire, *Holy Lives* (particularly pp. 49, 88).

5. Robert Martin-Achard, 'Resurrection', *ABD* 5.683.

6. Robert Martin-Achard, *From Death to Life: A Study of the Development of the Doctrine of the Resurrection in the Old Testament* (trans. John P. Smith; Edinburgh and London: Oliver and Boyd, 1960), p. 16.

7. Compare Gen. 2.7; 3.19; Job 4.12-21; 10.1-17; 21.19-26; 34.10-15; Sir. 17.25-32; Ps. 103.13-18.

8. Konrad Schaefer, *Psalms* (Berit Olam; Collegeville, Minn.: Liturgical, 2001), p. 226.

¹ Lord, you have been our dwelling place
    in all generations.
² Before the mountains were brought forth,
    or ever you had formed the earth and the world,
    from everlasting to everlasting you are God.
³ You turn us back to dust,
    and say, "Turn back, you mortals."
⁴ For a thousand years in your sight
    are like yesterday when it is past,
    or like a watch in the night.
⁵ You sweep them away; they are like a dream,
    like grass that is renewed in the morning;
⁶ in the morning it flourishes and is renewed;
    in the evening it fades and withers.
⁷ For we are consumed by your anger;
    by your wrath we are overwhelmed.
⁸ You have set our iniquities before you,
    our secret sins in the light of your countenance.
⁹ For all our days pass away under your wrath;
    our years come to an end like a sigh.
¹⁰ The days of our life are seventy years,
    or perhaps eighty, if we are strong;
    even then their span is only toil and trouble;
    they are soon gone, and we fly away.
¹¹ Who considers the power of your anger?
    Your wrath is as great as the fear that is due you.
¹² So teach us to count our days
    that we may gain a wise heart.
¹³ Turn, O Lord! How long?
    Have compassion on your servants!
¹⁴ Satisfy us in the morning with your steadfast love,
    so that we may rejoice and be glad all our days.
¹⁵ Make us glad as many days as you have afflicted us,
    and as many years as we have seen evil.
¹⁶ Let your work be manifest to your servants,
    and your glorious power to their children.
¹⁷ Let the favor of the Lord our God be upon us,
    and prosper for us the work of our hands—
    O prosper the work of our hands!

                    (Ps. 90.1-17)

Figure 12   Ps. 90.1-17

death conceivable to the psalmist is progeny (v. 16) and the work of one's hands (v. 17).[9]

Other texts in the Hebrew Canon portray the afterlife in terms of immortality. However, this immortality is not, by and large, a state that one eagerly awaits, because life continues only in a greatly diminished form. A dead person lives on not as a physical body, but as a 'shade' in a

---

9. Compare Psalm 103. For the alternative suggestion that progeny serves as the functional equivalent of immortality in the Hebrew Bible, see Jon D. Levenson, 'The Resurrection of the Dead and the Construction of Personal Identity in Ancient Israel' in *Congress Volume: Basel 2001* (ed. A. Lemaire; VTSup, 92; Boston and Leiden: Brill Academic, 2002), pp. 305–22.

³ When the Lord has given you rest from your pain and turmoil and the hard service with which you were made to serve, ⁴ you will take up this taunt against the king of Babylon:...

⁸ The cypresses exult over you,
        the cedars of Lebanon, saying,
"Since you were laid low,
        no one comes to cut us down."
⁹ Sheol beneath is stirred up
        to meet you when you come;
it rouses the shades (רְפָאִים) to greet you,
        all who were leaders of the earth;
it raises from their thrones
        all who were kings of the nations.
¹⁰ All of them will speak
        and say to you:
"You too have become as weak as we!
    You have become like us!"
                (Isa. 14.3-4a, 8-10)

Figure 13   Isa. 14.3-4a, 8-10

place referred to as 'Sheol' (שְׁאוֹל) or less often as 'Abaddon' (אֲבַדּוֹן). A collection of oracles in Isaiah 14 are particularly illustrative (see Figure 13).

The land of Sheol, here depicted as being 'beneath' the land of the living (Isa. 14.9), is home to the 'shades' of the dead (14.9). This passage highlights the contrast between those who are 'leaders of the earth' (14.9) – such as the king of Babylon (14.4) – and their ultimate destiny as weaklings: 'You too have become as weak as we!' (14.10) Isaiah's taunt plays on the Hebrew word that means the 'shades' (*repha'im* רְפָאִים) and the root from which this word derives (*rph'* רפא), meaning 'to weaken'.[10] In this portrayal of the afterlife, dead humans are only a weak representation, a shadow, of their earthly existence.

The mystical land of Sheol in and of itself is not very inviting. Like the shades, Sheol represents only a dark shadow of the glory that is the earth (see Figure 14).

The author of this text associates the dwelling place of the dead with themes of gloom and darkness (Job 10.21, 22) from which the character of Job is 'never to return' (10.21). Despite its dreary presentation, immortality is the dominant view of the afterlife in the Hebrew Canon.[11]

In comparison to immortality, Hebrew Bible texts that evoke the theme of resurrection are few. This section of the study examines four passages of the Hebrew Bible dating from the eighth to the fourth century B.C.E. in which resurrection figures as a predominant theme. Each of these passages derives from prophetic literature, whether that literature recalls the

10.   See Ernest Klein, *A Comprehensive Etymological Dictionary of the Hebrew Language for Readers of English* (New York: Macmillan, 1987), s.v. רְפָאִים and רפאII.
11.   See also Job 7.9-10; 16.22; 17.11-16; 40.10-14; Pss. 6.5; 16.10; 30.9; 55.23; 88.1-18; Eccl. 12.1-7 (esp. 12.5); Isa. 38.18; and Ezek. 32.17-32.

[20] Are not the days of my life few?
   Let me alone, that I may find a little comfort
[21] before I go, never to return,
   to the land of gloom and deep darkness,
[22] the land of gloom and chaos,
   where light is like darkness.

(Job 10.20-22)

Figure 14   Job 10.20-22

ministry of a prominent prophet via collected and edited oracles (Hos. 6.1-3; Ezek. 37.1-13), or saga cycles (1 Kgs 17.17-24; 2 Kgs 4.8-37).[12]

The question of whether or not a belief in resurrection prompted these and other references to resurrection was a topic of extensive research and debate in the 1970s and early 1980s.[13] The debate is currently experiencing a revival.[14] However, this question is not a primary consideration of this study. Whether or not these texts were intended to be read metaphorically, authors of the Hellenistic period – particularly in Hellenistic Jewish communities – may have found these verses to be a resource for their own construction of resurrection narratives. My reading of these texts accentuates (1) the presence of motifs that accompany the expression of resurrection in each text, as well as both (2) the function and (3) the placement of the text in the larger book.

4.1.1 Hosea 6.1-3 – A Song of Hope

Verses 1–3 of Hosea 6 contain what is quite likely the earliest surviving text of the Hebrew Bible to engage motifs related to resurrection. In these verses, a song dating from the Syro-Ephraimite War (735–733 B.C.E.) calls Israel to hope despite the recent assault on this people wrought by

---

12.   I will treat other passages summarily or in the notes.

13.   See Martin-Achard, *From Death to Life* (1960); Mitchell Dahood, *Psalms* 101–150 (AB 17A; New York: Doubleday, 1970), pp. xli–lii; Bruce Vawter, 'Intimations of Immortality and the Old Testament', *JBL* 91 (June 1972), pp. 158–71; Hans W. Wolff, *Anthropology of the Old Testament* (trans. Margaret Kohl; Philadelphia: Fortress, 1974), p. 11; Lloyd R. Bailey, *Biblical Perspectives on Death* (OBT; Philadelphia: Fortress, 1979); Francis I. Andersen and David N. Freedman, *Hosea* (AB 24; New York: Doubleday, 1980), pp. 420–1; and Leonard J. Greenspoon, 'The Origin of the Idea of Resurrection', in Baruch Halpern and Jon D. Levenson (eds), *Traditions in Transformation: Turning Points in Biblical Faith* (Winona Lake, Ind.: Eisenbrauns, 1981), pp. 310–11.

14.   See Simcha P. Raphael, *Jewish Views of the Afterlife* (Northvale, N.J.: Jason Aronson, 1996); Neil Gillman, *The Death of Death: Resurrection and Immortality in Jewish Thought* (Woodstock, Ver.: Jewish Lights, 1997); Friedrich Avemarie and Hermann Lichtenberger, eds, *Auferstehung = Resurrection: The Fourth Durham-Tübingen Research Symposium: Resurrection, Transfiguration and Exaltation in the Old Testament, Ancient Judaism and Early Christianity* (WUNT, 135; Tübingen: J.C.B. Mohr [Paul Siebeck], 2001); Leila L. Bronner, 'The Resurrection Motif in the Hebrew Bible: Allusions or Illusions', *JBQ* 30 (2002), pp. 143–54; Jon D. Levenson, 'Resurrection in the Torah? A Reconsideration', *CTIR* 6 (2002), pp. 2–29.

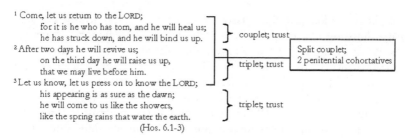

Figure 15   Hos. 6.1-3

Assyrian warriors under Tiglath-Pileser.[15] Unlike the prose resurrection narratives of Greco-Roman novelistic literature, Hos. 6.1-3 is 'an artfully crafted song',[16] perhaps more akin to the contemporaneous, calculated poetry of Homeric verse, though its effects are achieved not through dactylic hexameter but rather through the coupling and trebling of poetic lines[17] (see Figure 15).

This seemingly random arrangement does not detract from the poetic quality of the passage. In his analysis, Douglas Stuart notes that such variation of couplets and triplets 'is normal in Hebrew poetry, especially of the earlier periods'.[18] In this context, the message of the oracle is one of hope. Despite the recent military defeat, Hosea's song declares that YHWH will again revive and restore the people of Israel to the state of prosperity they enjoyed before the Assyrians ravaged their land.[19]

4.1.1.1 *Motifs of Resurrection*

An examination of resurrection and its accompanying motifs in Hos. 6.1-3 allows for the discernment of differences and similarities between this treatment of resurrection and the Epic topos of resurrection. The song opens with an exhortation to 'return to the Lord' (v. 1). Apparently the

15. See Albrecht Alt, 'Hosea 5.8–6.6: Ein Krieg und Seine Folgen in Prophetischer Beleuchtung', on pp. 163–87 of vol. 2 of his *Kleine Schriften zur Geschichte des Volkes Israel* (Munich: C.H. Beck, 3rd edn, 1964). In his *ABD* article on 'Hosea', Choon L. Seow affirms that 'Albrecht Alt's thesis that this [Syro-Ephraimite] war lies in the background of 5.8–6.6 is accepted by most scholars' (*ABD* 3.294).

16. Douglas Stuart, *Hosea-Jonah* (WBC, 31; Waco, Texas: Word, 1987), p. 101. The broader context of Hosea 5.8–7.1 suggests that vv. 1–3 of ch. 6 originally existed as an independent piece – the entirety of the passage 'takes the form of a series of divine speeches, with the single exception of 6.1–3', which is associated to the context by the catchword 'tear' (שרף) in 5.14. See also Hans W. Wolff, *Hosea* (Hermeneia; trans. Gary Stansell; Philadelphia: Fortress, 1974), p. 108: 'A priestly penitential song in 6.1–3 interrupts the prophetic genres.'

17. Stuart, *Hosea*, p. 101.

18. Stuart, *Hosea*, p. 101.

19. See Marvin A. Sweeney, *The Twelve Prophets* (Berit Olam; Collegeville, Minnesota: Liturgical, 2000), p. 70; Wolff, *Hosea*, pp. 116–17.

people have broken off their association with YHWH. Many scholars classify the song as 'penitential'[20] on the basis of a category of similar songs in the extant Hebrew Psalter, designated as such in the early twentieth century by form critics Hermann Gunkel and Sigmund Mowinckel.[21] However, only obliquely in the cohortative to 'return'[22] (v. 1) do the lines convey a 'sense of sorrow for sins or fault', presumably for ceasing to worship YHWH.[23] In contrast, the psalmist devotes the entire second and third lines to the cause of the breach that results in a need to 'return' – the people have been 'torn' and 'struck down' (v. 1). Hosea unabashedly attributes this abusive activity to YHWH himself: 'it is he who has torn ... he has struck down' (v. 1). This interpretation of divine activity leaves little wonder as to why the people have broken off relationship with their deity: a perceived *breach of trust* resulting from a dire situation promulgated by YHWH himself has drawn the people away from worship of the divinity.

The two references to mortal wounding in this passage in Hosea convey the motif of *death*. The Hebrew verb טָרַף ('torn'; v. 1) carries a connotation of being torn in pieces or rent limb from limb, an image frequently applied to the activity of wild beasts.[24] The Greek translation of this word in the Septuagint, ἥρπακεν ('seized'), similarly connotes a violent death as a result of wild animals (e.g. *Il.* 17.62) or of attacking enemy warriors (e.g. *Il.* 3.444), though the verb also can have comparatively less violent connotations akin to simply snatching something up hastily.[25] In the second reference, the victims are 'struck down' (Hebrew ךְ; v. 1), which is a Hebrew verb form that connotes divine activity of 'smiting' or 'striking dead' with great frequency.[26] The word representing this term in the Septuagint (πατάσσω) usually refers to 'a deadly blow' (cf. Judg. 9.43; 1 Kgs 17.9; et al.), though not always.[27]

The possibility that the language of abuse in Hos. 6.1 refers to death is strengthened by the statement that follows in v. 2: YHWH will 'revive' and 'raise up' the people. Here the text introduces the motif of a return to

---

20. See Wolff, *Hosea*, pp. 116–17; Stuart, *Hosea*, pp. 106–7.

21. See Psalms 6, 32, 38, 51, 102, and 130 and motifs noted by Sigmund Mowinckel, *The Psalms in Israel's Worship* (trans. D.R. Ap-Thomas; two volumes in one; Sheffield, Engl.: JSOT, 1992), 1.193–246, as well as Hermann Gunkel and Joachim Begrich, *Introduction to Psalms: The Genres of the Religious Lyric of Israel* (MLBS; trans. James D. Nogalski; Macon, Geor.: Mercer University Press, 1998), pp. 121–98.

22. So also Wolff, *Hosea*, p. 117.

23. Merriam-Webster, *Webster's Third New International Dictionary*, s.v. 'penitential'.

24. See *HALAT* 2.380, s.v. טָרַף; also Andersen and Freedman: 'it is not a mild but a fatal injury that Yahweh inflicts' (*Hosea*, p. 419).

25. See LSJ, pp. 245–6, s.v. ἁρπάζω.

26. The verb is in the *hifil* binyan. See *HALAT* 2.697-698, s.v. נכה, hif.

27. LSJ, 1347, s.v. πατάσσω, II a-b.

life or *resurrection*. In the Septuagint, the Greek expression that represents 'raising up' is a form of the verb ἀνίστημι, a word that occurs following allusions to death.[28]

The third and final verse of the song reasserts the opening cohortative: although they have suffered so extremely at the hands of their deity, Hosea exhorts the people to 'press on to know YHWH' (v. 3). The song is as legitimizing as it is penitential: it seeks to *reestablish divine communion*. Despite the harm the people have experienced, they will see that YHWH no longer brings injury, but 'spring rains' to water the earth (v. 3).

4.1.1.2 *The Function and Placement of the Resurrection Theme*
The function and placement of the song in its literary context are far from certain because of 'the peculiar way the sayings have been strung together' in chs 4 through 11 of the book.[29] Within this string of sayings, scholars identify a subsection that begins at Hos. 5.8 and incorporates the oracular song.[30] However, there is little agreement beyond this general observation. For example, Hans W. Wolff has suggested that in the present form of the text, the priestly song has the subordinate function of illustrating the prophet's preceding claim that it is only 'in their distress that they will beg my favor' (Hos. 5.15), thus giving 'bold relief to Hosea's rejoinder in the question in v 4a' that follows the insertion.[31] Douglas Stuart identifies the song as one of 'three expressions of hope' (Hos. 5.15; 6.1-3; 6.11–7.1a) in Hos. 5.8–7.1a, 'reflecting in microcosm the overall structure of the book'.[32] Gail Yee, however, seems to overlook the hopeful tone of Hos. 5.15 and 6.11–7.1a in her suggestion that the passage Hos. 6.1-3 works with other expressions of hope in 10.12 and 11.10-11 'as the first in a series of contrapuntal voices strategically arranged by a later redactor to prepare for the conclusion of the book'.[33] Indeed, even if a rhythm of expressions of hope could be discerned within the oracles, Hos. 6.1-3 would constitute the only occurrence of the themes of death and revival within the oracles as a whole.

---

28. See, for example, the Gospel of Mark (5.42; 8.31; 9.9, 10, 27, 31; 10.34; 12.18-27). Furthermore, in the Gospel this verb repeatedly occurs in tandem with a reference to three days (Mk 8.31; 9.31; 10.33), just as the Hosean text associates revival with a time frame of three days ('on the third day he will raise us up'; Hos. 6.2).

29. Wolff, *Hosea*, xxx.

30. Wolff, *Hosea*, p. 108; Stuart, *Hosea-Jonah*, pp. 99–100; Alt, 'Hosea 5.8–6.6'.

31. Wolff, *Hosea*, p. 109.

32. Stuart, *Hosea*, p. 100.

33. Gale A. Yee, 'Hosea' in *The New Interpreter's Bible* (Nashville: Abingdon, 1994), 7.249.

4.1.1.3 *Conclusion*

My reading of the themes of death and a return to life in the biblical book of Hosea elicits several characteristics of their presentation that will typify other biblical texts as well. The initial theme is a *breach of trust* which has resulted from death. The source of divine power itself is implicated in the death (Hos. 6.1). The second theme is *death*, expressed in brute terms (v. 1) originally intended to inspire hope for healing within an Israelite community facing a brutal, imperialistic attack in the eighth century B.C.E. A *resurrection* theme follows immediately (v. 2). As a result of the equivocal presentation of death, this resurrection can be read literally or otherwise. In this text resurrection is a promised event of the future. Also, the return to life will involve not any one individual, but the nation of Israel as a whole. When resurrection occurs, there is a *reestablishment of communion* that was initially broken (v. 3; cf. Hos. 5.14; 6.1). Finally, the function and placement of the passage are difficult to determine in its present context within a loose agglomeration of prophecies. Unlike the repeated use of themes of death and a return to life at several strategic points throughout the Epic tradition, the passage Hos. 6.1-3 represents a unique use of the themes within a series of oracles that lack clear definition. These themes do not serve to mark strategic points in the structure of Hosea.

4.1.2 *Ezekiel 37.1-14 – A Prophetic Vision*

Ezekiel's famous vision of the valley of dry bones (Ezek. 37.1-14) is a second text within the Hebrew canon in which themes of death and resurrection are prominent. The vision originates more than a century after the time of Hosea, in the early or middle years of the sixth century B.C.E.[34] Like the song in Hosea, Ezekiel's vision portrays the restoration of the people of Judah following a period of national distress. Many of the Israelites have been forced out of their own land and into exile in Babylon. Nevertheless, the prophet of Ezekiel 37.1-14 declares that YHWH will resurrect the people:

Moshe Greenberg has noted how the narrative of this vision is 'constructed in suspenseful steps'.[35] Verses 1–3 introduce a question from YHWH that creates tension: 'Can these bones live?' (v. 3). The tension is substantially resolved in vv. 4–8 as the bones receive everything necessary for a return to life ... except life-giving breath. YHWH provides this breath in vv. 9–10 so that the narrative culminates not just with an individual, but with a 'vast multitude' that has been restored to life. In

---

34. See Andrew Mein, *Ezekiel and the Ethics of Exile* (OTM; Oxford, New York: Oxford University Press, 2001).

35. See Moshe Greenberg, *Ezekiel 21-37* (AB, 22A; New York: Doubleday, 1997), pp. 747–8.

conclusion, vv. 11–14 explain the metaphor: 'these bones are the whole house of Israel' (v. 11). After an analysis of the primary motifs employed in this passage, I will explore the function and placement of the narrative in the book as a whole.

4.1.2.1 *Motifs of Resurrection*

Ezekiel's vision begins with a striking expression of the motif of *death* as YHWH places the prophet in a valley that is 'full of bones' (v. 1). The narration by the prophet presents the death in plain imagery: 'there were very many bones lying in the valley, and they were very dry' (v. 2). No explicit statement in the text serves to qualify this death.[36] Rather, the emphasis is upon describing death as stark and definite.

In v. 3, the text juxtaposes this vivid metaphor of death with YHWH's pointed question: 'Can these bones live?' This challenge transforms the valley into a type of playing field upon which YHWH will demonstrate divine abilities for the purpose of ending a *breach of trust*. YHWH's own people, the house of Israel, feel that their hope is lost (v. 11). Through the proclamation of the prophet, sinews, flesh, and breath enliven the bones, resulting in their *resurrection* (vv. 4–10). Consequently, *communion* with YHWH as a divine source is *reestablished*. In fact, YHWH's legitimacy is explicitly asserted twice – in v. 13 and v. 14 – as the text expounds the significance of the vision: 'You shall know that I am YHWH …. You shall know that I will act.'

4.1.2.2 *The Function and Placement of the Resurrection Theme*

Through the metaphor, Ezekiel proposes 'that under such conditions [as exile] the sole basis for hope lies in the superhuman and miraculous power of his God ….'[37] The driving purpose behind the vision is the impartation of hope. Such a function, however, does not promote the narrative to a particularly prominent position within the collection of prophecies as a whole. Certainly the book of Ezekiel demonstrates more evidence of an intentional arrangement than does the book of Hosea. The collection of prophecies in its present form suggests broad divisions on the basis of theme, with chs 1–24 containing oracles of doom, chs 25–32 consisting of prophecies against the nations, and chs 33–48 preserving a compilation of oracles of salvation.[38] Within these oracles of salvation, Ezekiel 34–39 contains a series of visions that promises (1) protection against wicked

---

36. Eichrodt marshals an impressive list of texts in which 'bones' are metaphorical representations of the center of vitality and strength (*Theology of the Old Testament* (trans. J.A. Baker; OTL; Philadelphia: Westminster, 1961–7), p. 2.146. Greenberg (*Ezekiel*, 749) notes the prominence of a literalistic, individualistic reading of the vision in the Hellenistic period, as does Block, *The Book of Ezekiel*, pp. 388–91.

37. Eichrodt, *Ezekiel*, 510.

38. Greenberg, *Ezekiel 1–20*, 6.

shepherds provided by YHWH and true servants of YHWH (ch. 34), (2) the restoration of the land (chs 35–36), (3) new life and unity for the people (ch. 37), and concludes with (4) protection from the enemy by the mysterious agency of YHWH himself (chs 38–39).[39] Ezekiel's vision of resurrection is one of two short visions that follow a lengthy passage about shepherds and an even longer text regarding the restoration of the land. After these brief interludes, the series culminates in an extended treatment of themes of military might. The resurrection oracle does not occur at a particularly strategic point in the text, even within this series of visions.

4.1.2.3 *Conclusion*

The same themes I observe in my treatment of resurrection in the Hosean song recur in this prophetic vision by Ezekiel. This vision begins with the theme of *death*, expressed in stark images of dry bones (Ezek. 37.1-2; cf. Hos. 6.1). A question from YHWH introduces the theme of a *reestablishment of communion* (Ezek. 37.3; cf. Hos. 6.3). The vision effects this reestablishment through the theme of *resurrection* (Ezek. 37.4-10; cf. Hos. 6.2), a return to life that involves not any one individual, but the nation of Israel as a whole. In Ezekiel's passage, the identification of the bones as 'the whole house of Israel' whose 'hope is lost' communicates the theme of a *breach of trust* (Ezek. 37.11). The implication is that YHWH has left his people as good as dead. Following this 'flashback' to the initial breach of trust, the theme of resurrection is asserted (37.12) and the divine source is emphatically reaffirmed (37.13-14). As a prophetic oracle, Ezekiel's vision clearly conveys hope to the people in a time of crisis. The function of the narrative with the book of Ezekiel, however, is less certain. The author does not position the theme in a location that is identifiably significant.

4.1.3 *1 Kings 17.17-24 – Resurrection Narrative*

Sometime between the eighth and fourth centuries B.C.E., the traditions of the prophets Elisha and Elijah (1 Kings 17 – 2 Kings 13) attained written form.[40] The influence of these traditions upon the Gospel of Mark is

---

39. See Walther Zimmerli, *Ezekiel 1* (trans. Ronald E. Clemens; Hermeneia; Philadelphia: Fortress, 1979), 2.

40. See Terence Fretheim, *First and Second Kings* (WestBC; Louisville, Ky.: Westminster John Knox, 1999), p. 7; Volkmar Fritz, *1 & 2 Kings* (trans. Anselm Hagedorn; CC; Minneapolis: Fortress, 2003), p. 2; Antony F. Campbell, *Of Prophets and Kings: A Late Ninth Century Document (1 Samuel 1 – 2 Kings 10)* (CBQMS, 17; Washington, D.C.: Catholic Biblical Association of America, 1986); Steven L. McKenzie, *The Trouble with Kings: The Composition of the Book of Kings in the Deuteronomistic History* (VTSup, 42; New York and Leiden: Brill, 1991); Judith A. Todd, 'The Pre-Deuteronomistic Elijah Cycle' in

evident in its details[41] and episodes.[42] In fact, two episodes in the Elijah/ Elisha cycles tell of a prophet who raises a child from the dead (1 Kgs 17.17-24; 2 Kgs 4.31-37), just as the Gospel of Mark contains two narratives in which Jesus raises a child from the dead (Mk 5.21-43 and 9.18-29).[43] In the passage 1 Kgs 17.17-24, Elijah resurrects the son of a woman who hosts the prophet during his stay in Zarephath.

The narrative form of this text differs from the song and vision that I have already considered in this chapter. However, the narrative derives from Hebrew prophetic tradition. Perhaps it is due to a common, prophetic source that the primary themes I have observed in the oracles of Hosea and Ezekiel recur in this prophetic narrative.

4.1.3.1 *Motifs of Resurrection*

The agent of the resurrection in this text is a prophet. Elijah, as divine representative, effects what Hosea and Ezekiel ascribe to YHWH. Despite this mediation, however, the motifs of resurrection I have previously identified are constant. Agency does not seem to play a determinative role in the presentation of the resurrection theme.[44]

The severe illness of the child prompts the woman to implicate Elijah: 'What have you against me ... to cause the death of my son?!' (1 Kgs 17.18). Yet in the verses immediately preceding, Elijah has provided the woman with food (17.8-16). Regardless, she implicates this source of divine power in the death of her son. The death has *broken the trust* the woman previously held in the divine representative.

Coote (ed.), *Elijah and Elisha in Socioliterary Perspective*, pp. 1–35; Antony F. Campbell and Mark A. O'Brien, *Unfolding the Deuteronomistic History: Origins, Upgrades, Present Text* (Minneapolis: Fortress, 2000).

41. See, for example, the description of John the Baptist's clothing in Mk 1.6 and the parallel description of Elijah in 2 Kgs 1.8.

42. For example, both texts tell of a feeding of the multitudes (cf. 2 Kgs 4.42-44, Mk 6.32-44, and Mk 8.1-9). See Raymond E. Brown, 'Jesus and Elisha', *Perspectives* 12 (1971), pp. 85–99 (as Joel Marcus, *Mark 1–8* [AB, 27; New York: Doubleday, 2000], pp. 156–7) and Silvia Pellegrini (*Elija – Wegbereiter des Gottessohnes: Eine Textsemiotische Untersuchung im Markusevangelium* [HBS, 26; Freiburg, Switz.; New York: Herder, 2000]). A study by Wolfgang Roth, *Hebrew Gospel: Cracking the Code of Mark* (Oak Park, Ill.: Meyer-Stone, 1988), which argues that the Gospel of Mark is composed according to a pattern established in 1 Kings 17 – 2 Kings 13, is insightfully criticized by Ron N. Liburd in *Word and World* 10 (1990), pp. 94–9, and has received little scholarly attention since its publication. See, rather, Jacob Chacko Naluparayil, *The Identity of Jesus in Mark: An Essay on Narrative Christology* (SBFA, 49; Jerusalem: Franciscan, 2000).

43. The only other occurrence of the motif of resurrection in these traditions is a brief mention of a man who resurrects during his own burial (2 Kgs 13.20-21).

44. A similar point can be made regarding the Epic topos. In Callirhoë's first resurrection, Chaereas' approach and kiss effect a return to life in themes that are identifiable in resurrections (both Homeric and Hellenistic) which the gods provoke (*Callir.* 1.1.14–16; see Sections 2.4.4–8).

The *death* described here is set forth in absolute terms. Both the widow (v. 18) and the prophet (v. 20) unequivocally describe the boy as dead. Nevertheless, the child's 'life comes into him again' (v. 21) and he *revives* (v. 22). The transformation achieved in the widow is just as stark as that of the child. She ceases her accusations that the prophet intends harm (v. 18), *reestablishing* instead that Elijah is a man of God (v. 24). She now 'knows' that Elijah is a man of God (v. 24).[45]

4.1.3.2 *The Function and Placement of the Resurrection Theme*

The resurrection narrative serves as the final miracle within a series of miracles that serve to introduce the figure of Elijah.[46] First, Elijah accurately predicts the advent of a drought (17.1-7), then he miraculously provides food for the widow (17.8-16), and 'after this' he raises the boy from the dead (17.17-24). Once the narrative has introduced Elijah, he is content to delay his next feat for a period of three years (18.1). Such placement and function of a resurrection narrative resemble the placement and function of several of the resurrection narratives that occur throughout Homeric and novelistic Greco-Roman texts.[47]

Certainly, the positioning neither necessitates nor even suggests a justification limited to epic influence. In such contexts as the description of miraculous deeds, expressions of death and raising naturally assume the role of a final, culminating act. In a world of mortals facing certain death at one point or another, few miracles surpass the raising of the dead! What is striking in these biblical texts, rather, is the infrequency with which the resurrection theme occurs at a significant turning point. Of the four resurrection narratives examined in detail in this study, this narrative is the only one that occurs at a significant turning point in the storyline. This situation changes dramatically in texts compiled later than the fourth century B.C.E., as I will demonstrate in Section 4.2.

4.1.3.3 *Conclusion*

In 1 Kgs 17.17-24, strong expressions of *death* (v. 17; cf. 17.18, 20) prompt the theme of a *breach of trust* on the part of the divine source (v. 18). An act of *resurrection* (vv. 21-23) results in the *reaffirmation* of the divine source (v. 24). Among the resurrection narratives examined in this study,

45. In three of the texts I have analyzed, the Hebrew verb יָדַע ('to know') is integral to this theme (Hos. 6.3; Ezek. 37.3, 13, 14; 1 Kgs 17.24).

46. My observations do not necessarily exclude the influence of traditional modes upon this narration, read generally as an ancient miracle report (see, for example, Alexander Rofé, *The Prophetical Stories: The Narratives About the Prophets in the Hebrew Bible, Their Literary Types and History* [PPFBR; Jerusalem: Magnes, 1988], p. 134). However, I do assert the influence of the particular expression of certain themes insofar as this text relates specifically to resurrection.

47. See Chapter 3.

this narrative is unique in its placement – it is the only account of death and raising that occurs at a strategic point in the sequence of events. Taken as a whole, the narrative functions to legitimize Elijah as a prophet of YHWH, for the element of death is in no way qualified.

4.1.4 *2 Kings 4.18-37 – Resurrection Narrative*
Elijah's successor, Elisha, is the perpetrator of a second resurrection in the prophetic narratives.[48] Like Elijah, Elisha raises the son of a woman who hosts the prophet as he travels, though not in Zarephath, but Shunem (2 Kgs 4.32-37). The Shunammite woman has borne a child in her old age according to the prophecy of Elisha himself (2 Kgs 4.8-17). However, the child dies before reaching maturity (2 Kgs 4.18-37). The lengthy resurrection narrative employs many elements that are not prominent or present in other resurrection narratives of the Hebrew Canon. However, the elements I identify in a Prophetic resurrection topos assert themselves as well.

4.1.4.1 *Motifs of Resurrection*
A sense of intense pain dominates the opening lines of this artful narrative. The author emphasizes this pain through a repetition of the boy's complaint – 'Oh my head, my head' (v. 19) – producing a 'mental stammer' that sends pain palpitating throughout this initial description.[49] So intense is the pain, in fact, that a servant must carry the boy to his mother, where he soon dies (v. 20).

The woman travels to the prophet, who has demonstrated divine power to her previously in his accurate prophecy that she will have a son (vv. 8-17). Now her first words implicate the prophet in the boy's death: 'Did I ask my lord for a son? Did I not say, "Do not mislead me?"' (v. 28). Once again, the death of a child has *broken the trust* that a parent previously held in a divine representative.

Verses 31 and 32 reassert the theme of *death* initially introduced in v. 20: the child has not awakened, but instead shows 'no sound or sign of life' lying 'dead on his bed'. In fact, he has lain in this condition throughout his mother's ten- to twenty-mile trek from Shunem up Mount Carmel and back again. Death is once more presented in unambiguous terms. Nevertheless, the boy *resurrects*, as demonstrated through a process of becoming warm (v. 34), sneezing seven times (v. 35), and opening his eyes (v. 35).

When Elisha returns the resurrected boy to the mother, she neither

---

48. On the 'striking similarities' between this text at 1 Kgs 17.17-24, see Mordechai Cogan, *1 Kings* (AB 10; New York: Doubleday, 2000), pp. 432–3.
49. See Robert Alter, *Art of Biblical Narrative* (New York: Basic Books, 1981), p. 92; Wire, *Holy Lives*, p. 93.

marvels at the event nor offers praise to YHWH. The focus, rather, is upon the *reestablishment of communion* with the prophet as an agent of the divine: 'She came and fell at his feet, bowing to the ground; then she took her son and left' (v. 37). Such a pointed summary statement accentuates the overriding purpose of the narrative to 'establish [Elisha's] authority as a prophet of YHWH'.[50]

4.1.4.2 *The Function and Placement of the Resurrection Theme*
The narrative functions neither as part of the introduction of Elisha, who has been introduced several chapters earlier (1 Kings 19), nor as a climax in the sequence of events. Elisha performs many miracles in 2 Kings 2–13, including a cluster of deeds that extends from 2 Kgs 2.1 through 2 Kgs 8.15. There are four miracles in 2 Kings 4, of which this resurrection is simply the second.

4.1.4.3 *Conclusion*
A sense of throbbing pain dominates the opening of the narrative (2 Kgs 4.18-19), prefacing a presentation of *death* (4.20) that is quite unambiguous (vv. 31-32). This death leads to a *breach of trust* in which the source of divine power is implicated (v. 28). However, as a result of the boy's *resurrection* (vv. 33-35), the prophet's authority as divine medium is *reestablished* (v. 37). This narrative has three key characteristics that are distinct from resurrection narratives in the epic tradition. First, the account does not signal an apparently significant point in the story. Second, there is no emotive-reactive crowd present. Third and perhaps most importantly, death is presented in unqualified terms.

4.1.5 *The Resurrection Theme in Other Hebrew Bible Texts*
Although I do not claim that all treatments of resurrection are handled similarly throughout the Hebrew Canon, many other biblical texts present the themes of death and resurrection within a constellation of motifs similar to the four passages I have just highlighted. In Psalm 22, for example, there is an expression of a breach of trust that implicates a divine source (e.g. Ps. 22.1-2: 'My God, my God, why have you forsaken me ...?') along with a theme of stark, unqualified death (22.14-18). YHWH engenders resurrection (22.19-21, 29), leading to a reestablishment of YHWH's divine power (22.22-28, 30-31). The theme of resurrection also leads up to reestablishing communion with the divine in Psalm 16 (see esp. vv. 10-11) and Psalm 49 (see esp. v. 15), among others.[51]

---

50. Keith W. Whitelam, 'Elisha', *ABD* 2.472.

51. See also Isa. 53.10-12. Here, the fourth 'Servant Song' initiates themes of death and return which result from a violent act of YHWH: 'Yet it was the will of the LORD to crush him with pain.' The same verse then evokes a sense of death ('you make his life an offering

Apocalyptic literature in the canon, written during periods of intense persecution, also invokes the resurrection theme as a means of legitimizing their worship despite their circumstances. Sometime after the fall of Jerusalem, 'as the delay of Yahweh's victory became apparent to some of Isaiah's disciples',[52] a salvation oracle was incorporated into the Isaianic tradition which proclaimed that, despite the hopeless situation, Israel's 'dead shall live' and 'their corpses shall rise' (Isa. 26.19). The oracle is immediately preceded by an accusation directed at YHWH for inflicting pain, a breach of trust: 'Like a woman with child, who writhes and cries out in her pangs when she is near her time, so were we *because of you, O LORD* ...' (Isa. 26.17-18). Following the resurrection, YHWH acts to reestablish communion with the people: 'The LORD comes out from his place to punish the inhabitants of the earth for their iniquity ... the LORD with his cruel and great and strong sword will punish Leviathan ... On that day: A pleasant vineyard, sing about it! I, the LORD, am its keeper ...' (Isa. 26.21–27.3).

The twelfth chapter of Daniel describes a 'time of anguish such as has never occurred' (Dan. 12.1) of which YHWH is apparently aware, for YHWH has revealed it to his prophet. However, YHWH will eventually reestablish Israel's worship of the deity by extending divine actions even to those martyrs who will die in the anguish: 'many of those who sleep in the dust of the earth shall awake, some to everlasting life, and some to shame and everlasting contempt' (Dan. 12.2).[53]

4.1.6 *A Comparison of the Prophetic and Epic Topoi*
My review of these texts identifies one constellation of themes associated with the expression of resurrection within the traditions of the Hebrew Canon, which I am calling the Prophetic resurrection topos. In this section, I will compare these themes with the Epic resurrection topos that I have identified within Hellenistic and Homeric texts (see Chapter 3). Following this written summary, Table 8 charts the elements of the Prophetic resurrection topos, correlating the basic themes to specific

---

for sin') and return ('he shall see his offspring, and shall prolong his days') resulting in a 'knowledge' of YHWH's goodness (Isa. 53.11) that is akin to the 'knowledge' asserted in Hos. 6.3, Ezek. 37.13-14, and 1 Kgs 7.24.

In Job 19.20-29, treatment of these themes also begins with a *breach of trust* on the part of YHWH: 'Have pity on me, have pity on me, O you my friends, for the hand of God has touched me! Why do you, like God, pursue me, never satisfied with my flesh?' (vv. 21-22). Yet, the author declares, 'after my skin has been thus destroyed [*death*], then in my flesh I shall see God [*resurrection*], whom I shall see on my side, and my eyes shall behold, and not another' [*reestablishment*] (vv. 26-27).

52. Millar, 'Isaiah 24–27', *ABD* 3.490.
53. See John J. Collins, *Daniel*, pp. 29–38.

verses in each of the four texts analyzed in this chapter as well as the text of Psalm 22.

In the Hebrew Canon, resurrection narratives *often present the theme of death in stark, absolute terms*. Such a presentation furthers what seems to be the overarching purpose of the themes overall, reestablishing a source of power. In this context, the themes describe the divine power as sufficient to raise even those who are in some sense – either metaphorically or in actuality – absolutely dead. The Hebrew texts do not qualify the nature of the death at the level of internal narrative or dialogue, as the texts of the Greco-Roman tradition do: Andromache is distraught '*even to death*' and Callirhoë has the '*appearance of* death' (see Table 7). Death in the Hebrew Canon, in comparison, is as stark as 'very dry' bones (Ezek. 37.2) and bodies that lie 'dead on the bed' (2 Kgs 4.32).

An expression of *a breach of trust between a source of divine power and adherents* is another recurring theme that accompanies the themes of death and resurrection throughout the Hebrew Canon. This breach of trust often relates directly to the theme of death – the adherent loses faith because the divine power or agent of divine power is thought to have inflicted or allowed death. In fact, *the narratives often directly implicate the divinity as instrumental in death*.

The breach of trust also relates directly to the theme of resurrection: *trust is regained once the prophet or YHWH reverses the effects of death through resurrection*. Like the Epic resurrection topos, the theme of resurrection produces a type of enlightenment. In the Prophetic resurrection topos, however, the enlightenment is specific and lasting: resurrection informs the adherent of the divinity's goodness and reestablishes trust in the divinity.

Two of the themes that are frequently found in an Epic resurrection topos are not noticeably operative in texts of resurrection within the Hebrew Canon. First, in ancient Greek texts, confusion results from either a direct physical wound or some unexpected news. This confusion manifests itself as a lack of knowledge or physical aimlessness (see Table 7). The emphasis in the Hebrew Canon, however, is upon *a physical wound without a concomitant manifestation as confusion*.[54] Second, in Hebrew Bible texts *the presence of the crowd does not occur alongside the theme of*

---

54. Note that in Ezekiel 37, the bones are not 'scattered' as though to convey a sense of confusion, but simply lying (37.2). Leslie C. Allen's translation of על־פני הבקעה as 'strewn over the plain' is unwarranted (*Ezekiel 20-48* [WBC 29; Waco, Texas: Word, 1982], p. 181). The preposition על־פני occurs 135 times throughout the Hebrew Bible as a standard preposition of location ('on'). The words occur in contexts of order as well as disorder (e.g. Gen. 7.3).

resurrection.[55] Homeric texts of resurrection often incorporate a crowd as an expression of the reintegration of the resurrected one into society. Hellenistic novelistic resurrection narratives very regularly employ the crowd as a means of heightening the emotions an author would attribute to the event. In most resurrection texts of the Hebrew Bible, however, the crowd is either not present or their reaction receives no treatment.

Finally, three points related to the broader context of writings of the Hebrew Canon are also significant for a comparison of these topoi. First, the Prophetic resurrection topos is distinct in its theological application which advances from theodicy to legitimization, functioning as a reestablishment of a communion with YHWH. Second, *the resurrection theme does not regularly serve to highlight strategic points in narrative structure.*[56] The theme serves as simply one expression of divine power among many. In contrast, epic resurrection narratives move more generally from confusion to enlightenment. Within their broader context, these texts serve to accentuate the introduction of a major character, a turning point, or the climax of the story, often associating a character with a particular deity or divine influence in general. And third, themes of death and revival in Hebrew Bible texts are rare in comparison to the epic tradition.[57]

I have summarized my findings regarding the Prophetic resurrection topos in Table 8.

4.1.7 *Conclusion*

The theme of resurrection in the Hebrew Bible often finds expression through a constellation of similar motifs. This pattern may evolve as the result of the influence of the 'Classical' prophet Hosea, whose leadership of the community in a time of despair and exile provided a model of hope for future prophets and writers. Although I do not claim that all treatments of resurrection were handled similarly in ancient Hebrew culture, my identification of the constellation does incorporate the primary expressions of resurrection in the Hebrew Canon, providing points of comparison that will prove illuminating for my reading of Hellenistic Jewish literature in the next section and the Gospel of Mark in Chapter 5.

55. A few expressions of the resurrection theme do incorporate what might be read as crowds. The emphasis in their inclusion lies not in the emotion they exhibit, as much as in the witness they provide. See, for example, Ps. 22.22-31.

56. The exception in the resurrection narrative at 1 Kgs 17.17-24 is unusual: it serves as the climax of the introduction of Elijah to the plot.

57. See Chapter 3 for a survey of these themes in the epic tradition.

TABLE 8: Resurrection Motifs in the Hebrew Canon				
Text	**Breach**	**Stark Death**	**Resurrection**	**Reestablishment**
Hos. 6.1-3	It is he who has torn... he has struck down. (Hos. 6.1)	He... has torn, ...he has struck. (Hos. 6.1)	He will revive us... he will raise us up, that we may live before him. (Hos. 6.2)	Press on to know YHWH. (Hos. 6.3)
Ezek. 37.1-14	Our hope is lost; we are cut off completely. (Ezek 37.11)	And they [the bones] were very dry. (Ezek 37.1-2)	The breath came into them, and they lived, and stood on their feet, a vast multitude. (Ezek 37.10)	You shall know that I am the LORD,... you shall know that I, the LORD, have spoken and will act. (Ezek 37.13-14)
1 Kgs 17.17-24	She then said to Elijah, "What have you against me, O man of God?" (1 Kgs 17.18)	"You have come to... cause the death of my son!" He cried out to the Lord, "O Lord my God, have you brought calamity... by killing her son?" (1 Kgs 17.19-20)	The life of the child came into him again, and he revived. (1 Kgs 17.22)	"Now I know that you are a man of God, and that the word of the Lord in your mouth is truth." (1 Kgs 17.24)
2 Kgs 4.18-37	Then she said, "Did I ask my lord for a son? Did I not say, Do not mislead me?" (2 Kgs 4.28)	He carried him and brought him to his mother; the child sat on her lap until noon, and he died... there was no sound or sign of life.... When Elisha came into the house, he saw the child lying dead on his bed (2 Kgs 4.31-32)	... He got up on the bed and lay upon the child, putting his mouth upon his mouth, his eyes upon his eyes, and his hands upon his hands; and while he lay bent over him, the flesh of the child became warm. He got down, walked once to and fro in the room, then got up again and bent over him; the child sneezed seven times, and the child opened his eyes. (2 Kgs 4.33-35)	She came and fell at his feet, bowing to the ground. (2 Kgs 4.37)
Ps. 22.1-31	My God, my God, why have you forsaken me? (Ps. 22.1)	I am poured out like water, and all my bones are out of joint; my heart is like wax; it is melted within my breast; my mouth is dried up like a potsherd, and my tongue sticks to my jaws; you lay me in the dust of death. (Ps. 22.14-15)	To him, indeed, shall all who sleep in the earth bow down; before him shall bow all who go down to the dust, and I shall live for him. (Ps. 22.29)	... You have rescued me. I will tell of your name to my brothers and sisters; in the midst of the congregation I will praise you.... Posterity will serve him.... (Ps. 22.21-22, 30)

4.2 *Resurrection Themes in the Literature of Hellenistic Judaism*

The conquests of Alexander the Great initiated a spread of Greek culture that dominated the Eastern Mediterranean from the fourth century B.C.E. to the early Byzantine period.[58] Novelistic Jewish literature manifests the effects of this Hellenization. Apparently, Hellenistic Jewish storytellers

---

58. Recent studies are numerous. Among them, see John Pairman Brown, *Ancient Israel and Ancient Greece*; Pieter W. van der Horst, *Japheth in the Tents of Shem: Studies on Jewish Hellenism in Antiquity* (CBET, 32; Sterling, Vir.: Peeters, 2002); Carsten Claussen, *Versammlung, Gemeinde, Synagoge: Das hellenistisch-jüdische Umfeld der frühchristlichen Gemeinden* (SUNT, 27; Göttingen: Vandenhoeck & Ruprecht, 2002); John J. Collins and Gregory E. Sterling, eds, *Hellenism in the Land of Israel* (CJA, 13; Notre Dame, Ind.: University of Notre Dame Press, 2001); Gruen, *Heritage and Hellenism*; Lee I. Levine, *Judaism and Hellenism in Antiquity: Conflict or Confluence?* (SLJS; Seattle: University of

assimilate aspects of Hebrew, Hellenistic, and other cultures, for a reading of resurrection narratives in extant Hellenistic Jewish literature illustrates this amalgamation. Both resurrection topoi – the Epic topos and the Prophetic topos – occur in novelistic Jewish literature of the Hellenistic period. In this section, I will read five novelistic Jewish texts that present resurrection narratives: *1 En.* 25.1-7, Tob. 8.9-18, Add. Est. 15.6-16, *Jos. Asen.* 9.1–17.6, and 2 Macc. 7.1-42. The reading from *1 Enoch* – an apocalyptic text without a significant display of novelistic traits – presents resurrection in the terms of the Prophetic topos. My reading of other, more novelistic texts, however, reveals a different presentation of resurrection. In these texts, characteristics of the Epic topos become dominant, though certain elements of the Prophetic topos remain.

4.2.1 1 Enoch *25.1-7 – An Apocalyptic Vision*

Apocalyptic literature flourished within early Jewish communities from around 250 B.C.E. to 250 C.E. During this time many people suffered as a result of the chaos that followed the death of Alexander the Great when rulers such as Antiochus IV Epiphanes, King of Seleucia from 175 to 164 B.C.E., forcibly imposed Hellenism in order to consolidate power despite efforts on the part of Jewish communities to preserve Judean religion and culture.[59] Robert R. Wilson describes the widely acknowledged relationship between apocalyptic literature and periods of persecution or trauma:

> Wars, famines, climatic changes, national economic reversals, and the shock of sudden cross-cultural contact can all lead to unusually widespread and severe feelings of deprivation. Not only do such periods of social upheaval produce political and social inequities that lead to genuine cases of deprivation, but crises such as wars and clashes with other cultures provide opportunities for people to compare their own situation with that of the outsiders. These comparisons may lead to feelings of relative deprivation and fuel social unrest. Times of social crisis frequently give rise to apocalyptic groups, for in such times feelings of deprivation are increased beyond tolerable levels ....[60]

Washington Press, 1998); Jacob Shevit and Yaacov Shevit, *Athens in Jerusalem: Classical Antiquity and Hellenism in the Making of the Modern Secular Jew* (trans. Chaya Naar and Niki Werner; Portland, Ore.: Littman Library of Jewish Civilization, 1997).

59. For a portrait of Antiochus IV, see 1 Macc. 1.10-64; 2 Macc. 4.7–5.27 as well as comments in Polybius, *Hist.* 26.1; Diodorus Siculus, *Bibl.* 29.32; and Livy, *Hist.* 41.20; and Othmar Keel, 'Die Kultischen Massnahmen Antiochus IV: Religionsverfolgung und/oder Reformversuch? Eine Skizze', in Othmar Keel (ed.), *Hellenismus und Judentum: Vier Studien zu Daniel 7 und zur Religionsnot unter Antiochus IV*, pp. 87–121.

60. Robert R. Wilson, 'The Biblical Roots of Apocalyptic' in Amanat and Bernardsson (eds), *Imagining the End: Visions of Apocalypse from the Ancient Middle East to Modern*

Sustained, intense feelings of deprivation that characterized the troubled times experienced in the region of Judea renewed a general sense that any basis for trust in the divine had been breached. Apocalyptic writings attempted to reestablish the worship of YHWH in the face of this intense persecution and even martyrdom through the assertion of eventual divine revenge upon the enemy, a cataclysmic end of the world, and occasionally through the promise of bodily resurrection.

The first 36 chapters of *1 Enoch*, also known as *The Book of Watchers*, are quintessentially apocalyptic. Many scholars believe that the traditions represented in these chapters extend a hope for resurrection to victims in the conflicts of the Diadochi (323–302 B.C.E.). Scribes later gathered these traditions into the literary unit of *1 Enoch* 1–36, perhaps in an attempt to provide encouragement to the inhabitants of Judea who suffered in the Seleucid-Ptolemaic fight for hegemony in this region during the first half of the third century B.C.E.[61] Perhaps it is due to this early date that elements of the Prophetic topos dominate the presentation of the resurrection theme in this text.

4.2.1.1 *Motifs of Resurrection*

In *1 Enoch*, motifs of resurrection extend from ch. 9 through ch. 25.[62] The *Book of Watchers* opens with an introductory prophecy by the righteous patriarch Enoch (cf. Gen. 5.18-24) who proclaims revelations of judgment on the basis of visions that are interpreted by angels (*1 Enoch* 1–5). A prophetic interpretation of portions of Genesis follows. YHWH will allow fallen angels to corrupt humanity (*1 En.* 6–11; cf. Gen. 6.1-4). Despite the faithful cries of humanity, however, YHWH fails to respond, resulting in a *breach of trust*:

> [10] ... [T]hose who have died will bring their suit up to the gate of heaven. Their groaning has ascended (into heaven), but they could not get out from before the face of the oppression that is being wrought on earth. [11] And you know everything (even) before it came to existence, and you see (this thing) (but) you do not tell us what is proper for us

America, p. 59. An extensive bibliography is included on pp. 393–405 of this volume. See also Paul D. Hanson, 'Apocalypses and Apocalypticism', *ABD* 1.280 as well as David Seed (ed.), *Imagining Apocalypse: Studies in Cultural Crisis*.

61.   This idea, originally argued by George W.E. Nickelsburg in his article, 'Apocalyptic and Myth in *1 Enoch* 6–11', (*JBL* 96 [1977], p. 389), and reasserted in his recent commentary on this text (*1 Enoch* [Hermeneia; 2 vols; Minneapolis: Fortress, 2001], p. 25), has been recently reaffirmed in John J. Collins, *Apocalyptic Imagination* (BRS; Grand Rapids, Mich. and Cambridge, Engl.: Eerdmans; Livonia, Mich.: Dove, 2nd edn, 1998), pp. 49–51 and Larry R. Helyer, *Exploring Jewish Literature of the Second Temple Period: A Guide for New Testament Students* (CCBS; Downers Grove, Ill.: InterVarsity Press, 2002), p. 85.

62.   See Nickelburg, *1 Enoch*, 1.213.

that we may do regarding it.

(1 En. 9.10-11)

Even though the 'groaning' of these righteous sufferers has 'ascended into heaven', they still 'could not get out before the face of the oppression' (v. 10). The lawsuit that the dead ones bring up to heaven directly implicates YHWH, who 'knows everything before' yet does not help out the people (v. 11).

Following this prophecy, Enoch ascends to the heavenly throne room, where the oracle announces YHWH's punishment of the behavior of the fallen angels (*1 Enoch* 12–16). From there, the archangel Uriel guides Enoch to the west, to the place of the punishment of the fallen angels (chs 17–19). Next, seven archangels accompany Enoch eastward (ch. 20), passing once more the place where the angels are punished (ch. 21) and continuing onward to two mountains. One mountain holds the souls of the *dead* until the eschaton (ch. 22).[63] Another mountain houses the Tree of Life until the restoration of Jerusalem (chs 24–26; cf. Gen. 2.4–3.24). The angel Michael explains to Enoch that, at that restoration, the fragrance of this holy tree will *resurrect* the souls of the righteous dead to their embodied selves:

> [1] And he (the angel Michael) said unto me, Enoch, 'What is it that you are asking me concerning the fragrance of this tree and you are so inquisitive about?' [2] At that moment, I answered, saying, 'I am desirous of knowing everything, but specially about this thing.' [3] He answered, saying, 'This tall mountain which you saw whose summit resembles the throne of God is (indeed) his throne, on which the Holy and Great Lord of Glory, the Eternal King, will sit when he descends to visit the earth with goodness. [4] And as for this fragrant tree, not a single human being has the authority to touch it until the great judgment, when he shall take vengeance on all and conclude (everything) forever. [5] This is for the righteous and the pious. And the elect will be presented with its fruit for life. He will plant it in the direction of the northeast, upon the holy place – in the direction of the house of the Lord, the Eternal King. [6] Then they shall be glad and rejoice in gladness, and they shall enter into the holy (place); its fragrance shall (penetrate) their bones, long life will they live on earth, such as your fathers lived in their days.'

(1 En. 25.1-6 [E. Isaac, OTP])

Immediately following this resurrection, worship of YHWH is once again reestablished. Despite the persecution, Enoch models the praise that is ultimately due YHWH:

> [7] At that moment, I blessed the God of Glory, the Eternal King, for he

---

63. See Nickelsburg, *1 Enoch*, 306.

has prepared such things for the righteous people, as he had created (them) and given it to them.

(*1 En.* 25.7 [E. Isaac, *OTP*])

The reference to resurrection extends an assurance of salvation to any who would identify themselves as 'the righteous and the pious' (v. 5) yet who suffer for such an identity.

4.2.1.2 *Conclusion*

The reference to resurrection in *1 Enoch* follows the sequence of resurrection motifs that I identify in the Prophetic topos. A *breach of trust* that initially prompts the sequence is asserted in ch. 9 (*1 En.* 9.10-11) after which the prophet Enoch tours the habitations of the *dead* (ch. 22). *Resurrection* is explicit (*1 En.* 25.6), resulting in reestablished communion with YHWH (*1 En.* 25.7).

Three other indications also suggest the dominant influence of the Prophetic topos upon this resurrection. First, like earlier narratives of resurrection in the Hebrew Canon (e.g. Ezekiel 37), the presentation of death is stark, portraying the dead metaphorically as 'bones' (*1 En.* 25.6). Second, like Ezekiel 37 and other apocalyptic literature, the narrative functions to engender hope within an embattled community. Third, Nickelsburg's postulation that 'these chapters (22; 24.2–27.2) provide a scenario that was probably taken for granted by the author of Dan. 12.2' suggests the influence of a Prophetic topos similar to what I have previously suggested about resurrection in general and the tradition in Dan. 12.1-2 in particular.[64]

Furthermore, note in comparison that several key elements of the Epic topos are clearly lacking. First, a responsive crowd is not included in the narration. Second, the consideration of resurrection does not occur at a turning point, climax, or any other seemingly strategic point in the narrative. The angel guide does not mention the resurrection at the beginning of the short venture west (*1 Enoch* 17), at the beginning of the longer journey east (chs 20–21), at some climactic central turning point, or at the end of the journey (ch. 32). Instead, the author associates resurrection within a sequence of several trees – in Jerusalem (ch. 26), in a valley of judgment (ch. 27), in mountains to the east (ch. 28), etc. – that culminates with the 'beautiful and pleasant' tree of wisdom (*1 En.* 32.3-6). And, finally, there is no attempt to qualify the death under consideration.

4.2.2 *Tobit: The Resurrection of Tobias*

In four novelistic Jewish texts written between the second century B.C.E. and the first century C.E., a resurrection narrative occurs at a strategic

---

64. Nickelsburg, *1 Enoch*, 304. See also Section 5.1.4.

point in each story. The book of Tobit joined the Septuagintal tradition sometime in the early second century B.C.E.[65] At this date, certain incipient effects of Hellenization become manifest insofar as the story presents a combined form of resurrection narration. The Prophetic topos is at work within the book of Tobit to reestablish the worship of YHWH. However, the Epic topos dominates the overall presentation of the narrative.

The opening chapter of the book of Tobit sets the story within a historical context that resonates with the feelings of desperation so characteristic of the times. The Assyrians have driven the namesake of the text and his wife Anna from their kosher life in Galilee (Tob. 1.1-9) into a life of servitude in Gentile Nineveh (1.10-22). There the couple and their only son, Tobias, struggle to live according to the traditions and ordinances of their faith (2.1-8). When some well-aimed sparrow droppings produce blindness in Tobit, he is unable either to work or to perform righteous deeds (2.9-14), leaving him praying for a quick death (3.1-6).[66] 'On that same day', a young woman in Media named Sarah also prays for a quick death.[67] She suffers under the powers of the wicked demon Asmodeus who has killed seven of Sarah's husbands out of jealousy, each on the night of their wedding (3.1-15). In response to all these troubles, the Lord sends the angel Raphael to the aid of both Tobit and Sarah (3.16-17).

Raphael appears on the scene just as Tobit prepares to send his son on a journey from Nineveh to northeastern Media in order to obtain a substantial sum of money that Tobit has left with a friend there (4.1–5.3).[68] The angel, disguised as Azariah, a kinsman of Tobit, serves the necessary role of seasoned escort, and the journey begins (5.4–6.1a). Along the way, the two travelers catch a magical fish whose entrails ward off demons and heal the blind (6.1b-9). Then 'Azariah' tells Tobias about a mutual relative, Sarah, and her desire for a husband (6.10-16). Tobias also learns of the demon's jealousy and the power of the fish's entrails (6.17-18). When the two men come to Ecbatana, they meet Raguel and Edna, Sarah's parents (7.1-11). Despite the danger inherent in the action, Raguel gives Sarah to Tobias as wife (7.12-16). Tension mounts as the

---

65. See Table 1.

66. Themes of life and death mark a significant turning point here. Tobit's words in verse 6 ('Do not, O Lord, turn your face away from me') evoke Psalm 22.24 ('he did not hide his face from me, but heard when I cried to him' cf. 2 Chr. 30.9; Isa. 64.6), hinting at life despite the pleas of death. At this point in the story, 'the scene shifts from Nineveh to Ecbatana, from Tobit to Sarah' (Fitzmyer, *Tobit* [CEJL; New York and Berlin: de Gruyter, 2003], p. 148).

67. Throughout the narrative, temporal markers maintain the rapid narrative pace so typical of novelistic literature. See especially Tobit 2.12; 3.7, 10, 16; 4.1, et al. in light of Section 1.2.3.

68. See Section 1.4.1.

young couple enter their bedroom (8.1). Fish entrails are spread, and prayers are said (8.2-8). This key point of Sarah's story assumes the form of a resurrection narrative at Tob. 8.9-18.

4.2.2.1 *Motifs of Resurrection*

The narrative projects the resurrection themes in a manner comparable to the Homeric and Hellenistic narratives I have examined in Chapter 3, though the resemblance is not as strong as in other, later texts that I will consider below. All of the activity occurs within the *confusion* of dark night, including a group of servants carrying out Raguel's orders to dig Tobias' grave (v. 9). Such activity, as well as explicit comments by characters in the story, provoke images of *death*. Raguel states, '*it is possible* that he will die' (v. 11), and therefore makes plans for a quick burial '*if* he is dead' (v. 12). Note in particular how the death is *qualified* by explicit comments of a character within the story world of the narrative in a manner characteristic of the Epic topos.

With the lighting of a lamp comes the good news that – despite all expectations – Tobias lives (v. 14). The Greek text of Rahlfs' Septuagint presents this news of life in succinct terms: 'She announced to them, "He lives," and Raguel praised God' (ἀπήγγειλεν αὐτοῖς ὅτι ζῇ καὶ εὐλόγησεν Ραγουηλ τὸν θεόν[69]; vv. 14-15). This staccato declaration is comparable to several of the resurrection narratives in Chariton's novel, which also engage the Greek verb ζάω in similar declarations regarding the return of characters who are thought to be dead. Consider, for example, the interaction of the heroes of that novel following the resurrection of Chaereas at the central turning point of the novel: 'Chaereas himself stepped forward. Callirhoë, on seeing him, cried out, "Chaereas, are you alive?"' (Χαιρέα, ζῇς; *Callir*. 5.8.1).[70]

The final statement of the Tobit narrative asserts themes of *enlightenment* in terms comparable to the expression of confusion at the onset of the narrative. The dawn of day reverses the dark death of the opening (Tob. v. 18). Moreover, the servants who dug the grave now fill it in, empty, just as the sun rises. The scene closes with an image of a fresh patch of dirt visible by the light of the breaking day.

Throughout the progress of the narrative, servants participate as a *crowd* of witnesses. This function is most readily apparent in the figure of the maid, whose express purpose is to announce that Tobias is alive to the awaiting crowd (v. 14). Following the resurrection, the crowd emotes joy and praise: 'They blessed the God of heaven' (v. 15).

---

69. Rahlfs, *Septuaginta*.

70. See also the use of the verb ζάω in *Callir*. 1.8.4, 3.2.7, 3.4.15, 4.4.7, 4.5.8, 5.2.4, 5.6.10, 5.7.8, 7.5.5, 8.6.8 [2x], 8.7.7.

4.2.2.2 *Conclusion*

The elements of the text identified in this section of the study suggest the influence of the Epic topos of resurrection upon a Jewish text. All four elements of this topos are present. The narrative begins in confusion and progresses through themes of death and resurrection to enlightenment.[71] An emotive crowd is present. The resurrection occurs at a clearly strategic point in the narrative structure of the story: the plot line involving Sarah's demonization has come to an end; she now has a living husband. And the death in the narrative is highly qualified.

Yet elements of the Prophetic topos are also present. Raguel's suggestion that the demon may kill Tobias in v. 10 of ch. 8 implicates a failure on the part of YHWH, who may not protect the faithful young man. (After all, YHWH has failed to protect seven others [Tob. 3.1-15].) Then, once death is avoided and resurrection assured, communion with YHWH is reestablished, and Raguel sings praises (8.15-17). The text presents a combined form of resurrection narrative. The Prophetic topos is operative and reestablishes the worship of YHWH. However, the Epic topos dominates insofar as a crowd is operative, confusion is present, and the placement of the resurrection at a significant point in the narrative, and the element of death is distinctly qualified.

4.2.3 *Additions to Esther: Esther's Death and Revival*

When Lysimachus of Jerusalem translated Esther into Greek (Add. Esth. 11.1) some time in the second or first century B.C.E., he incorporated six additional sections (A–F) that enhance the Hebrew story with novelistic quality.[72] 'Thanks largely to Addition D', the introduction to this text in the *New Oxford Annotated Bible* states, 'the climax of the Greek version is reached when God miraculously changes to gentleness the king's 'fierce anger' at Esther's unannounced entrance.'[73] Lysimachus marks this climax with a resurrection narrative at Add. Esth. 15.6-16 (Addition D). This account bears a strong resemblance to the narrative that Chariton considers to be Callirhoë's first resurrection.[74] Like Callirhoë, Esther suffers a lifeless faint and a return to life at a pivotal moment in her relationship with the man who will become her husband. The narrative seems to draw primarily upon the Epic topos of resurrection. Nevertheless, elements of the Prophetic topos are present.

---

71. See Wills, *Jewish Novel*, pp. 68–92.
72. See Wills, *Jewish Novel*, pp. 93–131.
73. Mary Joan Winn Leith, introduction to *Esther* (The Greek Version Containing the Additional Chapters) in Michael D. Coogan, et al. (eds), *The New Oxford Annotated Bible*, p. 54 APOCRYPHA.
74. See Section 2.4.

4.2.3.1 *Motifs of Resurrection*

The king's appearance, both terrifying (v. 6) and splendid (v. 7), evokes *confusion* in Esther, causing her to falter. The theme of *death* arises as Esther turns pale, faints, and finally collapses (v. 7). Perhaps in imitation of the final resurrection climax of *The Odyssey* in which Odysseus springs to the aid of his fainting father, here the king jumps forward and takes Esther in his arms.[75] Although she initially revives (v. 8), she remains unable to speak for some time (vv. 8-11). Despite these several indications, *the theme of death is still not absolute.*

As Esther lies in her moribund state, the king proclaims life to her. 'You shall not die', he declares (v. 10). His comforting words bring Esther back to her senses (vv. 9-11). In fact, her first words may imply that – in death – she has had an encounter with the divine. She has seen an 'angel', full of 'glory' and 'grace' (vv. 13-14). Esther's vision also indicates that she has been *enlightened* regarding God's work of transformation on behalf of the king. She saw the king 'like an angel of God' whose 'countenance is full of grace' (vv. 13-14). His demeanor has been reversed from terrifying, fierce anger (vv. 6-7) to gentleness (v. 8), and as a result of her enlightenment, Esther is aware of the transformation of the king.

In the concluding line, a *crowd* of servants compassionately offers comfort, imbuing the closure of the scene with emotions of well-being (v. 16). This crowd plays the emotive role that characterizes an Epic topos of resurrection.

4.2.3.2 *Conclusion*

A common depiction of the lifeless faint of a woman in the presence of a desired man in both Esther's death and resurrection and the first resurrection of Callirhoë suggests that the Epic resurrection topos exerts an influence upon this text. Specific characters of the narrative support the conjecture. Esther's emotional state progresses from confusion (v. 6) to a theme of death which is qualified in such a way that dying and fainting are conflated in the passage (v. 7). Images of resurrection illustrate her enlightenment (vv. 10-14). At the conclusion of the scene, unlike resurrections of the prophetic tradition, the author incorporates an emotive crowd (v. 16). Furthermore, the resurrection serves as 'the climax of the Greek version'.[76]

Nevertheless, the presence of elements of the Prophetic topos is also manifest. Esther's speech implies that YHWH is the cause of her fainting death, for it is YHWH who changes the king's countenance (v. 8) so that she loses consciousness (v. 13). The divine is reestablished in that – despite the deadly terror YHWH's transformation of the king evokes – his face is

---

75. See Section 3.2.3.
76. Leith, p. 54 APOCRYPHA.

at the same instant 'full of grace' (v. 14). This passage, therefore, like the resurrection narrative in Tobit, seems to present a hybrid form of resurrection narration.

4.2.4 *2 Maccabees 7.1-43 – Active Reestablishment of Resurrection Hope*
Most likely during the reign of Alexander Janneus (103–76 B.C.E.), a redactor compiled Jason of Cyrene's five-volume history of the Maccabean uprising in Israel into a single book that is now known as 2 Maccabees (2 Macc. 2.23).[77] Jonathan A. Goldstein notes that both works – the extended history and its epitome – were originally composed as novelistic literature:

> The surviving fragments demonstrate that popular writers would play strongly upon the reader's emotions, with vivid portrayals of atrocities and heroism and with copious use of sensational language and rhetoric, especially when presenting the feelings of the characters . ... The writer of a Greek popular history was free to show where his sympathies lay, to give exaggerated statistics, and to include minute descriptions of tortures and to compose sensational speeches of martyrs which no witness could have survived to report.[78]

Within this novelistic history of the Judean people in the second century B.C.E., the author has included a dramatic resurrection narrative that demonstrates the combined influence of both Prophetic and Epic topoi in the Hellenistic period. However, unlike the previous two resurrection narratives I have analyzed, the Prophetic topos is dominant in this text.

4.2.4.1 *Motifs of Resurrection*
The seventh chapter of 2 Maccabees details the fabulous trial and martyrdom of seven Jewish brothers and their mother under Antiochus IV Epiphanes. Elements characteristic of the treatment of resurrection throughout the Hebrew Canon are present. The theme of a *breach of trust* underlies the situation as a whole, for 'the Lord God is watching' (2 Macc. 7.6) as seven faithful brothers and their mother who reared them in the faith are tortured to death (2 Macc. 7.1-6).

The first brother is faithful to the end, and dies as God looks on. Unlike the highly qualified presentation of death in the Epic topos of resurrection, the recurring *deaths* in this narrative are neither explicitly qualified nor expressed via metaphor – their presentation is vivid in sight, sound, and smell. Antiochus cuts off the scalp, hands, feet, and tongue of each of

---

77. See Jan Willem van Henten, *The Maccabean Martyrs as Saviours of the Jewish People: A Study of 2 and 4 Maccabees* (SJSJ, 57; New York and Leiden: Brill, 1997).
78. Jonathan A. Goldstein, *II Maccabees* (AB, 41A; New York: Doubleday, 1983), pp. 20–1.

[35] Vengeance is mine, and recompense,
　　for the time when their foot shall slip;
　　because the day of their calamity is at hand,
　　their doom comes swiftly.
[36] Indeed the LORD will vindicate his people,
**　　have compassion on his servants,**
　　when he sees that their power is gone,
　　neither bond nor free remaining.
[37] Then he will say: Where are their gods,
　　the rock in which they took refuge,
[38] who ate the fat of their sacrifices,
　　and drank the wine of their libations?
　　Let them rise up and help you,
　　let them be your protection!
[39] See now that I, even I, am he;
　　there is no god besides me.
I kill and I make alive;
I wound and I heal;
　　and no one can deliver from my hand.

[40] For I lift up my hand to heaven,
　　and swear: As I live forever,
[41] when I whet my flashing sword,
　　and my hand takes hold on judgment;
　　I will take vengeance on my adversaries,
　　and will repay those who hate me.
[42] I will make my arrows drunk with blood,
　　and my sword shall devour flesh—
　　with the blood of the slain and the captives,
　　from the long-haired enemy.
[43] Praise, O heavens, his people,
**　　worship him, all you gods!**
　　For he will avenge the blood of his children,
　　and take vengeance on his adversaries;
　　he will repay those who hate him,
　　and cleanse the land for his people.
(Deut. 32.35-43)

Figure 16　Deut. 32.35-43

the brothers (2 Macc. 7.4-5, 8, 10, 13, 15, 18, 39) and presumably the mother as well (7.41) before pan-frying them to death.

Themes of *resurrection* and *reestablished communion* arise as early as the death of the first brother, who quotes from a song of Moses (v. 6). The specific quote derives from Deut. 32.36 but, according to Goldstein, alludes to themes of the entire song, including the themes of resurrection and reestablishment[79] (see Figure 16).

Goldstein observes that – given this allusion – the Judean audience of 2 Maccabees 7 is led 'to imagine the martyrs as fixing their attention upon the promise in Deut 32 ... that God is always mindful of Israel ... (Deut. 32.15-30). God will take vengeance on the enemy (32.35, 41-43) for whom there is no escape (32.39), and [God] will resurrect and restore the maimed martyrs (32.39).'[80] Reestablished communion is manifest in the acclamations of the people (32.43), who witness to their belief that – despite YHWH's present actions – the deity is worthy of praise.

The final words of the second brother amplify these themes (2 Macc. 7.7-9). YHWH's legitimacy receives affirmation in the praise of this brother, which in turn explicitly affirms a resurrection to 'an everlasting renewal of life' (v. 9). During the final words of the third and fourth brothers, the physical nature of resurrection is explicated (2 Macc. 7.10-14). Through a graphically physical representation, the third brother claims that YHWH will restore even amputated body parts (v. 11). The fourth brother continues the progression by explicitly naming the source of their hope: 'resurrection to life!' (v. 14). In their praises, both brothers reestablish communion with YHWH.

79.　Goldstein, *II Maccabees*, p. 303.
80.　Goldstein, *II Maccabees*, p. 303.

This overarching 'sequence of ideas' progresses yet further in the events surrounding the death of the seventh brother.[81] Extensive proclamations by mother and son highlight ideas of physical resurrection (vv. 27-29) and divine vengeance (vv. 30-38). Even in his death, the last son to suffer establishes his communion with the 'almighty, all-seeing God' (v. 35).

4.2.4.2 *Conclusion*

This resurrection narrative in the Prophetic topos serves to defend divine goodness and justice in the midst of dire circumstances through motifs of a breach of trust and reestablished communion. This topos seems to dominate the narrative. No crowds are present or reactive – only the family, king, torturers, and YHWH receive mention. Also characteristic of the Prophetic topos, on the other hand, is the fact that the element of death in the narrative is not qualified, but rather presented in stark fullness. Moreover, the Epic motifs of confusion and enlightenment do not play a significant role. Rather than confusion, the victims manifest lucidity as they deal with their present situation and describe the resurrection future that awaits them throughout the narrative.[82] Nevertheless, one prominent characteristic leads me to conclude that Hellenistic influence is discernible even in this history of the Judean people: 'the account of the martyrs' deaths in 2 Macc. 6.18–7.42 is both the climax of the account of Antiochus' cruelty and the turning point of the historical drama'.[83] As with the previous resurrection narratives in the Hellenistic Jewish novels, the form of this narrative is a combination of the Prophetic and the Epic topoi.

4.2.5 *Joseph and Aseneth: Aseneth's Death and Return*

The fifth and final extended resurrection narrative I will consider from the Hellenistic Jewish novels also combines Prophetic and Epic topoi. However, unlike 2 Maccabees 7, this narrative is highly characteristic of the Epic topos despite the particularly biblical nature of its context. The resurrection occurs in the novelistic writing *Joseph and Aseneth*,[84] which

---

81. See Goldstein, *II Maccabees*, pp. 303–4.

82. Note, in particular, the description of the mother before her final speech (2 Macc. 7.21). The passage does not include confusion, as I have observed in the Epic resurrection topos. (Compare the analysis of *Od.* 5.423–6 and 436–7 in Section 3.2.1.2. See also *Il.* 5.110–20.)

83. George W.E. Nickelsburg, *Jewish Literature Between the Bible and the Mishnah: A Historical and Literary Introduction* (Philadelphia: Fortress, 1981), p. 119.

84. Along with scholars Charles Burchard ('Joseph and Aseneth', *OTP* 2.180-181), Randall Chestnutt (*From Death to Life: Conversion in Joseph and Aseneth* [JSPSUP, 16; Sheffield, Engl.: Sheffield Academic, 1995], pp. 65–9), Edith M. Humphrey (*Joseph and Aseneth*, pp. 17–28), and Lawrence M. Wills (*AJN*, pp. 121–62), this study works from a longer text-type of the novel, assuming this version to be earlier than a shorter version

develops the biblical story of Joseph, the beloved son of Jacob (Genesis 37–50; introduced in *Jos. Asen.* 1.1-3) to include his courtship of and marriage to a beautiful Egyptian woman, Aseneth (introduced in 1.4-14).[85] Aseneth dwells securely at the top of a private tower on her father's estate, 'where her virginity was being fostered' (2.12; cf. 2.1-20).[86] Heroine and hero first meet each other as Joseph visits the household for dinner (3.1–8.2). When Aseneth spies Joseph arriving on his chariot, 'her soul [is] crushed, and her knees [are] paralyzed, and her entire body tremble[s], and she [is] filled with great fear' (6.1).[87] Joseph also eyes Aseneth, but one thing stands between the two lovers: Aseneth must convert to Judaism (8.3-11). Her eventual conversion is a strategic turning point in the narrative structure that the author highlights through themes of death and a return to life.

4.2.5.1 *Motifs of Resurrection*

After their initial meeting, Joseph leaves for the evening and Aseneth 'retires in *confusion*'[88]: [9.1] And Aseneth rejoiced exceedingly ... and fell on her bed exhausted,[89] because in her there was joy and distress and much fear and trembling and continuous sweating ... (*Jos. Asen.* 9.1 [Wills, *AJN*]).

Although she retires alone, the narrator asserts the presence of a reactive *crowd* through a group of attendants that are attentive to her desperate situation. This crowd and its presentation are comparable to the crowd present at Callirhoë's first resurrection (*Callir.* 1.1.14–16):

> [10.5] Closing the door firmly behind her and securing the iron bolt, she [Aseneth] groaned and wept bitterly. [6] Now one of the virgins, whom Aseneth loved more than all the virgins[90] and had adopted as a sister,

---

witnessed in certain manuscripts. Ross Shepard Kraemer has recently argued that Marc Philonenko's shorter text-type (*Joseph et Aséneth: Introduction Texte Critique Traduction et Notes* [SPB, 13; New York and Leiden: Brill, 1968]), which she dates to the third or fourth centuries CE, is earlier (Kraemer, *When Aseneth Met Joseph*, pp. 6–9; Kraemer, 'The Book of Aseneth' in Schüssler Fiorenza [ed.], *Searching the Scriptures, Volume Two: A Feminist Commentary*, pp. 859–63). Note, however, Humphrey's assessment of Kraemer's work (*Joseph and Aseneth*, pp. 17–28).

85.   The introduction identifies Aseneth as the most beautiful woman in the region (1.6) in a manner similar to Chariton's introduction of Callirhoë (*Callir.* 1.1.2).

86.   On the centrality of virginity in Greek romance novels, see Reardon, 'General Introduction', in *CAGN*, p. 2.

87.   The parallels to the Greek novels are manifest. See, as a sampling, *Callir.* 1.1.14, 4.1.9, et al.; *Eph. Tale* 1.3.1; *Golden Ass* 5.22.3; etc. The expression parallels the Homeric λύτο γούνατα καὶ φίλον ἦτορ (see Ch. 2, n. 108.).

88.   Charles Burchard summarizes the first two sentences of *Jos. Asen.* 9 (ital. mine). See *OTP* 2.214.

89.   As Callirhoë (*Callir.* 1.1.14).

90.   'Aseneth has a favorite slave just as Callirhoë (*Callir.* 1.4.1 etc.)' (*OTP* 2.215, n. 10j).

heard the groaning and immediately woke the others. They came to Aseneth's door but found it closed. [7] Hearing her moaning and weeping, they called out, 'What is wrong, mistress? Why do you sound so ill? Is something troubling you? Open the door so that we may see what is wrong!' [8] 'My head is throbbing with pain,' answered Aseneth through the closed door, 'and I must lie quiet in my bed. I am not strong enough to rise and open the door, my body is so weak. But go, each of you, back to your rooms and rest, and allow me to lie quietly.'

(*Jos. Asen.* 10.5–8 [Wills, *AJN*])

Burchard translates the inquiry of the crowd as follows: 'What have you, mistress, and why do you *feel so sad,* and *what is it that is bothering you?'* (*Jos. Asen.* 10.7).[91] Through their questions, the crowd reasserts and thereby strengthens the emotions that accompany the scene, a traditionally epic role of the crowd in resurrection narratives.

In addition to these references to a general malaise of body (10.8; cf. *Callir.* 1.1.14), the intensity of Aseneth's ritual of conversion evokes images of *death* and burial:

[10.18] At daybreak, when Aseneth got up, she saw that a great pool of mud had formed from her tears and the ashes. [19] Falling on her face again in the ashes, she remained there until nightfall. [20] In the same way she passed the next seven days; she did not eat bread or drink water in the seven days. [11.1] But when dawn came on the eighth day, the birds were singing and the dogs barking at passersby. Exhausted and spent from her fast of seven days, Aseneth was barely able to lift her head from where she was lying amid the ashes on the floor ....

(*Jos. Asen.* 10.18–11.1 [Wills, *AJN*])

More like a corpse than a living person, Aseneth lies in a muddy mixture (*Jos. Asen.* 10.18; 11.1) all night and all day (10.19–20) for more than a week (10.20; 11.1). Several extensive prayers sustain this conversion experience over hundreds of lines of verse (11.3–13.12). Throughout these penitential prayers, images of death arise frequently:

[12.8] O Lord, extend your hands to me as a benevolent father,
And snatch me up off the earth,
[9] For now a savage old lion is after me –
The father of the Egyptian gods –
And his children [are those who are driven mad by idols.
I despise them because they are children of the lion.]
[10] Their father, [the lion, is in a rage and pursuing me,]
But you, Lord, save me from his hands
And pluck me up from out of his mouth,
Lest he grasp me like a lion and rip me to pieces,

91. τί σοί ἐστι δέσποινα καί διά τί σὺ σκυθρωπάζεις καί τί ἐστι τὸ ἐνοχλοῦν σοι; For Burchard's translation, see *OTP* 2.215 (ital. mine).

> And throw me into a roaring flame,
> [And the fire throw me into the hurricane,
> And the hurricanes surround me with darkness,
> And cast me out into the depths of the sea.
> The eternal] sea monster will swallow me whole
> [And I shall perish for all time.
> Save me, lord, before all these things overtake me ....]
>
> (*Jos. Asen.* 12.8-10 [Wills, *AJN*])

Death is clearly present in metaphors of a ravaging lion (12.8-10) who will not only 'rip [Aseneth] to pieces' (12.10) but also threatens a series of other fatal events by which Aseneth will 'perish for all time' (12.10).[92]

As a result of her prayers, the 'chief of the angels' descends from heaven (14.1-7). His commands and exhortations evoke a theme of *resurrection*. First, he orders Aseneth to stand up from the mire in which she lies, to wash her hands and face with 'living water' (14.13), and to put on a new linen robe (14.8-17). He *enlightens* her regarding her resurrection:

> [15.3] Have courage, Aseneth, [chaste virgin]. Your name has been inscribed in the Book of Life [in heaven; at the very beginning of the book your name has been inscribed by my hand,] never to be erased. [4] From this day forth you shall be made new, reformed, given a new life (ἀναζωοποιήσας), eating [blessed] bread of life, drinking from the [blessed] cup of incorruptibility. [5] Have courage, Aseneth, [chaste virgin.] I have given you today as a bride to Joseph, and he shall be your groom forever ....
>
> (*Jos. Asen.* 15.3-5 [Wills, *AJN*])

The angel gives Aseneth a new life, an expression Charles Burchard translates 'made alive again' based on the Greek verb ἀναζωοποιέω present in the earliest (eleventh-twelfth century C.E.) Greek manuscript (A) of the Vatican Library, as well as several other ancient Greek manuscripts (P, F, W, B, D).[93]

Before the angel leaves, the author intensifies the sense of blessing through the return of the *crowd*. Aseneth desires to have her attendants present not only to witness this miracle and her marvelous transformation, but to receive a blessing from the mysterious man.

> [17.4] Aseneth said to the man, 'Lord, seven virgins, born on the same

---

92. The imagery of tearing is highly reminiscent of the metaphors regarding death in Hos. 6.1. See Section 4.1.1. See also *Jos. Asen.* 11.18; 13.8.

93. See *OTP* 2.226, n. 15i, as well as the translation. See also Philonenko, *Joseph et Aséneth*, p. 182, n. 10. The Greek text of the longest text-type is available on pp. 851–9 of Albert-Marie Denis, *Concordance grecque des pseudépigraphes d'Ancien Testament: Concordance, corpus des textes, indices* (Louvain-la-Neuve: Université Catholique de Louvain, 1987), though it lacks critical apparatus (available in part in Philonenko, *Joseph et Aséneth*, pp. 128–220).

[11.17b] Surely the Lord will be furious
If I call upon his holy name in my sins.
[18] What then is such a wretch as I to do?
I will dare to open my mouth to him
And call upon his name!
And even if the Lord **strikes** [πατάξει] me in his fury
Surely **he will heal** [ἰάσεται] me again,
And **if he chastises me with his whips,**
He will also **turn his face to me in his mercy.**
And if he is enraged over my sins,
He will be reconciled to me again and forgive
each one.

Therefore I will dare to open my mouth to
him.

(*Jos. Asen.* 11.17b-18 [Wills, *AJN*])

[1] Come, let us return to the LORD;
 for **it is he who has torn,**
 and **he will heal** [LXX: ἰάσεται] **us**;
 he has struck down [LXX: πατάξει],
 and **he will bind us up.**

[2] After two days **he will revive us**;
 on the third day he will raise us up,
 that we may live before him.

[3] **Let us know, let us press on to know the LORD;**
 his appearing is as sure as the dawn;
 he will come to us like the showers,
 like the spring rains that water the earth.

(Hos. 6.1-3)

Figure 17   YHWH Strikes and Restores

night as I, and raised with me from my youth, are here. They serve me, and I love them [as my sisters.] Allow me to call them so that you may bless them as you have me.' [5] 'Call them', he said. [6] So Aseneth called [the seven virgins and presented them to the man,] who blessed them and ... the man disappeared from before her eyes ....

(*Jos. Asen.* 17.4-6 [Wills, *AJN*])

True to the Epic topos, the presence of the crowd evokes emotions. In this narrative, they introduce not only sisterly love (17.4), but also the sense of blessing (17.6) to counter the intense death experience.

4.2.5.2 Conclusion

The presentation of Aseneth's confusion, the crowd, her resurrection and her enlightenment suggests that the Epic topos exerts significant influence upon the extended resurrection narrative that functions to mark a strategic point in the narrative structure of the story, the conversion of Aseneth.[94] However, this resurrection narrative also incorporates the Prophetic topos. The element of death at *Jos. Asen.* 12.8-10 is stark, presented in terms of a ravaging lion as at Hos. 6.1. Elsewhere, also, Aseneth's prayer of confession incorporates themes that parallel resurrection themes of the classic prophet Hosea (see Figure 17).

This brief segment of Aseneth's prayer describes the potential of a divine wrath (*Jos. Asen.* 11.17b) that may lead to the physical abuse of Aseneth (11.18). This imagery of YHWH's maltreatment and the subsequent healing closely parallel Hosea 6.1-3, suggesting that the Hosean text is appreciated for its theme of resurrection at the turn of the Common Era. Note that Aseneth's resurrection (*Jos. Asen.* 11.18) –

94. As with Chariton, the author of *Joseph and Aseneth* revels in the dramatic value of the resurrection event. Compare Ch. 3, n. 17.

anticipated by the parallel (Hosea 6.2) – is not as quickly asserted in *Joseph and Aseneth* as it is in Hosea. The novelistic author only declares reconciliation (*Jos. Asen.* 11.18), postponing resurrection until the resolution that arrives at the height of the conversion experience (15.4). So the Prophetic topos provides allusions here for the element of death alone, while the Epic topos seems to influence the placement as well as other elements of the resurrection narrative.

4.2.6 *Conclusion: Resurrection Themes in Jewish Apocalyptic and Novelistic Literature*

I have traced themes of death and a return to life in five Jewish texts from the Hellenistic period. Although the Prophetic topos identified in biblical texts predominates in the apocalyptic writings of *1 Enoch* (third century B.C.E.), the influence of the Epic topos is apparent in the resurrection narratives of Jewish texts from the Hellenistic period. Hybridity becomes a dominant characteristic as early as Tobit and the Additions to Esther, with the Epic topos giving shape to themes of death and raising in these texts. The apocalyptic setting of 2 Maccabees, which calls its readers to have faith in YHWH despite the abuses of Antiochus IV Epiphanes, may play a significant role in the prevalence of the Prophetic topos in chapter 7 of its story. Even the biblical retelling of Joseph is a hybrid of epic and biblical influences, with the Epic topos dominant.

4.3 *Conclusion*

A resurrection topos defined in large part by the classic prophet Hosea exerted an influence from the eighth century B.C.E. down through the biblical prophets and beyond, as evidenced in a rewritten story about *Joseph and Aseneth* from the first century C.E. However, with the advent of Hellenization, this topos most often operated in combination with a resurrection topos from the Epic tradition. Hybridity marks the texts. In fact, in most of the Hellenistic Jewish novels of this study, the Epic resurrection topos dominates.

As I will demonstrate in the next chapter, the Gospel of Mark fits into this literary context with remarkable ease. Although the biblical influence upon the Gospel is manifest – as I have demonstrated at the outset of this chapter – the resurrection topos that clearly dominates the Gospel is the Epic topos. These observations provide impetus for the study of this Gospel in relationship to novelistic literature based not only on Jewish novelistic literature, but also on novelistic literature for which Homeric tradition plays a prominent role.

Chapter 5

RESURRECTION IN THE GOSPEL OF MARK

Resurrection is a predominant motif in the Gospel of Mark, occurring at significant points throughout the narrative. The motif accentuates the irony of the Gospel by highlighting both the power of Jesus' ministry (Section 5.1) as well as the subsequent failure of his disciples as that failure is both assured (Sections 5.2) and realized (Section 5.3).[1] The occurrence of resurrection narratives at significant junctures in the story suggests the influence of the Epic topos. Also indicative of epic influence is the qualification of death in many of these narratives. Yet the influence of the Prophetic topos is manifest as well, as certain salient characteristics of these narratives indicate. The Gospel, like other Hellenistic novelistic literature, is a hybrid text. What is surprising in the case of Mark, however, is the dominant presence of elements of the Epic topos, suggesting that novelistic techniques based in the Homeric tradition significantly affected the telling of Mark's story.

5.1 *The Power of Jesus' Ministry*

With a style that is characteristic of Hellenistic novelistic literature, the events of Mark's Gospel begin *in medias res*.[2] John the Baptizer proclaims a baptism of repentance (Mk 1.1-8), which Jesus then receives in a show of glory (1.9-11). The introduction of Jesus may be compared with the introductions of Diomedes, Aeneas, Sarpedon, Odysseus, and others in which a divine sponsor rescues the hero from near death (1.12-13; see Section 3.2.1). Following this introduction, Jesus begins his ministry in Galilee (1.14-15), calling four disciples (1.16-20) as he heals and teaches many in the region (1.21-45). So extensive is the attention he attracts that a series of controversies develop between Jesus and the religious

---

1. See Theodore J. Weeden (*Traditions in Conflict* [Philadelphia: Fortress, 1971]), who reads the disciples as representative of enemies of the author; Elizabeth Struthers Malbon ('Texts and Contexts: Interpreting the Disciples in Mark', *Semeia* 62 [1993], pp. 81–102), who reads the disciples 'pastorally' as fallible but justifiable; and Robert M. Fowler (*Let the Reader*, pp. 73–80) and Mary A. Tolbert, who read the effect of the disciples as a function of their response to the main character (Tolbert, *Sowing*, p. 97, n.13).

2. See Section 1.5.1.; Ch.1, n. 158.

authorities of the area. They reject the 'new teaching' of this rabbi (1.27; see 2.22) and initiate a conspiracy against him (2.1–3.6).

Nevertheless, Jesus' popularity grows (3.7-12, et al.). He chooses 12 disciples, proclaiming that 'whoever does the will of God' (3.35) is part of his ministry (3.13-35). Before sending out his disciples, however, Jesus continues to demonstrate his ability to teach through a collection of parables that are all related to seeds and sowing (4.1-34; cf. Mk 1.22). He also continues to demonstrate his own power in a series of miracles which extends in the Gospel from the end of ch. 4 to the end of ch. 5. In just 50 verses, Jesus calms a storm at sea (4.35-41), heals a demoniac (5.1-20), cures a woman who suffers from chronic bleeding (5.25-34), and even raises Jairus' daughter from the dead (5.21-24, 35-43). Through these miracles, Mark's audience gains an appreciation of the extensive abilities of the central character of the story, who exerts authority not only over nature and sickness, but even over death itself. The narrative of the resurrection of Jairus' daughter is the first resurrection narrative of the Gospel.

The influence of the Epic topos is apparent in the placement of this resurrection narration as the fourth and final miracle in a sequence of four, accentuating the power of Jesus' ministry (Section 5.1.1). In fact, the elements of the Epic topos dominate the motifs in this resurrection, though elements of the Prophetic topos are also present, indicating the hybrid nature of the text (Section 5.1.2).

5.1.1 *The Function and Placement of the Resurrection Theme*

Scholars frequently identify two extended narrative units in the opening chapters of Mark's Gospel[3] (see Figure 18).

In the first unit (1.1–3.6), impressive teachings and miraculous events demonstrate Jesus' extraordinary power. A series of miracles produces results that are increasingly visible and tangible. Jesus heals some who are 'sick' and 'demon-possessed' (1.29-34). Then he heals the more manifest illness of leprosy (1.40-45), followed by the restoration of the legs of a man who could not walk (2.1-12) and the full restoration of a visibly 'withered' hand of another man (3.1-5). In the final miracle of the series, which Jesus describes as a case of life and death (3.4), he demonstrates his power over death (3.5).[4] However, despite this manifestation of power, a response of

---

3. Paul J. Achtemeier, 'Mark, Gospel of', *ABD* 4.546. See also Dennis C. Duling and Norman Perrin, *The New Testament: Proclamation and Parenesis, Myth and History* (Fort Worth: Harcourt Brace College, 3rd edn, 1994), pp. 306–8; Raymond E. Brown, *An Introduction to the New Testament* (ABRL; New York: Doubleday, 1997), pp. 128–35.

4. Though perhaps not as remarkable as the resurrection theme, stories in novelistic writing that convey hope for life over death frequently mark significant points. See Ch. 4, n. 66.

1. Jesus appears, preaching God's reign (1:1-3:6)
   A. John the Baptist appears; the story begins (1:1-8)
   B. Jesus introduced (1:9-15)
   C. Jesus' ministry begins; he chooses disciples (1:16-20)
   D. Jesus teaches and heals (1:21-45)
   E. Jesus rejected; conflict with religious authorities (2:1-3:6)
2. Jesus ministers in Galilee (3:7-6:6a)
   A. Jesus designates 12 (3:7-19)
   B. Jesus designates true followers (3:20-35)
   C. Jesus teaches in parables (4:1-34)
   D. Jesus performs mighty acts (4:35-5:43)
   E. Jesus rejected; conflict with his own (6:1-6a)

Figure 18   Achtemeier Outline, Mark 1–6

rejection concludes the unit. The Pharisees and Herodians conspire how they might kill him (3.6).[5]

Like the first unit, the second unit also describes impressive teachings and miraculous events that reveal Jesus' extraordinary power. And, once again, a series of miracles culminates with an exhibition of Jesus' power over life and death as Jesus raises Jairus' daughter from the dead (5.21-24, 35-43).[6] The resurrection narrative holds a strategic position as the final miracle in this second series. Yet again, however, Mark's hero encounters rejection – this time by people from his own hometown (6.1-6a).

A redactional-critical analysis of the story of raising Jairus' daughter suggests that the author has transformed a common tradition about Jesus into a resurrection narrative in order to accentuate this strategic point. The basic tradition, a healing of an official's child/slave, occurs in all four Gospels. Lawrence Wills notes an impressive list of similarities between the tradition in Jn 4.46-54 and in Mark's raising of Jairus' daughter.[7] This tradition also finds expression in the healing of the centurion's servant in Q (Mt. 8.5-13//Lk. 7.1-10). Below I have added my own summary of the Q material to the key elements that Wills identifies in John and Mark (see Figure 19).

In each healing, common elements occur in a consistent order: an official beseeches Jesus concerning an ailing servant or child; Jesus then responds by healing the sick person. Note how Mark intensifies the tradition by transforming the recovery – present in the concluding line of Matthew, Luke, and John – into a death that precedes the ultimate

---

5.   See also Brown, *Introduction*, p. 130, and Duling and Perrin, *New Testament*, p. 308. Tolbert identifies four healings and a controversy (Mk 1.16–2.12) followed by four controversies and a healing (2.13–3.6), forming 'a nice inclusio ... rounding out the whole section ...' (*Sowing*, p. 132; see also p. 311).

6.   In Tolbert's schema, the story regarding Jairus' daughter serves as the final narrative of a miracle before an extended repetition (6.1-34) encloses the material of a second major unit (3.7–6.34; see *Sowing*, p. 312, IIC2b4-IIC3).

7.   Wills, *Quest*, p. 83.

Mt. 8.5-13	Lk. 7.1-10	Jn 4.46-54	Mk 5.21-24, 35-43
centurion	centurion who built synagogue	royal official	Jairus, leader of the synagogue
beseeches Jesus	sends servant beseeching Jesus	beseeches Jesus	beseeches Jesus
concerning slave near death	concerning sick slave	concerning son near death	concerning daughter near death
Jesus: "I will come heal"	Jesus approaches	Jesus: "Your son lives"	
man: "I am not worthy"	man: "I am not worthy"	man believes	
Jesus: "Let it be"	Jesus: "Such faith!"	Jesus goes to son	Jesus goes to daughter
		as they are walking, servants come	as they are walking, people come
servant has recovered	servant has recovered	saying that he has recovered	*saying that she has died*

Figure 19   Mark Intensified the Tradition

healing (at Mk 5.41-42). This change transforms the healing story into a resurrection narrative that accentuates the completion of this second series of miracles.

The author also shapes this narrative as one of several 'intercalations', or insertions, which occur throughout Mark's Gospel.[8] This literary device splits a narrative into two halves (5.21-24 and 35-43), with a story about a woman who suffers from a hemorrhage inserted in the middle. The suspense engendered within this intercalation works together with the resurrection narrative to accentuate this strategic point of the structure of the Gospel.[9]

5.1.2 *Motifs of Resurrection*

The significant influence of the Epic topos is apparent not only in the placement of the resurrection narrative, but also in the elements of the narrative of Mk 5.21-24, 35-43. In this section I will demonstrate that although this narrative is hybrid insofar as both prophetic and epic elements exert characteristic influences, the Epic resurrection topos dominates. Specifically, I will note several functions that the crowds serve which are comparable to the function of crowds in the epic tradition and Hellenistic novelistic literature (Section 5.1.2.1). Also strikingly characteristic of the epic tradition is the highly qualified nature of the death in the account (Section 5.1.2.2). Novelistic characteristics of the resurrection proper not only outweigh characteristics of the Prophetic topos, but also suggest an authorial sensitivity to patterns similar to those of the Epic topos (Section 5.1.2.3). The only aspect of this resurrection narrative that suggests the influence of the Prophetic topos is an emphasis upon a transition from fear to faith. This overall progression in the narrative is comparable to the dynamics that accompany the transition from a breach of trust to reestablished communion (Section 5.1.2.4).

---

8.   See pp. 58–63 of John R. Donahue, *Are You the Christ? The Trial Narrative in the Gospel of Mark* (SBLDS 10; Missoula, Mont.: Scholars, 1973). See also Kermode, *Genesis of Secrecy*, 127–37. On intercalations in novelistic literature, see Ch.1, n. 174.

9.   The 'intercalation' that Roth (*Hebrew Gospel*, p. 38) reads in 2 Kings 4 may relate to the interaction of the woman to be healed with the servant Gehazi at the beginning and end of the narrative. However, there is not a shift of miracles comparable to the dramatic shift in Mark 5.

5.1.2.1 *The Crowd*

The transitional statement leading into the resurrection narrative incorporates the crowd as part of the initial portrayal of the scene (v. 21). Four other comments by the narrator further assert the presence of the crowd: once in the transition to the interlude regarding the bleeding woman (v. 24) and three times in the midst of her healing (vv. 27, 30, 31). The author repeatedly states that the crowd 'presses in' on Jesus (v. 24, 31), asserting their presence 'as an indication of popularity'[10] in a move that is highly characteristic of the epic tradition and Hellenistic novelistic literature.[11]

Jesus allows 'no one to follow him except Peter, James, and John' (v. 37), but once he arrives at the house for the resurrection, another crowd replaces the first crowd.[12] This crowd consists of mourners who cause a 'commotion ... weeping and wailing loudly' (v. 38).[13] Their commotion evokes Jesus' response that 'the child is not dead but sleeping', a response that the crowd in turn ridicules (vv. 39-40). As throughout novelistic literature, the author's use of the crowd 'focuses on the dramatic possibilities', providing a situation in which death can be qualified.[14]

In a third and final change of crowd, the author of Mark shows Jesus removing this crowd from the scene of the resurrection (v. 40). This final move is highly atypical for this Gospel: Jesus typically heals within and among crowds, as I have just shown regarding the healing of the bleeding woman.[15] Yet in resurrection narratives of the Prophetic topos, prophets such as Elijah and Elisha take the same action of clearing the resurrection scene, establishing an exclusive, indoor setting for the resurrection (1 Kgs 17.19; 2 Kgs 4.33).[16] The Prophetic topos accounts for this atypical setting

---

10. Ascough, 'Narrative', p. 76.

11. See Sections 1.3.2 and 2.4.10.

12. 'In the present setting', Robert A. Guelich comments, 'this action excludes the large crowd of 5.21, 24, 27, 32' (*Mark 1–8.26* [WBC 34A; Dallas: Word, 1989], p. 300).

13. Gustav Stählin argues for the distinctively Semitic nature of such a group, grossly overstating his case: 'the Orient was *always* the model for this type of utterance' (Gustav Stählin, κοπετός, κτλ., TDNT, 3.833 [ital. mine]). However, the Epic tradition includes acts of mourning with the same characteristics as those which are described in this Markan text. As I have noted in Section 2.4, the death of Andromache evokes a throng of mourning sisters and wives (*Il.* 22.473). In fact, after her resurrection, Andromache herself wails for her dead husband (22.477). At the death (and eventual resurrection) of Achilles, Thetis and a large crowd of goddesses utter shrill cries and 'beat their breasts' in lamentation (18.13–70). See Gail Holst-Warhaft, *Dangerous Voices: Women's Laments and Greek Literature* (New York and London: Routledge, 1992).

14. Lawrence M. Wills, 'The Depiction of Jews in Acts', *JBL* 110 (1991), p. 650.

15. Mk 5.21, 24, 27, 30, 31. See also Mk 1.33-34; 2.4; 3.9-10.

16. See Sections 4.1.3 and 4.1.4. Jesus withdraws from the crowd for the accomplishment of two other miracles in the Gospel of Mark: the healing of the deaf mute in the Decapolis (Mk 7.33) and the healing of a blind man at Bethsaida (8.23). Only in this resurrection scene, however, does Jesus dismiss the crowd *outside* so that he performs the miracle alone *inside*.

of isolation. Note, however, that this suggestion of isolation does not ultimately affect the narrative. Despite his formal action of dismissing the crowd, a truly emotive and reactive crowd remains. Unlike the resurrection stories of the Prophetic tradition, the parents are allowed to stay as well as some of Jesus' disciples.[17] 'The child's father and mother and those who were with him' – being Peter, James, and John – fill the interior space (Mk 5.40). In true epic fashion, the remaining crowd of observers functions as audience. They are demonstrably 'overcome with amazement' (v. 42) in response to Jesus' miracle.[18] The Prophetic topos and its characteristic isolation have been effectively overshadowed by the influence of epic and novelistic characteristics.

5.1.2.2 *Death*

My preceding redaction-critical analysis of this passage indicates that Mark transforms a tradition of healing into a resurrection narrative through the introduction of the element of death. He further develops this element by means of the messengers from Jairus' house (v. 35), the lamenting crowd (vv. 38, 39), and the prostrate positioning of the body (cf. vv. 39, 41), all of which suggest that the girl is dead. Notice, however, that the main character, Jesus, asserts the contrary: 'the child is not dead, but sleeping' (καθεύδει; v. 39). This specific euphemism for death indicates the influence of the Prophetic topos, in which 'sleeping' in the context of a stark death occurs repeatedly, as in the description of the boy who lies 'not yet awakened' (2 Kgs 4.31) as well as in the second verse of Daniel 12: 'Many of those who sleep (LXX: τῶν καθευδόντων) in the dust of the earth shall awake.' However, the stark terms which accompany the euphemism of sleep in the Prophetic topos ('dead on the bed'; 2 Kgs 4.31) are not found in this narrative. Rather, an accompanying statement by Jesus asserts that 'the child is not dead', a declaration that seems strangely counterproductive within a miracle that would demonstrate the powers of a prophet. The statement introduces an ambiguity into the narrative that has long puzzled Markan scholars.[19] Yet such an ambiguity is a salient

---

The specific setting inside of a building is highlighted in both of the resurrection narratives in 2 Kings. 'This sort of restriction of the audience for a miracle is attested ... elsewhere ... in the OT (1 Kgs 17.19; 2 Kgs 4.33)' (Marcus, *Mark 1–8*, pp. 370–1).

17. Guelich, *Mark 1–8.26*, p. 303.

18. See Ascough, 'Narrative', p. 74–6.

19. In the 1920s, Cuthbert H. Turner read the account as a resuscitation of a girl who had been in a coma (*A New Commentary on Holy Scripture* [ed. C. Gore, H.L. Goudge, A. Guillaume, London: SPCK, New York: Macmillan, n.d.; repr. as *The Gospel according to St. Mark* [London: SPCK, New York: Macmillan, 1928], p. 30). In the 1950s, C.E.B. Cranfield argued that the story is an account of the resurrection of a girl who is literally dead (Cranfield, *The Gospel according to Saint Mark: An Introduction and Commentary* [CGTS; New York and Cambridge, Engl.: Cambridge University Press, 1959], pp. 188–9). And, in the

characteristic of the element of death within the Epic topos. Just as Callirhoë is described as '*nearly* expired' (*Callir*. 1.1.14) or manifests the '*appearance* of death' (1.5.1), so here Jesus declares that 'the child is *not* dead', and is consequently laughed at by the crowd. The death is qualified, as the death element is throughout the Epic topos. Once again, characteristics of the Epic topos overshadow accompanying elements of the Prophetic topos.

5.1.2.3 *Resurrection*

Jesus calls the girl to rise, takes her by the hand, and she awakens (Mk 5.41-42).[20] In Robert Guelich's view, 'Jesus' taking the parents with him to the child, grasping her hand and directly commanding her to arise belies any direct influence of the OT stories on this account.'[21] Yet to conclude that these details belie any influence whatsoever – including indirect influence – would be to overstate the case, for as Guelich himself notes, 'The ... backdrop for this miracle lies in the stories of Elijah and Elisha .... Both Elijah and Elisha isolated themselves with the dead child [and] prayed for God's help.'[22] Rather, the Prophetic topos has been transformed by novelistic influences. These specific actions, though not a part of the prophetic tradition, emphasize physical action and direct address in the narrative in a manner that is characteristic of novelistic literature.[23]

The influence of the Epic topos may also be present in the phrasing of the resurrection event. In particular, some similar terminology describing Jesus' actions recurs three times throughout the Gospel, once in a narrative of healing (Mk 1.31) and twice in narratives about resurrection (5.41; 9.27) (see Figure 20).

---

same decade, Vincent Taylor's assessment of the text produced the most repeated though oxymoronic conclusion regarding the interpretation of this passage: 'It is clear that the saying is one of great ambiguity' (*The Gospel According to St. Mark: The Greek Text with Introduction, Notes, and Indexes* [London: Macmillan, 1952], p. 295). C.S. Mann concludes that 'Mark's text appears to be *almost deliberately ambiguous*' (*Mark* [AB, 27; New York: Doubleday, 1986], p. 287 [ital. mine]). See also William L. Lane, *The Gospel According to Mark: The English Text with Introduction, Exposition and Notes* (NICNT, 2; Grand Rapids, Mich.: Eerdmans, 1974), p. 196; Hugh Anderson, *The Gospel of Mark* (NCB; London: Oliphants, 1976), p. 155; and Joel Marcus, *Mark 1–8*, p. 371: 'a pregnant sentence that seem to run counter to the evidence of everyone's sense'.

20. The inclusion of the command to rise in Aramaic ('talitha cum'; Mark 5.41) does not suggest the influence of a Prophetic resurrection topos. Aramaic phrases occur repeatedly throughout the Gospel (3.17; 7.11, 34; 11.9-10; 14.36; 15.22, 34). The mingling of Aramaic and Greek within one text supports my contention that this hybrid text draws upon a variety of influences.

21. Guelich, *Mark 1–8.26*, p. 303.

22. Guelich, *Mark 1–8.26*, p. 303.

23. See Section 1.2.2.

1.31 καὶ προσελθὼν **ἤγειρεν** αὐτὴν **κρατήσας τῆς χειρός**· καὶ ἀφῆκεν αὐτὴν ὁ πυρετός....
5.41 καὶ **κρατήσας τῆς χειρὸς** τοῦ παιδίου λέγει αὐτῇ,... **ἔγειρε.** καὶ εὐθὺς **ἀνέστη**....
9.27 ὁ δὲ Ἰησοῦς **κρατήσας τῆς χειρὸς** αὐτοῦ   **ἤγειρεν** αὐτόν, καὶ **ἀνέστη**.

Figure 20   Raising Tradition I

These verbal parallels serve as a kind of 'linguistic scar ... physical evidence of the artistic skill involved'.[24] They indicate that this author is sensitive to literary patterns and the specific way in which those patterns are expressed.[25] The recurrence of specific literary phrases within resurrection narratives is a characteristic of the Epic topos, particularly reminiscent of the way in which Chariton associated Callirhoë's 'second resurrection' (*Callir.* 1.8.1) with that of her first (1.1.14–15).[26] Note in addition that these similar descriptions are not contained within a single pericope, but span the majority of the story, as Chariton's attention to the resurrection theme spans his story.[27] Such similarities suggest that the shape of Mark's story has been influenced by exposure to epic tradition, particularly as that tradition finds expression in novelistic literature.[28]

5.1.2.4 *The General Progression of the Narrative:*
Breach to Reestablished Communion

The transformation associated with resurrection in the prophetic tradition – a progression from a breach of trust to reestablished communion –

24. Conte, *Rhetoric of Imitation*, p. 62. See also E.J. Pryke, *Redactional Style, in the Marcan Gospel: A Study of Syntax and Vocabulary as Guides to Redaction in Mark* (New York: Cambridge University Press, 1978). p. 121; Peabody, *Mark as Composer*, p. 47 [Table 44]. The recurrent theme of 'fear versus faith' may provide another narrative link between the two texts: Compare the statement 'Do not be afraid; only believe' (Mk 5.36) with the following interaction: ' "If you can believe; all things are possible to him who believes ...." "I believe, help my unbelief" ' (9.23-24).

25. Other indications of an authorial sensitivity to literary patterns are found in the aforementioned series of controversies and miracles, the collection of parables about the ground, and the intercalated traditions, though Mark may have inherited some of these patternings from the tradition that precedes the Gospel. See Tolbert, *Sowing the Gospel*.

26. See Section 3.2.1.3, esp. Ch. 3, n. 47. In the Prophetic topos, I note the recurrence of a single word only. See Ch. 3, n.45.

27. As surveyed in Chapter Three, Chariton's primary resurrections occur in Books 1, 5 and 8. For a more detailed consideration of resurrection throughout Chariton's story, see Ch. 3, n. 17.

28. Given these similarities, a reader might expect major characters or the hero to undergo near death and a return to life at key points in the narrative, whereas in Mark seemingly minor characters die and are raised. In fact, the author of Mark seems to work with such an expectation on the part of the reader for characters such as Jairus' daughter are, in fact the major characters of the story. As Tolbert notes, 'after the three healings of Mk 5.1–43, the audience should have identified the Gospel group illustrating the good earth type as those who are healed' (*Sowing*, p. 181). In Mark, 'the nameless masses who [come] forth for healing [are] the human representatives of the fruitful ground of God's kingdom' (*Sowing*, p. 181).

resonates with the narrative presentation of the raising of Jairus' daughter.[29] The feature of this narrative that evokes the Prophetic topos is a breach of trust that parallels the resurrection narrative of the prophet Elisha (2 Kgs 4.18-37).[30] Just as Jairus approaches Jesus regarding his child (Mk 5.22-23), so in the Elisha narrative, a parent approaches a prophet regarding a child who is near death (2 Kgs 4.20-28). Both parental figures entrust their critical situation to the prophet. In the Jairus story, an extended series of events forestalls the response of the prophet (Mk 5.25-34), as in the prophetic narrative (2 Kgs 4.22-27). Once the response of the prophet is finally secured, the issue of a breach of trust immediately arises. In Mark 5, people from Jairus' home suggest that the leader has entrusted his child to Jesus in vain: 'Your daughter is dead. Why trouble the teacher any further?' (5.35).[31] Joel Marcus also notes the breach:

> Previously, when Jairus made his request for aid, there was still a basis for hope; now there seems to be none .... The time for emergency medical procedures is past; now it is time to call in the professional mourners. 'Why bother the teacher any more?' the messengers add cruelly. The girl's death thus challenges Jesus' credibility sharply: why, readers might wonder, has he been wasting his time on a woman whose illness was not life-threatening, thus allowing the life of the young girl to slip away? Is his sense of triage so amiss?[32]

The questions Marcus posits of the readers reflect the same frustration exhibited in texts such as 2 Kgs 4.28 when the parent proclaims, 'Did I ask my lord for a son? Did I not say, "Do not mislead me?"' (5.28).

Following the resurrection in the prophetic tradition of 2 Kings 4, the resultant theme of reestablishment is prominent: the parent 'came and fell at [the prophet's] feet, bowing to the ground' (Mk 5.37). In Mark, the sense of restored faith is not as blatant. Jairus neither declares that Jesus is a son of God (cf. 1 Kgs 17.24) nor even falls once more at Jesus' feet, as he does at the opening of the scene (Mk 5.22). However, three references in the text evoke a general sense of restored communion in terms of the Prophetic topos. First, Jesus' exhortation to 'believe' (5.36) is reminiscent

29. The name Jairus means 'he will enlighten' in Hebrew (see *HALAT* 1.24-25), suggesting the influence of the Epic topos and the typical progression from confusion to enlightenment. However, 'the problem is that ... the functions associated with the name Jairus would be more proper to Jesus', who enlightens Jairus, 'than to the synagogue leader' himself, enlightened though he may become (Donahue and Harrington, *Gospel*, p. 173). The specification of the name 'Jairus' does not seem to relate to themes of the Epic resurrection topos.

30. See Section 4.1.4.

31. Also, in both narratives the prophets isolate themselves with the child, pray for God's help, and heal through touch. According to Guelich, these similarities 'could hardly be overlooked by one familiar with the OT' (Guelich, *Mark*, p. 304).

32. Marcus, *Mark 1-8*, p. 370.

of other prophets involved with resurrection such as Hosea, who calls his people to believe in YHWH's reviving power (Hos. 6.3), and Ezekiel, who exhorts Israelites to have faith that dead bones will live again (Ezek. 37.12-13). Second, at the conclusion of the narrative everyone present is 'overcome with amazement' (Mk 5.42). This expression, ἐξέστησαν ἐκστάσει μεγάλῃ, derives from the prophetic tradition, occurring in the Septuagintal translations of 2 Kgs 4.13 as well as Ezek. 26.16, 27.35, and 32.10. The use of the expression here is particularly significant because this is the one and only time that Mark employs this phrase in his description of characters who are 'amazed' or who 'marvel', even though such a reaction occurs no less than 21 times in the story.[33] Third, although the conclusive command to 'give (the girl) something to eat' (Mk 5.43) may simply be a demonstration that the girl has been healed, such a display is unnecessary because Mark has already established the healing in the description of the child as walking (5.42).[34] Moreover, the specificity of this command – to eat – has prompted some scholars to refer to the action as an 'anomaly'[35] or to claim that the order 'has puzzled interpreters'.[36] Attention to the Prophetic topos is helpful in this regard. Note that the resurrection in 1 Kgs 17.17-24 is followed by a feeding miracle that emphasizes the provision of food (see 1 Kgs 18.1-46). Also, as I demonstrate in the columns below, a feeding miracle by Elisha following the resurrection of 2 Kgs 4.18-37 manifests multiple verbal parallels to Jesus' command following the resurrection of Jairus' daughter to 'give her something to eat' (Mk 5.43) (see Figure 21).

Following the resurrection narrative in 2 Kings 4, two instances of the verb 'to give' (δίδωμι) are followed by the verb 'to eat' (ἐσθίω, aor. ἔφαγον). So the final command to 'give her something to eat' in Mark's resurrection narrative echoes the closing of two prominent resurrection narratives in the Prophetic topos; yet under the dominant sway of the epic tradition this prophetic tradition is reduced to a single 'stroke of the brush'.

Despite these multiple indications of the influence of the Prophetic

33.   Elsewhere Mark employs the Greek verbs ἐκπλήσσω (1.22; 6.2; 7.37; 10.26; 11.18), (ἐκ)θαμβέομαι (1.27; 9.15; 10.24, 32; 14.33; 16.5), and θαυμάζω (5.20; 6.6; 12.17; 15.5, 44). Three times he uses the verb ἐξίστημι by itself (2.12; 3.21; 6.51), and once he employs the noun ἔκστασις with the verb ἔχω (16.8).

34.   'The order to give the girl something to eat is generally seen as a concluding element that provides unmistakable evidence of how effective the intervention has been, but the fact that the girl begins walking about immediately after getting out of bed could surely be seen as more than enough proof of that' (Bas M.F. van Iersel, *Mark: A Reader-Response Commentary* [JSNTSS, 164; trans. W.H. Bisscheroux; Sheffield, Engl.: Sheffield Academic, 1998], pp. 209–10).

35.   Guelich, *Mark*, p. 304.

36.   Donahue and Harrington, *Gospel*, p. 178.

| Mk 5.43 | // | 2 Kgs 4.42-44 |

καὶ εἶπεν **δοθῆναι** αὐτῇ **φαγεῖν**   καὶ εἶπεν **δότε** τῷ λαῷ καὶ **ἐσθιέτωσαν** 43 καὶ
εἶπεν ὁ λειτουργὸς αὐτοῦ τί **δῶ** τοῦτο ἐνώπιον
ἑκατὸν ἀνδρῶν καὶ εἶπεν **δὸς** τῷ λαῷ καὶ
ἐσθιέτωσαν ὅτι τάδε λέγει κύριος **φάγονται**
καὶ καταλείψουσιν 44 καὶ **ἔφαγον** καὶ κατέλιπον
κατὰ τὸ ῥῆμα κυρίου.

Figure 21   Something to Eat

topos, the text does not describe an obvious reconciliation between Jairus
and Jesus. Rather, Mark includes Jairus' response within the reaction of
an emotive crowd (Mk 5.40) which I identify as an element of the Epic
topos. Jairus' reestablished communion is obfuscated, illuminating further
influence of the Epic topos.[37]

5.1.3 Conclusion

Salient characteristics of the narrative of the raising of Jairus' daughter in
Mark 5, such as the working of a prophet in isolation and the qualified
expression of death, indicate the influence of both Prophetic and Epic
resurrection topoi. The Epic resurrection topos dominates the narrative.
In line with this tradition, the resurrection occurs at a strategic point in
the story, accentuating the power of Jesus' ministry. Also, three crowds
are operative, each employed for their value as a literary device: (1) to
indicate Jesus' popularity, (2) to prompt a key response, and (3) to
function as an audience. In addition, the element of death in the narrative
is qualified through Jesus' statement that the child is not dead in
combination with the mocking response of a crowd. Yet this resurrection
narrative also manifests the influence of the Prophetic resurrection topos,
in narrative events highly reminiscent of the story of Elisha (2 Kgs 4.17-
38) particularly involving a sense of trust betrayed (2 Kgs 4.28). Several
specific phrases and a transitional command at the end of the narrative
allude to resurrection narratives of the Prophetic topos, though the Epic
topos has weakened the portrayal of the reestablished communion (Mk
5.43). Overall, hybridity characterizes Mark's narration of the resurrection of Jairus' daughter such that the narrative is neither exclusively
'Jewish' nor 'Greek', but rather a Hellenistic amalgamation of resurrection traditions. Although the Epic topos is dominant, influences from
both topoi – the Epic and the Prophetic – operate within the narrative.

37. The obfuscation of this element may also serve Mark's purpose of contrasting Jesus'
humble disinterest in 'personal renown and glory' to the prideful ambitions of the disciples.
See Tolbert, *Sowing*, p. 227.

5.2 *The Failure of the Disciples Assured*

Having provided his disciples with significant teaching and demonstra-tions of authority, Jesus initiates a new phase of his ministry as he sends forth 12 disciples (Mk 6.7-13, 30-32). Mark accentuates the significance of this event by intercalating the sending with a narrative in which resurrection occurs as a primary theme: the resurrection of John the Baptist (6.14-29). Immediately following the sending of Jesus' disciples, the text informs us that the King of Judea, Herod himself, has heard the rumor that Jesus is John the Baptist 'raised from the dead' (6.14). Though other theories regarding the person and nature of Jesus also circulate (6.15), Herod's conclusion of the matter reasserts the resurrection theme: 'John the Baptist has been raised from the dead' (6.16). The association of the two prophets does not bode well for Jesus, because Herod had become so annoyed with John the Baptist that he eventually ordered the death of that prophet (6.17-28). As gruesome and horrific as the story is, a final note adds a glimmer of hope – at his death, John has left behind a generation of disciples who continue to care for his ministry and teaching (6.29).[38] The close proximity of this note to the return of Jesus' disciples (6.30-32) raises the question as to whether or not they will be so faithful, a question that receives a conclusive answer at the next significant point in the text that is also accentuated via themes of resurrection.

Once the teacher and disciples are reunited, Jesus continues to set the example, feeding the multitudes and performing miracles (6.33-56), teaching about the biblical law (7.1-23), and performing more miracles then feeding the multitudes once again (7.24–8.10).[39] Despite this ministry, both the Pharisees (8.11-13) and his own disciples (6.52; 7.18; 8.14-21) repeatedly misunderstand Jesus. Even though Jesus heals a blind man (8.22-26), explicitly teaches the disciples (8.27-9.1; 9.30-31), is transfigured before them (9.2-13), and raises a little boy from the dead (9.14-27), the disciples *still* do not understand (9.28-32). This final lack of understanding is particularly telling: clearly, the disciples are bound for failure.

Mark's text accentuates this significant turning point by setting the failure of the disciples within a context that is rife with references to resurrection. Following the mysterious transfiguration on the mountain (9.1-8), Jesus tells his disciples Peter, James, and John 'to tell no one about what they had seen, until after the Son of Man had *risen from the dead*. So they kept the matter to themselves, questioning what this *raising from the dead* could mean' (9.9-10). As they descend from the mountain, Jesus also makes some cryptic remarks which suggest that Elijah himself has in some

---

38.   The recurring image of a head on a platter contributes to the novelistic quality of the text. See Section 1.3.5.

39.   Here is another inclusio. See Tolbert, *Sowing*, p. 312.

3. Jesus and the disciples under way (6.7-8.21)
    A.   Jesus sends out 12; John is killed (6.7-29)
    B.   Jesus feeds and heals (6.30-56)
    C.   Jesus teaches about the Law (7.1-23)
    D.   Jesus heals and feeds (7.24-8.10)
    E.   Jesus misunderstood by disciples and Pharisees (8.11-21)
4. Jesus heals blind eyes; teachings on the life of discipleship (8.22-10.52)
    A.   Jesus heals blind eyes (8.22-26)
    B.   First Passion prediction and attendant events (8.27-9.29)
    C.   Second Passion prediction and attendant events (9.30-10.31)
    D.   Third Passion prediction and attendant events (10.32-45)
    E.   Jesus heals blind eyes (10.46-52)

Figure 22   Achtemeier Outline, Mark 6–10

way risen from the dead (9.11-13). Then, once they come down from the mountain, they enter yet another expression of this theme in a resurrection narrative at Mk 9.14-29. The influence of the Epic topos is apparent in that this resurrection narration strategically occurs at the point in which the failure of the disciples is assured (Section 5.2.1). Prominent elements within the narrative indicate that both Prophetic and Epic topoi have a substantial impact on the narration, though once again elements of an Epic topos dominate (Section 5.2.2).

5.2.1 *The Function and Placement of the Resurrection Theme*
Many biblical scholars fail to perceive the climactic position of this resurrection narrative because of a pervasive paradigm among Markan studies that views Mk 6.7–8.21 as dedicated to the themes of the misunderstanding of the disciples and Mk 8.22–10.52 as a separate section in which three passion predictions are enveloped in a repeated motif of the blind coming to see. Achtemeier's *ABD* article on the Gospel of Mark outlines this oft-repeated structure as indicated above:[40]

The sections are each bracketed by similar miracles: a feeding of the multitudes brackets the third major section and the healing of blind eyes brackets the fourth major section. Working within this structure, Georges Minette de Tillesse identifies the resurrection of the boy from the crowd as a significant point in the narrative: 'Marc a voulu faire allusion à une mort et à une résurrection, présages et symboles de celles de Jésus. Cela semble d'autant plus clair que le guérison de l'épileptique se situe au coeur de la section dominée par les trois grandes prédictions de la passion.'[41]

A stronger sense of the significance of the resurrection narrative in Mk 9.14-29 emerges with the recognition that the theme of misunderstanding, represented in Section 3E of Achtemeier's outline, extends beyond ch. 8 of the Gospel. In their *Introduction to the New Testament*, Dennis Duling

40.   Achtemeier, 'Mark, Gospel of', *ABD* 4.546.
41.   Georges Minette de Tillesse, *Le Secret messianique dans l'Évangile de Marc* (Lectio Divina, 47; Paris: Éditions du Cerf, 1968), p. 97.

52   'they did not *understand*..., but their *hearts were hardened*' (1)
18   '...are you also without *understanding*?' (2)
15, 21   'Do you not yet perceive or *understand*? Are your *hearts hardened*...?'
            'Do you not yet *understand*?' (3)

Figure 23   Misunderstanding Tradition I

32   'But they did not *understand* what he was saying and were afraid to
            ask him.' (4)

Figure 24   Misunderstanding Tradition II

and Norman Perrin fail to incorporate Mk 9.32 when they assert that
'[Mark] is developing the theme of the misunderstanding and failure of the
disciples that comes to a climax in ch. 8'[42] (see Figure 23).

This schema is misleading, because the motif of misunderstanding does
not end in ch. 8 but in ch. 9 when the disciples are shown – without
question – to not understand. My analysis would add the following verse
to complete the climax which Duling/Perrin note (Figure 24).

Recognition that the sequence culminates at Mk 9.32 suggests an
outline such as the following (Figure 25).

An inclusio becomes apparent in that (1) the *statement* that the disciples
did not understand becomes (2–3) a *question* on the part of Jesus before
returning to end with (4) this lack of understanding as a *statement* of fact.
Through this strategic sequence in his narrative, Mark communicates a
characteristic of the disciples that is crucial for the appreciation of his
story: the disciples will never understand. Jesus' 'faithless generation' (Mk
9.19) is populated by inherent failures who will abandon Jesus (14.50) and
ultimately fail in their calling (16.8).[43] In order to communicate this failure
clearly and thereby prepare his audience for the tragic end of his story, the
author highlights this strategic point with a resurrection narrative.[44] Such

---

42. Duling and Perrin, *New Testament*, 309. And see Guelich (*Mark*, 268), who also
terminates the list at 8.21.

43. As Tolbert notes, Jesus here 'expresses his greatest frustration yet in the narrative'
(*Sowing*, p. 187). Indeed, this declaration constitutes the apex of Jesus' frustration with the
disciples in the story, which will focus upon the death in Jerusalem shortly hereafter for the
second half of the story (Mark 11–16).

44. A comparison of the characteristics of the turning points at Mk 3.1-6 (see Section
5.1.1) and 11.19-23 (the entry into Jerusalem) elicits secondary indications that 9.30-32 marks
a strategic point in the narrative. In each of these passages, the *author emphasizes Jesus'*
extraordinary power over life and death in the healing of a withered hand (3.1-6), the raising of
the boy from the crowd (9.30-32), and the condemnation of a fig tree (11.19-23). Note also
that each of these three narratives employs the verb 'to wither' (ξηραίνω) in their description
of the death over which Jesus demonstrates his power. Antoinette C. Wire has commented
informally that, in the hot and arid climate of the ancient Near East, death manifests itself
not so much by rotting or molding as by withering. A third perspective by which this
narrative may be seen to be positioned strategically is made by Charles Hedrick, who notes

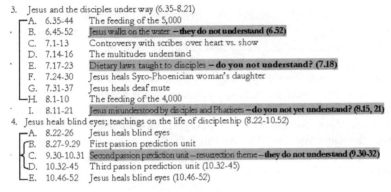

3. Jesus and the disciples under way (6.35-8.21)
- A. 6.35-44   The feeding of the 5,000
- B. 6.45-52   Jesus walks on the water — **they do not understand (6.52)**
- C. 7.1-13   Controversy with scribes over heart vs. show
- D. 7.14-16   The multitudes understand
- E. 7.17-23   Dietary laws taught to disciples — **do you not understand? (7.18)**
- F. 7.24-30   Jesus heals Syro-Phoenician woman's daughter
- G. 7.31-37   Jesus heals deaf mute
- H. 8.1-10   The feeding of the 4,000
- I. 8.11-21   Jesus misunderstood by disciples and Pharisees — **do you not yet understand? (8.15, 21)**

4. Jesus heals blind eyes; teachings on the life of discipleship (8.22-10.52)
- A. 8.22-26   Jesus heals blind eyes
- B. 8.27-9.29   First passion prediction unit
- C. 9.30-10.31   Second passion prediction unit — resurrection theme — **they do not understand (9.30-32)**
- D. 10.32-45   Third passion prediction unit (10.32-45)
- E. 10.46-52   Jesus heals blind eyes (10.46-52)

Figure 25   Climactic Misunderstandings

a strategic placement suggests that the Epic topos plays a significant role in the narration.

5.2.2 *Motifs of Resurrection*

Distinctive features within this narrative reassert the influence of both Prophetic and Epic resurrection topoi upon the telling of this episode. An analysis of these motifs indicates more prominent influence from the Epic topos. The presence and function of the crowd, the overall movement from confusion to a point of enlightenment, and a qualification of death are formative in the narrative (Sections 5.2.2.1–5.2.2.5).

5.2.2.1 *The Crowd*

As throughout novelistic Hellenistic literature, the crowd is particularly conspicuous in this narrative, serving in roles I have identified in several expressions of the Epic topos. For example, in the same way that Chaereas' enemies 'incite the crowd to anger' following the apparent death of Callirhoë (*Callir.* 1.5.3), so at the beginning of this narrative Jesus' enemies, the scribes, incite the crowd in an argument (v. 14).[45] The emotive function that is repeatedly operative in conjunction with the crowds of the Epic topos is also effective here, calling attention to the incredible event at hand: the crowd is 'immediately overcome with awe' when Jesus arrives and they run forward to greet him (v. 15).[46] Following some description of interaction with the crowd, the Markan text asserts that Jesus exorcises the boy 'when he saw that a crowd came running

---

how the direction of travel shifts from a northward movement (Mk 8.27) toward the south (Mk 9.30, 33), ('What is a Gospel: Geography, Time, and Narrative Structure', *PRS* 10 [1983], p. 266).

45. See Ascough, 'Narrative', pp. 78–9.
46. See Table 7.

together' (v. 25). This assertion may strike the audience as incongruous due to the fact that, clearly, the crowd is already present. Perhaps this activity is a function of the irony that occurs throughout Mark: contrary to Jesus' wishes, an insistent crowd repeatedly acknowledges him.[47] The immediate context, however, suggests that an imitation of the Epic resurrection topos may provide the motivation for reasserting the crowd and their dramatic reaction, thereby drawing attention to this significant point in the story, for the exorcism and resurrection that Jesus performs begin in the same verse (v. 25). As throughout this tradition, the element of an active crowd heightens the dramatic effect of Epic resurrection narration.[48]

5.2.2.2 *Confusion*

In the Epic tradition, which I traced in Chapter Three, confusion abounds as a resurrection narrative opens. In this central resurrection narrative, Mark attributes confusion not only to the crowd, but also to Jesus and the disciples as this episode begins. The narrative opens with a panoramic scene from the vantage point of Jesus, James, Peter, and John as they look down from the foot of the mountain: 'they saw a great crowd around them [the other disciples], and some scribes arguing with them' (Mk v. 14). When Jesus arrives, this confused mass turns to him for clarity (v. 15). However, clarity does not come immediately. Jesus must ply the crowd with questions: 'What are you arguing about ...?' (v. 16) 'How long has this been happening ...?' (v. 21).

In the Epic topos, the element of confusion typically involves the one who is to be resurrected, and this narrative is no exception.[49] Four distinct references develop a strong sense of the boy's confusion through terms that are remarkably graphic: (1) a spirit of confusion 'seizes [the boy] and dashes him down' (cf. vv. 17-18); (2) he falls on the ground and rolls about, foaming at the mouth (v. 20); (3) in the past, his confused state has driven him into fire and water (v. 22); and (4) the spirit causes him to cry out and convulse (v. 26).[50] So extreme is the confusion of the boy, in fact, that the theme of death intermingles with the element of confusion.

5.2.2.3 *Death*

The motif of death begins with the initial description of the boy's ailment as one that causes him to 'become rigid' (v. 18). Modern readers of

---

47. See, most prominently, Mark 1.35-37, 44, 45; 3.9, 12-13, 19-20; 5.31; 6.31; and elsewhere.

48. See Table 7.

49. See Table 7.

50. In Section 1.3.5 I have noted such violent descriptions to be a characteristic of novelistic Hellenistic literature in general.

English might associate the verb with concepts of rigor mortis and death. A similar association seems to be operative in Mark's text, for he again uses the Greek verb ξηραίνω, meaning 'to shrivel' or 'to wither', suggesting that something is being 'killed by drought'.[51] The Gospel of Mark twice employs the verb in a context of death: (1) in a parable about a sower whose seeds grow into a plant that chokes to death (Mk 4.6) and (2) in the description of a fig tree killed by a curse from Jesus (11.20). Mark's description of the young boy from the crowd in this terminology suggests that he, too, may die.

The continuing commentary regarding the boy's ailment extends the theme of death with graphic and morbid imagery. A reference to convulsions that 'often cast him into the fire' (9.22) conjures up horrific images of flames igniting a terrified boy who cannot control his flailing body even to save his life. The text seems to revel in this horror as it continues, asserting that the confusion also 'often cast him ... into the water, to destroy him' (v. 22). These comments paint a picture of a convulsing boy choking within a body of water, barely escaping death, perhaps because he spews the water out of his mouth and nose so as not to drown.[52] Death is not only present here, but imminent and vivid.[53]

The subsequent exorcism that Jesus performs evokes this element of death in a manner that is highly reminiscent of the Epic resurrection topos: 'most' of but not the entire crowd says 'he is dead' after the boy ceases convulsing and appears in all respects '*like* a corpse' (v. 26).[54] The qualifying effect of this expression is apparent in the variant interpretations of modern commentators, many of whom read this qualification as a *dismissal* of the element of death,[55] while others note an allusion to death,[56] and only a very few recent studies find death and its reversal to be

---

51. So DBAG, s.v. ξηραίνω. See n. 44 of this chapter.

52. Compare Odysseus at *Od.* 5.455–457. See Section 3.2.1.2 of this study.

53. Hans D. Betz notes that the portrayals of the sick person in exorcism scenes in both Lucian's *Lover of Lies* (16) and his *Peregrinus* (44) utilize a vocabulary that is similar to the violent descriptions in this very passage in the Gospel of Mark: κυλίειν und ἀφρίζειν zusammen.' (Betz [ed.], *Lukian*, p. 148, n. 2). On violence in novelistic literature and the Gospel of Mark, see Section 1.3.5.

54. The recurrence of this linguistic element ('like a corpse') evokes Conte's comment on the novelistic text, *Satyricon*: 'linguistic elements serve to reinforce the allusions' (Conte, *Hidden Author*, p. 16). Notice also the resumptive work of the declaration regarding death in the middle of v. 26: perhaps the author has transformed a healing narrative into a resurrection narrative once more, as I have noted in Section 5.1.1.

55. See Joseph A. Alexander, *Commentary on the Gospel of Mark* (New York: Charles Scribner and Sons, 1864; repr., Grand Rapids, Mich.: Zondervan, 1955], p. 252); Turner, *Gospel*, p. 44.

56. See Anderson, *Gospel*, p. 231; Lane, *Gospel*, pp. 334–5).

1.31   καὶ προσελθὼν **ἤγειρεν** αὐτὴν **κρατήσας τῆς χειρός**· καὶ ἀφῆκεν αὐτὴν ὁ πυρετός....
5.41   καὶ **κρατήσας τῆς χειρὸς** τοῦ παιδίου λέγει αὐτῇ,.... **ἔγειρε.** καὶ εὐθὺς **ἀνέστη**....
9.27   ὁ δὲ Ἰησοῦς **κρατήσας τῆς χειρὸς** αὐτοῦ   **ἤγειρεν** αὐτόν, καὶ **ἀνέστη**.

Figure 26   Raising Tradition II

an integral part of this narrative.[57] This study reveals, however, that the strong qualification is the result of a long-standing tradition from as early as the songs of Homer – an Epic resurrection topos.

5.2.2.4 *Resurrection*

When the anticipated element of resurrection occurs, its treatment is brief and to the point: 'Jesus took him by the hand and lifted him up, and he was able to stand' (Mk 9.27). However, the relatedness of the verses to previous Markan narration suggests that this author was sensitive to literary patterns and the specific way in which those patterns are expressed (see Figure 26).

As the narration of the raising of Jairus' daughter (5.41), so the high degree of similarity in the wording of the resurrection of the boy from the crowd (9.27) also suggests that the author of the Gospel associated the two resurrection narratives with one another in a manner reminiscent of the way in which Chariton associated Callirhoë's 'second resurrection' (*Callir.* 1.8.1) with that of her first (1.1.14–15). Such literary signals considered in addition to the repeated patterns of the topoi, recurring phraseology unique to such narratives, and explicit comments by authors furthers my suggestion that for storytellers of the ancient world, including the author of the Gospel of Mark, the resurrection topos was a favored tool within a storyteller's 'box of tricks' for accentuating a key point in a narrative structure.[58]

5.2.2.5 *Enlightenment*

Once Jesus takes the boy by the hand and lifts him up, the confusion that had previously cast him down on the ground, into fire, and into water is no more: he is 'able to stand' (Mk 9.27). Though Hector 'spins' 'like a top' in a confused state before his death and return to life (*Il.* 14.413), his enlightenment allows him to command the swiftest of horses (*Il.* 15.263–169). Chaereas, when confused, does not know whether to fall or stand (*Callir.* 1.1.7). Yet in his enlightenment he aggressively runs forward

---

57.   Donahue and Harrington (*Gospel*, pp. 279–80; ital. mine): 'The language of lifting up (*egeirein*) evokes the idea of resurrection – a motif *confirmed* by the addition of another 'resurrection' verb, *anistemi* ('arose'), immediately afterward.'

58.   See my comments regarding Mk 5.41 in Section 5.1.2.3 as well as the notes regarding the 'box of tricks' of Greco-Roman storytellers at Section 1.7 (esp. Ch. 3, n. 58).

(1.1.15). Confusion causes Callirhoë to fling herself upon her bed (1.1.14), but her enlightenment makes her 'taller and stronger' (1.1.16). When confusion returns to her before the final resurrection narrative of Chariton's novel, she curls up in a ball upon the ground (7.6.8–9). Following her enlightenment, she 'moves with dignity' (8.1.12). So the young boy in Mark's story no longer falls to the ground flailing, but in his enlightenment is able to stand (Mk 9.27). This physical manifestation of the shift from confusion to enlightenment, along with the other notable aspects of the narrative which I have observed in this section, all seem to derive from mimesis as the story lives within the Epic topos.[59]

Note that not only the young boy experiences a type of enlightenment, but even Jesus does as his questions end and he gains clarity into the situation (9.21). Only the disciples remain confused, still asking questions (9.28). Jesus gives them an answer, but there is no confirmation that they understand its implications. This emphasis upon their continued confusion stands in service of a strategic point in the narrative that is explicit in v. 32 of the chapter: 'but they did not understand what he was saying and were afraid to ask him'.

5.2.3 *Conclusion*

Elements of an Epic topos of resurrection narration dominate the presentation of this second climactic resurrection. Confusion, a death that is highly qualified, resurrection, enlightenment, and an emotive crowd constitute the primary constellation of motifs in this narrative. Yet the significant sway of the Epic topos does not altogether eliminate the influence of the Prophetic topos, as is apparent in the expression of a breach of trust immediately after the attention of the prophet/healer is obtained. In 1 Kings 17, the widow of Zarephath first asks Elijah: 'What have you against me, O man of God ... to cause the death of my son?' (1 Kgs 17.18). In 2 Kings 4, the parent proclaims, 'Did I ask my lord for a son? Did I not say, Do not mislead me?' (2 Kgs 4.28). And also here in Mark 9 the miracle begins with an accusation by the father that trust has been breached: 'I asked your disciples to cast it out, but they could not do so' (Mk 9.18).[60] In this particular expression of the Prophetic topos, the narrative does not reestablish the disciples as representatives of the divine. Far from an oversight, this omission serves Mark's purposes well: he prepares his audience for their complete failure and the tragic end of his story, to which I now turn.

---

59. For further examples, see Table 7.

60. Resurrection themes in Hos. 6.1-3 and Ezek. 37.1-14 also incorporate accusations that trust has been breached. See Table 8.

5.3 *The Failure of the Disciples Realized*

The resurrection narrative involving Jesus provides the climax of Mark's story as a whole. The disciples do, in fact, fail Jesus who – in contrast to John the Baptist (Mk 6.29) – dies alone with no disciples to continue his ministry (16.8).[61] In this subsection, as previously, I will first demonstrate how the influence of the Epic topos is apparent in that this resurrection narration occurs at such a strategic point in the narrative structure of the Gospel (Section 5.3.1). Then I will read the text of the narrative, illustrating how elements of both the Epic topos primarily, as well as elements of the Prophetic topos, have very likely influenced the presentation of this hybrid Hellenistic text (Section 5.3.2).

5.3.1 *The Function and Placement of the Resurrection Theme*

Following the fourth and final statement about the disciples' lack of understanding (Mk 9.32), the group travels to Capernaum where Jesus teaches about the priorities of the Kingdom of God (9.33–10.31). He also gives his third passion prediction (10.32-34), after which James and John ask for seats of glory (10.35-40), prompting Jesus to assert teachings about servanthood (10.41-45). The unit that begins with the healing of a blind man (8.22-26) and culminates in a strong demonstration of the disciples' own 'blindness' (9.32) then closes with another story of the healing of a blind man (10.46-52).

Eventually Jesus and his disciples arrive at Jerusalem where they receive a welcome by the people but confrontation from Jewish leaders (11–12). In Mark 11 – just as Jesus first enters Jerusalem to face his trials and death – he once again demonstrates his power over life and death in his interaction with a fig tree (11.12-14, 19-23).[62] Several issues arise between Jesus and the leaders, the centerpiece of which is resurrection (12.18-27). These observations, originally proposed by Joanna Dewey,[63] have recently been slightly modified and represented as follows.

The structure indicates the significance of resurrection not only as an effective dramatic element but also as a key topic of debate during this period, a role that related texts of the period corroborate.[64] Indeed, the attention paid to resurrection in public discourse may very well contribute

---

61. For an insightful analysis of the possible significance of Jesus' lonely death for his ancient audience, see Tolbert, *Sowing*, pp. 284–8.

62. At other key points in the narrative structure, the author emphasizes Jesus' extraordinary power over life and death in the healing of a withered hand (Mk 3.1-6) and the raising of the boy from the crowd (9.30-32). See n. 44 of this chapter.

63. *Markan Public Debate: Literary Technique, Concentric Structure, and Theology in Mark 2.1-3.6* (SBLDS, 48; Chico, Ca.: Scholars, 1980), pp. 156–63.

64. See also Acts 5.17; 23.8; Josephus, *Ant.* 18.2.4 and *War* 2.8.14.

A   **11:17-33**   *The source and nature of Jesus' authority questioned*
 B   **12:1-9**   *Parable of the wicked tenants; God's judgment*
  C   **12:10-12**   *Psalm citation: Jesus' ultimate vindication proclaimed*
   D   **12:13-17**   *Debate/teaching: The things of God to be given to God*
    E   **12:18-27**   *THE REALITY OF THE RESURRECTION*
   D'   **12:28-34**   *Debate/teaching: Commands to love God and neighbor*
  C'   **12:35-37**   *Psalm citation: Jesus' ultimate vindication proclaimed*
 B'   **12:38-40**   *Warning against scribes; God's judgment*
A'   **12:41-44**   *True nature of authority exemplified by poor widow*

Figure 27

to the usefulness of the theme in highlighting significant points in a narrative.[65]

Once he is at the Temple itself, Jesus proclaims the nature of its end, as well as the end of 'heaven and earth' (Mark 13; esp. 13.31). Talk of Jesus' arrest in v. 1 of ch. 14 introduces the Passion Narrative proper. The verse also marks the beginning of a series of specific time references, the likes of which often characterize the climactic finish of novelistic literature.[66] The plot against Jesus receives clarification (14.1-11), and a final supper with his disciples precedes a prayer time in the garden at Gethsemane (14.12-31).

In the garden, the failure of the disciples begins in earnest: despite Jesus' repeated requests to remain awake, the disciples fall asleep three times (14.32-42).[67] When Jesus is arrested in the garden, the male disciples flee in fear (14.43-52). In the same instance that Jesus undergoes a religious trial, one of his foremost disciples denies him three times (14.53-72).[68] Following a political trial, a solitary Jesus is condemned to crucifixion (15.1-15).[69] As he is nailed to his cross, Jesus endures torture and mockery without the defense of supporters (15.16-32).[70] Only after his death (15.33-39) does the text mention Jesus' female disciples (15.40–16.8), whose visit to the tomb reasserts the failure of the male disciples. 'Who will roll away the stone for us?' (16.2). Yet even the female followers fail in their discipleship, as emphasized through the presence of the theme of resurrection. In response to a final, climactic resurrection announcement, the women flee in fear, sharing the news with no one (16.6–8).[71]

---

65.   See Section 6.2.2.
66.   Tolbert, *Sowing*, p. 75. See Section 1.2.3.
67.   Recall that ternary repetition is a characteristic of novelistic literature.
68.   Another set of three.
69.   Trials are a common theme in novelistic literature. See Section 1.3.3.
70.   Torture is also a common theme in novelistic literature. See Section 1.3.5.
71.   As indicated by manuscript and literary evidence, Mk 16.8 most likely represents the end of the Gospel. See Paul L. Danove, *The End of Mark's Story: A Methodological Study* (BIS, 3; New York and Leiden: Brill, 1993).

5.3.2 *Motifs of Resurrection*

The hybridity of this final narrative is particularly thorough – both the Epic and Prophetic topoi exert a recognizable influence upon the final resurrection narrative of the Gospel. Once again, however, the Epic topos dominates the presentation, as I will demonstrate in my consideration of the elements of confusion and enlightenment (Section 5.3.2.1), a breach of trust and reestablished communion (Section 5.3.2.2), death (Section 5.3.2.3), resurrection (Section 5.3.2.4), and the crowd (Section 5.3.2.5).

5.3.2.1 *Confusion and Enlightenment*

Themes of darkness and light enclose the narrative of Jesus' death and return to life as an expression of the epic elements of confusion and enlightenment. Just before his death, darkness reigns supreme: 'When it was noon, darkness came over the whole land until three in the afternoon' (Mk 15.33). Then, as Jesus resurrects following the death sequence, light prevails: 'And very early on the first day of the week, when the sun had risen, they went to the tomb' (16.2). Even though the author mentions that the day is 'very early', he is certain to clarify the point with the additional phrase, 'when the sun had risen' (16.2).

Certainly, themes of light and darkness are prominent in the Hebrew Canon, particularly in Second Isaiah in connection with the Suffering Servant figure.[72] However, in Hebrew Canon texts the themes of darkness and light occur either individually[73] or as correlatives within a single statement: 'I will turn the darkness before them into light.'[74] The themes do not frame resurrection narratives or any other extended narratives, as they do in the Epic topos when expressing confusion and enlightenment. In particular, in the Epic topos these motifs find expression in allusions to the time of day, as here in Mark's narrative. Chariton's novel, for example, portrays the confusion of Callirhoë's second resurrection in terms of darkness and light. Callirhoë's confusion arises because she 'sits in darkness' 'late in the evening' (*Callir.* 1.4.8, 11). After she has been reunited with Chaereas, however, Chariton explicitly notes that Chaereas 'did not even wait until evening before coming to the royal chamber' to enlighten Callirhoë on his whereabouts since their separation (8.1.13). In the resurrection narrative in the book of Tobit (Tob. 8.9-18), Raguel's servants spend the night digging Tobias' grave (8.9), but with the lighting of a lamp comes the good news that Tobias lives (8.14).[75] Note the closing verse in particular – Tobit explicitly 'order[s] his servants to fill in the

---

72. See, for example, Isa. 5.30; 42.16; 45.7; 60.2.
73. As at Gen. 1.2-3; Exod. 10.21-23; Isa. 8.22; 48.15 [LXX]; 50.2; Jer. 15.9; 33.19-21; Ezek. 32.8; Joel 2.2, 31; Amos 8.9-10; Zeph. 1.15; Mal. 4.2 [LXX].
74. Isa. 42.16; see also Isa. 45.7 and elsewhere.
75. See my analysis in Section 4.2.2.

grave *before daybreak'* (8.19; ital. mine). So the scene closes with an image of a fresh patch of dirt visible by the light of the breaking day. Like these resurrection narratives of the Epic topos, the Gospel of Mark also opens the final resurrection narrative in the confusion of darkness (Mk 15.33) then later emphasizes light through allusion at the point of resurrection: 'when the sun had risen' (16.2).

5.3.2.2 *Breach of Trust and Reestablished Communion*

Elements of the Prophetic topos also frame the presentation of Jesus' death and return to life. A dramatic cry stemming from a breach of trust immediately follows the opening reference to darkness: 'At three o'clock Jesus cried out with a loud voice, "Eloi, Eloi, lema sabachthani?" which means, "My God, my God, why have you forsaken me?"' (Mk 15.34). Just as the resurrection narratives of the Hebrew Bible implicate YHWH or the prophets of YHWH for the death element of that narrative, so Jesus, as he hangs on a cross, implicates YHWH for his pending death. One indication of the author's awareness of this effect is the fact that he draws the quotation from Psalm 22, a song that manifests themes of the Prophetic resurrection topos.[76] The end of the Markan narrative is less explicit. The proclamation of the stranger at the tomb indirectly reestablishes Jesus' communion with God: 'He has been raised,' the stranger declares (Mk 16.6). YHWH has righted Jesus' unjust situation. The assumption is that the communion of the two has been reestablished.

5.3.2.3 *Death*

In the description of the death, the author twice employs the verb ἐκπνέω (15.37, 39), a compound of a root (πνέω) that occurs frequently in the Epic resurrection topos:

> [37] Then Jesus gave a loud cry and breathed his last (ἐξέπνευσεν). [38] And the curtain of the temple was torn in two, from top to bottom. [39] Now when the centurion, who stood facing him, saw that in this way he breathed his last (ἐξέπνευσεν), he said, 'Truly this man was God's Son!'
>
> Mk 15.37-39

The same form of this verb describes the death in Callirhoë's first resurrection narrative (ἐκπνέω, *Callir.* 1.1.14). Forms of the root occur in resurrection narratives throughout Homer and novelistic Hellenistic literature.[77]

---

76. See Table 8. In my reading, the presence of these several elements significantly overshadows any brief allusion to the death of Hector, whose soul flees 'bewailing' at the point of death (cf. MacDonald, *Homeric Epics*, p. 185).

77. Some prominent examples include ἀμπνέω/ἐμπνέω (*Il.* 5.697; 11.359; 14.436; 15.60, 262; 22.475; *Od.* 5.458; 24.349; *Callir.* 2.5.10), ἀναπνέω (*Callir.* 1.8.1), and ἐπιπνέω (*Il.* 5.698). The occurrence of the root in verb form twice in this narrative is particularly

In the tradition of the Prophetic topos, the description of Jesus' death is stark and final. There is no qualification of the death. In fact, the interchange between Joseph of Arimathea and Pilate works diligently against any such qualification, strongly asserting that Jesus has died at Mk 15.42-47. A thorough-going, three-part process verifies that Jesus is indisputably dead: (1) Pilate wonders if Jesus is dead (v. 44), (2) asks if he has been dead for some time (v. 44), and (3) explicitly learns that he is, indeed, dead (v. 45).[78]

Contrary to the assertions of many biblical scholars, I argue that the impetus behind such an emphatic presentation is not apologetic, but an indication of the influence of the Prophetic topos. If this text held apologetic value, then surely the Gospel of Matthew – which is explicitly concerned about apologetic issues such as whether or not 'his disciples came by night and stole him away' (Mt. 28.13) – would not have omitted the passage *in toto*, preserving only a single parallel to Mk 15.37.[79] Neither is any apologetic value for this passage affirmed by the Gospel of Luke, which omits the passage in its entirety, simply describing Jesus as having 'breathed his last' (Lk. 23.46). Among the Synoptic Gospels, only the Gospel of Mark reasserts the final breath of Jesus twice (Mk 15.37, 39) before its unique three-part emphasis upon the absolute nature of his death (15.44 [2x], 45).

I suggest that these details result from the influence of the Prophetic topos. Ezekiel's vision portrays death unambiguously through the barest of remnants, 'bones' (Ezek. 37.1), 'and they were very dry' (37.2). In 1 Kings 17, both the widow (1 Kgs 17.18) and – just a few verses later – the prophet unequivocally describe the widow's son as dead (17.20). And in 2 Kings 4 there are three references to the lifeless condition of the child (2 Kgs 4.20, 31, 32). The author of the Gospel has learned from the Prophetic topos that by portraying death as stark and absolute his text also will effectively encourage the praise value of YHWH who – by overcoming even the starkest of deaths – is proclaimed to be powerful and worthy of praise.

---

noteworthy as the root occurs nowhere else in the Gospel of Mark. Also within the vein of the Epic topos, the declaration of the Roman soldier at the cross of Jesus (Mk 15.39) parallels the declaration of the Romans after Habrocomes returns from his crucifixion in a resurrection narrative of the novelistic *An Ephesian Tale*: 'the gods were looking after' Habrocomes (Xenophon, *An Ephesian Tale* 4.2 [Anderson, *CAGN*]).

78. MacDonald argues that parallels to the burial of Hector (*Il.* 24) may provide a backdrop for the construction of this narrative (*Homeric Epics*, pp. 185–87). See, however, Section 6.1.2.

79. The Gospel of Matthew furthers this apologetic purpose by arguing against a hypothetical assertion that the body was stolen. See Mt. 28.4, 11-15.

5.3.2.4 *Resurrection*

At the point of resurrection, also, the influence of both the Epic and the Prophetic topoi are discernible in the pericope Mk 16.1-8. The influence of the Prophetic topos is veiled within the temporal reference that precedes the resurrection announcement: it is 'the first day of the week' (Mk 16.2). Following the crucifixion (15.42), the narrator informs us that Jesus' death has occurred on 'the day before the sabbath'. Counting from this day, the resurrection happens 'on the third day', [80] thereby associating Jesus' resurrection story with Hosea's classical resurrection narrative (see Hos. 6.2).[81]

In comparison to this subtle and partial influence of the Prophetic topos, the influence of the Epic topos upon this passage is surprisingly direct and quite extensive. The author situates his resurrection proclamation within the trope of an 'empty tomb story', such as occurs in Chariton's popular novel:[82]

[1] Chaereas waited for dawn to visit the tomb, ostensibly to bring wreaths and libations, but really in order to kill himself. He could not bear separation from Callirhoë and considered death the only cure for his sorrow. When he arrived, he discovered that the stones had been moved and that the entrance was wide open. [2] He was astonished at what had happened. Rumor swiftly brought the shocking news to Syracuse, and everyone hastened to the tomb, but no one ventured to go inside until Hermocrates gave the order. The man sent in gave a full and true account. [3] It seemed unbelievable that not even the corpse was lying there. Then Chaereas himself decided to go in, eager to see Callirhoë once more even though she was dead. But on searching the tomb he could find nothing. [4] Many others entered incredulously after him. All were baffled, and one of those inside said, 'The funeral

80. Donahue and Harrington, *Gospel*, p. 459. Each of the predictions of Jesus' resurrection envisages a raising that will occur 'after three days' (Mk 8.31; 9.31; 10.34) rather than 'on the third day'. However, the terms may be synonymous. Or the reference in Jesus' prophecies may indicate an unspecific amount of 'some' time, as Johannes B. Bauer, 'Drei Tage', *Biblica* 39 (1958), 354–8.

81. See Section 4.1.1. On the 'classical' influence of the Hosean oracles, see n. 3 of the Preface to Part II.

82. I analyze Chariton's empty tomb story as part of Callirhoë's second resurrection narrative in Section 3.1.2.1. See also Elias J. Bickerman, 'Das Leere Grab' on pp. 70–81 of vol. 3 of *Studies in Jewish and Christian History* (AGJU 9; New York and Leiden: Brill, 1986); Neill Q. Hamilton, 'Resurrection Tradition and the Composition of Mark', *JBL* 84 (1965), pp. 415–21 [419]); Ludger Schenke, *Auferstehungsverkundigung und leeres Grab: eine traditionsgeschichtliche Untersuchung von Mk 16, 1–8* (SB, 33; Stuttgart: Katholisches Bibelwerk, 1968); Adela Yarbro Collins, *The Beginning of the Gospel: Probings of Mark in Context* (Minneapolis: Fortress, 1992), pp. 119–48; and Daniel A. Smith, 'Revisiting the Empty Tomb: The Post-Mortem Vindication of Jesus in Mark and Q', *NovT* 45 (2003), 128–37.

offerings have been stolen! This is the work of tomb robbers. But where is the corpse?' Many different speculations were entertained by the crowd. But Chaereas, looking up to heaven, stretched forth his hands ....

(*Callir*. 3.3.1–4)

Chariton's account of Callirhoë's empty tomb shares many of the elements of the empty tomb story in the Gospel of Mark (Mk 16.4-6). In both narratives, characters visit the tomb of a loved one to find the entrance unexpectedly open.[83] Upon further investigation, it is determined that the tomb is in fact empty.[84] And, for both narratives, this emptiness results in the final conclusion that divine intervention has brought a corpse back to life. Although these similarities – in addition to the common provenance, date, and novelistic style of the two texts – may suggest that the author of the Gospel of Mark emulates Chariton, given the observations of this study, the more probable situation is that both authors operate within a culture of mimetic storytelling that values resurrection narration as a literary device.[85]

5.3.2.5 *The Crowd*

In a manner familiar to novelistic Hellenistic tradition, Mark's resurrection narrative of Jesus employs an emotive crowd that exhibits alarm (16.5), terror, amazement, and eventually fear (16.8). In fact, the reaction of the crowd to Jesus' death exemplifies the diversity of Hellenistic culture that has produced such a hybrid text as the Gospel of Mark. While the 'bystanders' are familiar with biblical traditions regarding the return of Elijah, their knowledge of Aramaic is so poor that they fail to understand even the first line of a psalm: Jesus calls not to Elijah but to YHWH ('Eloi'; 15.35-36).[86]

5.3.3 *Conclusion*

Both Prophetic and Epic topoi of resurrection narration exert significant influence upon the presentation of the death and return to life of Jesus. Along the lines of the Prophetic tradition, Jesus confronts the divine with a breach of trust, and the relationship is ultimately reestablished. Death is absolute, and resurrection occurs 'on the third day' (Hos. 6.2). The Epic

83. Chariton describes 'stones shaken [down]', and Mark tells of a single 'stone rolled away'.

84. In Chariton the investigation is the work of witnesses at the scene, including Chaereas himself; in Mark the investigation is made by a mysterious man in white and three women at the tomb.

85. See Sections 2.3 and 2.4.

86. See, for example, Mal. 4.5; S-B 4.773-77; Morris M. Faierstein, 'Why Do the Scribes Say that Elijah Comes First?' *JBL* 100 (1981), pp. 75–86.

topos, however, plays a significant role that is even more formative on the narrative. In the course of his death and return to life, Jesus advances through the confusion of darkness to the enlightenment of the dawn. Resurrection is accompanied by an extensive story of an empty tomb, and an emotive crowd guides reactions throughout the text. Furthermore, the resurrection occurs at the final turning point of the story, a distinguishing contribution of the Epic topos. The study of the resurrection narrative of Jesus provides yet another example of some of the insights to be gained by taking seriously Mark's participation within a culture shaped by Epic traditions and novelistic literature as well as by biblical texts.

5.4 *Conclusion*

The treatments of the theme of resurrection in the Gospel of Mark indicate that the author was familiar with both Epic and Prophetic modes of resurrection narration. In each of my readings of resurrection traditions in this Gospel, Epic traditions exert a greater influence upon the resurrection narratives than biblical traditions. This influence is manifest not only within the individual narratives, but also in the occurrences of resurrection themes throughout the story as a whole. Extended resurrection narratives occur at strategic points in the story, highlighting the overall structure of the Gospel as it progresses from the ministry of Jesus (Mk 5.21-24, 35-43), to the failure of the disciples (9.14-29), and ultimately to Jesus' lonely death and resurrection lacking the support of followers (15.33–16.8). Although this conclusion is striking in light of Mark's close work with biblical texts, the paucity of references to resurrection within those texts – particularly in contrast to the fascination for death and return that the Epic tradition held – render the conclusion justifiable.[87]

---

87. Regarding an Epic fascination for death and the afterlife, see Section 2.5.

Part III Theory: Implications for Interpretation

Chapter 6

LITERARY AND HISTORICAL IMPLICATIONS

I have organized a review of the primary implications of this study for interpreting the Gospel of Mark into two heuristic – though by no means mutually exclusive – categories. In general terms, the study contributes to a modern appreciation of the ancient *literary* context of the Gospel of Mark (Section 6.1) as well as to increased awareness of specific aspects of the *historical* setting in which the Gospel was written (Section 6.2). Literarily, my observations regarding the deployment of resurrection narratives at climactic points throughout Mark's story provide new evidence for the theory that the Gospel participates in the genre of ancient novelistic literature (Section 6.1.1). The study also provides a model for appreciating the nature and role of Homeric influence in the Hellenistic period (Section 6.1.2). Historically, the study contributes to a growing awareness of the fluidity that characterizes 'Jewish' and 'Greek' influences upon the literature of Hellenistic Judaism (Section 6.2.1). In this section I also consider a possible rationale for the increased occurrence of resurrection narratives in novelistic literature at this time (Section 6.2.2). Finally, I conclude with some reflections upon the significance of the study for the postmodern Christian church of the twenty-first century (Section 6.3).

6.1 *Situating Mark Literarily: The Contributions of this Study*

In Chapter 3 of this study, I demonstrate how some authors of novelistic literature strategically deploy resurrection narratives at significant points throughout their plot in imitation of a Homeric pattern. In Chapter 5 I argue that the author of the Gospel of Mark also places resurrection narratives at significant points throughout his text. In this chapter I will explain how this observation regarding the Gospel of Mark contributes new evidence to the theory that the Markan Gospel participates in the genre of novelistic literature (Section 6.1.1).[1] In fact, this evidence may be the most compelling evidence to date because, according to Conte and Most, *imitatio* and the strategic deployment of *topoi* are primary indicators of genre in the ancient world. Another literary contribution

---

1. In Chapter 1 I review other indications that Mark participates in novelistic literature.

of this study is the model it provides for an appreciation of Homeric influence upon Hellenistic novelistic literature (Section 6.1.2). I propose the approach of this study as a cautious alternative to the extravagant claims that frequent the work and conclusions of scholars who attempt to identify Homeric influence in the Gospel of Mark.

6.1.1 *More Evidence of Markan Participation in Novelistic Literature*

Classical scholars Gian Biagio Conte and Glenn Most have spent a lifetime exploring the nature and use of genre in the Greco-Roman world.[2] Throughout their writings, these scholars consistently argue against an understanding of genre as any one particular 'recipe' of structure and/or content. Rather than formal patterns established as though according to 'handbooks of composition',[3] Conte and Most assert that the primary influences upon generic communication in ancient literature are literary imitation and the strategic deployment of *topoi*:

> [G]enres function within texts as a way of reducing complexity and thereby not only enriching, but even enabling literary communication: for, by guiding *imitatio* and identifying as pertinent the strategic deployment of *topoi* and of conspicuous stylistic and thematic features, they select only certain contexts out of the potentially infinite horizon of possible ones.[4]

For Conte and Most, genre *enriches and even enables communication*.[5] Their definition asserts the position that – without a sense for which genre

---

2. The observation applies primarily to Conte. '[M]y reflection on literary genres has been constant at least since 1976 or 1977', he writes in a collection of seminal essays published in 1994 (Gian Biagio Conte, *Genres and Readers: Lucretius, Love Elegy, Pliny's Encyclopedia* [trans. Glenn W. Most; Baltimore: Johns Hopkins University Press, 1994], p. 132). Glenn Most has 'worked closely with Conte for many years', and has translated much of his work from Italian into English (Charles Segal, 'Foreward: Literary History as Literary Theory', in Conte, *Genres and Readers*, p. xv).

Although Conte's primary area of study is the field of classical Roman poetry, his work on genre has implications applicable to a broad range of Greco-Roman literature. The inclusion of Conte's article on 'genre' in the *Oxford Classical Dictionary* also attests in part to the far-reaching influence of his work (*OCD*, 630–631). See his study of Petronius' *Satyricon* (Conte, *The Hidden Author*) for a demonstration of the relevance that his generic theories hold for novelistic literature.

Other influential scholars skeptical of a unitary approach in generic analysis include F. Kermode, E.D. Hirsch, Alistair Fowler, and Francis Cairns.

3. See Conte, *Genres and Readers*, 106.

4. Conte and Most, 'Genre', *OCD*, 631. A fuller treatment of genre in the Greco-Roman world is available in Conte's monograph, *Genres and Readers*.

5. See also Alistair Fowler, a prominent theorist of modern genre, who writes that 'genre primarily has to do with communication' (*Kinds of Literature: An Introduction to the Theory of Genres and Modes* [Oxford: Clarendon; Cambridge, Mass. and London: Harvard University Press, 1982], 22).

is operative at any given point of a text – a reader may have little sense of what that text intends to communicate or how it is meant to be used. Furthermore, the definition asserts that genre enables communication through four aspects of an ancient text: (1) *imitatio*, (2) the strategic deployment of topoi, (3) conspicuous stylistic features, and (4) conspicuous thematic features.

In Chapter 1 of this study I consider the third and fourth aspects of Conte and Most's definition of genre. My observations of the ways in which the Gospel of Mark shares many conspicuous stylistic features with other novelistic literature – including parataxis, asyndeton, and a lively narrative pace that slows only for the paranormal and the intensely emotional – serves as an initial indication of a generic relationship between the Gospel and novelistic literature.[6] In addition to stylistics, conspicuous motifs and themes that the Gospel of Mark shares with novelistic literature – such as violence, torture, crucifixion, resurrection, the divine realm, travel, history, and crowds, among others – further suggest a generic relationship between Mark and novelistic texts.[7] These features are characteristics of genre that often receive attention as part of an analysis of generic relationships.

The unique contribution of Conte and Most, however, is their recognition of the primary influence of *imitatio* and the strategic deployment of *topoi* in the determination of genre, the first and second aspect of the definition of genre that these scholars detail in the extended quote above. If these factors are as primary as Conte and Most suggest, then my observations regarding resurrection topoi in Chapters 3 through 5 of this study present evidence of Mark's participation in the genre of novelistic literature that is even more compelling than the evidence in Chapter 1. In Chapters 3 to 5 I demonstrate that both novelistic literature and the Gospel of Mark strategically deploy a topos of resurrection in imitation of a Homeric progenitor. So both novelistic literature and the Gospel of Mark manifest all four primary characteristics of genre identified by Conte and Most in the *Oxford Classical Dictionary*: conspicuous stylistic and thematic features, a guiding *imitatio*, and the strategic deployment of the resurrection topos.

Furthermore, Mark's participation in the genre of novelistic literature enables literary communication. For example, following the fast-paced, paratactic beginning *in medias res*, the audience might expect a central turning point and a final recognition.[8] Additional communication occurs as these expectations are fulfilled, unfulfilled, or fulfilled in an unusual manner. This study has demonstrated that an audience might also expect

6. See Sections 1.2 and 1.3.1.
7. See Sections 1.3–1.4.
8. As in *Callirhoë*. See Section 1.5.

themes of death and resurrection at significant points in the plot. For the audience of the Gospel of Mark, the fulfillment of this expectation allows for additional communication about the irony of the Gospel in which a remarkably powerful teacher and healer is ultimately abandoned by his disciples.

The generic communication of the Gospel as a whole, however, remains to be explored. What communication might be inherent in the text's expression of a historical-biographical subject in the genre of novelistic fiction literature? Douglas Templeton grapples with this question in his book, *The New Testament as True Fiction*: 'Although it is a novel Mark is writing and not a history, nevertheless, because the hero is, by the best account (for there are worse), a historical figure, the novel is not a novel *tout court*, but a historical novel and, thus a mixture of fact and fiction.'[9] Such an assessment would put the Gospel in the league of generic forebears such as Ctesias of Cnidus' *History of Persia* from the fourth century B.C.E. or *Third Maccabees* at the turn of the Common Era.[10] Yet Mark is clearly also biographical, as is the novelistic *Life of Aesop* (turn of the Common Era).[11] The precedent for such a combination of material content may be found in Xenophon of Athens' *Cyropaedia* (fourth century B.C.E.) as well as Artapanus' *On Moses* (third-second century B.C.E.). Therefore, the mixture of content in the Gospel of Mark fits comfortably within the genre of novelistic literature, yet not within modern conceptions of fact and fiction.[12]

Certainly, the communication of history or biography through the means of the ancient novelistic genre is not the communication of 'objective historical facts'. Bowersock's survey of Greco-Roman literature describes a predominant conception of history at the time as 'a fiction, or rhetoric, or whatever'. For Bowersock, it was not until the second century that writers like Celsus and Lucian of Samosata grew concerned that certain fictional aspects of the story of Jesus (in particular) were not being treated as appropriately fictional.[13] Yet, as the studies of several scholars

---

9.   Douglas A. Templeton, *The New Testament as True Fiction: Literature, Literary Criticism, Aesthetics* (PTT, 3; Sheffield, Engl.: Sheffield Academic, 1999), p. 139. On the mixture of fact and fiction in novelistic literature, see also J.R. Morgan, 'Make-Believe and Make Believe: The Fictionality of the Greek Novels' in Gill (ed.), *Lies and Fiction in the Ancient World*, pp. 175–229 and, on pp. 230–44 of the same volume, D.C. Feeney, 'Epilogue: Towards an Account of the Ancient World's Concepts of Fictive Beliefs'.

10.   The information about the novelistic literature mentioned in this passage is drawn from Table 1.

11.   See Wills, *Quest*. Apollonius of Tyana is best placed after Mark, in the third century C.E. (See Koskenniemi, 'Apollonius of Tyana'.)

12.   On the diversity of content in novelistic writing, see Section 1.7.

13.   Bowersock, *Fiction*, pp. 1–27. The quotation is from p. 12. D.C. Feeney would disagree. Citing the first century (C.E.) rhetorician Quintilian, Feeney demonstrates that 'there was some kind of interest in a category of fiction in the ancient tradition':

indicate, history in novelistic form does seek to make an authentic communication of one kind or another.

D.C. Feeney argues that the ancients 'were, in particular, much more concerned about the *moral worth* and *philosophical value* of making fictional statements than about the logical status of those statements'.[14] The end – expressions of morals and philosophy – justified the means – fictional statements. Furthermore, the perceived need for justification was markedly less prominent in the ancient world than according to post-Enlightenment standards.[15] According to Feeney's appreciation of novelistic literature, therefore, Mark's employment of a fictional genre may communicate that his text is more concerned with moral and philosophical issues than with an exposition of what actually happened.

Lawrence Wills suggests a communication similar to morals and philosophy on the part of novelistic literature as he likens the Jewish novels to 'pious example stories'.[16] Yet Wills would also broaden the list of possible generic communications: 'The category *"entertaining and exhilarating"* brought the novels and historical novels together and outweighed the importance of distinguishing what is fiction from what is non-fiction.'[17] Perhaps the novelistic genre of the Gospel communicates that the primary interest of Mark's story is entertainment.

J.R. Morgan's consideration of fiction in Mark's Gospel in particular would add an emphasis upon *faith* to the list of possible generic communications. Morgan suggests that Mark may emulate the novelistic genre because faith is an integral part of the fictive worlds that fiction writings create. 'Religion and the novel are in the same market', Morgan notes, because both 'depict not the world as it is, but the world as it ought to be'.[18] So, although the Gospel relates the story of the person Jesus, who has experienced a violent death at the hands of the authorities, expression

---

We have three types of narrative: myth, which you get in tragedies and poems, and which is removed not only from the truth but even from the appearance of truth; fictitious story [*argumentum* = Greek *plasma*], which comedies invent, false but verisimilitudinous; and history, in which there is an exposition of something which actually happened.

Quintilian, *Inst. Or.* 2.4.2 [Feeney, 'Epilogue', p. 232]

Note, however, that Quintilian seeks to describe *all* narrative, not simply popular novelistic literature. There are no examples of 'history' as described by Quintilian, among the ancient novelistic writers. See also Pseudo-Cicero, *Rhet. ad Herr.* 1.8.12–13.

14. Feeney, 'Epilogue', p. 234 (ital. mine).

15. Feeney's point of comparison is not post-Enlightenment, but 'Christian culture' (see 'Epilogue', p. 241).

16. Wills, *Jewish Novel*, p. 12. On pp. 217–24 of the same book, Wills argues for the 'fictitious' nature of novels such as Judith and Esther.

17. Wills, *Jewish Novel*, p. 12 (ital. mine).

18. Morgan, 'Make-Believe', p. 229.

of the story within a novelistic text introduces a certain 'comfort in the knowledge that everything is safe in the hands of a rational power' that is characteristic of fiction literature.[19] Precisely because the genre is based in fiction, 'to read and to believe is a gesture of faith: faith in the possibility that reality could be like a Greek novel'.[20]

Primarily, however, I would suggest that the presence of novelistic stylistics and themes communicates that the story has a greater interest in *rhetoric* than in standards of historical verification. Through his use of novelistic stylistics, Mark communicates his desire to use his story for purposes of persuasion. Mark seeks *to influence as large an audience as possible*, including even the most inexperienced readers.[21] Such a concern for rhetoric over 'historical reporting' is not at all surprising in light of Mark's literary context. In her essay on 'The Rise of the Greek Novel', Consuelo Ruiz-Montero reminds us that 'the novel as genre is born, like the rest of the literature of the age, in a rhetorical-literary context'.[22] The Gospel of Mark as a Hellenistic writing is certainly not to be excluded from this description. Foundational studies of ancient literacy by classical scholar Walter Ong repeatedly assert that the language of ancient culture is inherently rhetorical.[23] Such a rhetorical-literary context had little, if any, use for 'objective history'. Kenneth Sack's short treatment of Hellenistic historiography in the *Oxford Classical Dictionary* pays much attention to the significant influence of rhetoric in novelistic history:

> Rhetoric played an important role in the development of [historical] narrative [in the Hellenistic world]. Historians had, since Thucydides, added speeches for variety, colour and dramatic tension. Isocrates ... influenced Theopompus and Ephorus to include also character assessments in passing moral and practical judgements on their subjects ....[24]

By writing in a form of novelistic literature, the author communicates that his concern for historicity is intrinsically subordinate to his concern for rhetoric.

The Gospel of Mark is also profoundly rhetorical. Robert Fowler's study of the Gospel demonstrates how the rhetoric of the Gospel

---

19.   Morgan, 'Make-Believe', p. 229.
20.   Morgan, 'Make-Believe', p. 229.
21.   See Section 1.1.
22.   Ruiz-Montero, 'The Rise of the Greek Novel', *NAW*, p. 68.
23.   For an introduction to the subject as well as a recent bibliography, see the reprint of Walter Ong, *Orality and Literacy: The Technologizing of the Word* (New Accents; London, New York: Methuen, 1982; reprinted Philadelphia: Taylor and Francis, 2002).
24.   Kenneth S. Sacks, 'historiography, Hellenistic', *OCD*, p. 715. Ancient texts do not make a strong distinction between history and fiction. See also Bowersock, *Fiction as History*; D.C. Feeney, 'Epilogue: Towards an Account of the Ancient World's Concepts of Fictive Beliefs'.

functions not merely to persuade, but also to 'construct its own reader'.[25] Fowler suggests that if one were to chart the emphases of the Gospel along two poles – the historically referential and the pragmatically rhetorical – one would discover the profoundly rhetorical nature of Mark's Gospel:

> The language of Mark's Gospel functions primarily along the rhetorical axis, with an emphasis on the pole of the reader .... Numerous passages in the Gospel do not function referentially. Rather, they function pragmatically ... molding and shaping its implied reader. The Gospel is not so much designed to construct its own world as it is designed to construct its own reader.[26]

Douglas Templeton makes a similar observation, which he identifies as a result of the peculiar blend of history and fiction that characterizes the bulk of Mark's narrative: 'the Jesus of popular fancy Mark creates on the model of the popular fancy ....'[27] Certainly Mark's novelistic stylistics are strikingly rudimentary in comparison to most Hellenistic historians – indeed, even in comparison to most popular literature.[28] The author of the Gospel employs these stylistics for the purpose of reaching a wide audience[29] so that his story might be enjoyed by the multitudes.[30] Through this preference for even the simplest of novelistic forms, the author of the Gospel communicates his concern to persuade as wide an audience as possible – indeed, to proclaim his good news 'to all the nations' (Mk 13.10).

6.1.2 *Discerning Homeric Influence in Hellenistic Novelistic Literature*
In addition to these contributions to the momentous question of Markan genre, this study also presents a nuanced approach to the much-debated issue of Homeric influence upon the Gospel of Mark. Garnering his inspiration from the extensive influence of Homer on education in the Hellenistic period, Dennis R. MacDonald argues that Homer, more than any other contemporary literature, is the 'primary literary inspiration' for Mark's 'prose epic modeled largely after *The Odyssey* and the ending of

---

25. Fowler, *Let the Reader*, p. 57.

26. Fowler, *Let the Reader*, p. 57. Here Fowler draws upon poles defined in an insightful study by Paul A. Hernadi entitled 'Literary Theory: A Compass for Critics' (*CI* 3 [1976], pp. 369–86).

27. Templeton, *True Fiction*, p. 64. See Templeton's Chapter 6 ('A Pigeon and the Solidity of Thin Air') for further reflections upon Mark as poet.

28. See, for example, the excerpt of Appian in Section 1.2.2.

29. See Section 1.1.

30. Compare the attention given to the multitudes in the text itself at Mk 1.5, 28, 33, 37, 45; 2.2, 13, 15; 3.6, 7; et al.

The Iliad.[31] Robert B. Coote and Mary P. Coote question the nature and extent of the Homeric influence that MacDonald asserts, citing Jewish Scripture as primary: 'the contrast between the prominence of references to Jewish Scripture and the magnitude of their significance and the obscurity of references to Homer – between substantiality and fragility – is extreme.'[32] While affirming the likelihood that Homeric literature influenced the Gospel of Mark as a Hellenistic text, Coote and Coote are also aware of the challenges of identifying such an influence:

> The biggest challenge now facing the project of finding Homer in Mark is to show how imitation of Homer, invisible though it was, contributed to the wider array of Mark's interconnected themes .... How does this imitation relate to Mark's use of what was, unlike Homer, his 'primary literary inspiration', the Jewish Scriptures?[33]

The present study claims to have identified several indications of the influence of Homeric literature upon Mark: the positioning of resurrection narratives at strategic points throughout Mark's story[34] as well as the qualification of the motif of death and the presence of an emotive crowd, phenomena that occur throughout Homeric literature but manifest themselves only rarely in the Hebrew Canon.[35] The 'invisibility' of this influence is affirmed in the general impact that these phenomena had upon much novelistic literature of the period: the Homeric texts may have directly influenced the author of the Gospel, or Homeric influence may

31.   MacDonald, *Homeric Epics*, p. 3.

32.   Coote and Coote, 'Homer', pp. 193–4. See n. 20 of Coote, 'Homer', p. 196 for an extensive and recent bibliography of 'significant books and articles on the use of the Scriptures in the New Testament'. For Mark in particular, see Marcus, *Way of the Lord*, 1 (as quoted at the opening of Chapter 4 of this study).

33.   Coote and Coote, 'Homer', p. 200. Hilhorst and Lalleman's critique of MacDonald's thesis that the novelistic *Acts of Andrew* represents a 'Christianized Homer' introduces other criticisms relevant to MacDonald's work with Mark: 'At best some of the parallels can make an intertextual relationship credible, but none of them suffices to prove that the author of the original *AA* has sought to produce a "baptized Odysseus" or a "baptized Socrates."' See MacDonald, *Christianizing Homer* and the critique by A. Hilhorst and Pieter J. Lalleman, 'The Acts of Andrew and Matthias: Is It Part of the Original *Acts of Andrew?*' in Bremmer (ed.), *The Apocryphal Acts of Andrew*, p. 13.

34.   'Petronius plays a subtle game: he does not force the models upon the reader's attention, but simply hints at them faintly through generic features, like vague suggestions of a direction to follow. Each model that he evokes is close enough to the narrative situation for some sort of comparison to be possible, but at the same time it must not be too near, to make sure the story does not lose its own narrative autonomy .... Petronius tends to use only a few major *structural* elements in order to evoke a famous literary model' (Conte, *Hidden Author*, p. 4, 16; italics mine).

35.   1 Kgs 17.17-24 is a resurrection narrative that highlights the introduction of a primary character. See Section 4.1.3.

have resulted indirectly from general Homeric trends manifest throughout contemporaneous novelistic literature.

One function of Homeric epic in particular may indicate an influence that is more direct than indirect. Mark's deployment of the resurrection topos, rooted in Homeric literature as it is, may have served as part of Mark's communication that his story, also, is an epic to be recognized as the new scripture of the community. Conte's studies of ancient literature identify an 'epic code, ... the narrative elements and descriptive devices that belong to the genre from Homer on ....' at work throughout the ancient world. [36] According to Conte, this epic code:

> allows a community to consolidate its historical experiences, conferring sense on them, until they become an exemplary system that is recognized as the community's new cultural text or scripture. Such a code is a source and a story of interconnected values, vividly displayed in the actions of heroes, on which the community can draw as an organic arrangement of its own cultural foundations.
>
> The epic code is the preliminary level of that elaboration whose purpose is *the literary organization, in narrative form, of collective cultural values*. Essentially, it is a function rather than a set of contents. Obviously, though, cultural history offers not abstract forms of organization but values and contents made concretely available – single epic texts.[37]

So Mark's placement of narratives of death and revival at strategic points throughout his story, the inclusion of emotive-reactive crowds, and the qualification of the element of death in two of the three narratives may contribute to an authorial communication that the story is not intended as history, nor even simply as story, but rather as an epic that conveys the values of his community in narrative form. Mark claims that his story is a story of representative Christian existence, providing his community with a sense of its foundations and values that is much needed after the fall of the Jerusalem Temple in 70 C.E. Mark's story is to be the new 'cultural scripture' for his community.

In this view, the Gospel of Mark functions analogously to the letters of Paul in the early Christian communities. Gerd Theissen describes the phenomenon in this way:

> If we ask why the evangelists wrote, in my view we find in them the same motivation as that of Paul in writing his letters. In critical phases he wanted to influence his communities to think like him and to guide them. That challenged him as a writer. The same motivation to produce literature is also at work among the evangelists. They too wanted to

---

36. Conte, *Rhetoric of Imitation*, p. 13. For an appreciation of the topos of resurrection as part of the epic code, see Section 3.2.

37. Conte, *Rhetoric of Imitation*, pp. 142–3 (ital. mine).

guide communities in and after crises. They do so not by giving direct instructions in letters, but in an indirect way by telling a story about Jesus.[38]

An appeal to an epic code in addition to the biblical traditions that resound throughout Mark's story would legitimize the foundational story for audience members of the diverse Hellenistic world who might not ascribe import to biblical traditions. Templeton's theory regarding the generic communication of Mark's Gospel also points to communal formation. For Templeton, the novelistic genre communicates an interest in *constituting* people. Mark is not interested in history, but fiction (< Latin *facere*, to make or create), that is, the molding and shaping of the audience, drawing upon 'the power of art both to modify our grasp of the real and even partly to *constitute*' his ancient audience's grasp of the real.[39]

Such an understanding of Mark's relationship to Homeric literature meets 'a challenge that proponents of the primacy of Homer in Mark appear at present disinclined to take up' in that the theory identifies one possible way in which Homeric literature 'contribute(s) to the wider array of Mark's interconnected themes ... and relate(s) to Mark's use of ... the Jewish Scriptures'.[40] Through his use of both the Epic resurrection topos and Jewish scriptures, Mark informs his diverse audience that his story is a foundational narrative for the establishment of the culture of his Christian community.

6.1.3 *Conclusion*

The specific demonstration of literary imitation and the strategic deployment of topoi that this study presents provide compelling new evidence that Mark participates in the genre of novelistic literature. Mark's Gospel is not primarily a history or biography of the life of Jesus, but rather an entertaining story of good news aimed at the wide audience of non-elite people of the ancient Hellenistic world. The combined influence of epic and prophetic traditions on the story further suggests not only this goal, but also a desire to establish an epic norm that would serve as 'an exemplary system, ... recognized as the community's new cultural text or scripture' in order to establish the identity of the diverse community.[41] The author of the Gospel of Mark molds the details of

---

38. Gerhard Theissen, *Fortress Introduction to the New Testament* [Minneapolis: Fortress, 2003], p. 118. See also Helmut Koester, 'Apostel und Gemeinde in den Briefen an die Thessalonischer', in Lührmann and Strecker (eds), *Kirche: Festschrift für Günther Bornkamm zum 75. Geburtstag*, pp. 287–98.

39. Templeton, *True Fiction*, p. 65.

40. Coote and Coote, 'Homer', p. 200.

41. Conte, *Rhetoric of Imitation*, p. 142.

Jesus' life in order to best convey an experience and shape the identity of a young, diverse community.[42] Indeed, this point is conveyed through the authority of the central character Jesus as he gives post-resurrection instructions (Mk 9.9, 13.10) and commissions the disciples to return to Galilee (Mk 16.7; cf. 14.28) for their continued existence in a manner that is consonant with this new scripture of the community.

6.2 *Situating Mark Historically: The Contributions of this Study*

At the end of Part I, I identified studies by scholars Porter and Brown, who argue for Greek influence upon Jewish and early Christian ideas of resurrection.[43] The observations of this study suggest a historical development of the idea that comes closest to the reconstruction proffered by Brown. The influence of Greek epic and culture foster the further development of a biblical motif of resurrection.[44] In addition to this broad appreciation of the existence and influence of the Epic resurrection topos upon Mark's Gospel, this study addresses two historical issues that are otherwise significant for Markan studies. The first issue takes up a call to nuance modern conceptions of ethnicity in antiquity (Section 6.2.1). Mark's Gospel has often been read as though fixed and rigid conceptions of ethnicity and race existed in the Hellenistic period of history. Intricate patterns of things 'Jewish' and things 'Greek' are identified to reveal subtle communications in the Gospel. This study, through its in-depth examination of resurrection topoi, contributes to a growing scholarly appreciation for the fluidity that characterizes the conception of cultural traditions in the Hellenistic period. The second issue related to the historical context of Mark is theoretical, seeking to determine the impetus behind the profusion of resurrection narratives throughout the Hellenistic period (Section 6.2.2).

6.2.1 *The Hybrid Cultures of the Hellenistic Period*
In the 1970s and '80s, a significant number of Markan studies identified 'Jewish' and 'Gentile' communications in the Gospel, hypothesizing a conflicted Jewish/Gentile identity in need of reconciliation. An assortment of early Christian cultural reconciliation programs was hypothesized that continue to have an influence on current Markan scholarship. For

42. See Conte, *Rhetoric of Imitation*, p. 108.

43. Martin argues for a Greek notion of resurrection that predates Christianity, but holds that Jewish eschatology rather than Greek mythology, was formative upon the early Christians. See Section 2.5.

44. In my view, Porter's analysis does not give sufficient recognition to biblical influences. Note that John P. Brown also unnecessarily limits the biblical expression to 'the Psalms' (Brown, *Ancient Israel*, p. 24).

example, in his study of geography in the Gospel, Werner Kelber reads the presentation of Jesus' ministry in Mk 4.35–8.21 as an attempt on the part of the author to reconcile Jewish and Gentile facets of the identity of his Hellenistic Jewish community. Kelber argues that a 'duplication of traditional material' available to the author provided comparable miracle stories which the author could juxtapose in both Jewish and Gentile settings.[45] The initial crossing of the sea (4.35-41) brings Jesus to the land of the Gerasenes, where – Kelber asserts – 'a definite Gentile coloring of the territory' includes the specific designation of the land as the Decapolis.[46] The situation reverses, however, after Jesus and his disciples 'cross again to the other side' (5.21): 'As clearly as the Decapolis exorcism was painted in Gentile colors, so are the two miracles of the raising of Jairus' daughter and the woman with a hemorrhage placed into a recognizably Jewish milieu'.[47] Kelber's analysis follows the text back and forth across the Sea of Galilee to arrive at the conclusion that:

> ... in 4.35–8.21 Mark comes to terms with the Gentile mission and the ethnic identity of his community .... The boat trips are designed to dramatize ... a unitive movement, alternating between the two sides of the sea. The lake, losing its forces as a barrier, is transposed into a symbol of unity, bridging the gulf between Jewish and Gentile Christians. The two are the one. Galilee is no longer ethnically confined to either a Jewish or a Gentile Christian identity, rather 'all of Galilee' is where Jewish Christians and Gentile Christians live together in the newness of the Kingdom.[48]

The final statement asserts a dichotomy between 'Jewish Christians and Gentile Christians'.

Jean-Marie van Cangh studied geographical and linguistic elements in the twin traditions regarding the multiplication of the loaves in Mark's Gospel (6.30-44; 8.1-10, 17-21) in his argument that the coloring of the two stories allows for the representation of Jewish and Greek identities.

> Ce qui nous semble évident, c'est que Marc a placé *rédactionnellement* la première multiplication des pains en territoire juif et la seconde en territoire païen .... Cette inconséquence dans l'itinéraire de Jésus s'explique du fait que Marc a voulu intégrer deux théologies en partie contradictoires ....[49]

---

45. Werner Kelber, *The Kingdom in Mark: A New Place and A New Time* (Philadelphia: Fortress, 1974), p. 63.

46. Kelber, *Kingdom*, p. 51.

47. Kelber, *Kingdom*, p. 52.

48. Kelber, *Kingdom*, p. 62–3.

49. Jean-Marie van Cangh, *La Multiplication des Pains et L'Eucharistie* (Lectio Divina, 86; Paris: Éditions du Cerf, 1975), p. 131. Van Cangh's study makes no reference to Kelber's work.

Citing van Cangh, Donald Senior affirms the conclusion regarding the author's desire to integrate the two identities: 'The first story ... takes place in *Jewish* territory .... The second feeding ... is clearly a feeding of *Gentiles*: Jesus returns to Jewish territory on the other side of the lake only at Mk 8.10. Thus the Markan Jesus feeds both Jews *and* Gentiles.'[50]

More recently, Donahue and Harrington describe Jesus' movement at the beginning of Mark 5 as progressing 'from the western (Jewish) side of the lake to the eastern (Gentile) side'.[51] Daniel Marguerat has identified 'a programme of the theological integration' in Luke-Acts and Josephus between early Jewish tradition and a Hellenistic readership.[52]

Such proposals, however, pose an artificial dichotomy that fails to recognize how any expression of Judaism in the first century – be it Christian or otherwise – 'is itself a species of Hellenism'.[53] For John J. Collins and Erich Gruen, the dynamics of the Jewish response to Hellenistic culture in the period after the conquests of Alexander the Great are difficult to discern, for Hellenism was 'the sea in which [the early Jews] swam and was an integral part of their identity'.[54] Buell and Johnson Hodge's reading of Paul's letters elicits a sense for 'the fluidity and messiness of ethnoracial categories'.[55]

In its reading of resurrection narratives from pre-Hellenistic into the Hellenistic period, this study supports the conclusions of scholars such as Collins, Gruen, Boyarin, Buell and Johnson Hodge, among others.[56]

---

50. Donald Senior, 'The Eucharist in Mark: Mission, Reconciliation, Hope,' *BTB* 12 (1982), pp. 67–71 (68–9). See also Donahue and Harrington: 'Here the disciples are challenged to see Jesus as the one bread who unites both Jews and Gentiles' (*Gospel*, p. 254).

51. Donahue and Harrington, *Gospel of Mark*, p. 157.

52. Daniel Marguerat, *The First Christian Historian: Writing the 'Acts of the Apostles'* (trans. Ken McKinney, Gregory J. Laughtery, and Richard Bauckham; SNTSMS, 121; New York and Cambridge, Engl.: Cambridge University Press, 2002), p. 66.

In his argumentation against reading Mark as a 'Greek novel', Michael Vines asserts a 'cultural difference' between Mark as Jewish literature and the novels as Greek literature: 'In Jewish and Christian literature, interest in the alienated individual does not overwhelm a concern for the larger community as it does in the Greek novel .... The cultural difference between these two groups of readers is more pronounced than Tolbert seems to allow' (Vines, *Problem*, pp. 20–1).

53. Boyarin, *Border Crossings*, p. 235, n. 73.

54. John J. Collins, *Between Athens and Jerusalem: Jewish Identity in the Hellenistic Diaspora* (BRS; Grand Rapids, Mich. and Cambridge, Engl.: Eerdmans, 2nd edn, 2000), p. 261. Erich S. Gruen's study of Jewish identity in the Hellenistic period concludes that the Jews 'were part and parcel of Hellenistic societies in the Diaspora ... not so much permeated by the culture of the Greeks as they were an example of it' (*Heritage and Hellenism*, p. 292). Boyarin affirms Gruen's point: ' "Judaism" is a species of Hellenism' (*Border Lines*, p. 235, n. 73).

55. Buell and Johnson Hodge, 'Politics of Interpretation', p. 251.

56. See, for example, the collection of essays in Adam H. Becker and Annette Yoshkio Reed (eds), *The Ways That Never Parted: Jews and Christians in Late Antiquity and the Early Middle Ages* (TSAJ 95; Tübingen: J.C.B. Mohr [Paul Siebeck], 2003).

Within the pre-Hellenistic period, the Epic and Prophetic topoi maintain broad characteristics which I have identified in Chapter 3 and in the beginning of Chapter 4. However, in Hellenistic literature such as Tobit, Greek Esther and the Gospel of Mark, traditional and ethnic characteristics blend and merge in such a way as to become increasingly difficult to identify.[57]

6.2.2 *Why Resurrection?*

Scholarly studies of resurrection in the Hellenistic period suggest a variety of factors that contributed to the increased use of resurrection themes at the time. For example, John J. Collins describes the idea of resurrection as one means by which certain early Jewish communities might have coped with increased religious persecution, particularly manifest in apocalyptic literature.[58] John P. Brown notes the sharing of culture and ideas at the time as another potential impetus.[59] Observations in Part I of this study suggest that increased literacy within popular culture might also have served as a catalyst for the increased occurrence of resurrection themes in Hellenistic texts in comparison to earlier periods since resurrection was a popular theme.[60] In this section I will focus upon the contribution that the reading in Part II of this study contributes to this question. These texts suggest that the prominence of resurrection narratives in the Hellenistic period is one of the outcomes of this significantly increased rate of change related to the social and ethnic mobility of the period.

Whether one characterizes the influence of Hellenistic culture following the conquests of Alexander the Great as a period of cultural diffusion ('Hellenism') or cultural imperialization ('Hellenization'), the rapid rate of change that marks this period is practically undisputed.[61] In the

---

57. A similar study has been undertaken by Loveday Alexander, who compares the literary presentation of battles in classical Greek (Herodotus, Thucydides) and biblical literature (Josh. 6) with the Hellenistic text of the Gospel of Luke to conclude that 'where there is a significant difference between the two traditions, Luke follows the biblical approach to historiography almost every time' (Loveday C.A. Alexander, 'Marathon or Jericho? Reading Acts in Dialogue with Biblical and Greek Historiography', in Clines and Moore (eds), *Auguries: The Jubilee Volume of the Sheffield Department of Biblical Studies*, pp. 92–125 (119). See also O. Wesley Allen's study, *The Death of Herod: The Narrative and Theological Function of Retribution in Luke-Acts* (SBLDS, 158; Atlanta: Scholars, 1997), a monograph that traces the motif of the death of the tyrant in classical Greek (Herodotus, etc.) and biblical (2 Chronicles, etc.) narratives for a comparison with the Gospel of Luke.

58. Collins, *Apocalyptic Imagination*, pp. 112–13. Also notable is Nickelsburg, *Resurrection*, pp. 11–42.

59. Brown, *Ancient Israel*, p. 24.

60. See Chapter 2.

61. Bowersock argues against the word 'Hellenization' because of its suggestion of cultural imperialism: 'The very notion of Hellenization ... is a useless barometer for assessing Greek culture. There is not even a word for it in classical or Byzantine Greek. Hellenism was

Hellenistic world, 'physical, ethnic, and social mobility were the order of the day .... Such mobility fired cultural exchange and assimilation to hitherto unheard of levels.'[62] The resurrection narratives this study has examined frequently reflect radical changes related, in particular, to social and ethnic mobility. However, the narratives do more than merely *reflect*. In Jewish and early Christian literature, resurrection narratives also *project* hope for political change in the midst of this dynamism.

Issues of social change provide the context for the majority of resurrection narratives examined in the course of this study. In Tob. 8.9-18, themes of resurrection occur in conjunction with marriage, a primary means of social change. In Add. Esth. 15.1-16, the heroine's acceptance among the ranks of the king prompts her death and return to life. Note how Chariton associates Callirhoë's second 'death' with a loss of social status via her desperate prayer to Aphrodite:

> [8] 'Then you delivered me into the hands of tomb robbers and brought me from the tomb to the sea and subjected me to pirates more awful than the waves. For this I was given my famed beauty, that the pirate Theron might win a high price for me! [9] I have been sold in an isolated place and was not even brought to the city as any other slave might be, for you were afraid, Fortune, that if any saw me, they might judge me nobly born. That is why I have been handed over like a mere chattel to I know not whom, whether Greeks or orientals or brigands once more.'
>
> As she beat her breast with her fist, she saw on her ring the image of Chaereas, and kissing it, she said, 'Chaereas, now I am truly lost to you, separated by so vast a sea. [10] You are repenting in grief as you sit by the empty tomb, bearing witness to my chastity after my death, while I, the daughter of Hermocrates, your wife, have today been sold to a master!'

(Chariton, *Callir.* 1.14.8–10 [Goold, LCL 481])

---

a language and culture in which peoples of the most diverse kind could participate. That is exactly what makes it so remarkable. Hellenization is ... a modern idea, reflecting modern forms of cultural domination' (*Hellenism in Late Antiquity* [JL, 18; Ann Arbor: University of Michigan Press, 1990], p. 7).

Peter Green, on the other hand, asserts that 'Hellenization meant the interpenetration of Greek and Oriental culture .... The customary method of diffusion was by way of imposed rule, military settlements, commercial exploitation, by men who brought their language, culture, and administration with them, and enforced their authority by means of a mercenary army. Exploitation exacerbated poverty, so that resistance was often felt at all social levels, with an abused peasantry rallying behind a dispossessed aristocracy or priesthood. The conquerors' artificial islands of culture were at first no more acceptable than a wrongly matched heart transplant' (Green, *Alexander*, p. 323).

62. Tolbert, *Sowing*, p. 38.

In her death, Callirhoë's social status drops from 'famed beauty' (*Callir.* 1.14.8) and noble birth (1.14.9) as 'the daughter of Hermocrates' (1.14.10) to 'mere chattel' (1.14.9) 'sold to a master' (1.14.10). Nevertheless, through her resurrection, Callirhoë regains her noble status. Dressed 'in Tyrian purple', her father reclaims her before all of the people of Syracuse (8.6.7–8). The story of *Joseph and Aseneth* also relates resurrection to a change of social status, though the status relates specifically to conversion:

> In *Joseph & Aseneth* the language of renewal and restoration to life simply denotes advancement from the nothingness of heathen existence to the glorious existence of the one who worships God ... The change is one of status, not of essential nature. The emphasis is on the contrast between Aseneth's former status and her present status, and the contrast is so radical that it is best expressed with the language of re-creation.[63]

Within the social mobility of the Hellenistic world, the changes that result from acceptance within a new society – familial, royal, or religious – are sufficiently radical to find expression in terms of resurrection.

In Jewish and early Christian resurrection narratives, such radical change is not primarily social, but rather political change. Facing oppression from the Roman Empire, groups such as the early Jews and Christians wanted to see change and to see it happen dramatically, such that hope of change found expression in resurrection.[64] In his recent study of *The Resurrection of the Son of God*, Nicholas T. Wright identifies a 'note' that 'runs from at least Daniel and 2 Maccabees through Paul and John to Ignatius, the Apocalypse of Peter, Justin, Tertullian and Irenaeus, that resurrection is a revolutionary doctrine which has to do with the creator's overthrow of the kingdoms of the world'.[65] One of the ways in which the author of the Gospel of Mark, in particular, dramatizes the hope that a new kingdom, 'the kingdom of God', is 'at hand' (Mk 1.15) is through resurrection narratives. For Mark, the hope is for a kingdom that will radically change the sicknesses (5.21-24, 35-43), afflictions (9.14-29), and injustices (15.33-47) of the present world system, resulting in a new world in which God brings new life (16.1-8). Ultimately, 'resurrection means that God acts to reclaim the real world to which the Herods and the Caesars have staked their false claims. The resurrection [of Jesus] is the

---

63. Chestnutt, *From Death to Life*, pp. 148–9.

64. For a detailed study of the composition of the Gospel 'in Rome ... in the latter months of 71 in response to the stressful situation that existed for the Christians of that city', see Brian J. Incigneri, *The Gospel to the Romans: The Setting and Rhetoric of Mark's Gospel* (BIS, 65; Boston and Leiden: Brill Academic, 2003), p. 2.

65. N.T. Wright, *The Resurrection of the Son of God* (COQG; London: SPCK, 2003), p. 549.

beginning of the new creation, the beginning of a new phase in the history of Israel and the world.'[66]

Because radical change abounded in the Hellenistic era, resurrection narratives played a significant role in popular, novelistic literature of the period. These narratives are unique in their ability to contain and convey – in appropriately dramatic terms – both the radical experiences of social change that abounded at this time as well as the hopes for radical, political change that arose in communities such as those of the early Christians.

6.2.3 *Conclusion*

The hybrid nature of resurrection narratives throughout the Gospel of Mark sustains the academic contention that the historic period in which the Gospel was composed was one of great diversity and change. In times such as this, Hellenistic communities identified with expressions of resurrection in part as a result of their unique ability to convey through story the dynamics that accompany occasions of dramatic change.

6.3 *Conclusion*

My reading of themes of death followed by a return to life on earth within literature that bears a close relationship to the Gospel of Mark suggests several new observations about the literary-historical context of the Gospel in general and the literary patterning of the Gospel in particular. I have traced two basic topoi of resurrection operative among storytellers in the ancient Eastern Mediterranean. Numerous resurrection narratives in Homeric epic and the prophetic literature of the Hebrew Bible intimate the existence of recurring constellations of motifs in the period – resurrection topoi. The Epic resurrection topos typically begins in confusion and progresses through death and resurrection to arrive at a place of enlightenment. In the Prophetic resurrection topos, resurrection themes begin with a breach of trust on the part of the divine and progress through death and resurrection to conclude with the reestablishment of the divine communion.

Early in the Hellenistic period, these traditions begin a process of blending that extended to the writing of the Gospel of Mark and beyond. Elements of both the Epic and Prophetic resurrection topoi are present in

---

66. Robert H. Smith, '(W)right Thinking on the Resurrection (?)', *Dialog* 43 (Sept. 2004), pp. 244–51. For an extended reading of political subversion in the Gospel of Mark, see Richard A. Horsley, *Hearing the Whole Story: The Politics of Plot in Mark's Gospel* (Louisville, Ky.: Westminster John Knox, 2001): 'Mark's story presents the renewal of Israel under the enabling kingdom of God spearheaded by Jesus as the fulfillment of the history and hopes of the people of Israel' (p. 235). Horsley analyzes the resurrection narratives as 'a program of village community renewal' written for imperially subjected people (pp. 94–7).

Jewish novelistic writings of the Hellenistic period, such as Tobit, Greek Esther, and *Joseph & Aseneth*. Rather strikingly, the Epic topos dominates, manifesting its influence not only in the elements of resurrection narration, but also in the occurrence of these narratives at strategic points in the story. The Gospel of Mark participates in this trend. In this Gospel, resurrections – in which death is often qualified and crowds react – occur at points in the story that highlight the ironic presentation of Jesus' powerful ministry and the disciples' failure to appreciate that ministry.

In his study of the genre of the Gospel of Mark in light of certain literary theories of Russian scholar Mikhail Bakhtin, Michael E. Vines makes the proposition 'that the chronotope of the Gospel of Mark most closely resembles that of the Jewish novels', to which he hastily adds that 'this is not to deny other influences on the composition of the Gospel'.[67] Further on he notes: 'In the context of the first century, it would not be surprising to find that Mark, to one degree or another, borrowed from both Greek and Jewish literary forms.'[68] The present study also attempts to relate the Gospel of Mark to the novelistic literature of its day. My own starting point is not modern literary theories such as Bakhtin's chronotope, but rather a specific theme drawn directly from the literary-historical context of the Gospel: the theme of resurrection. My reading of ancient texts that bear a close literary-historical relationship to the Gospel of Mark discerns both Epic and Prophetic topoi working together in such a manner that any position which would assign either Jewish or Greek characteristics to the Gospel as a whole (as Vines) seems misguided. Furthermore, contrary to Vines' assertion that Mark is a Jewish novel, the resurrection narratives in the Gospel exhibit a greater influence on the part of an Epic topos than on the part of a Prophetic topos. Once again, 'the Gospels seem to lie "between" several genres', suggesting that Mark's Gospel most closely resembles the open genre of Hellenistic novelistic literature.[69]

Consequently, scholars of the New Testament have new incentive to explore ancient works of novelistic literature in their efforts to better appreciate the literary nature of the Gospel of Mark and the Gospels which derive from it. The observations made regarding the nature and placement of resurrection narratives in the Gospel of Mark constitute just one example of some of the insights to be gained by taking seriously Mark's participation within novelistic literature. There are other themes and topoi of novelistic literature that might profitably be explored for further appreciation of the generic dynamics and communications of the

---

67. Vines, *Problem*, p. 153.
68. Vines, *Problem*, p. 163.
69. Wills, *Quest*, p. 11. See also Section 1.7 of the present study.

Gospel of Mark. Observations regarding the strategic deployment in ancient novelistic literature of motifs of travel, recognition, torture, incarnation, dreams, daughters, heroic monologues, and the role of 'Rumor' or fast-spreading news, among others, may contribute to a greater appreciation of the nature, structure, and the heritage of Mark's Gospel.

Since its composition, this Gospel has continued to speak to people of various and diverse backgrounds spanning multiple generations. As a result of this history, the Gospel is both a type of 'constitution' and a 'classic' of Christian literature.[70] Indeed, I would suggest that – despite the centuries – Mark's deployment of the resurrection stories communicates two primary Christian values that continue to merit repetition within the postmodern church of the twenty-first century. First, the resurrection narratives in the Gospel of Mark communicate hope for change that results in a new world system in which sickness (Mk 5.21-24, 35-43), affliction (9.14-29), and injustice (15.33-47) are replaced by a renewed life that arises as a result of divine power (16.1-8). Second, the popular, novelistic style of the Gospel indicates that Mark intended his message of God's love for as wide an audience as possible.

May the Gospel of Mark, and the symbols of resurrection that this Christian classic employs, continue to call the widest possible audience to hold out hope in the power of the divine to effect positive change for the future.

---

70. See Sallie MacFague, *Life Abundant: Rethinking Theology and Ecology for a Planet in Peril* (Minneapolis: Fortress, 2001), pp. 58–60.

BIBLIOGRAPHY

Abma, Richtsje, *Bonds of Love: Studies of Prophetic Texts with Marriage Imagery* (SSN, 40; Assen: Van Gorcum, 1999).

Achilles Tatius, *Leucippe and Clitophon* (ed., trans. by Stephen Gaselee; LCL, 45; London: Harvard University Press, 1947).

Achtemeier, Paul J., 'Mark, Gospel of', in Freedman (ed.), *ABD*, 2.541-57.

Aescuylus, *Agamemnon*, in Smyth (ed.), *Agamemnon; Libation-Bearers; Eumenides; Fragments*, 1–152.

Alexander, Joseph A., *Commentary on the Gospel of Mark* (repr., Grand Rapids, Mich.: Zondervan, 1955).

Alexander, Loveday C.A., 'Marathon or Jericho? Reading Acts in Dialogue with Biblical and Greek Historiography', in Clines and Moore (eds), *Auguries*, 92–125.

Allen, Leslie C., *Ezekiel 20-48* (WBC, 29; Waco, Texas: Word, 1982).

Allison, Dale C., *Testament of Abraham* (CEJL; Berlin: de Gruyter, 2003).

Alt, Albrecht, 'Hosea 5.8-6.6: Ein Krieg und Seine Folgen in Prophetischer Beleuchtung', in Albrecht Alt, *Kleine Schriften zur Geschichte des Volkes Israel* (2 vols; Munich: C.H. Beck, 3rd edn, 1964), 2.163-87.

Alter, Robert, *Art of Biblical Narrative* (New York: Basic Books, 1981).

Amanat, Abbas, and Magnus Bernardsson (eds), *Imagining the End: Visions of Apocalypse from the Ancient Middle East to Modern America* (London: I.B. Tauris, 2002).

Andersen, Francis I., and David N. Freedman, *Hosea* (AB, 24; New York: Doubleday, 1980).

Anderson, Graham, 'The Greek Novel', in Reardon (ed.), *Erotica Antiqua*, 165–71.

—'Introduction' to Xenophon of Ephesus, *An Ephesian Tale* in *CAGN*, 125–8.

Anderson, Hugh, *The Gospel of Mark* (NCB; London: Oliphants, 1976).

Ando, Clifford, *Imperial Ideology and Provincial Loyalty in the Roman Empire* (CCT, 6; Berkeley: University of California Press, 2000).

Antonius Diogenes, *The Wonders beyond Thule* in Stephens and Winkler (eds), *Ancient Greek Novels: The Fragments*, 101–72.

Apollodorus, *Bibliotheca (The Library)* (ed., trans. James G. Frazer; 2 vols; LCL, 121–2; London: Harvard University Press, 1960).

Appian, *Roman History* (ed., trans. Horace White; 4 vols; LCL, 2–5; London: Harvard University Press, 1912).

Apuleius, *The Golden Ass* (trans. Jack Lindsay; Indiana University Greek and Latin Classics; Indianapolis: Indiana University Press, 1960).

—*Les Métamorphoses* (ed. Donald S. Robertson; trans. Paul Vallette; 3 vols; Paris: Budé, 1940–5).

Aristotle, *Poetics* in Halliwell (ed.), *Aristotle: Poetics; Longius: On the Sublime; Demetrius: On Style*, 1–142.

—*Politics* (ed., trans. Harris Rackham; LCL, 264; London: Harvard University Press, 1932).

—*The Art of Rhetoric* (ed., trans. John H. Freese; LCL, 193; London: Harvard University Press, 1926).

Arnim, Hans Friedrich A. von, *Stoicorum Veterum Fragmenta* (Leipzig: B.G. Teubner, 1921–4).

Ascough, Richard S., 'Narrative Technique and Generic Designation: Crowd Scenes in Luke-Acts and in Chariton', *CBQ* 58 (Jan 1996), 69–81.

Aune, David E. (ed.), *Greco-Roman Literature and the New Testament: Selected Forms and Genres* (SBS, 21; Atlanta: Scholars, 1988).

Avemarie, Friedrich, and Hermann Lichtenberger (eds), *Auferstehung = Resurrection: The Fourth Durham-Tübingen Research Symposium* (WUNT, 135; Tübingen: J.C.B. Mohr [Paul Siebeck], 2001).

Bailey, Lloyd R, *Biblical Perspectives on Death* (OBT; Philadelphia: Fortress, 1979).

Baltzer, Klaus, *Die Biographie der Propheten* (Neukirchen-Vluyn: Neukirchener, 1975).

Bartol, Krystyna, 'From Cyzicus to Samothracians: On the Allusion to the Homeric Verse in *Anth. Pal.* 11.346', *Eos* 82 (1994), 31–6.

Bauer, Johannes B., 'Drei Tage', *Biblica* 39 (1958), 354–8.

Becker, Adam H. and Reed, Annette Yoshkio (eds), *The Ways That Never Parted: Jews and Christians in Late Antiquity and the Early Middle Ages* (TSAJ 95; Tübingen: J.C.B. Mohr [Paul Siebeck], 2003).

Betz, Hans D., *Lukian von Samosata und das neue Testament: Religionsgeschichtliche und paränetische Parallelen* (TU, 76; Berlin: Akademie, 1961).

Bickerman, Elias J., 'Das Leere Grab', *ZNW* 23 (1924), 281–91; reprinted in Elias J. Bickerman, *Studies in Jewish and Christian History* (AGJU, 9; Leiden: Brill, 1986), 3.70–81.

Block, Daniel I., *The Book of Ezekiel: Chapters 25–48* (NICOT; Cambridge, Engl.: Eerdmans, 1997).

Boadt, Lawrence, *Reading the Old Testament: An Introduction* (Mahwah, N.J.; New York: Paulist, 1984).

Booth, Wayne C., *A Rhetoric of Irony* (Chicago: University of Chicago Press, 1974).

Borrell, Augusti, *The Good News of Peter's Denial: A Narrative and Rhetorical Reading of Mark 14.54, 66-72* (trans. Sean Conlon; ISFCJ; Atlanta: Scholars, 1998).

Bowersock, Glen W., *Fiction as History: Nero to Julian* (SCL, 58; Berkeley: University of California Press, 1994).

—*Hellenism in Late Antiquity* (JL, 18; Ann Arbor: University of Michigan Press, 1990).

Bowie, Ewen L., 'The Ancient Readers of the Greek Novels', in NAW, 87–106.

—'The Greek Novel', in Easterling and Knox (eds), *Greek Literature*, 683–99.

—'Novel, Greek', in *OCD*, 1049–50.

Boyarin, Daniel, *Border Lines: The Partition of Judaeo-Christianity* (DRLAR; Philadelphia: University of Pennsylvania Press, 2004).

Bremmer, Jan N., *The Apocryphal Acts of Andrew* (SAAA, 5; Leuven, Belgium: Peeters, 2000).

Bronner, Leila L., 'The Resurrection Motif in the Hebrew Bible: Allusions or Illusions', *JBQ* 30 (2002), 143–54.

Brown, John Pairman, *Ancient Israel and Ancient Greece: Religion, Politics and Culture* (Minneapolis: Fortress, 2003).

Brown, Raymond E., *An Introduction to the New Testament* (Anchor Bible Reference Library; New York: Doubleday, 1997).

—'Jesus and Elisha', *Perspectives* 12 (1971), 85–99.

Bruce, F.F., *Paul: Apostle of the Heart Set Free* (Exeter: Paternoster; Grand Rapids, Mich.: Eerdmans, 1977).

Büchsel, Friedrich, 'γίνομαι, γένεσις, γένος, γένημα, ἀπογίνομαι, παλιγγενεσία', in Kittel and Friedrich (eds), *Theological Dictionary of the New Testament*, 1.681–9.

Buell, Denise Kimber, and Caroline Johnson Hodge, 'The Politics of Interpretation: The Rhetoric of Race and Ethnicity in Paul', *JBL* 123 (2004), 235–51.

Bultmann, Rudolf, *The History of the Synoptic Tradition* (trans. John Marsh; New York: Harper and Row, 1972).

Burchard, Charles, 'Joseph and Aseneth', in Charlesworth (ed.), *Old Testament Pseudepigrapha*, 2.177–247.

Calame, Claude, *Le Récit en Grèce Antique* (Semiotique; Paris: Klincksieck, 1986).

[Pseudo-]Callisthenes, *The Alexander Romance* in Merkelbach (ed.), *Die Quellen des griechischen Alexanderromans*, 227–83.

Camery-Hoggatt, Jerry, *Irony in Mark's Gospel: Text and Subtext* (SNTSMS, 72; Cambridge, Engl.: Cambridge University Press, 1992).

Campbell, Antony F., *Of Prophets and Kings: A Late Ninth Century Document (1 Samuel 1 – 2 Kings 10* (CBQMS, 17; Washington, D.C.: Catholic Biblical Association of America, 1986).

Cancik, Hubert (ed.), *Markus-Philologie: Historische, literargeschichtliche und stilistische Untersuchungen zum zweiten Evangelium* (WUNT, 33; Tübingen: J.C.B. Mohr [Paul Siebeck], 1984).

Cancik, Hubert, and Helmuth Schneider (eds), *Brill's New Pauly: Encyclopaedia of the Ancient World* (Boston and Leiden: Brill Academic, 2001–).

Cangh, Jean-Marie van, *La Multiplication des Pains et L'Eucharistie* (Lectio Divina, 86; Paris: Éditions du Cerf, 1975).

Carroll, Robert P. (ed.), *Text as Pretext: Essays in Honour of Robert Davidson* (JSOTSup, 138; Sheffield, Engl.: JSOT, 1992).

Chariton, *Callirhoë* (ed., trans. George P. Goold; LCL, 481; London: Harvard University Press, 1995).

Charlesworth, James H. (ed.), *The Old Testament Pseudepigrapha* (2 vols; New York: Doubleday, 1985).

Chestnutt, Randall, *From Death to Life: Conversion in Joseph and Aseneth* (JSPSup, 16; Sheffield, Engl.: Sheffield Academic, 1995).

Cicero, *Brutus*, in Hendrickson and Hubbell (eds), *Brutus; Orator*, 1–296.

[Pseudo-]Cicero, *Rhetorica ad Herennium* (ed., trans., Harry Caplan; LCL, 403; London: Harvard University Press, 1954).

Claussen, Carsten, *Versammlung, Gemeinde, Synagoge: Das hellenistisch-jüdische Umfeld der frühchristlichen Gemeinden* (SUNT, 27; Göttingen: Vandenhoeck & Ruprecht, 2002).

Clines, David J.A., and Stephen D. Moore (eds), *Auguries: The Jubilee Volume of the Sheffield Department of Biblical Studies* (JSOTSup 269; Sheffield, Engl.: Sheffield Academic, 1998).

Coffey, Michael, *Roman Satire* (Bristol: Bristol Classical, 2nd edn, 1989).

Cogan, Mordechai, *1 Kings* (AB, 10; New York: Doubleday, 2000).

Collins, Adela Yarbro, *The Beginning of the Gospel: Probings of Mark in Context* (Minneapolis: Fortress, 1992).

Collins, John J., *The Apocalyptic Imagination: An Introduction to Jewish Apocalyptic Literature* (BRS; Grand Rapids, Mich.: Eerdmans, 2nd edn, 1998).

—*Between Athens and Jerusalem: Jewish Identity in the Hellenistic Diaspora* (The Bible Resource Series; Grand Rapids, Mich.: Eerdmans, 2nd edn, 2000).

—*Daniel* (ed. Frank M. Cross; Hermeneia; Minneapolis: Fortress, 1993).

Collins, John J., and Gregory E. Sterling (eds), *Hellenism in the Land of Israel* (CJA, 13; Notre Dame, Ind.: University of Notre Dame Press, 2001).

Colson, Francis H. (ed.), *On Abraham; On Joseph; On Moses* (LCL, 289; London: Harvard University Press, 1950).

Colson, Francis H., and George H. Whitaker (eds), *On the Cherubim; The Sacrifices of Abel and Cain; The Worse Attacks the Better; On the Posterity and Exile of Cain; On the Giants* (LCL, 227; London: Harvard University Press, 1981).

Conte, Gian Biagio, *Genres and Readers: Lucretius, Love Elegy, Pliny's Encyclopedia* (trans. Glenn W. Most; Baltimore: Johns Hopkins University Press, 1994).

—*The Hidden Author: An Interpretation of Petronius' Satyricon* (SCL, 60; Berkeley: University of California Press, 1996).

—*The Rhetoric of Imitation: Genre and Poetic Memory in Virgil and Other Latin Poets* (ed. Charles Segal; CSCP, 44; London: Cornell University Press, 2nd edn, 1996).

Conte, Gian Biagio, and Glenn W. Most, 'Genre', in *OCD*, 630–1.

Conybeare, Frederick C. (ed., trans.), *Life of Apollonius of Tyana, The Epistles of Apollonius, and The Treatise of Eusebius* (LCL, 16–17; London: Harvard University Press, 1960).

Coogan, Michael D. (ed.), *The New Oxford Annotated Bible* (Oxford: Oxford University Press, 3rd edn 'with the Apocryphal/ Deuterocanonical Books', 2001).

Coote, Robert B., 'Mark 1.1: ἀρχή, Scriptural Lemma', in Carroll (ed.), *Text as Pretext*, 86–90.

Coote, Robert B. (ed.), *Elijah and Elisha in Socioliterary Perspective* (Semeia Studies; Atlanta: Scholars, 1992).

Coote, Robert B., and Mary P. Coote, 'Homer and Scripture in the Gospel of Mark', in Hearon (ed.), *Distant Voices Drawing Near*, 189–201.

Cranfield, C.E.B., *The Gospel according to Saint Mark: An Introduction and Commentary* (CGTS; Cambridge, Engl.: Cambridge University Press, 1959).

Crawford, David S., *Papyri Michaelidae, Being a Catalogue of the Greek and Latin Papyri, Tablets, and Ostraca in the Library of Mr. G.A. Michaelidis of Cairo* (Aberdeen: Aberdeen University Press, 1955).

Cullmann, Oscar, 'Immortality of the Soul or Resurrection of the Dead', in Stendhal, *Immortality and Resurrection*, 9–53.

Curtius, Ernst Robert, *European Literature and the Latin Middle Ages* (trans. Willard R. Trask; Bollingen Series, 36; Princeton, N.J.: Princeton University Press, 1953).

Dahood, Mitchell, *Psalms 101–150* (AB, 17A; New York: Doubleday, 1970).

Danove, Paul L., *The End of Mark's Story: A Methodological Study* (Biblical Interpretation Series, 3; Leiden: Brill, 1993).

Denis, Albert-Marie, *Concordance Grecque des Pseudépigraphes d'Ancien Testament: Concordance, Corpus des Textes, Indices* (Louvain-la-Neuve: Université Catholique de Louvain, 1987).

Dewey, Joanna, *Markan Public Debate: Literary Technique, Concentric Structure, and Theology in Mark 2.1-3.6* (SBLDS, 48; Chico, Ca.: Scholars, 1980).

Diodorus Siculus, *Bibliotheke* (ed., trans., Charles H. Oldfather, Charles Lawton Sherman, C. Bradford Welles, Russel M. Geer, and Francis R. Walton; LCL 279, 303, 340, 375, 377, 384, 389–90, 399, 409, 422–23; 12 vols; London: Harvard University Press, 1933–67).

Donahue, John R., *Are You the Christ? The Trial Narrative in the Gospel of Mark* (SBLDS, 10; Missoula, Mont.: Scholars, 1973).

Donahue, John R., and Daniel J. Harrington, *The Gospel of Mark* (Sacra Pagina Series, 2; Collegeville, Minn.: Liturgical, 2002).

Donbaz, Veysel, 'Two Neo-Assyrian Stelae in the Antakya and Kahramanmaras Museums', *ARRIM* 8 (1990), 4–24.

Duling, Dennis C., and Norman Perrin, *The New Testament: Proclamation and Parenesis, Myth and History* (Fort Worth: Harcourt Brace College, 3rd edn, 1994).

Durand, Jean-Marie (ed.), *La femme dans le Proche-Orient Antique: Compte rendu de la XXXIIIe* (RAI, 33; Paris: Editions Recherche sur les Civilisations, 1987).

Dwyer, Timothy, *The Motif of Wonder in the Gospel of Mark* (JSNTSup, 128; Sheffield, Engl.: Sheffield Academic, 1996).

Easterling, Patricia E., and Bernard M.W. Knox (eds), *Greek Literature* (CHCL, 1; Cambridge, Engl.: Cambridge University Press, 1985).

Eichrodt, Walther, *Ezekiel: A Commentary* (trans. Cosslett Quin; OTL; Philadelphia: Westminster, 1970).

—*Theology of the Old Testament* (trans. J.A. Baker; OTL; 2 vols; Philadelphia: Westminster, 1961–7).

Elliott, James K. (ed.), *The Apocryphal New Testament: A Collection of Apocryphal Christian Literature in an English Translation* (Oxford: Clarendon; Oxford: Oxford University Press, 1993).

Emmerson, Grace I., *Hosea: An Israelite Prophet in Judean Perspective* (JSOTSup, 28; Sheffield, Engl.: JSOT, 1984).

Engberg-Pedersen, Troels (ed.), *Paul Beyond the Judaism/Hellenism Divide* (Louisville, Ky.: Westminster John Knox, 2001).

Eriksen, Roy, *Contexts of Pre-Novel Narrative: The European Tradition* (AS, 114; Berlin: de Gruyter, 1994).

Erim, Kenan T., *Aphrodisias: City of Venus Aphrodite* (London: Muller, Blond & White, 1986).

Euripides, *Alcestis* (ed. Antonio Garzya; Bibliotheca Scriptorum Graecorum et Romanorum Teubneriana; Leipzig: B.G. Teubner, 1983).

—*Hippolytus* (ed. Walter Stockert; Bibliotheca Scriptorum Graecorum et Romanorum Teubneriana; Leipzig: B.G. Teubner, 1994).

Evans, Craig A., ' "Peter Warming Himself": The Problem of an Editorial "Seam" ', *JBL* 101 (1982), 245–9.

Faierstein, Morris M., 'Why Do the Scribes Say that Elijah Comes First?', *JBL* 100 (1981), 75–86.

Feagin, Glyndle M., *Irony and the Kingdom in Mark: A Literary-Critical Study* (MBPS, 56; Lewiston, N.Y.: Edwin Mellen, 1997).

Feeney, D.C., 'Epilogue: Towards an Account of the Ancient World's Concepts of Fictive Beliefs', in Gill and Wiseman (eds), *Lies and Fiction in the Ancient World*, 175–229.

Fiorenza, Elisabeth Schüssler, with Ann Brock and Shelly Matthews, *Searching the Scriptures, Volume Two: A Feminist Commentary* (2 vols; New York: Crossroad, 1993).

Fitzgerald, John T. (ed.), *Greco-Roman Perspectives on Friendship* (RBS, 34; Atlanta: Scholars, 1997).

Fitzmyer, Joseph A., *Tobit* (CEJL; Berlin: de Gruyter, 2003).

Focant, Camille (ed.), *The Synoptic Gospels: Source Criticism and the New Literary Criticism* (BETL, 110; Leuven, Belgium: Leuven University Press, 1993).

Foley, John Miles, *The Singer of Tales in Performance* (VPT; Indianapolis: Indiana University Press, 1996).

Fortenbaugh, William W., Pamela M. Huby, Robert W. Sharples, and Dimitri Gutas, *Theophrastus of Eresus: Sources for his Life, Writings, Thought, and Influence* (2 vols; Leiden: Brill, 1992).

Fowler, Alistair, *Kinds of Literature: An Introduction to the Theory of Genres and Modes* (Oxford: Clarendon; London: Harvard University Press, 1982).

Fowler, Robert M., *Let the Reader Understand: Reader-Response Criticism and the Gospel of Mark* (Harrisburg, Penn.: Trinity, 1996).

Frame, Douglas, *The Myth of Return in Early Greek Epic* (New Haven, Conn.: Yale University Press, 1978).

France, Richard T., *The Gospel of Mark: A Commentary on the Greek Text* (NIGTC; Cambridge, Engl.: Eerdmans; Carlisle, Pa.: Paternoster, 2002).

Frazer, James G., *Publii Ovidii Nasonis, Fastorum Libri Sex (The Fasti* of Ovid), Edited with a Translation and Commentary in Five Volumes *(5 vols; London: Macmillan, 1929)*.

Freedman, David N. (ed.), *ABD* (6 vols; New York: Doubleday, 1992).

Fretheim, Terence, *First and Second Kings* (WestBC; Louisville, Ky.: Westminster John Knox, 1999).

Friesen, Steven J., 'Poverty in Pauline Studies: Beyond the So-called New Consensus', *JSNT* 26 (2004), 323–61.

Fritz, Volkmar, *1 & 2 Kings* (trans. Anselm Hagedorn; CC; Minneapolis: Fortress, 2003).

Gamble, Harry Y., *Books and Readers in the Early Church: A History of Early Christian Texts* (New Haven: Yale University Press, 1995).

Giangrande, Giuseppe, 'On the Origins of the Greek Romance: The Birth of a Literary Form', *Eranos* 60 (1962), 132–59.

Gill, Christopher, 'Introduction' to Longus, *Daphnis and Chloe* in *CAGN*, 285–8.

Gill, Christopher, and T.P. Wiseman (eds), *Lies and Fiction in the Ancient World* (Austin: University of Texas Press, 1993).

Gillman, Neil, *The Death of Death: Resurrection and Immortality in Jewish Thought* (Woodstock, Ver.: Jewish Lights, 1997).

Goldstein, Jonathan A., *II Maccabees* (AB, 41A; New York: Doubleday, 1983).

Goold, George P. (ed., trans.), *Callirhoë* (LCL, 481; London: Harvard University Press, 1995).

Gould, John P.A., 'Herodotus', in *OCD*, 696–8.

Gowler, David B., *New Boundaries in Old Territory: Form and Social Rhetoric in Mark* (ESEC, 3; New York: Peter Lang, 1999).

Green, Peter, *Alexander to Actium: The Historical Evolution of the Hellenistic Age* (HCS, 1; Berkeley, Los Angeles: University of California Press, 1990).

Greenberg, Moshe, *Ezekiel 21-37* (AB, 22A; New York: Doubleday, 1997).

Grenfell, Bernard P., Arthur S. Hunt, and David G. Hogarth (eds), with a chapter by Grafton Milne, *Fayûm Towns and their Papyri* (EEFGRB, 3; London: Offices of the Egypt Exploration Fund, 1900).

Gruen, Erich S., *Heritage and Hellenism: The Reinvention of Jewish Tradition* (HCS, 30; Berkeley: University of California Press, 1998).

Grundmann, Walter, *Das Evangelium nach Markus* (THNT, 2; Berlin: Evangelische Verlagsanstalt, 1977).

Guelich, Robert, 'The Gospel Genre', in Stuhlmacher (ed.), *The Gospel and the Gospels*, 173–208.

—*Mark 1–8.26* (WBC, 34A; Dallas: Word, 1989).

Gunkel, Hermann, and Joachim Begrich, *Introduction to Psalms: the Genres of the Religious Lyric of Israel* (trans. James D. Nogalski; MLBS; Macon, Georgia: Mercer University Press, 1998).

Hägg, Tomas, *Narrative Technique in Ancient Greek Romances: Studies of Chariton, Xenophon Ephesius and Achilles Tatius* (Stockholm: Svenska Institutet i Athen, 1971).

—*The Novel in Antiquity* (Berkeley and Los Angeles: University of California Press, English edn, 1983).

—'Orality, Literacy, and the "Readership" of the Early Greek Novel', in Eriksen (ed.), *Contexts of Pre-Novel Narrative: The European Tradition*, 47–81.

Hahn, Ferdinand (ed.), *Zur Formgeschichte des Evangeliums* (WdF, 81; Darmstadt: Wissenschaftliche Buchgesellschaft, 1985).

Halpern, Baruch, and Jon D. Levenson (eds), *Traditions in Transformation: Turning Points in Biblical Faith* (Winona Lake, Ind.: Eisenbrauns, 1981).

Hamilton, Neill Q., 'Resurrection Tradition and the Composition of Mark', *JBL* 84 (1965), 415–21.

Hansen, William (ed.), *Anthology of Ancient Greek Popular Literature* (Indianapolis: Indiana University Press, 1998).

Hanson, James S., *The Endangered Promises: Conflict in Mark* (SBLDS, 171; Atlanta: Society of Biblical Literature, 2000).

Harrison, Thomas, *Divinity and History: The Religion of Herodotus* (OCM; Oxford: Clarendon; Oxford: Oxford University Press, 2000).

Hatina, Thomas R., *In Search of a Context: The Function of Scripture in Mark's Narrative* (JSNTSup, 232; SSEJC, 8; Sheffield, Engl.: Sheffield Academic, 2002).

Hearon, Holly E. (ed.), *Distant Voices Drawing Near: Essays in Honor of Antoinette Clark Wire*. (Collegeville, Minn.: Liturgical, 2004).

Hedrick, Charles W., 'Representing Prayer in Mark and Chariton's *Chaereas and Callirhoë*', *PRS* 22 (1995), 239–57.

—'What is a Gospel: Geography, Time, and Narrative Structure', *PRS* 10 (1983), 255–68.

Heinrichs, Albert, 'Clymenus', in *OCD*, 353.

Heinze, Richard, 'Petron und der griechische Roman', *Hermes* 34 (1899), 494–519.

Heliodorus, *An Ethiopian Story* (trans. J.R. Morgan), in *CAGN*, 349–588.

Helyer, Larry R., *Exploring Jewish Literature of the Second Temple Period: A Guide for New Testament Students* (CCBS; Downers Grove, Ill.: InterVarsity, 2002).

Henten, Jan Willem van, *The Maccabean Martyrs as Saviours of the Jewish People: A Study of 2 and 4 Maccabees* (JSJSup, 57; Leiden: Brill, 1997).

Hernadi, Paul, 'Literary Theory: A Compass for Critics', *Critical Inquiry* 3 (1976), 369–86.

Herodotus, *Historiai (The Persian Wars)* (trans. Alfred D. Godley; LCL, 117–20; 4 vols; London: Harvard University Press, 1982).

Highet, Gilbert, 'Reciprocity (Greece0', in *OCD*, 1295.

Hilhorst, A. and Pieter J. Lalleman, 'The Acts of Andrew and Matthias: Is It Part of the Original *Acts of Andrew*?', in Bremmer (ed.), *The Apocryphal Acts of Andrew*, 1–14.

Hirsch, E.D., *Validity in Interpretation* (New Haven, Conn.: Yale University Press, 1967).

Hock, Ronald F., 'Homer in Greco-Roman Education', in MacDonald (ed.), *Mimesis and Intertextuality in Antiquity and Christianity*, 56–77.

—'An Extraordinary Friend in Chariton's *Callirhoe*: The Importance of Friendship in the Greek Romances', in Fitzgerald (ed.), *Greco-Roman Perspectives on Friendship*, 145–62.

—'The Greek Novel', in Aune (ed.), *Greco-Roman Literature and the New Testament*, 127–46.

Holst-Warhaft, Gail, *Dangerous Voices: Women's Laments and Greek Literature* (London: Routledge, 1992).

Holzberg, Niklas, *Antike Roman: Eine Einführung* (Dusseldorf: Artemis & Winkler, 2nd edn, 2001).

Homer, *The Iliad*. (ed., trans., Augustus T. Murray; rev. William F. Wyatt; LCL, 170–171; 2 vols; London: Harvard University Press, 2nd edn, 1999).

—*The Odyssey* (ed., trans., Augustus T. Murray; rev. George E. Dimock; LCL, 104–105; 2 vols; London: Harvard University Press, 2nd edn, 1995).

Hornblower, Simon, and Antony Spawforth (eds), *The Oxford Classical Dictionary* (Oxford: Oxford University Press, 3rd rev. edn, 2002).

Horsley, Richard A., *Hearing the Whole Story: The Politics of Plot in Mark's Gospel* (Louisville, Ky.: Westminster John Knox, 2001).

Horst, Pieter W. van der, *Japheth in the Tents of Shem: Studies on Jewish Hellenism in Antiquity* (CBET, 32; Sterling, Vir.: Peeters, 2002).

—*The Sentences of Pseudo-Phocylides* (SVTP, 4; Leiden: Brill, 1978).

Horst, Pieter W. van der, and Michael A. Knibb (eds), *Studies on the Testament of Job* (SNTSMS, 66; Cambridge, Engl.: Cambridge University Press, 1989).

Huffington, Arianna, *The Gods of Greece* (New York: Atlantic Monthly, 1993).

Humphrey, Edith M., *Joseph and Aseneth* (GAP; Sheffield, Engl.: Sheffield Academic, 2000).

Hunink, Vincent, 'Comedy in Apuleius' Apology', *GCN* 9 (1998), 97–113.

Hunter, Lynette (ed.), *Toward a Definition of Topos*: Approaches to Analogical Reasoning (London: Macmillan, 1991).

Huprich, Amy L., 'John 20.11-18: The Recognition/reunion Scene and its Parallels in Greek Romance', in *Proceedings of the Eastern Great Lakes and Midwest Biblical Societies* 15 (Buffalo: Canisius College Press, 1995), 15–20.

Hyginus, *Poetica Astronomica* (ed. Ghislaine Viré; Bibliotheca Scriptorum Graecorum et Romanorum Teubneriana; Leipzig: B.G. Teubner, 1992).

—*Fabulae* (ed. Peter K. Marshall; Bibliotheca Scriptorum Graecorum et Romanorum Teubneriana; Munich and Leipzig: K.G. Saur, rev. ed.; 2002).

Iamblichus, *Babyloniaka*, in Stephens and Winkler (eds), *Ancient Greek Novels: The* Fragments, 179–245.

Iersel, Bas M.F. van, *Mark: A Reader-Response Commentary* (trans. W.H. Bisscheroux; JSNTSup, 164; Sheffield, Engl.: Sheffield Academic, 1998).

Incigneri, Brian J., *The Gospel to the Romans: The Setting and Rhetoric of Mark's Gospel* (BIS, 65; Boston and Leiden: Brill Academic, 2003).

Janko, Richard, *The Iliad, a Commentary: Volume 4 (Books 13–16)* (ed. Geoffrey S. Kirk; Cambridge, Engl.: Cambridge University Press, 1992).

Johnson, Sara Raup, *Historical Fictions and Hellenistic Jewish Identity: Third Maccabees in Its Cultural Context* (HCS, 43; Berkeley: University of California Press, forthcoming).

Josephus, *Against Apion*, in Thackeray (ed.), *The Life; Against Apion*, 161–412.

Keck, Leander E. (ed.), *The New Interpreter's Bible: General Aricles and Introduction, Commentary, and Reflections for Each Book of the Bible Including the Apocryphal/Deuterocanonical Books in Twelve Volumes* (12 vols; Nashville: Abingdon, 1994).

Keel, Othmar, 'Die Kultischen Massnahmen Antiochus IV: Religionsverfolgung und/oder Reformversuch? Eine Skizze', in Keel (ed.), *Hellenismus und Judentum*, 87–121.

Keel, Othmar, and Urs Staub, *Hellenismus und Judentum: Vier Studien zu Daniel 7 und zur Religionsnot unter Antiochus IV* (OBO, 178; Göttingen: Vandenhoeck and Ruprecht, 2000).

Kelber, Werner H., *The Kingdom in Mark: A New Place and A New Time* (Philadelphia: Fortress, 1974).

—*The Oral and the Written Gospel: The Hermeneutics of Speaking and Writing in the Synoptic Tradition, Mark, Paul and Q* (VPT; Indianapolis: Indiana University Press, 2nd edn, 1997).

Kerényi, Karoly, *Die griechisch-orientalische Romanliteratur in religions-geschichtlicher Beleuchtung* (Tübingen: Mohr, 1927; 2nd edn: Darmstadt: Wissenschaftliche Buchgesellschaft, 1962; 3rd edn: Darmstadt: Wissenschaftliche Buchgesellschaft, 1973).

Kermode, Frank, *The Genesis of Secrecy: On the Interpretation of Narrative* (CENL; London: Harvard University Press, 1979).

—*The Sense of an Ending: Studies in the Theory of Fiction* (Oxford: Oxford University Press, 2nd edn, 2000).

Keyes, Clinton W. (ed., trans.), *On the Republic (De Re Publica); On the Laws (De Legibus)* (LCL, 213; London: Harvard University Press, 1928).

Kittel, Gerhard, and Gerhard Friedrich (eds), *The Theological Dictionary of the New Testament* (trans. Geoffrey W. Bromiley; 10 vols; Grand Rapids, Mich.: Eerdmans, 1964–76).

Klauser, Theodor (ed.), *Reallexicon für Antike und Christentum, Band I: AundO – Bauen* (Stuttgart: Hiersemann, 1950).

Klein, Jacob, 'The Birth of a Crown Prince in the Temple: A Neo-Sumerian Literary Topos', in Durand (ed.), *La femme dans le Proche-Orient Antique*, 97–106.

Koehler, Ludwig, and Walter Baumgartner, *Hebrew and Aramaic Lexicon of the Old Testament* (ed., trans. Mervyn E.J. Richardson; rev. Walter Baumgartner and Johann J. Stamm; 5 vols; Leiden: Brill, 1994).

Koester, Helmut, *Ancient Christian Gospels: Their History and Development* (Philadelphia: Trinity; London: SCM, 1990).

—'Apostel und Gemeinde in den Briefen an die Thessalonischer', in Lührmann and Strecker (eds), *Kirche*, 287–98.

Koskenniemi, Erkki, 'Apollonius of Tyana: A Typical ΘΕΙΟΣ ΑΝΗΡ?', *JBL* 117 (1998), 455–67.

Kraemer, Ross S., 'The Book of Aseneth', in Fiorenza, Brock, and Matthews (eds), *Searching the Scriptures*, 859–88.

—*When Aseneth Met Joseph: A Late Antique Tale of the Biblical Patriarch and his Egyptian Wife, Reconsidered* (Oxford: Oxford University Press, 1998).

Lane, William L., *The Gospel According to Mark: The English Text with Introduction, Exposition and Notes* (NICNT, 2; Grand Rapids, Mich.: Eerdmans, 1974).

Leith, Mary Joan Winn, 'Introduction to Esther (The Greek Version Containing the Additional Chapters)', in Coogan (ed.), *New Oxford Annotated Bible*, 53–54 APOCRYPHA.

Lemaire, Andre (ed.), *Congress Volume: Basel 2001* (VTSup, 92; Boston and Leiden: Brill Academic, 2002).

Lesky, Albin, 'Prose Romance and Epistolography', in Willis and de Heer (eds), *A History of Greek Literature*, 857–70.

Levenson, Jon D., 'Resurrection in the Torah? A Reconsideration', *Center of Theological Inquiry Reflections* 6 (2002), 2–29.

—'The Resurrection of the Dead and the Construction of Personal Identity in Ancient Israel', in Lemaire (ed.), *Congress Volume: Basel 2001*, 305–22.

Levine, Lee I., *Judaism and Hellenism in Antiquity: Conflict or Confluence?* (SLJS; Seattle: University of Washington Press, 1998).

Liburd, Ron N., 'Hebrew Gospel: Cracking the Code of Mark, by Wolfgang Roth', *Word and World* 10 (1990), 94–9.

Livy, *History (Ab Urbe Condita)* (ed., trans. John Briscoe, Thomas A. Dorey, and Patricius G. Walsh; Bibliotheca Scriptorum Graecorum et Romanorum Teubneriana; 6 vols; Leipzig: B.G. Teubner, 1998).

Lollianus, *Phoinikika*, in Stephens and Winkler (eds), *Ancient Greek Novels: The Fragments*, 314–57.

[Pseudo-]Longinus, *On the Sublime*, in Fyfe (ed., trans.), *Aristotle, Poetics; Longinus, On the Sublime; Demetrius, On Style*, 143–308.

Longus, *Daphnis and Chloë* (ed., trans. Michael D. Reeve; Bibliotheca

Scriptorum Graecorum et Romanorum Teubneriana; Munich and Leipzig: K.G. Saur, 1998).

Lucian, *Complete Works* (ed., trans. Austin M. Harmon, K. Kilburn and Mathew D. McLeod; LCL, 14, 54, 130, 162, 302, 430–32; 8 vols; London: Harvard University Press, 1921–67).

Lucke, Christina, 'Zum Charitontext auf Papyrus', *ZPE* 58 (1985), 21–33.

Lührmann, Dieter, 'Biographie des Gerechten als Evangelium: Vorstellungen zu einem MarkusKommentar', *Wort und Dienst* 14 (1977), 25–50.

Lührmann, Dieter, and Georg Strecker (eds), *Kirche: Festschrift für Günther Bornkamm zum 75. Geburtstag* (Tübingen: J.C.B. Mohr [Paul Siebeck], 1980).

MacDonald, Dennis R., *Christianizing Homer: The Odyssey*, Plato, and *The Acts of Andrew* (Oxford: Oxford University Press, 1994).

—*The Homeric Epics and the Gospel of Mark* (New Haven, Conn.: Yale University Press, 2000).

MacDonald, Dennis R. (ed.), *Mimesis and Intertextuality in Antiquity and Christianity* (SAC; Harrisburg, Penn.: Trinity, 2001).

MacFague, Sallie, *Life Abundant: Rethinking Theology and Ecology for a Planet in Peril* (Minneapolis: Fortress, 2001).

MacQueen, Bruce D., *Myth, Rhetoric, and Fiction: A Reading of Longus' Daphnis and* Chloë (Lincoln, Neb.: University of Nebraska Press, 1990).

Mainville, Odette and Daniel Marguerat (eds), *Résurrection: L'après-mort dans le monde ancien et le Nouveau Testament* (MB, 45; Montreal: Médiaspaul; Geneva: Éditions Labor et Fides; 2001).

Malbon, Elizabeth Struthers, 'Texts and Contexts: Interpreting the Disciples in Mark', *Semeia* 62 (1993), 81–102.

Mann, C.S., *Mark* (AB, 27; New York: Doubleday, 1986).

March, Jennifer R., 'Sarpedon', in *OCD*, 1357.

Marcus, Joel, *Mark 1–8* (AB, 27; New York: Doubleday, 2000).

—*The Way of the Lord: Christological Exegesis of the Old Testament in the Gospel of Mark* (ed. John Riches; SNTU;. Edinburgh: T & T Clark, 1993).

Marguerat, Daniel, *The First Christian Historian: Writing the 'Acts of the Apostles.'* (trans. Ken McKinney, Gregory J. Laughtery, and Richard Bauckham; SNTSMS, 121; Cambridge, Engl.: Cambridge University Press, 2002).

Martin, Dale B., *The Corinthian Body* (New Haven, Conn.: Yale University Press, 1995).

Martin-Achard, Robert, *From Death to Life: A Study of the Development of the Doctrine of the Resurrection in the Old Testament* (trans. John P. Smith; Edinburgh and London: Oliver and Boyd, 1960).

—'Resurrection (Old Testament)', in Freedman (ed.), *ABD*, 5.680-84.

McKenzie, Steven L., *The Trouble with Kings: The Composition of the Book of Kings in the Deuteronomistic History* (VTSup, 42; Leiden: Brill, 1991).

Meggitt, Justin J., *Paul, Poverty and Survival* (SNTU; Edinburgh: T&T Clark, 1998).

Mein, Andrew, *Ezekiel and the Ethics of Exile* (OTM; Oxford: Oxford University Press, 2001).

Merkelbach, Reinhold, *Die Quellen des griechischen Alexanderromans* (ed., trans. Reinhold Merkelbach; Zetemata 9. Munich: Beck, 2nd edn, 1977).

—*Roman und Mysterium in der Antike* (Munich and Berlin: C.H. Beck, 1962).

Merklein, H., 'Mark 16,1–8 als Epilog des Markusevangeliums', in Focant (ed.), *The Synoptic Gospels: Source Criticism and the New Literary Criticism*, 209–38.

Merriam-Webster, *Webster's Third New International Dictionary* (unabr.; Springfield: Merriam-Webster, rev., 2002).

Metiochus and Parthenope (trans. Gerald N. Sandy) in *CAGN*, 813–15.

Michel, Raphael, 'Clymenus', in Cancik (ed.), *Brill's New Pauly*, 352.

Millar, William R., 'Isaiah 24–27 (Little Apocalypse0', s.v. 'Isaiah, Book of', in Freedman (ed.), *ABD*, 3.488-90.

Miller, Frank J. (ed., trans.), *Hercules Furens. Troades. Medea. Hippolytus or Phaedra. Oedipus* (LCL, 62; London: Harvard University Press, 1988).

Miller, Patricia Cox, *Dreams in Late Antiquity: Studies in the Imagination of a Culture* (Princeton: Princeton University Press, 1994).

Minette de Tillesse, Georges, *Le Secret messianique dans l'Évangile de Marc* (Lectio Divina, 47; Paris: Éditions du Cerf, 1968).

Momigliano, Arnaldo, 'The Place of Herodotus in the History of Historiography', *History* 43 (1958), 1–13.

Moore, Carey A., *Daniel, Esther, and Jeremiah: The Additions* (AB, 44; New York: Doubleday, 1977).

—*Esther* (AB 7b; New York: Doubleday, 1971).

—*Judith* (AB, 40; New York: Doubleday, 1985).

Morgan, J.R., 'Heliodoros', in *NAW*, 417–56.

—'Make-Believe and Make Believe: The Fictionality of the Greek Novels', in Gill and Wiseman (eds), *Lies and Fiction in the Ancient World*, 175–229.

Morgan, Teresa, *Literate Education in the Hellenistic and Roman Worlds* (CCS; Cambridge, Engl.: Cambridge University Press, 1998).

Mowinckel, Sigmund, *The Psalms in Israel's Worship* (trans. D.R. Ap-Thomas; two volumes in one; Sheffield, Engl.: JSOT, 1992).

Müller, Carl W., 'Chariton von Aphrodisias und die Theorie des Romans in der Antike', *A&A* 22 (1976), 115–36.

Munck, Johannes, *The Acts of the Apostles* (AB, 31; New York: Doubleday, 1967).

Nagy, Gregory, *Greek Mythology and Poetics* (M&P; London: Cornell University Press, 1990).

Naluparayil, Jacob Chacko, *The Identity of Jesus in Mark: An Essay on Narrative Christology* (SBFA, 49; Jerusalem: Franciscan, 2000).

Neirynck, Frans, *Duality in Mark: Contributions to the Study of the Markan Redaction* (BETL, 31; Leuven, Belgium: Leuven University Press, 1972).

Nickelsburg George W.E., *1 Enoch* (Hermeneia; 2 vols; Minneapolis: Fortress, 2001).

—'Apocalyptic and Myth in 1 Enoch 6–11', *JBL* 96 (1977), 383–405.

—*Resurrection, Immortality, and Eternal Life in Intertestamental Judaism* (HTS 26; London: Harvard University Press, 1972).

Nikolainen, Aimo T., *Der Auferstehungsglauben in der Bibel und ihrer Umwelt* (AASF, B49.3; B59.3; 266; 3 vols; Helsinki: Suomalainen Tiedeakatemia, 1944–92).

Ninus Romance, in Stephens and Winkler (eds), *Ancient Greek Novels*, 23–71.

Nock, Arthur D., 'Greek Novels and Egyptian Religion', *Gnomon* 4 (1928), 485–92.

Oakes, Peter, 'Constructing Poverty Scales for Graeco-Roman Society: A Response to Steven Friesen's "Poverty in Pauline Studies" ', *JSNT* 26 (2004), 367–71.

Oepke, Albrecht, 'Augerstehung II (des Menschen)', in Klauser (ed.), *RAC*, 1.930-38.

Ong, Walter J., *Interfaces of the Word: Studies in the Evolution of Consciousness and Culture* (London: Cornell University Press, 1977).

—*Orality and Literacy: The Technologizing of the Word* (New Accents; London: Methuen, 1982; repr. Philadelphia: Taylor and Francis, 2002).

Orton, David E. (ed.), *Prophecy in the Hebrew Bible: Selected Studies from Vetus Testamentum* (BRBS, 5; Leiden: Brill, 2000).

Ovid, *Amores* in Showerman (ed.), *Heroides; Amores*, 313–508.

—*Fasti (Publii Ovidii Nasonis, Fastorum Libri Sex)* (ed., trans. James G. Frazer; 5 vols; London: Macmillan, 1929).

—*Fasti* (ed., trans. James G. Frazer; rev. George P. Goold; LCL, 253; London: Harvard University Press, 2nd edn, 1989).

Pauly, August, Georg Wissowa, and Wilhelm Kroll (ed.), *Paulys Real-Encyclopädie der Klassischen Altertumswissenschaft: Neue Bearbeitung und der Mitwirkung zahlreicher Fachgenossen* (24 vols; Stuttgart: J.B. Metzler, 1893–1963).

Papanikolaou, Antonius D., *Chariton-Studien: Untersuchungen zur*

Sprache und Chronologie der griechischen Romane (Hypomnemata, 57; Göttingen: Vandenhoeck and Ruprecht, 1973).

Peck, Harold T. (ed.), *Harper's Dictionary of Classical Literature and Antiquities* (New York: Cooper Square, 1962).

Pellegrini, Silvia, *Elija – Wegbereiter des Gottessohnes: Eine Textsemiotische Untersuchung im Markusevangelium* (HBS, 26; Freiburg, Switz.: Herder, 2000).

Persius, *Satires*, in Ramsay (ed.), *Juvenal and Persius*, 309–401.

Persson, Axel W., *Zur Textgeschichte Xenophons* (LUA, 1.10.2; Lund, Sweden: C.W.K. Gleerup, 1915).

Perry, Ben E., *Aesopica* (2 vols; New York: Arno, 1980).

—*Ancient Romances: A Literary-Historical Account of Their Origins* (SCL, 37; Berkeley: University of California Press, 1967).

—'Chariton and his Romance from a Literary-Historical Point of View', *AJPh* 51 (1930), 99–134.

—'Some Addenda to the Life of Aesop', *ByzZ* 59 (1966), 285–304.

Pervo, Richard I., *Profit with Delight: The Literary Genre of the Acts of the Apostles* (Philadelphia: Fortress, 1987).

Pesch, Rudolf, 'Jairus (Mk 5,22/Lk 8,41)', *BZ* 14 (1970), 252–6.

Petri, Remy, *Über den Roman des Chariton* (BKP, 9; Meisenheim an Glan: A. Hain, 1963).

Petronius, *Satyricon*, in Heseltine (ed.), *Petronius; Seneca, Apocolocyntosis*, 1–321.

Philo, *On the Cherubim*, in Colson and Whitaker (eds), *On the Cherubim, et al.*, 3–87.

Philonenko, Marc, *Joseph et Aséneth: Introduction Texte Critique Traduction et Notes* (SPB, 13; Leiden: Brill, 1968).

Philostratus, *Das Leben des Apollonios von Tyana* (trans. Vroni Mumprecht; ST; Munich: Artemis, 1983).

Photius, *Bibliothèque* (Ed., trans. René Henry; 9 vols; Paris: Société d'édition Les Belles lettres, 1959–91).

—*The Wonders beyond Thule* (trans. Gerald N. Sandy), in *CAGN*, 777–82.

Plepelits, Karl, *Chariton von Aphrodisias: Kallirhoë, Eingeleitet, Übersetzt und Erläutert* (BGL, 6; Stuttgart: Anton Hiersemann, 1976).

Pliny, *Natural History* (ed., trans. Harris Rackham, William H.S. Jones, Alfred C. Andrews, and D.E. Eichholz; LCL, 330, 352–3, 370–1, 392–4, 418–19; 10 vols; London: Harvard University Press, 1947–1963).

Plutarch, *Moralia* (ed., trans. Frank C. Babbitt, William C. Helmbold, Phillip H. de Lacy, Benedict Einarson, Paul A. Clement, Herbert B. Hoffleit, Edwin L. Minar, Jr., Francis H. Sandbach, Harold N. Fowler, Lionel Pearson, and Harold Cherniss; LCL, 197, 222, 245, 305–6, 321, 337, 405–6, 424–9, 470; 15 vols; London: Harvard University Press, 1927–1976).

—*Lives* (ed., trans. Bernadotte Perrin; LCL, 46–7, 65, 80, 87, 98–103; 11 vols; London: Harvard University Press, 1914–1926).

Polybius, *The Histories* (ed., trans. William R. Paton; LCL, 128, 137–8, 159–61; 6 vols; London: Harvard University Press, 1922–1927).

Porter, Stanley E., 'Resurrection, the Greeks and the New Testament', in Porter, Hayes, and Tombs (eds), *Resurrection*, 52–81.

Porter, Stanley E., Michael A. Hayes, and David Tombs (eds), *Resurrection* (JSNTSup, 186; Sheffield, Engl.: Sheffield Academic, 1999).

Propertius, *Elegies* (ed., trans. George P. Goold; LCL, 18; London: Harvard University Press, 1990).

—*The Poems* (ed., trans. Guy Lee; Oxford: Clarendon, 1994).

Pryke, E.J., *Redactional Style, in the Marcan Gospel: A Study of Syntax and Vocabulary as Guides to Redaction in Mark* (New York: Cambridge University Press, 1978).

Quintilian, *Institutio Oratoria (The Orator's Education)* (ed., trans. Donald A. Russell; LCL, 124N-127N, 494N; 5 vols; London: Harvard University Press, 2001).

Radford, Jean, *The Progress of Romance: The Politics of Popular Fiction* (HWS, London: Routledge and Kegan Paul, 1986).

Rahlfs, Alfred (ed.), *Septuaginta: id est, Vetus Testamentum Graece Juxta LXX Interpretes* (2 vols. in one; Stuttgart: Deutsche Bibelgesellschaft, 1979).

Ramsay, George G. (ed., trans.), *Juvenal and Persius* (LCL, 91; London: Harvard University Press, 1940).

Raphael, Simcha P., *Jewish Views of the Afterlife* (Northvale, N.J.: Jason Aronson, 1996).

Reardon, Bryan P., 'Chariton', in *NAW*, 309–35.

—*Courants Littéraires Grecs des IIe et IIIe Siècles après J.-C.* (ALUN, 3; Paris: Les Belles Lettres, 1971).

—*The Form of Greek Romance* (Princeton: Princeton University Press, 1991).

—'General Introduction', in *CAGN*, 1–16.

—'Introduction' to Lucian, *A True Story* in *CAGN*, 619–20.

Reardon, Bryan P. (ed.), *Collected Ancient Greek Novels* (Berkeley: University of California Press, 1989).

—*Erotica Antiqua* (AICAN; Bangor, Wales: University College of North Wales Press, 1977).

Reiser, Marius, 'Der Alexanderroman und das Markusevangelium', in Cancik (ed.), *Markus-Philologie*, 131–63.

—'Die Stellung der Evangelien in der antiken Literaturgeschichte', *ZNW* 90 (1999), 1–27.

—*Syntax und Stil des Markusevangeliums im Licht der hellenistischen*

Volksliteratur (WUNT, 2.11; Tübingen: J.C.B. Mohr [Paul Siebeck], 1984).

Rhoads, David, Joanna Dewey, and Donald Michie, *Mark as Story: An Introduction to the Narrative of a Gospel* (Minneapolis: Fortress, 2nd edn, 1999).

Robbins, Vernon K., *Jesus the Teacher: A Socio-Rhetorical Interpretation of Mark* (Philadelphia: Fortress, 1984).

—'Summons and Outline in Mark: The Three-Step Progression', *Novum Testamentum* 23 (1981), 97–114. Repr. in Gowler (ed.), *New Boundaries in Old Territory*, 118–35.

—'Text and Context in Recent Studies of the Gospel of Mark', *RSR* 17 (Jan 1991), 16–22.

Robins, William R., 'Romance and Renunciation at the Turn of the Fifth Century', *JECS* 8 (2000), 531–57.

Rofé, Alexander, *The Prophetical Stories: The Narratives about the Prophets in the Hebrew Bible, Their Literary Types and History* (PPFBR; Jerusalem: Magnes, 1988).

Rohde, Erwin, *Der griechische Roman und seine Vorläufer* (Leipzig: Breitkopf und Hartel, 1876; 2nd edn: 1900; 3rd edn: 1914; 4th edn: Darmstadt: Wissenschaftliche Buchgesellschaft, 1960; 5th edn: Hildesheim: Georg Olms, 1974).

Roth, Wolfgang, *Hebrew Gospel: Cracking the Code of Mark* (Oak Park, Ill.: Meyer-Stone, 1988).

Ruge, Walter, 'Kyzikos', in *RE*, 12.227-33.

Ruiz-Montero, Consuelo, 'Aspects of the Vocabulary of Chariton of Aphrodisias', *CQ* 41 (1991), 484-89.

—'The Rise of the Greek Novel', in *NAW*, 29–85.

Sacks, David, *A Dictionary of the Ancient World* (OPR; Oxford: Oxford University Press, 1995).

Sacks, Kenneth S., 'Historiography, Hellenistic', in *OCD*, 715–16.

Sandy, Gerald N., 'Introduction' to *Metiochus and Parthenope*, in *CAGN*, 813–15.

—'Introduction' to *Ninus Romance*, in *CAGN*, 803–4.

—'Introduction' to Lollianus, *A Phoenician Story*, in *CAGN*, 809–10.

Schaefer, Konrad, *Psalms* (Berit Olam; Collegeville, Minn.: Liturgical, 2001).

Schenke, Ludger, *Auferstehungsverkundigung und leeres Grab: eine traditionsgeschichtliche Untersuchung von Mk 16,1–8* (SB, 33; Stuttgart: Katholisches Bibelwerk, 1968).

Schmeling, Gareth (ed.), *The Novel in the Ancient World* (Boston and Leiden: Brill Academic, rev., 2003).

—'The Satyrica of Petronius', in *NAW*, 457–90.

—*Xenophon of Ephesus* (TWAS, 613; Boston: Twayne, 1980).

Schmid, Wilhelm, 'Chariton', in *RE*, 3: 2168–71.

Schmidt, Hans (ed.), *Eucharisterion: Studien zur Religion und Literatur des Alten und Neuen Testament: Hermann Gunkel zum 60 Geburtstage* (2 vols; Göttingen: Vandenhoeck and Ruprecht, 1923).

Schmidt, Karl L., 'Die Stellung der Evangelien in der allgemeinen Literaturgeschichte', in Schmidt (ed.), *Eucharisterion*, 2.50-134. Repr. in Schmidt, *Neues Testament, Judentum, Kirche*, 37–130. Repr. in Hahn (ed.), *Zur Formgeschichte des Evangeliums*, 126–228. Repr. as Schmidt, *The Place of the Gospels in the General History of Literature* (trans. Byron R. McCane; Columbia, S.C.: University of South Carolina Press, 2002).

Schneemelcher, Wilhelm (ed.), *New Testament Apocrypha* (trans. Robert McLachlan Wilson; rev. Edgar Hennecke; 2 vols; Louisville, Ky.: Westminster John Knox, 1992).

Schulz-Rauch, Martin, *Hosea und Jeremia: Zur Wirkungsgeschichte des Hoseabuches* (CTM, A16; Stuttgart: Calwer, 1996).

Seed, David (ed.), *Imagining Apocalypse: Studies in Cultural Crisis* (New York: St. Martin's, 2000).

Seneca, Lucius Annaeus, 'Hippolytus', in Miller (ed.), *Hercules Furens, et al.*, 317–423.

Senior, Donald, 'The Eucharist in Mark: Mission, Reconciliation, Hope', *BTB* 12 (1982), 67–71.

Seow, Choon L., 'Hosea', in Freedman (ed.), *ABD*, 3.291-97.

Shelton, Jo-Ann, *As the Romans Did: A Sourcebook in Roman Social History* (Oxford: Oxford University Press, 2nd edn, 1998).

Shevit, Jacob, *Athens in Jerusalem: Classical Antiquity and Hellenism in the Making of the Modern Secular Jew* (trans. Chaya Naar and Niki Werner; Portland, Ore.: Littman Library of Jewish Civilization, 1997).

Showerman, Grant (ed., trans.), *Heroides; Amores* (LCL, 41; London: Harvard University Press, 1914).

Sidebottom, E.M., 'The So-called Divine Passive in the Gospel Tradition', *ExpTimes* 87 (1978), 200–04.

Smith, Daniel A., 'Revisiting the Empty Tomb: The Post-Mortem Vindication of Jesus in Mark and Q', *NovT* 45 (2003), 123–37.

Smith, Robert H., '(W)right Thinking on the Resurrection (?)', *Dialog*, forthcoming.

Smyth, Herbert W., *Greek Grammar* (rev. Gordon M. Messing; London: Harvard University Press, 1984).

Sophocles, *Electra*, in Lloyd-Jones (ed.), *Ajax; Electra; Oedipus Tyrannus*, 165–322.

Stadter, Philip A., 'Setting Plutarch in his Context', in Stadter and Van der Stockt (eds), *Sage and Emperor*, 1–26.

Stählin, Gustav, 'κοπετός, κτλ', in Kittel and Friedrich (eds), *Theological Dictionary of the New Testament*, 8.830-52.

Stendhal, Krister, *Immortality and Resurrection* (Ingersoll Lectures; New York: Macmillan, 1965).

Stephens, Susan A., and John J. Winkler (eds), *Ancient Greek Novels: The Fragments* (Princeton: Princeton University Press, 1995).

Stewart, Zeph, *Essays on Religion and the Ancient World* (London: Harvard University Press, 1972).

Stone, Michael E., 'The Book of Enoch and Judaism in the Third Century B.C.E.', *CBQ* 40 [1978], 479–92.

Strabo, *Geography* (ed., trans. Horace L. Jones; LCL, 49–50, 182, 196, 211, 223, 241, 267; 8 vols; London: Harvard University Press, 1917–1928).

Stuart, Douglas, *Hosea-Jonah* (WBC, 31; Waco, Texas: Word, 1987).

Stuhlmacher, Peter (ed.), *The Gospel and the Gospels* (Grand Rapids, Mich.: Eerdmanns, 1991).

Suidas, *Suidae Lexicon* (ed. Ada Adler; Lexicographi Graeci Recogniti et Apparatu Critico Instructi, 1; 5 vols; Leipzig: B.G. Teubner, 1928–1938).

Sullivan, John P., 'Introduction' to Pseudo-Lucian, *The Ass* in *CAGN*, 589–92.

Sweeney, Marvin A., *The Twelve Prophets* (Berit Olam; Collegeville, Minn.: Liturgical, 2000).

Taylor, Vincent, *The Gospel According to St. Mark: The Greek Text with Introduction, Notes, and Indexes* (London: Macmillan, 1952).

Templeton, Douglas A., *The New Testament as True Fiction: Literature, Literary Criticism, Aesthetics* (PT, 3; Sheffield, Engl.: Sheffield Academic, 1999).

Theissen, Gerhard, *Fortress Introduction to the New Testament* (Minneapolis: Fortress, 2003).

Thomas, Christine M., *The Acts of Peter*, Gospel Literature and the Ancient Novel: Rewriting the Past (Oxford: Oxford University Press, 2003).

Thomas, Rosalind, *Herodotus in Context: Ethnography, Science and the Arts of Persuasion* (Cambridge, Engl.: Cambridge University Press, 2000).

Todd, Judith A., 'The Pre-Deuteronomistic Elijah Cycle', in Coote (ed.), *Elijah and Elisha in Socioliterary Perspective*, 1–35.

Tolbert, Mary Ann, *Sowing the Gospel: Mark's World in Literary-Historical Perspective* (Minneapolis: Fortress, 1989).

Too, Yun Lee (ed.), *Education in Greek and Roman Antiquity* (Leiden: Brill, 2001).

Turner, Cuthbert H., *The Gospel according to St. Mark*; London: SPCK; New York: Macmillan, 1928).

Vawter, Bruce, 'Intimations of Immortality and the Old Testament', *JBL* 91 (1972), 158–71.

Virgil, *The Aeneid: A Verse Translation* (trans. Allen Mandelbaum; Berkeley: University of California Press, 1981).

Votaw, Clyde W., 'The Gospels and Contemporary Biographies', *AJT* 19 (1915), 45–73, 217–49. Repr. *The Gospels and Contemporary Biographies in the Greco-Roman World* (Facet Books: Biblical Series, 27; Philadelphia: Fortress, 1970).

Vines, Michael E., *The Problem of Markan Genre: The Gospel of Mark and the Jewish Novel* (SBLAB, 3; Boston and Leiden: Brill Academic, 2002).

Weber, Gregor, *Dichtung und Höfische Gesellschaft: Die Rezeption von Zeitgeschichte am Hof der Ersten Drei Ptolemäer* (HE, 62; Stuttgart: Steiner, 1993).

Weeden, Theodore J., *Traditions in Conflict* (Philadelphia: Fortress, 1971).

Weider, Andreas, *Ehemetaphorik in prophetischer Verkündigung: Hos 1–3 und seine Wirkungsgeschichte im Jeremiabuch* (FzB, 71; Würzburg: Echter, 1993).

Wernicke, Konrad, 'Boreas', in *RE*, 3.720-30.

West, Martin L., *Studies in the Text and Transmission of the Iliad* (Munich and Leipzig: K.G. Saur, 2001).

Whitelam, Keith W., 'Elisha', in Freedman (ed.), *ABD*, 2.472-73.

Wilamowitz-Moellendorff, Ulrich von, 'Asianismus und Atticismus', *Hermes* 35 (1900), 1–52.

—'Die griechische Literatur des Altertums', in Wilamowitz-Moellendorff, Krumbacher, Wackernagel, Leo, Norden, Skutsch (eds), *Die Griechische und Lateinische Literatur und Sprache*, 3–238.

Wilamowitz-Moellendorff, Ulrich von, K. Krumbacher, J. Wackernagel, F. Leo, E. Norden, F. Skutsch (eds) *Die Griechische und Lateinische Literatur und Sprache* (KGEZ, 1.8; Berlin and Leipzig: B.G. Teubner, 3rd edn, 1912).

Willcock, Malcolm M, 'Homer', in *OCD*, 718–20.

Willis, James, and Cornelis de Heer (eds), *A History of Greek Literature* (London: Methuen, 1966; repr. Indianapolis: Hackett, 1996).

Wills, Lawrence M., *Ancient Jewish Novels: An Anthology* (Oxford: Oxford University Press, 2002).

—'The Depiction of Jews in Acts', *JBL* 110 (1991), 631–54.

—'The Depiction of Slavery in the Ancient Novel', *Semeia* 83/84 (1998), 113–32.

—*The Jew in the Court of the Foreign King: Ancient Jewish Court Legends* (HDR, 26; Minneapolis: Fortress, 1990).

—*The Jewish Novel in the Ancient World* (M&P; London: Cornell University Press, 1995).

—*The Quest of the Historical Gospel: Mark, John and the Origins of the Gospel Genre* (London: Routledge, 1997).

Wilson, Robert R., 'The Biblical Roots of Apocalyptic', in Amanat and Bernardsson (eds), *Imagining the End*, 56–66.

Wire, Antoinette C., *Holy Lives, Holy Deaths: A Close Hearing of Early Jewish Storytellers* (SBL, 1; Atlanta: Society of Biblical Literature, 2002).

Wolff, Hans W., *Hosea* (trans. Gary Stansell; Hermeneia; Philadelphia: Fortress, 1974).

—*Anthropology of the Old Testament* (trans. Margaret Kohl; Philadelphia: Fortress, 1974).

Worthington, Ian (ed.), *Demosthenes: Statesman and Orator* (London: Routledge, 2000).

Wright, N.T., *The Resurrection of the Son of God* (COQG; London: SPCK, 2003).

Wright, Wilmer C. (ed., trans.), *Philostratus, Eunapius* (LCL, 134; 2 vols; London: Harvard University Press, rev. ed., 1952).

Xenophon (of Athens), *Hellenica* (ed., trans. Carleton L. Brownson; LCL, 88–89; 2 vols; London: Harvard University Press, 1985–6.

Xenophon (of Ephesus), *Ephesiacorum Libri I-V de Amoribus Anthiae et Abrocomae* (ed., trans. Antonius D. Papanikolaou; Bibliotheca Scriptorum Graecorum et Romanorum Teubneriana; Leipzig: B.G. Teubner, 1973).

Yee, Gale A., *Composition and Tradition in the Book of Hosea: A Redaction Critical Investigation* (SBLDS, 102; Altanta: Scholars, 1987).

—'Hosea', in Keck (ed.), *The New Interpreter's Bible*, 7.195-298.

Zimmerli, Walther, *Ezekiel 1* (trans. Ronald E. Clemens; Hermeneia; Philadelphia: Fortress, 1979).

INDEX OF REFERENCES

INDEX OF AUTHORS